Praise for R

'*Next to Nature* offers a lifetime of thought, walking and reading ... [it] is next to perfect, and to be cherished as a companion for the dark winter and beyond'

The Times, Best Books of 2022

'One of our best writers ... *Next to Nature* is a hoard of observation, gossip and stories designed to take you through the year, with something rich and strange on every page'

Hilary Spurling, *The Spectator*, Books of the Year

'Ronald Blythe's eye and voice bring the countryside alive like a Brueghel painting. To immerse yourself in this East Anglian year is be reminded of why we love and value the rhythms and realities of rural life. Bliss'

Stephen Fry

'We can see [in *Next to Nature*] the qualities that have earned him the reverence from two generations of nature writers: close observation, close engagement and identification with place (specifically the Essex–Suffolk border); a degree of learning remarkable in both depth and scope; a marvellously fluent and occasionally flashy style ... I know of no other nature writer whose work is so easy, and so pleasurable, to quote: at every turn, an exemplary phrase'

Times Literary Supplement

'Why is this great man not more feted? It would be difficult to find ... a sensibility which is richer or better fed, more deeply watered and manured, more drenched in Englishness'

Adam Nicolson

'One of our greatest nature writers ... exquisite'

Daily Mail

'Ronald Blythe [has] an exceptionally sharp eye for poignant situations and an equally fine ear for telling phrases'

Andrew Motion

'A book of priceless wisdom ... to read as the year unfolds. Mr Blythe has a great, often droll sense of humour ... and writes with a spry, unforced elegance'

Country Life

'A series of beautifully observed, lyrical pieces organised by season'

Country Living

Next to Nature

A Lifetime in the English Countryside

RONALD BLYTHE

INTRODUCED BY RICHARD MABEY
and contributions from Julia Blackburn, Mark Cocker,
Ian Collins, Maggi Hambling, James Hamilton-Paterson,
Alexandra Harris, Richard Holloway, Olivia Laing,
Robert Macfarlane, Vikram Seth, Hilary Spurling,
Frances Ward & Rowan Williams

JOHN MURRAY

First published in Great Britain in 2022 by John Murray (Publishers)
An Hachette UK company

This paperback edition published in 2023

1

Introduction © Richard Mabey
Monthly introductions © Julia Blackburn, Mark Cocker, Ian Collins, Maggi Hambling, James
Hamilton-Paterson, Alexandra Harris, Richard Holloway, Olivia Laing, Robert Macfarlane,
Hilary Spurling, Frances Ward, Rowan Williams 'For Ronald Blythe' © Vikram Seth

Diary entries originally published in the UK by the Canterbury Press, an imprint of Hymns
Ancient & Modern Ltd of 13a Hellesdon Park Road, Norwich, Norfolk NR6 5DR

Extract from *Beowulf* (1999) by Seamus Heaney, reproduced by permission of Faber and Faber Ltd.
Extracts from 'Ash Wednesday' and 'Little Gidding' by T. S. Eliot from *The Complete
Poems and Plays* (2004), reproduced by permission of Faber and Faber Ltd.
Excerpt from 'The Journey of the Magi' by W. R. Rodgers from *Poems* (1993) is reproduced by
kind permission of the author's Estate and The Gallery Press. www.gallerypress.com
Extract from 'Christmas' by John Betjeman from *Collected Poems*
(2006), reproduced by permission of John Murray Press.
Extract from *Letters from Menabilly* (1992) by Daphne du Maurier, reproduced
by permission of Curtis Brown Ltd, London, on behalf of The Chichester
Partnership. Copyright 1992 © The Chichester Partnership.
Every reasonable effort has been made to trace copyright holders, but if
there are any errors or omissions, John Murray will be pleased to insert the
appropriate acknowledgement in any subsequent printings or editions.

A CIP catalogue record for this title is available from the British Library

Paperback ISBN 9781399804691
eBook ISBN 9781399804677

Typeset in Bembo by Hewer Text UK Ltd, Edinburgh
Printed and bound in Great Britain by Clays Ltd, Elcograf, S.p.A.

John Murray policy is to use papers that are natural, renewable and recyclable products and
made from wood grown in sustainable forests. The logging and manufacturing processes
are expected to conform to the environmental regulations of the country of origin.

John Murray (Publishers)
Carmelite House
50 Victoria Embankment
London EC4Y 0DZ

www.johnmurraypress.co.uk

For Flea, Amanda, Amélie, Caroline D, Caroline P, Chris, Colin, Emily, Linda, Luke, Natasha, Ruth, Suzanne, Thea, William and Zoe

Contents

Introduction

One May evening a few years back I had an excited phone call from Ronnie announcing that a nightingale was singing in his garden. It was a spectacular piece of news, our totem bird come to bless the home thicket. I drove over from the Chilterns the next day, but the bird had moved on. I wasn't that disappointed. There were other nightingales not far off, and what had touched me most was that phone call. Ronnie's vespers message was a touch of nightingale music itself. Here was East Anglia's senior troubadour proclaiming to his distant friend that there was another ornament for his nest in the Stour Valley.

I've known Ronnie since the end of the sixties. We met when he was living in Debach, some thirty miles to the east, and enjoying the success of his classic portrait of English village life *Akenfield*. Almost the first words he uttered to me were a gothic story about the prodigious plants in his pond. And these nuggets of anecdote – a one-line exclamation about unseasonal weather, a professorial caption to a view on a walk, a bird on the line – have been one of the great joys of our friendship. Vivid, alert, intimate, sometimes startlingly strange, they are his way of seeing, and writing. They have the air of dispatches, datelined 'the home front'. In his seminal essay 'An Inherited Perspective', Ronnie talks of 'the indigenous eye', and how a writer's 'feeling for nature and the landscape of man deepens when it remains hedged about by familiar considerations ... From childhood on, what he sees, he is.' Ronnie's familiar *terroir*, his home front, is the farming countryside, half in Essex, half in Suffolk, that encircles the village of Wormingford. His dispatches from it have become the best literary accounts of the English rural scene in the twenty-first century.

Ronnie has been a lay reader at the local churches, and a short while after that nightingale evening the *Church Times* invited him to contribute a weekly 'Word from Wormingford' column. It would be a kind of journal, in which observations on the demands of the garden, a farmer's funeral and the echoes of a long-ago war, would be entwined with reflections on the liturgy. No other writer could have pulled it off, this calendar in which the barriers between past and present, sacred and secular dissolve, so that a profundity by an Apostle can shade into anxieties over a fish pie. It resembles Virginia Woolf's ideal diary, which she felt should be 'like some old desk ... in which one flings a mass of odds and ends', and then comes back a year or two later to find that 'the collection had sorted itself out and refined itself and coalesced ... into a mould, transparent enough to reflect the light of our life'. The column ran between 1993 and 2017 and generated a series of books, from which this current volume is a selection.

When I read these pieces I'm humbled by Ronnie's astounding recall. How could anyone have read so many books, and seemingly remembered them by heart? Remote passages of scripture, bon mots from novels, entries in ancient parish registers, all tumble from him as effortlessly as greetings in the lane. He has, of course, an Alexandrian library, but these aren't cribbed quotes. His memory is extraordinary, and heightened I think by his capacity for historical empathy, so that the feelings of a prophet or a painter can, momentarily, become his own,

The memories are as acute for his own past, so this collection is also a fragmentary autobiography. He was born into a family of poor farmworkers in Acton, only ten miles from the house he was eventually to inherit in Wormingford. He romped in barns and rode derelict tractors like any country child, but while he was still at first school he was off walking, exploring the lacework of lanes, haunting Suffolk's medieval churches and peering over the walls of great houses and artists' hideouts. He read the tombstones and For Sale notices and village signs of a countryside that John Constable had known, and which was still worked by big Suffolk horses. And, of course, he retained every detail. He left school at fourteen to work in a bookshop and the process of his majestic self-education began. Soon he was into French poets and Lin Yutang, lying hidden in the grass with a book like John Clare, the poet he would later come to champion.

After the war (a veiled period in his life), he worked as a librarian in Colchester and wrote short stories and poems. And here, one day in the late '40s, he struck lucky. 'A tall woman in a WVS uniform asked me for a miniature score of Mozart's *Idomeneo*. She ran it close to her smoked glasses, opening it here and there, humming a line or two.' She was the artist Christine Kühlenthal, the wife of John Nash. It was a propitious meeting and helped Ronnie to edge deeper into the world of Suffolk's cultural royalty, which included the writer Adrian Bell, artists Cedric Morris and Arthur Lett-Haines, who ran the East Anglian School of Painting and Drawing, and eventually Benjamin Britten and his salon. A while later he moved into the Nash's farmhouse in Wormingford, Bottengoms, as an informal lodger. The whole process, he wrote later, 'was like pulling some threads in a workbox, and bringing out a tangle of unsuspected objects.'

Dear Bottengoms, the heart and hearth of this story. Approaching it from the south is like experiencing the prologue to a play. The half-mile-long track is pot-holed and capricious. There are hilly pastures, rabbits and horses to your right. As the trees close over, you feel as if you are entering a green bell-jar. By the side of an overgrown pond you are asked politely to park. And in front of you, glimpsed through a dense lattice of roses and irises and fruit trees, is the old house itself and tantalising views of the Stour valley beyond. Bottengoms is a sturdy, brick-built yeoman's farmstead. The current building dates from about 1600, but there were dwellings on the site long before that. Ronnie is acutely aware that he is a curator as much as an owner.

I first visited the house in 1978, just after John Nash had died and bequeathed it to Ronnie. He was looking exhausted after a year of caring for John, and well-meaning friends were urging him to move to a sensible town apartment in Sudbury or Cambridge. 'You'll rattle about in this big house!' they said. 'You're getting on [he was only fifty-six]. What if you fall ill, half a mile from the nearest road and no car?' I doubt I was the only person who urged him to ignore this advice and remember the resilient singleton he'd always been. He wore Bottengoms as comfortably as a favourite old jumper, and to have abandoned all the embedded memories and prospects, the plants tended and songbirds exalted, would have made him shrivel up.

When the artist Charlotte Verity came to paint the house and its garden in 2016/17, she did one view from the top of the rise to the east. Bottengoms has the look of an eyrie buried in the trees, with a single window squinting between the branches. This is Ronnie's lair, his eye on the world. He writes in Christine's old bedroom, with his back to that window, to avoid distraction. But for the rest of the time, a kind of distraction – an insatiable attention to and curiosity about the world around him – is his modus vivendi. He shares our late friend Roger Deakin's ability to 'see the extraordinary in the ordinary'.

Weather bedrocks and frames the days. Down in the bell-jar everything is amplified. Rains flood the track. Snowdrifts block it and cut Bottengoms off. Summer sun becomes heatwave. But Ronnie finds the extraordinary in all these tribulations. In a very hot June he remembers the summer of 1976 when his pond in Debach dried up completely, revealing 'its Victorian litter, muddy lamps, horse-chains, cracked crocks'. The past is always present for him.

In more clement spells, the draw of the outside is irresistible. He 'gets about', goes walking and looking – at clouds, crops, the light shining off new leaves. Or he may potter in the garden, attending to the irises and geraniums that John Nash was given by Cedric Morris, a plantsman as well as an artist. Or check on the state of the spring-fed creek that edges through the garden. It once flowed through the house and was the only source of water. 'You could see the wear it made on the kitchen floor' he once told me. And solitary though he may be, his world and writings are populated by visitors. They are always welcomed – fans from across the Atlantic chancing their luck, village ladies discussing the Flower Festival, local craftspeople clearing fallen trees and tending to the plumbing.

His farmer neighbours are old friends, but also heroic. He sees even the combine driver, hunched in his cab, as the inheritor of a contract with the earth that reaches back to Adam. 'Sometimes I hear them, the skinny labourers, clumping down from the bothy to feed the stock, the girls singing in the dairy, the barefoot children falling over the dogs, the mother shouting, the pot bubbling. All gone into the dark, says the poet. Or into the light, says somebody else.' Ronnie has always stood up for farmworkers, ancient and modern, and respected the dignity of their labour. He misses the noise and bustle and camaraderie that once filled the fields. I can't always sympathise with his view of farming, but we share a horror at the way modern agribusiness has degraded both natural and human life in the countryside. It's hard to navigate this paradox, and I've felt myself that constant tension between the bliss of a new spring and the suffering that can underlie it, between nature's imperatives and human need. Ronnie experiences this in the garden too. He's tugged both by his obligations to honour its creators' vision, and the demands of the riotous froth of cow parsley under the kitchen window, which 'dares me to touch it'. The cow parsley wins. In June he writes 'I have always been conscious of residents other than humanity who give this address and whose claim for shelter is historic'. He rescues a cloud of his 'cherished' hornets from a bedroom, using the old trick of a cup and a card.

One hot August day, he's sprawled in the deckchair, and a dragon-fly visits and alights on the hymnal in his lap. 'I clasp it stockstill. The dragonfly's wings are colourless and translucent, and I can read Binchester and Yattendon through them ... It shifts to *O qua juval*. It is a darter, a creature of speed and pause. I am a creature of sloth, and thus a scandal to Harold's bees as they assault the balsam.' I love these moments of whimsy when he puts opinions into the heads of other beings. It isn't the remotest bit anthropo-morphic (though maybe a mite animistic: even books shout 'Read me!' at him). I see them more as wry and mischievous framings of the image he holds of himself, and of his relationship with the outside world, whose independent agency is always honoured.

Nowhere more so than with his beloved cats. It's late December and snowing hard. Flakes are 'melting on the warm backs of beasts, leaving a sodden gloss. Max looks out in disgust before selecting the softest, warmest chair in the kitchen in which to winter. His green eyes close in prayer as he thanks God for creat-ing human to wait on cats.' Max and 'the white cat' (in fact there have been several white cats) are his familiars. Sometimes they would walk the fieldpaths with him, urging and scolding as they went.

I have walked and talked many paths with Ronnie, logging wild flowers, footstepping martyrs, and it strikes me that the experience is a metaphor for his writing. Things appear, are admired, spark free associations. There are diversions, clues to the past, distant prospects, brilliant images, giddy leaps of point of view. These are the ingredients and talking points of one lunch-time outing: whitebait and Guinness in Lavenham – young lovers in the bar – next day a party to hear wedding banns – 'banns' a medieval word for the prologue of a play – his wood restless with mating birds ...

The one thing absent from this panoply, so honestly autobio-graphical in so many ways, is any consideration of his inner life. The sensitive interpreter of others' pains and loves is silent about his own. 'Never you mind!' would be his blunt East Anglian retort. But I sense civic courtesy behind this diffidence, and have written elsewhere about his writings' contrast with the recent tides of self-indulgent memoirs and egotistical confessionals – the literature of the 'me' generation. Ronnie's personal writing offers something more valuable and honourable, the literature of 'us', where the 'I', so to speak, becomes the eye, fascinated with the world beyond itself. 'What he sees, he is.'

But there is an exception to this, too. Ronnie's knowledge and practice of scripture are evident in many of his writings. But only in these Wormingford columns does he openly declare his quite unselfconscious, unquestioning, sometimes irreverent, and just occasionally pagan-tinged Christian faith. And as a friend but a non-believer I have to make a reckoning with this. By unspoken common consent we have never discussed religion. But at a dinner with village friends once, I betrayed my metropolitan prejudices by insisting that the church no longer had any influence on everyday social life. Ronnie turned to me and said, quietly, 'Richard, you don't know what you are talking about.' And as far as Wormingford is concerned he was quite correct, as these pages abundantly show. It was the closest we have ever come to a row. But Ronnie has never been the least evangelical towards me, and I must return that respect. Many of his scriptural references are as foreign to me as Mandarin, but through the medium of our long friendship I can glimpse common threads in our beliefs: the immemorial virtues of kindness and cooperation, but also of toil; the way the land – be it Palestinian desert or Suffolk prairie farm – moulds us as much as we mould it; the worth and autonomy of all Creation's beings.

It's another early summer dusk, and Ronnie is about one of his vespers rituals, night-walking. And in a single perfect paragraph he captures both the essence of this book and his watchful, curious, compassionate, unifying and gratefully amazed vision of life. 'Wild roses festoon every hedge and cats emerge from ditches with golden glances at this late person. It is sultry and every window is wide. The church tower is a charcoal stump, just as it was during the summer nights that followed the Conquest. The clock face gives me its old-fashioned look. Gravestones are legible and there are dense scents. Young rabbits are dining off a wreath and other unidentifiable creatures rustle and fidget. Everywhere, it is all so perfectly interesting that one might never go to bed.'

Richard Mabey
Norfolk, 2022

JANUARY

In one of C. S. Lewis's novels, a young woman says that she fell in love with the man who is now her husband because they both liked weather; any kind of weather. She would have settled down very happily with Ronald Blythe. Noticing the great mobile spectrum of physical stimulus in the midst of which we live – the view, the temperature, the sound of snow or frozen soil under foot, the smell – is part of what Blythe's writing opens up for us with rare clarity.

And there are some seasons of the year when we are more aware than at other times that we are running our hands down the same surfaces as our ancestors. Midwinter is one of them. Easy in early January in the country, even in these dark days of climate chaos, to think that not much has changed since Hardy – or even Chaucer. Blythe nudges us back to look again at the iconic paintings of midwinter, especially those from the 'Little Ice Age' of the sixteenth and seventeenth centuries, reminding us that the exuberant outdoor activities depicted has something to do with the fact that it was probably simpler to get warm outside than indoors in those days. As he remarks in a very Blythian aside, our blood barely circulates at all today as we sit wrapped dozily in warm air.

Cold makes blood circulate; the great commemorations of the winter season, especially the feast of the Epiphany, are definitely blood-quickening moments – the Magi of the gospel story circling half the world to witness the mystery. Eliot's 'midwinter spring' is never far away in these pages.

Rowan Williams

The Approaching Snow

Approaching snow. I think I can smell it. The fields ache in the cold. A brave band of chrome yellow straight out of my old paintbox streaks across the sky. All the trees are still. At matins, sixteen of us crowd into the chancel to keep warm, like Bishop Heber's beasts of the stall. I expect that poor young man, torrid in India, longed for snow.

What we have to learn is to work at home during snow. Commuters should have a winter desk in their houses where, with today's gadgetry, they could turn in a good day's toil without struggling through drifts to the office. Schoolchildren, too. Approaching snow might be when the value of a meeting could be assessed.

Why is Duncan flying the Australian flag on his barn? It is a flag in shock. It flaps stiffly towards the freezing North Sea. I write with my back to what is to come because it will be, as always, strangely thrilling. David telephones. Have I got bread? He can get down in the Land Rover. The cat, languorous between curtain and glass, trades whiteness with whiteness.

Preaching at New Year, in quiet mid-flow on Doctor Johnson's resolutions, I have a feeling that I have done so before. It cannot be helped, however. And, anyway, that great Christian man should be heard alongside the Epiphany manifestation. He was an old man who could not change his ways. And, indeed, why should he?

He had practised his faith at huge inconvenience to himself. 'I have taken my wife's unpleasant friend into my house. I have taken a black boy into my house, fed him, taught him, and made him my son.'

Samuel Johnson was following the epistle of Paul to Philemon to the letter. And yet, like some January fool, he would resolve:

To apply to study.
To rise early.
To go to church.
To drink less.
To oppose laziness.
To put my books in order.

My mother told me how she would look up at his statue – a clumsy figure staring towards Fleet Street – when she went to Sunday school at St Clement Danes. He loved Christ, wrote beseeching prayers, and dismissed the Church's everlasting arguments with: 'Sir, I think all Christians, whether Papists or Protestants, agree in the essential articles, and that their differences are trivial, and rather political than religious.'

The snow is now very near. Fragments of the Christmas fall wait in the ditches to welcome it. The clouds cannot move. The roses rattle. With the oil tank full and the log corner high with split ash, and the fridge still mildly bursting, I feel like the husband-man and his eat, drink and be merry. Wonderful leftovers. What is more delectable than a half-eaten pie?

After the cards come the invites to the year's literature festivals, the requests to do this and that, the need to read, the services for Lent, and, in the year's good time, the spring flowers.

Distant friends ring. 'Are you snowed in? We are thinking of you.' How impatient they are.

Once Again

A multitude of green needles with minute white eyes are perforating the black mulch on the far bank – snowdrops, thousands of them. Armies of them will soon be swarming through the gully at Great Glemham where, it is said, the parson-poet George Crabbe originally introduced them. There is nothing like a snowdrop to obey Genesis 1, 22, to the letter. Also, the barn owl has zoomed over. Mighty mouser, he rushes from Maltings Farm towards the Grange at half-light like a predatory seraph, no sooner seen than gone. One New Year another parson-writer, Gilbert White, was complaining to a friend about the paucity of towers fit for jackdaws in Hampshire. 'We have many livings of two or three hundred pounds a year, whose houses of worship make little better appearance than dovecots. When I first saw Northamptonshire, Cambridgeshire and Huntingdonshire, and the Fens of Lincolnshire, I was amazed at the number of spires which presented themselves in every point of view.' The Selborne jackdaws were reduced to building their nests in old rabbit burrows. It was not good enough. The natural history of many an ancient church provided a winged accompaniment to its services. The countryside could not be kept out. It crept through the walls and made its way up into belfries.

I am past resolution. Or rather I am more a daily than a yearly resolver, getting up each morning determined to do this and not do that. Sometimes making a little list entitled 'To Be Done' and ticking off each achievement by evening. There have been too many New Year's Days riddled with failure for me to take them seriously any more. New Year has always been such a wild and portentous celebration that the church rather gave up trying to subdue it long ago. What it did was to take care that no great Christian feast should actually fall on New Year's Day, to get mixed up with pagan riotousness. But after centuries of no feast, that of the Circumcision and then that of the Name of Jesus, both banished from the Roman Calendar in 1969, arrived as though to remind the faithful that something had to be going on between the birth and the showing of the Saviour. At school we used to sing Lawrence Tuttiett's 'Father, let me dedicate all this year to thee.' He was rector of St Andrew's, Scotland and author of a history of 'Amen'. In what other calling would one find a master of snowdrops, an expert on jackdaws and an authority on Amen?

So be it. I have just remembered my most dutifully kept New Year's task, which is to list what flowers are still in bloom – always an astonishing number.

All Snug Within

Diaries begin. First, self-assessments, then by February a comfortable falling back into old habits. Sensible diarists like Lady Eleanor Butler had no truck with good resolutions and just settled down to a pleasant winter.

'Freezing hard. Windy. Cold, but very comfortable in the dressing room – and an excellent fire. Shutters closed. Curtains let down. Candles lighted – our pens and ink. Spent the evening very pleasantly reading *Tristram Shandy* aloud – adjourned to the library. Worked – laughed.'

Self-lacerating diarists such as Katherine Mansfield tore themselves to pieces. 2nd January 1922: 'I have not done the work I should have done . . . This is very bad. In fact I am disgusted with myself. There must be a change from now on. What I chiefly admire in Jane Austen is that what she promises, she performs . . .'

Ah, if only we all performed what we promised, how satisfying this would be. Nature does. Bulbs tip the surface and will bloom, catkin stubs on the January branch will tassel. The sun just showing above the hill will run up the sky. I observe it, drinking tea by the window through which the old farmers stared, generation after generation. Same sun, same hill, and Shakespeare sixty miles away, writing *A Winter's Tale*.

A letter from Shandy Hall, where my friend Patrick has become curator. He has sent me one of Laurence Sterne's sermons. It is florid stuff delivered by the sound of it from under a full periwig to a well-heeled congregation in St Michael le Belfry, York in 1747, to raise funds for a local charity school. The great comic novelist was being dead serious, which wasn't his style at all. He was preaching on 'The Case of Elijah and the Widow of Zerephath' – she of the never emptying cruse of oil, should you have forgotten. And here am I reading it in a room which would have been battered by farming when the glorious charity of *Tristram Shandy* burst on the scene, to do more for humanity than ever did its author when in the pulpit. 'Writing,' wrote Sterne, 'when properly managed (as you may be sure mine is) is but a different name for conversation.' We can only hope that he managed to talk his way into the pockets of his congregation. Georgian charity, how it makes us shudder.

A hundred sheep or more graze in Harold's field along the lane. It is a surprise and a treat to see them there in a now more or less animal-free landscape. It is one of those small discrete fields which still belong to the 'old people', i.e. the locals who have been here for ever and ever, who muster in force at the funeral of one of their kind, and who then reveal an unsuspected ownership of much of the village to the incomer, with his quarter of an acre property. The old people's acres would fetch a fortune with planning permission, not much when it is not granted. I like to see their meadows and fields in their modesty and occasional usefulness as they give their owners a ghostly reminder of the old independence. They are sometimes let for trifling sums, either for crops or grazing, and sometimes left to flower, which they do in a far better way than the set-aside. But, like Sterne, 'I pity the man who can travel from Dan to Beersheba, and cry, "'Tis all barren".'

Winter Wild

The first walk of the year. Over the great field which was once ten fields, or 'several', as they say here. 'Were there many there?' – 'Several.' Fine flints glitter in the set-aside, fine rosettes of thistle, fine puddles in the ridges to catch the clouds, fine gulls on their way to a bit of ploughing. That ultimate smudge down river must be Dedham tower. My little wood whistles and shakes as I come home to it and I am tempted to do some thinning with a bow-saw. But the cold is taking my ears off, so it must be desk work instead. An appalling thought enters my head. Supposing I had come home to one of those television house and garden makeovers, to tons of decking and a blue pagoda and that wild woman with the Rapunzel hair! But all is well. The postman's van is the only vehicle in sight.

My brother telephones from Australia. He is homesick for winter. 'It is 28 degrees here, if this means anything to you. Are you breaking the ice in the water-butt?' A few thin ice needles hang from the eaves. Do I remember skating on the North meadows? Do I! One needs some chilly memories to cheer one up when the stonework round the swimming pool burns one's bare feet. Ian then rings from Edinburgh, from his eyrie-like flat high up opposite the Scott Memorial in Princes Street. A torrent of bagpipers are wailing below and the cold, well he can't describe it. Oh to be in sultry Suffolk in January.

I write a bit then wrap up, go out once more and make a place for the oil tanker to park. Come in, type a page or two, read a chapter, listen to a story on the radio, water hyacinths, answer letters and call it a day. For such is the literary life. All go. The cards and holly are toppling but cannot be removed until Twelfth Night, one of those 'fire' dates when the symbolism of the old religion and Christianity ignite. There were bonfires in the January wheatfields right up until Kilvert's time. Epiphany light begins to steal into ours. In *Twelfth Night* Shakespeare is wishing us the ambiguity of the season. At the end of the play 'the whirligig of time' brings illuminations.

Keith the farmworker appears, plus his dogs and two little grandsons with Christmas lingering in their eyes. I think of Feste singing for the very first time, 'What's to come is still unsure'.

Hauntings

Seeing an ancient hall bedizened with Christmas lights from apex to moat, I thought how M. R. James would have disapproved. He remains our ghost-storyteller extraordinary, and for him the halls and churches of East Anglia were places of shadows, of half-seen things, of inexplicable sounds, of bumps in the day as well as in the night. 'If any of my stories succeed in causing their readers to feel pleasantly uncomfortable when walking along a solitary road at nightfall, or sitting over a dying fire in the small hours, my purpose in writing them will have been attained.' He is being disingenuous. Far from making us pleasantly uncomfortable he frightens the life out of us. He was successively the Provost of Eton and King's, and a master of decay, whether of building, landscape or person. He was too, of course, the son of a Victorian country rector. In youth he was strikingly like Stephen Fry in appearance. Although an excellent cranky historian, he saw himself as an antiquary, and although the dons and collectors and parsons of his tales are presented as conventional types, they are in fact scary examples of learned lonely bachelors going potty. M. R. James's masterpiece is 'Oh, Whistle, and I'll Come to You, My Lad'. He died after a visit to Kew Gardens in June 1935, leaving us edgy and wintry, and with afar from Pevsner view of our stained glass and flint towers.

New Year brought the ghosts out. The melancholy ever-rolling stream of Time through dark old rooms, the tilting photographs of past incumbents in damp vestries, the melting ice in dank shrubberies, the unwanted (or possibly longed for) companion catching one up in the foggy lane, and history seen as a medieval box of fun holy tricks to poke about in, these were among the experiences of January. A sense not of beginnings but of endings. The churchyard filled up with winter graves. Neighbours died but did not quite depart. The novelists and writers generally,

Charles Dickens, Le Fanu, had a field day. Old wives' tales came true, at least for little John Clare, humping flour from Maxey Mill and hardly daring to pass certain spots along the way. As children, we had to pass the Satan Tree, an innocent hawthorn of vast dimension which had been hung about with this libel for ages, though it was impossible to tell why. But there was a need to be frightened and it was a poor sort of village which lacked something that would put the wind up both inhabitant and traveller. Our trump card was Borley Rectory, just down the road. It had actually burnt down about the same time as M. R. James went to Paradise via Kew Gardens, but this did not exorcise its ghost, a nun, of course. My old friend James Turner and his wife occupied the coach house. I can hear him now, rattling out novels on his Remington typewriter, whilst the apple wood splintered in the grate. We were ardent Jamesians, though I was actually apostate, enjoying the horror but unbelieving, a sightseer in the haunted nest. The Turners were movers but they never took a house without a ghost. Nor at that time did it ever strike us that we should not be so entertained by the supernatural darkness when it was the Epiphany. There was so little light before gas and electricity, and so little could be done. No warmth except by the fireside. The flames danced and another world took shape.

Twelfth Night

Long ago, walking home, I was tempted to visit the poet Edward FitzGerald's grave on a winter's afternoon, just when the light was 'going', as we used to say. A young airman from the USAAF base with a little son in his arms was fumbling his way into the church. 'Where is the light?' he asked. Memorials glimmered all around. Light was taking its daily absence.

Since it is Twelfth Night, I take down the holly. Log fires have dulled its gloss. Crisped to a turn, it hisses from the beams to the bricks. The white cat has done for the Christmas cards. No sooner do I stand them up than she mows them down, believing this to be her duty.

I shove crushed wrapping-paper into a sack unceremoniously, empty ashes and remove wizened apples, when, without warning, an Epiphany sun blazes in, making the ancient interior look trashy and in need of a good putting-to-rights. But, as children, we took down the paper chains and folded up the paper bells with sadness. We watched the snowman drip into nothing, and witnessed his dying. Everything was different then, as it was bound to be.

The farmhouse was in 'full Christmas' when William Shakespeare wrote *Twelfth Night* to entertain King James at Whitehall. Food-wise, what could be salted away was preserved for the bitter months ahead. The winter's cold could be terrible. You had to clutch at health for all you were worth. You could become low.

'Keep good fires,' the Revd Sydney Smith advised a depressed friend. 'Winter wild, and winter drear, Surely wintertime is here', we sang in the village school. But in church we sang, 'Brightest and best of the sons of the morning'. Reginald Heber wrote this entrancing Epiphany hymn after discovering the *Olney Hymns*. He was so youthful, and, alas, so vulnerable to the destructive Indian heat. He listened to his hymn being sung in a Raj church below the Himalayas. It is exotic, and a far cry from Cowper's pleading 'Heal us, Emmanuel'.

Many old country people called Twelfth Night 'the real Christmas'. It was also a trickster time, when boys became girls and bonfires from the old gods challenged the light of Christ. When ice and snow made it impossible to work, play took over. See a typical Dutch winterscape: as it is far colder inside, everyone is outside, skating, running, drinking, shouting. In freezing Victorian classrooms, the children would be told to stand up and 'beat your arms' to get the circulation going. One reason for our present post-Twelfth Night aches is that our blood barely circulates. Families dine on sofas, not at tables. But then the Three Kings probably dined on a carpet.

I could pick a bunch of primroses. Not that I will; for their open presence near the house must not be disturbed. But here they are, about a dozen of them, in the Epiphany sunshine, forerunners of thousands. The sodden oak leaves of the rains are dry and conversational. The sky is a goldmine. Lots of mud about. The church smells of pine needles and wax, and damp uncollected cards. I am to lay at Christ's feet my 'burden of carefulness'. I know exactly what the writer is getting at. So should we all.

Richard Mabey's Wetland

Only in today's ecology would a Twelfth Night guest be sploshed off after a festive lunch to the local marsh. But then I was visiting my lifelong friend Richard Mabey and would not have expected to remain indoors when the wetlands called. All our meetings have been stretched out by giant walks, whatever the weather. This time it is pure wan winter-sun weather with just a nip of Norfolk. Rooks were lodging on the tips of oaks and the Waveney was putting in an occasional appearance. Just down the lane Diss was still dripping with the electric festoons of Christmas. But to the right were the marsh and its sucking sounds as Richard, Polly and myself did what Bunyan's hero would never have done without an urgent plea for divine protection, strode happily into the mud. No birdsong, no firm footing – 'Are you all right?' – and no sense, as our forebears would have said. And everywhere an abundance of old deaths and new life, of fallen wood and wild iris shoots, papery reeds and greening mulch. My toes were soon swimming around in a leaky shoe and were still doing so on the train home. But before then it was marshlight, not just that treacherous glimmer ahead which led the country people straight into the slough of despond, but the flat glinting surface of patchy water as it lay in a string of ponds and ruts ahead. This was a Mabey walk to rival his walk with me to Wormingford Mere where, although I don't like to boast, we have a dragon. When the Psalmist slipped, morally not ecologically, the Lord bent down and 'brought me up out of the muddy pit . . . and gave me a firm footing'. Our blessed mud is called, pejoratively, 'mire' in the King James Bible. It was something which soiled and held you. We three managed to remain upright.

Emerging, we saw the shadows of Diss and the Xanadu domes of the Bressingham Garden Centre, white in the fire of the sunset. We thought we could smell tea. I had meant to pay my respects to the Diss poet John Skelton before returning to Bottengoms but swift darkness intervened. He had been the wild Rector of the little town in 1502, writing poems like 'Philip Sparrow' and 'Ware the Hawk' in irregular lines called 'Skeltonics.' Reverend poets are apt to be misunderstood by their parishioners. I can even see today's apprehensive churchwardens, interviewing an applicant for the living, nervously wondering whether they might ask the delicate question, 'Are you a poet?' They made John Skelton Poet Laureate and he was able to sign himself 'Laureate Poet of Disse', an exquisite title. And he could be practical, once catching a man who used the nave of his church to train hawks in. Diss grew up round a great mere and is a true waterland place. Skelton himself is buried far-away in St Margaret's, Westminster, where he was seeking sanctuary from a furious Cardinal Wolsey whom he had lampooned. Richard, Polly and I talked about the Fens, and how they are apt to breed rebels and saints and fancy words. John Skelton, Laureate Parson of Disse, knew a girl who was

Benign, courteous, and meek,
With wordes well devised;

In you, who list to seek,
Be virtues well comprised.

Her name was Margery Wentworth. I see her catching his eye at
matins.

And the Waters Covered the Earth

Late cards continue to limp in. Mourners go about the churchyard removing dead flowers. Sacks of 'Christmas' await the
dustman. The lanes are all under water, the skies awash, the river
rising – were it not for the elder and willow line, who could tell
where the river was? London commuters splash their way to the
station, bravely making amphibious jokes. With dawn also come
mallard and swans, and white water as far as the eye can see. It
shines harshly. It has come to rule us. 'Flood-time!' it says. So we
make what we can of it, helpless as we are in its wake. Our modest
streams, Stour, Box, Brett, Linnet, Colne, are in an over-reaching
mood and are filling their valleys instead of just their beds.
Travellers come home with watery tales. But the ancient and wily
men who built most of our riverside farms and cottages for the
most part built them just out of reach of these annually flooding
streams. But even where they did get in, they were soon brushed
out again and could hardly make the ground floors damper than
they usually were, and all the year round.

I splosh in the direction of Garnons to survey this now just
occasional New Year flooding. Garnons is a manor perched on a
man-made Saxon mound and has always kept its footings dry.
Narrow knife-slits of sunlight cut into the rain clouds. It is the
Epiphany. White or gold? says the lectionary. Take your choice.
We hear the voices of John and Jeremiah, enlighteners and poets
both. We address God as 'the bright splendour whom the nations
seek'. We forget all the wet, the impassable roads, the roaring

ditches, for are we not at 'the source of every blessing?' and although it is such a dark day, the old church is luminous beyond candles, beyond all the lights we have switched on. Needles from the vanished tree wither among the armorials of the sanctuary tombs and the vestry sports the undertaker's new calendar. 'Sing unto the Lord a new song', we are told, but we sing Monsell and Heber and Prudentius, of course. It is the best we can do. Their rich language boosts the interior glow.

Back home, I search for one book and dislodge another which whispers, 'Read me instead'. It tumbles invitingly onto the carpet, a harlot of a volume. It is Rose Macaulay's *Last Letters to a Friend 1952–1958*, which I never knew I possessed. Gone the dark day now. High Anglicans surround me, Simon Phipps, and the genuflecting incumbents of Dame Rose's beloved London churches in which she spread her worship, driving to one or another daily in her little car, believed by her friends to be under divine protection as she was the worst driver in town, and richly rising from these pages the learned Christianity of half a century ago. Then I came to her account of the Epiphany floods of 1953 when half of Holland drowned and the North Sea swept into East Anglia for miles and inundated it from the Thames to the Wash, all its seaside towns and villages, drowning hundreds of people in a few hours.

Less tragic inundations invited her wit. 'We are having floods here; perhaps just a few men will be spared. I should like a voyage in an ark. I wish when in Turkey I had climbed Ararat and found splinters of the ancient ark, as travellers were used to do.' What she found in Turkey, of course, was the stuff, the theology if you like, of her masterly Christian novel *The Towers of Trebizond*. I can see it on a shelf out of the corner of my eye, but it won't do, I must get back to some galleys and be their slave. But I catch one of her frequent asides about the Epiphany. '*Stella ista sicut flamma coruscat* – That star sparkles like a flame. Why is it that Christ as light means more to me than any other aspect?'

Epiphany

Neighbours call. These are neighbourly days. Hugh the vet sits in the guest chair, having sploshed down the track. The ditches roar with rainfall, lakes are spreading across the lanes and the river will be rising under our bridge. Max gives Hugh a long, green-eyed stare which says, 'I am a perfectly healthy cat, so none of your tricks.' He is certainly a perfectly ungrateful cat. Hugh has brought me a summery photograph of the Little Horkesley road, the stretch which I hurry along to the bus, and which at this moment is pretty well immersed, but which in the picture is stripy with sunlight, with towering hedges and leafy oaks touching overhead. We talk of animals, of the coming and going of herds, of retirement, of a new year.

Frances arrives to show me the botany books which she kept sixty years ago when she was ten, text on the left, watercolour flowers on the right. 'Jan. 14th 1930. I found at Maiden-croft farm some Winter Aconites. They grow in moist bushy places and belong to the Buttercup family . . .' I pore over the little books when she has gone. Sea pinks from the Newlyn cliffs, cross-leaved heather from a Scottish glen. What a learned, erudite little girl, and what happened to my pressed-flower albums, I wonder? Clumsy, lumpy volumes, I dimly recall, many of the blooms more squashed than flattened and all of them plucked not a mile from home. Frances' botany reminded me of the seventeenth-century herbarium in the library of Shrewsbury School, all the local wild flowers which George Herbert could have seen growing in the Severn meadows, not crushed and dead like my childish pressings, but holding on to their hues and shapes. Herbert believed that rectories should be made paradisal with flowers and their gardens turned into medicine chests with herbs.

Peter-Paul and Kate arrive, along with someone whose arrival is imminent – 6 January, the Epiphany, to be precise. So close is the birth that I feel that he or she is present already. We talk of names. A broken-backed Cruden's *Concordance* contains in neat alphabetical order all the names in the Bible and we run through them while the pheasants bake. Kate sits bolt upright by the fire as mothers do when a son or daughter is imminent and the blazing wood covers her with a shooting rosy light. There are, I suggest, six possible names for an Epiphany child, three male, three female, and these are respectively considered as the oven spits and crackles. But of course the name of the imminent one has already been fixed, though it is not for me to ask it. So we fancifully speculate on the many generations of births which must have taken place in this farmhouse and give each other large helpings of everything as the wind howls and the clock ticks.

Unsearchable Riches

The Epiphany sunsets are furious, vast blazing caves of lurid light. Each evening they burn the field across which a dog fox trots, taking his time, trailing his brush through the inch-high corn. I cremated the Christmas holly according to custom. Dry as dust from twelve days in warm rooms, it hurries to become ashes. At night the stars are extra-shining, making the Stansted planes dim in comparison. Hard frosts having made the footpath walkable, I crackle my way to St Andrew's for a 10.30 Communion and for some of those 'solemn things of mystic meaning', as Prudentious called them. Old tombs stand in white grass; pheasants examine berry-less wreaths, wind comes round the tower like a scythe. The Epistle has St Paul making up his mind to release the starlight of Bethlehem into the world at large and to talk about the 'unsearchable riches of Christ' to anyone who would listen. The altar candles waver and make shrouds, the chancel heating hums expensively.

Back home, it being too good to be in, I cut down some dead cotoneaster, whose name means 'like a quince-tree', and 'staff-like' because its stems make good walking sticks. I saw up its slender logs for the stove. Then back to the study to write an Afterword for the Launcelot Fleming Lectures at Norwich.

Now and then I manage to find my way about an area, not with a street-plan, but with what I know of some celebrated resident's life. Thus I am walking with Coleridge in Highgate. It is new ground to me, and poorly lit at that. A self-imposed law says that I must not ask the way. I wander on and it is only when I read 'Millfield Lane' on a wall that I know where I am. For it is where in April 1819, on a Sunday afternoon, 'A loose, slack, not well-dressed youth met Mr Green and myself . . . It was John Keats.' 'Myself' was of course Mr Coleridge. So here they stood. Mr Green, who had tutored Keats at Guy's Hospital, introduced the two poets and they all walked on in a torrent of talk. I pass the buildings they passed. London, five miles away, does not look as it looked to them. Now it is the biggest pile of tinsel ever, glittering, clear. Then it was a fuming sulphurous pit afar off, fed as it was by a million sea coal fires. The smoke, as they called it. Nearby, doubly dark, is the fabulous cemetery where Engels stood by Karl Marx's grave, praising him to the skies. But now I come to the corner shop where an obliging chemist sold Coleridge all the laudanum, and finally to a glass noticeboard containing my name, and to Livia Gollancz gallantly welcoming me to the celebrated Highgate Literary and Scientific Institute. Both I and the pleasant Victorian room should be pent-up with revolution but all such passion has been long spent, and I talk bookishly to bookish people, and fancy I hear a great wind roaring by outside.

On Pendle Hill

A strange day. Two hours of brilliant sunshine, and many hours of freezing fog. Except it isn't freezing – just as cold, but liquid, lanes all sloppy mud, and the wetness being blown out of the trees by a slight wind.

I would have stayed indoors, but for urgent business with our village post office – for which God be praised. Heather emerges from what Thomas Hardy called 'her penetralia' to sell me three books of stamps, and I find myself remembering a lifetime of country shopkeepers who briefly emerged from a curtained holy-of-holies to serve me; and that never once have I seen inside these secret rooms. But then their potent mystery would be gone for ever. Heather and I tell each other what a ghastly day it is. And then she's gone.

Back at the farmhouse, Jonathan has taken my rubbish up to the top for the dustmen. It sways garishly on his muddy runabout, a basic little vehicle, which looks as if it is constructed out of Meccano. The dustmen are exacting, and have to be waited on hand and foot according to the conservation faith. It is a blue day: bottles, Whiskas tins, and *The Times*.

Ten thousand starlings fly over, all talking at once. And then comes the wondrous sight that I could not have seen yesterday, and can only just make out today, as the light is so bad: scores of matt-white snowdrop heads in the mulch below the quince tree.

The white cat sits on a brick surveying them, or rather surveying why I am hanging about in weather like this when it is teatime.

The Epiphany weeks pass. We are to remember George Fox. I went to find him once on Pendle Hill, in Lancashire. He had been travelling about for a decade before, aged 28, he saw Pendle Hill rising out of Bowland, like, William Penn said, 'a great auditory'. What a natural pulpit it would have made.

But, descending, Fox mounted a haystack and said nothing, not a word, to his expectant congregation of Seekers. This was the first Quaker sermon – silence. He had a young friend with him, Richard Farnsworth, who had been hurt in some way and so was unable to climb Pendle: how regularly people have climbed mountains to find God.

I must admit that when I climbed Pendle in the rain, I was as keen to take in that mighty view as that inner voice that would create the

Society of Friends. Also, I had been reading David Pownall's wonderful book *Between Ribble and Lune*, and was still caught up in his vision of Lancashire. And I, too, had left a companion at the bottom, my dear hospitable friend Allen, nice and dry in the car.

Thomas Carlyle wrote that perhaps the most remarkable incident in modern history is not the Diet of Worms, still less the Battle of Waterloo, but George Fox making himself a suit of Leather! And he quoted the quiet craftsman's words: 'Will all the shoe-wages under the Moon ferry me across into that far Land of Light? Only Meditation can, and devout Prayer to God. I will to the woods: the hollow of a tree will lodge me, wild berries feed me; and for Clothes, cannot I stitch myself one perennial suit of Leather?' Thus, continues Carlyle, 'from the lowest depth there is a path to the loftiest height'.

I suppose he meant from cobbling to Pendle Hill; from being a tradesman to being a prophet.

Gustav Holst and Martin Shaw

Market day. The village bus twists and turns through the lanes. On it are old folk, students, workmen, the woman who reads paperbacks all the way. There is an Italianate villa where the naval rating who helped to bury Rupert Brooke *en route* to Gallipoli lived; there is the hill where Martin Shaw composed 'Hills of the North, rejoice'. And there, across the liquid landscape, is the little house where my aunt spent her life making lace for the altar.

But, in the market town, the stone griffins on the church tower maintain their watch, seeing off goblins and foul fiends. I sense a new feeling of things not being as prosperous as they were. And, as always, faces from boyhood appear in the old street – not phantom features, but young faces grown old along with my own, especially in Waitrose.

The Epiphany proceeds. The Queen joins the Three Kings in the Chapel Royal; and in our three ancient parishes we sing and pray the journeying liturgy. Soon, we will be walking into Lent. Last midnight I wandered around the garden, staring at stars, and followed by the white cat. Stansted planes flew silently through golden clouds. An extra quietness prevailed. Snow was out of the question, and winter was no more than a name. But I checked the oil tank, and it answered with a half-full clunk.

Then came the clearing of desks for this year's work. Only not quite yet. Let January get into its stride. Hear some music. Answer letters. Remember that Keith is coming to decorate John Nash's studio, now my bedroom. He went to it every day at ten o'clock, and came down from it at four o'clock. His easel fronted a north light, and there was a single 40-watt bulb to encourage it. We never entered without permission, and he never left it without a kind of sadness. It was never swept or dusted, and cocoa-tin lids piled with ash were rarely emptied.

When he went away to fill up the sketchbooks, he cleared a space for me in which to write. But I never worked in his studio with its north light and half-light, but always in the sunshine. His pupils would enter this room with reverence, looking forward to the time when they, too, would attain its murk and hereditary litter and spiderwebs. For it takes an age to create one's own peerless dust and muddle.

I was once told the tale of Gustav Holst's reaction to the new composing room which his wife made ready for him when he was away. Glorious it was, with great windows on to the beautiful Thaxted countryside. But they said that he never wrote a note in it, and sat by the hearth in his old house, as he always did. His suite *The Planets* might soar to the skies, but it was created by the hearth.

Benjamin Britten worked in a window which faced the sea, and which at times was sprayed with it. But the local stationer sold postcards of the window, and, when visitors to Aldeburgh stood on the sea wall to watch him, he had to find a hiding place.

William Hazlitt, the great essayist who longed to be an artist, insisted that no one should approach an artist at work — that something sacred was happening at that moment. I once read 'Kubla Khan' in the room where Coleridge had written it, rocking his baby son to sleep at the same time. Nash walked to his studio in my room every day.

Painters and Trees

The last time trees were given free range throughout the Royal Academy was when it honoured John Nash with a retrospective, in the late '60s. He was the same age as David Hockney. His trees flourished in their modest fashion from Cornwall to Skye. But their roots, as it were, grew in Nash's homeland, Buckinghamshire. And particularly on the Chilterns and around the Aylesbury Plain.

As with Hockney, Nash carried the viewer into scenes of personal happiness — joy, even. It was a similar emotion to that experienced by being carried away by one of those marvellous watercolour posters on a '30s railway station platform. One knows that young people and old places cannot be as perfect as this, and yet the entire world is transfigured simply by looking at them.

Hockney, of course, is trailing his coat before the conceptionalists, the anti-smoking lobby, the painting-versus-photography argument, if this still exists, and anything that stands in the way of simple happiness.

His Yorkshire wold — German *Wald*, forest — is but a wooded lane, which he drives from Bridlington to look at obsessively time and time again, with a car-load of hi-tech aids. He is no primitive, no Alfred Wallis. Yet he creates traditional landscapes out of the most ordinary sights and the most sophisticated materials, and allows this unidentifiable joy of his to flood them.

Even his camera — the last word, we can be sure — is made to produce the wonder of a Box Brownie snap. His plants, including his trees, are essentially unbotanical. They conduct light and shade, leaf and hibernate, and are determinedly ordinary. They are what we miss when we are driving, not walking or staring, and were the subject-matter of Georgian poetry.

Visitors to this huge picture show will slow up by some verge, ditch, field, copse, and reconsider the purpose of their own existence. Or just to take a good look. The art critics could be thrown as they back-pedal. First California, and now this track.

I have lived most of my days under Gainsborough's and Constable's trees, and not figuratively; for many of them go on growing. Cornard Wood is just over the hill, as is Tendring Park. And I have sat beside John Nash as he sketched in the Stour Valley, and watched the willows in winter appearing on the sheet. Cigarette ash, too.

One of these crashed down in the recent gale, opening up sky and land. At night, I listen to the ashes groaning. 'That'll fall on you one of these days.' I doubt it. But it misses being a model. It is asking for attention and creaking: 'Look at me!' Hockney's wayside trees will be ill at ease in Piccadilly. But then so should we, now and then. Our joy should be elsewhere, maybe. Visionaries might be able to tell us, or an art exhibition — though no longer a station poster.

I tell another David about the tumbled willow, and he says: 'I'll bring my chainsaw.' Snowdrops are flooding where it has let in the light. You would hardly believe it was January. Paul Nash was given a camera in 1930, and photographed one of his significant images — *Monster Field*.

Tobias and the Sitter

Toby the artist has arrived from Swanage to paint my portrait. He looks round the old house for the 'best sitting place' and chooses the study window. Rainy panes flash with intermittent sunshine.

Toby is working on a series of portraits of rural people, mostly from Wessex, whose way of life is being destroyed by those who most admire it – the incomers. 'Each man kills the thing he loves.' Or, as a Dorset hurdle-maker told Toby, referring to the new race of village-dwellers, 'they love what they see and then they change it to what they left behind.'

He draws and paints for three days, and I hope is impressed by my professionalism as an artist's model, as I manage to chat and provide meal-breaks without moving, so to speak. And, of course, it is a treat to be in Dorset once more. It was Paul Nash's favourite place, and I myself made wonderful trips to it when I was helping to edit the New Wessex edition of Thomas Hardy, or writing about T. F. Powys. Or climbing Maiden Castle.

We talk about the way in which, not all that long ago, local people could get trapped in landscape: how it could destroy them, as it did in *The Return of the Native*.

Tall and serious, Toby paints away while the white cat, new to the smell of turpentine, considers this change of environment. My face, along with the hurdle-maker's and those of all the other country men and women who will sit for him, will hang in the Dorset County Museum in Dorchester.

This is an extraordinary institution, possessing, as it does, Thomas Hardy's study in a room-sized glass case. He used a different pen, I remember, for each novel, writing on its holder *Tess of the D'Urbervilles*, *The Woodlanders*, etc. But how strange that this most furtive of authors should have his very soul on display! Not that I wasn't glued to the glass when I entered the museum at 'seeing' not only the worn nibs, but the inky fingers pressing on, line after line, and the blotter working overtime.

Toby says that he has bought a boat named Selina and would like to change this, but it is unlucky. Ships are never rechristened. Which brings us to Tobias and the angel, and myself to sorting out Jacob and his angel, and the completely forgotten tale of Tobit, Tobias and Raphael. This is well worth anyone's glimpse of the Apocrypha.

Briefly, Tobit, a Jewish exile in Nineveh and blind, allows his son to travel with a guide named Azarius, who is in fact the angel Raphael.

Off they go, to Tobias's mother's grief, to find fish, which will provide the means for her son's happy marriage and her husband's sight. And, of course, Tobias has a dog, Dog Toby.

It is a great tale. I take the artist Tobias to see a portrait by John Constable at Nayland, just up the road, the model for which was his brother Golding, a young land agent. He stares upwards as the Christ, a natural-enough gesture for him, as he was usually walking through the Suffolk woods with his gun. Then back to the sitting.

It is etiquette not to remark on a work in progress or even to look at it. But when Tobias at last turns the canvas round, I am disconcerted by how far he has seen into me, and how correctly. And how truthful even my chair is! Off he goes in the wild, wild weather, the easel folded up in the car like a sleeping insect.

Being Barak

Each near-dawn, tea in hand, cat on the make, I sit watching the great hazel filter in the day. Its companion was coppiced two years ago, but, remembering how this tree let in the light with a gradualness that suited me, I stayed my hand. What petty power, I now think. It shames me to write it down. But there it is, the 40-foot hazel with its frothing catkins and fanning boughs, and the small man coming to.

At first – it is 6.30 and still January – it does no more than shift darkness. But by seven it is a mutation of sumptuous verticals of colour. Then the sun fires it, and the uncurtained window is too blazing to contemplate.

Yesterday, something very odd occurred. Forty or so men trotted over the hill and into the valley. Backpacked, not chattering like the crocodiles of ramblers, they were soldiers getting up steam – maybe for Afghanistan. Easy on their feet, they passed through the hazel screen so quickly that I might have imagined them.

Later this morning, I listen to Thomas Tallis's mighty motet for 40 voices. It is a music that overrides religious division and paltry argument. What price bank scares, what price anything that leaves out the eternal? Like the radio presenter, I heard it in Blythburgh Church ages ago, the forty voices waving and weaving their way to the painted angels, and out over the marshes. Having begun, they cannot end, at least in one's head, in one's devotions. How do the singers keep their places in this articulated glory?

Afterwards, dizzy with voices, I pick up fallen wood for the stove, and all the trees join in – although I am not so heavenly 'sent' not to see what needs lopping. Wild daffodils, those that Dorothy Wordsworth noted, are in bud under the plum.

During the debate about having judges or kings, Jotham tells a delightful tale about the trees' arguing over who should be their monarch. It is in Judges 9. 'The trees went forth on a time to anoint a king over them; and they said unto the olive tree [and to the fig, vine, and bramble], Reign thou over us.' And, being wise, as all trees are, they made their leafy excuses. No fear! Trees have better things to do than to reign over each other. And so had many of the Shechemites, it seems. After telling his tale, 'Jotham ran away', which is just like an author.

A noticeable thing, if I may say so, is how un-Bible-read the worshippers are these days. On Sunday, I preach on Barack

Obama's namesake, that Hebrew hero who saved his nation and whom the writer of Hebrews links with David. 'Arise, Barak, and lead' (Judges 5). Isn't this what they will have cried on Super Tuesday? He and a woman, Deborah, would rescue their country. So nothing is new.

Why do not so many of us read scripture for pleasure, or as a last resort on our desert island? Its stories are infinite; its poetry is enchanting. In it, the trees are enthroned and crowned as only nature can make them, and as they are in my old garden at this moment as the latest sap anoints them.

My lovely hazel (*Corylus avellana*) has high standing in the Christian universe; for did it not provide Dame Julian with her divine nut? A cock pheasant scuffles beneath it, kicking up black mould. 'You need to coppice that tree,' advises a passer-by. Do I?

Warm Winters

'What we need is a good hard frost,' says the unknown rider as she squelches up the track, her horse's hooves imprinting watery cicatrices in the mud. 'Yes,' I say supinely, for to be honest I find the warm January days blissful. I too squelch from bed to bed, from bush to tree whilst a blackbird sings aloft and unseasonal zephyrs mark my way as in a Handel opera. Snowdrops prick the earth and a couple of primroses are actually out. The air is brand new from whichever quarter it mildly blows. I thought I might walk to the church and ask the young pointer of pinnacles if he knew that mortar was once strengthened with 'malt liquor'. I must also enquire of the poet James Knox Whittet, late of Islay, and a welcome visitor to Bottengoms, whether he had heard of this use of his island's main export. He may well blanch at the thought of a single malt holding a church tower together.

But 'good hard frosts', snowfalls and bitter north winds, and Robin trying to keep himself warm, poor thing, will they be no more? Don't count on it. Little Ice Age or global warming, winter wild will come again. So make the most of a tropical January. The happiness of a bedroom window gaping across the fields all night and a cat asleep in the in-tray all day. The pleasure of the ditches rippling away, not with frigid gushes from the field-drains but with a sparkle. Sorting the Christmas cards into piles of needing a reply and not needing a reply. I spend some time admiring the pictures. Hardly any Pickwickian coaches, but quite a few Dutch villagers dancing about on the snow. And who would want to stay inside during the little Ice Age without windowpanes? Just shutters, and these blowing open. So put on every garment you possess and frolic by the river, play football – a favourite pitch was the frozen river – and drink a malt or two and by no means let the builder have it for bodging the cracks in the church.

Just twice have I been snowed-up down at the farmhouse. The first time I opened the front door on to a snow buttress and couldn't get out. And both times it was impossible to get up the track to the lane, a distance of about a mile, due to a filling-in with snowdrifts. The neighbours – people in this country always become frenzied during a big snowfall – were amazed that my telephone still worked and said that they placed food at the top 'if you can get to it'. In vain did I describe my deep freeze with its many packages bossily lettered, some of them, 'expiry date 1997' etc., and my laid-out apples, and my shelf-ful of jams and pickles, although I do not tell them about the wine as I have to preserve some kind of sobriety in my position. These epic snowfalls knew that an ancient house had to have some kind of drama in its long life. Had it not endured several centuries of the little Ice Age? One of them sans glass windows? Had not its thatch kept snug under a ton of snow and its eaves hung with icicles, and its inhabitants in January rushed from it into the cosy garden? Dark, dark it would have been, those Ice Age Epiphanies. And yet light. Not much light where that religious mob outside Parliament was concerned. And how British that their sacred fury should turn on the moral argument of a B & B. Such a nation has nothing to fear.

To Mount Bures for Epiphany matins and to daydream in that spiry little place and listen to the softly battering wind during the Lessons. We sing *Cantate Domino* – 'then shall all the trees of the wood rejoice before the Lord'. And it is so.

Ponds and Buses and Barrel-organs

Hard frosts accompany my reading of Henry Thoreau's *Walden*, with its memorable account of a hundred men cutting thousands of tons of ice from Walden Pond to store in such a way that two roasting Massachusetts' summers failed to melt it. 'Pond' – it covered over sixty acres! *Walden* is a young man's year in the wilderness during 1846, a delightful treatise on spartan living. Somewhat overwhelmed by Thoreau's pond, I 'cronched' – his word – over the white grass to look at mine. There are three of them, a couple where the garden begins and one where it ends. For time immemorial the plough horses drank deep at them somewhere about 3 p.m., or the end of their toiling day. In Walden the young hermit has a frequent argument with himself. 'Shall I go to heaven or a-fishing?' Even the saints must have asked themselves this question now and then. I sometimes think that God will ask us, 'That wonderful world of mine, why didn't you enjoy it more?'

The ice on my ponds is mere thin crackles around half-furled marsh marigold leaves, nothing extreme. A sunbeam would see it off. But the village stays wintry and even hibernatery. Some faint bustling in the shop, in the Crown, in Simon's carpentry shed, but that's about all. Half of us is in school, in the office, at the supermarket, in London. A minute part of us is on the farm. Why, we might be Ovington! Trying to discover the church key in that far west village, I must have knocked on a dozen unanswered doors before a girl on a bike called, 'They're out!' And the church key was where it always was – and where I soon found it. Cats sat in council-house windows, glad to have Ovington to themselves. An ancient man dug his garden but didn't look up. Ovington, population fifty-three. A murderer lived here, we were told as boys, meaning Lieutenant John Felton who, in 1628, walked from London to Portsmouth to rid England of the beautiful but bad Duke of Buckingham. An excellent woman, Mrs Brett, also lived here, as the little church bears witness, for it still has, inside and out, many of her Tractarian embellishments. She too walked far and significantly, for she was the secretary of Bishop Frank Weston of Zanzibar, one of the founders of the African Church and in many ways a precursor of Archbishop Trevor Huddleston. Bishop Frank and Mrs Brett challenging the imperialists, including Lord Milner himself, and then going on their way, she to Ovington with its old field church, its few folk and its son who with 'a tenpenny knife' altered history. Poor Bishop Weston also died from a knife wound which led to blood poisoning. His cook-boy had, with his permission, wielded it to relieve a carbuncle as they walked hundreds of miles through his diocese. He was fifty-three. It is not only old empires that were far flung, but also old villages.

Galanthus

I must go out to look at the snowdrops before the snow covers them. How coming snowstorms thrilled us as children. We would hear the grown-ups say, 'The sky is full of it', and we would rush to the hilltop to meet it halfway. 'Let it snow, let it snow!' we would holler. And the hill would be so quiet as it waited for the special snow silence. My snowdrops wait for it now, faintly trembling with pleasure, faces to the earth. Any minute it will fall on them, ravish them. Their name *Galanthus* means milk flower and it's milk which describes their particular whiteness, not snow. The whiteness of snow outdoes their milkiness. The few I gather open in minutes in the warm room. Isolated from the garden drifts their variant exposures are breathtakingly beautiful. I hold them up to look at what I would not be able to see outside and remember some of their species names, *Elwesi, Nivalis, Nivalis Viridispice* ... Their green-tipped bells have sprung, revealing all. There are snowdrop experts like my artist friend John Morley who are intimately acquainted with *Galanthus* society but I am on affectionate nodding terms with just a few of these first flowers. They drift in my wood, in the orchard, under the roses, along the lane, where the old farm buildings fell down, around the horse pond, where the postman turns his van, countless thousands of them. Snowdrops like to wander about a bit but still keep company.

They drift where I bury Mary's ashes in Little Horkesley churchyard and where generations of her family, the Bullocks, lie. Bullocks' corner it is known as. A stone has been removed to have her name added to it and she will not have to endure one of those stingy set in the grass tablets for the cremated. I have never understood why the latter should have doll's house memorials. Better to have one's name added to a marble book which suggests the divine roll-call than to rest under a tile. I have to cut a snowdrop slab in order to put Mary underground. Her ashes are grey as they slide from a plastic bag. I read John Donne's 'Bring us, O Lord, at our last awakening into the house and gate of heaven' over them to lend the practical business a bit of style. It is true winter and the bare trees clack. 'It is enough to cut you in half,' say the relations.

After which we take Helen to the Crown to celebrate her hundredth birthday. Just the handful of us who have known her for ever. Then back to her bungalow where a card from the Queen totters in pride of place on the mantelpiece. Bouquets cover her jigsaw table. Later, I walk home in the promised snowfall. The wind howls in my ears. The white cat, lengthways on the radiator, says something like, 'Thou fool' but when I set a match to the log fire she changes her tune and mouths, 'Thou angel'. A farmer and his family would have sat around this hearth when Shakespeare was writing *The Winter's Tale*, which is a play set in Bohemia. Flowers are mentioned but not snowdrops. The village people used to believe them to be unlucky and wouldn't have them in the house. White cats too were unlucky. Mine lies on her back and opens to the heat.

Snowfall

I know that it has arrived before I draw the curtains. Snow. Its silent voice fills the landscape. Snow is weather with a finger to its lips. A faint cold wind will be blowing towards the house in powdering drifts. John Nash, whose studio window this was, would have stood here to put the snow down, miraculously to me, on his snowy watercolour paper. There it would be, a favourite sight, snow-white on paper-white, and marked with a pheasant's starry footsteps. He is gone, the scene remains with its snow-laden willows toppling about a bit, and the flooded valley vaguely present through millions of flakes. They dance in the London commuters' headlights and settle on the cats, who for some purpose known only to them have left the warm kitchen to plunge about in the soaking whiteness like deceived girls making for the workhouse. The downfall is exhilarating the horses. They canter across the hillside, one of them sporting her winter blanket. 'Hast thou entered into the treasures of the snow?' enquires God of Job. 'No', say we all, men and beasts alike, though it is not for want of trying.

Later this snow morning we drive across a purified East Anglia on ebony motorways to Cambridge to hear a friend read her new poems. All is changed. Modest heights such as Tudy Camps and the Gogs are pretending to be the Himalayas. The windscreen wipers click like Chinese fans, throwing the snow off as fast as it comes. 'The clouds are full of it', we tell each other, this being something which is always said at such a time. Ours is a perilous enterprise for poetry's sake. Will the lane from Rodbridge to Cavendish be adrift when we return? It is the kind of lane down which Mr Woodhouse unwisely ventured to dinner when snow threatened.

It seems not quite right to celebrate Richard Rolle in January, though there he is in the Lectionary. He was the Yorkshire hermit whose love of Christ was too hot to handle by the medieval Church. Or perhaps it felt that it had to stand back from his fire. Rolle is our St John of the Cross, a saint of the interior song. The nuns at Hampole adored him, this passionate young man who did not care much for church services and sang on his doorstep.

I ask you, Lord Jesus,
to develop in me, your lover,
an immeasurable urge towards you,
an affection that is unbounded,
a longing that is unrestrained,
a fervour that throws discretion to the winds!

The Hampole nuns would have had him canonised – but no. So they beatified his memory. Some claim Richard Rolle to be the 'true father of English literature'. He was a wild boy who left Oxford without a degree, who lived as a hermit without being licensed to do so, and who wrote dazzlingly in English at a time when God expected Latin. Listening to poems in Girton College where I'm told there are now more men than women, fragments of Richard Rolle's enchanting book *The Fire of Love* become entangled with what I am hearing, which is quite a compliment to the poet reading her work. I think of Rolle's concept of the way we should love Christ: 'Reason cannot hold it in check, fear does not make it tremble, wise judgment does not temper it'. He was born in 1300 at Thornton-le-Dale, maybe during an Epiphany snowfall.

You who are the most lovely,
lovable and beautiful,
remember that it is through you
that I am no longer afraid of any passing power ...

Rolle's life and work are lessons on how not to get on in the Church.

Absent Relations

The question most asked if you live in a funny old house in the middle of nowhere is: 'Do you see ghosts?' No; but now and then I hear mothers calling 'Get up!' They stand at the bottom of the clumsy stairs, or the wonky ladder to the attic, threatening sleepy sons with dire consequences if they do not appear before they count ten. Feed the pigs. Go to school. What would their father say? Half-past five and still abed.

But at least these centuries of farmers' boys would not likely have put their parents down on paper. Many writers do, one way or another. Dickens immortalised – and forgave – his father in Mr Micawber. Edmund Gosse, an only son, in his masterpiece, *Father and Son*, revealed how far one could go in not giving hurt to a parent. Poor Mr Gosse Snr was a Creationist, and also a great scientist. Genesis told him one thing, the rocks, another. He and his fellow religionists once stood on the shore to await the Second Coming. One day Edmund told him that he did not believe a word of all this. Love continued between them, but something terrible, as well. It was not the usual row – literature saw to that. But what a fate, to breed an author!

The poet John Clare had to break it to his parents gently that he had written what he read to them because his mother 'knew not a single letter, and superstition went so far with her that she believed the higher parts of learning was the blackest arts of witchcraft'. Oh, the shame of it, to have a writer for a son! Or a daughter, of course. And, oh, the risk of it!

My friend Edward Blishen was able to take the risk. Love made it possible for him. 'Hate could be equally rewarding.' The plain truth was that his mother, Lizzie Pye, a servant girl and all unknowingly a great woman, was irresistible copy.

On the whole, writers find fathers easier to expose than they do mothers; not that exposure is necessarily a driving force – only the morality of telling the truth. To tell the truth about Mother, one had to cut into oneself as well as into her.

Edward and Lizzie seem to have been unflinching in this all their lives, which is not usually the case. But she had to grow old before he could, at least, show her to others as unsparingly as, since his boyhood, she had shown herself to him. For such a passionate writer, it was a long wait. Both he and his mother were touchers to the end – embracing, holding hands, giving little kisses: a warming existence. And this helped.

Iciness can be equally productive. Think of Ivy Compton-Burnett's *Mother and Son*. Yet there is a kind of natural avoidance, to the extent of caricature, in putting parents on the page. Once, Jesus shockingly rebuffed his mother – 'Woman, what have I to do with you?' The clinging nature of Jewish mothers?

With writers, of course, there is the painful nature of all ties, and their exploration, the putting them into words, and the breaking of taboos, the flight from them, and the inescapable tentacles of them, which the playwright Dodie Smith called *Dear Octopus*. Thus, from afar, in rooms where parents and children have insisted on dependence and independence for many generations, I might catch a cry or two. Although, of course, it might be the white cat.

FEBRUARY

*B*lythe's February brings us 'water-music': the music of field drains, the splosh of wet paths, the rush of the swollen Stour. It brings the 'hurtling darkness' of windy nights and, at the winter meeting-points of old and young, dead leaves raked from fresh-growing grass. Blythe walks the flinty track to and from his house, 'passing and re-passing' known and new things, mindful of the generations of people who have walked or slipped this way before. Those people and their necessary tasks – ditching, draining, hedge-laying – are here in these pages, their work preparing the 'handmade' landscape of the present.

In the patterning of the Christian year, February is shaped by its anticipatory relationship to Easter. We are preparing the way ahead and counting down – 'Septuagesima Sunday' marks seventy days to go – though for Blythe such number-work is joined by a sense of 'the immeasurable'. He catches the many moods of Shrovetide, partly a last carnival (feasts cooked on the Frost Fair ice), partly a sober anteroom to Lent. Then comes Ash Wednesday and the beginning of forty days echoing Christ's time in the desert. Through a lifetime's Lents, Blythe has been less interested in penance than in learning to appreciate simplicity. He notes shafts of warmth coming into a cold church, and the austere beauty of East Anglia's wild places. The emotional and narrative arc of the liturgy directs his eye to features of the Suffolk world around him.

For me, much of the joy of reading Blythe lies in following the associative logic that draws together apparently disparate observations. Often it works through delicate visual rhymes. Perhaps a tossed pancake at the local school joins the bright button of a Shrovetide sun with a stained-glass medallion symbolic of Christ. When foot-and-mouth spreads, and scientists model 'plumes' of airborne infection, Blythe thinks of 'vapour trails' across the country. He adds without comment that 'At Lenten

Compline our breath spirals in the cold church'. It's a bold leap, made with the swiftness of the metaphysical poets.

The method is non-schematic; nothing is goaded into line with a theme. Left to their own devices, Blythe's images are free to grow into metaphors or remain as vivid quotidian fragments, answering February's questions as they will. The final essay for the month moves antiphonally between prisons and open views, bars and plain glass. If we look back at February through this last window, the concern with seeing becomes clear. Opticians' spectacles, Damascene lights, the panes of a lost clerestory, the uncertain visions of the poet William Cowper, all rise up as possible emblems of Lenten insight in the cool, clear winter air.

There ought to be a more precise name than 'essay' for these pieces which are variously related to sermons, diary entries, letters, prose-poems and meditations. Blythe invokes a term used by Herbert, who asked 'where are my window-songs?' Set to the tune of other Februaries over centuries and yet highly distinct, these are Blythe's window-songs.

Alexandra Harris

Entrepreneur

We are in turmoil, which makes a change. Local tomato-growers are asking for planning permission to turn their acres into a Constable theme park. It will only need three-quarters of a million visitors a year to make it viable. There will be restaurants, car parks, playgrounds, toilets, everything you need for a day in the country. 'But where will they get all the Constables?' we ask. 'Aha!' reply the tomato-growers. To the further reality of everything they will offer being already here, the wild flowers, the woodland, the creatures, and most of all 'those scenes which made me a painter', as the great artist confessed, the theme parkers say, 'But what we propose is a marvellous business-like arrangement where you can enjoy all this without having to traipse along old footpaths, getting tired and muddy and all that.' Once, walking in Langham, the next village to that of the tomato-growers, John Constable told his wife that this countryside reminded him of Christ's saying, 'I am the resurrection and the life.' It was spring-time. And very soon it will be springtime once more, and the modest river will flow slowly to the North Sea, now and then pausing, as it were, to reflect some of the most celebrated views in English art, the Field Studies Centre at Flatford Mill, the nature reserves properly cared for by the Woodland and Wildlife Trusts, the ancient East Anglian towns and villages where both Constable's and Gainsborough's families made their living, through which another kind of river will stream, that of theme park traffic. Hence our yelling in the lanes and waving our Kalashnikovs.

By coincidence Ian and I found ourselves in Mistley the other day where an eighteenth-century attempt to turn the Stour estuary into a spa quite failed in spite of Robert Adam being commissioned to design the church. It was bitterly cold and scores of swans were grooming themselves on the bank. The wind blew in from the Arctic, and old ladies, wrapped like Innuits, dropped correct swan breakfast onto the surface of the water, where it was scooped up by whirling gulls. Mr Rigby the spa entrepreneur saw himself as the provider of a rivery theme park for the Quality. There would be fashionable sermons in Mr Adam's church, promenades along the Stour, carriage outings to the coast, though avoiding Harwich, of course, and meetings of the best society. But it all came to nothing, or near-bankruptcy, which is much the same thing. We actually went on to Harwich to see Captain Jones's house. It was he who captained the *Mayflower*. We stood, too, in wonder before the Electric Cinema, 1911, listening hard for the sound of Tom Mix and Mae West. One shilling this side, sixpence this side. An old man came to tell us that during the war he was let in free. We walked to Dovercourt, getting colder and colder. Vast ships crept into harbour. Below us was the seaweedy strand where Dr Johnson saw young James Boswell off to Holland after making him say his prayers. Boswell watched his new friend until he was out of sight.

On Sunday I preached on the Presentation, morning and evening, in one church then another. On those old watchers Simeon and Anna. Trevor, a teacher from Holland, was present at both services. The ringers attempted a quarter peel. Constable's uncles and aunts and cousins slept in the table-tombs in the graveyard. I imagined them by the river, hard folk making a living, and the labourers digging yet one more great ditch, it being February.

One of the Coldest Times Ever

Ages ago, when I was beginning to write, I put up a bravura defence of winter. 'Winter wild, and winter drear, Surely wintertime is here', we sang as children. I didn't believe it. Snow elated me. Black-ice ponds thrilled me. Thus, when I listened to the beginnings of the present blanket condemnation of winter by the weathermen, I was genuinely puzzled.

My defence of it was in a youthful 'literary middle', as I believe such thousand-word essays were called in the *Observer*. It was headed 'A good word for winter'. These provocative opinions, sharp and short, were in the tradition of William Hazlitt, the British Montaigne.

Sitting with my back to the hot sun as it blazes through the study window, and with boys and girls and frantic dogs tobogganing on the steep field, I find myself thinking that it would not go amiss for the young forecaster in his smart suit to point out what an indescribably beautiful day it has been. Of course, less so if one is on the road or on the train, when winter can be an inconvenient, or even dangerous loveliness. All the same, its 'dreariness' these days is usually more on the screen than outside.

And why do most seventeenth-century artists have everyone outside when it snows? This was one of the coldest times ever, as we know. For one thing, it was warmer than in the house. Just look at the unglazed windows, the rocking shutters, the miserable thread of smoke winding up into the blue from the hefty chimneys. Then see the frantic exercise outside. You can almost hear the shouts, the barks, the pleasure.

Such sounds were duplicated on my hill. It was Sunday, but no church, which made the day somehow unlicensed and strange, it being impossible to get up the farm track. It was deep in drifts, scribbled all over by bird feet and rabbit paws. And here was a fine something-before-Lent sermon lying unspoken on the table. And then I find that it is Septuagesima in the old language, when 'we may be mercifully delivered by thy goodness, for the glory of thy name'. When Henry, the Vicar, rings up at seven in the morning to say, 'No services today', for who could slide to church on such icy lanes? I reply that we must say our prayers at home. Yet it is odd, winter or no winter.

The first icicle of the season jabs from the guttering, a kind of black-white spike pointing to the earth. I scoop snow from a trough and scatter 'wild bird seed', which is what it says on the label. There now, I tell myself, I have done my bit. I have shown true regret for not taking matins, and I have fed the hungry. And I am enjoying, at long range, the happiness of the season. And the white cat on the sill wears a nimbus of snowy sunshine, and wisely declines an invitation to go out.

In Good King Charles's winter days, even the court joined the sliders on the Thames. The river was almost solid ice, and people lit bonfires on it, built temporary shops on it, skated to the sea or to Oxford on it. The big thing was to roast an ox on it. Many people in villages or towns perished from the cold, of course. They were called the poor. Many people, young and old, were exhilarated by the sharpness of life, not death. Walk carefully. See the briefly transformed view. And, as the Revd Sydney Smith advised, 'Keep good fires'.

How to Paint Towers

Cathedrals disturb our journeys. Who has not glanced up from a book on the train as it rushes past Durham or creeps into Ely and not only lost his place but his way? Throughout his life Claude Monet would leave Paris or his beloved Giverny to visit his father at Le Havre or his brother at Rouen, following the Seine all the route. In February 1892 he put up at an hotel whose windows faced the south-west front of Rouen Cathedral. Its immense tower with its needle-like spire, a fairly recent addition, could not be seen, cut off as it were by glazing-bars. Watching the daylight falling in continually altering hues on the grand entrance, shifting from viewpoint to viewpoint, he conceived an extraordinary set of pictures, thirty in all, which would record what happened to a building every hour. Thus one of the mightiest painterly concepts was achieved. It was the Irish writer George Moore who described Impressionism as 'the rapid noting of elusive appearance'. Thus Monet's *Cathedrals*, as these studies came to be called, which took him ten hours a day over nearly two years to complete, are some-thing other than Impressionistic. Suffice to see them as perfect statements on what atmosphere hourly does to stone.

This climatic vision of both architecture and its local land-scape wasn't new. John Constable understood it all his life and called it 'a science'. But it was left to Monet at the close of the nineteenth century to make this astonishing statement on it by showing Rouen Cathedral round the clock. He caused paint to give the time of day to a building, one which the viewer could almost set his watch by. He entitled his studies *Early afternoon; 2–3 pm*, etc. And it was exactly that. Constable called his painting of a cart and horse standing quiet and still in the millpond *Noon* but a friend dubbed it *The Hay Wain*. Artists like to give their world the time of day.

A monolithic church tower catches every light there is as I walk down my farm track. It is that of Stoke-by-Nayland church. It rises from a hill five miles off and for a minute or two it is framed by an oak and an ash before it vanishes altogether. I know exactly where to catch it as I bring down the paper and the milk, but I cannot 'know' its infinite variety, only marvel at its pinks and bloody reds, its translucent solidarity, its ability sometimes to be as golden as St Bernard's Jerusalem, or as gossamer as dragonflies' wings. Like Monet at Rouen, Constable painted it over and over again, once when the labourers were rioting, chalking-in a rain-bow over its pinnacles, a symbol of the divine providence. This tower is 120 feet high. We climbed it as boys, praying that Canon Clibbon wouldn't catch us, or worse his verger. 'Come you down you little B's!' We wanted to see Harwich Water from the top. It was up and up and round and round, the tower's dusty entrails clunking and groaning, and a strange interior wind hooting at us and, worst of all, the bell-ringers starting up to deafen us like poor Quasimodo, the hunchback of Notre-Dame.

We were in Stoke again last week, to find them clearing trees and 'rubbish' (wild plants) in order to let us see the tower from where Constable saw it. We made a pilgrimage to the south doors, a pair of tall silvery-grey carvings of amazing beauty, weathered by Suffolk hands, weighing a ton yet light as air. Doors which Constable's painty fingers would have opened. He and Monet let us view architecture in all the dispensations of daylight.

Now the floodlight sponsors of Stoke-by-Nayland tower – £6 at the Post Office – allow us night vision of its magnificence. During the last week of the old year 'Philip, so loved', and 'Wendy, Nicolette and James, the best family anyone could wish for', are celebrated. Their names fill the niches left empty by topped saints and crowd the shields of forgotten lords. 'You have kept the church lit,' says the magazine. So have we, say the sun and rain, the mists and winds. Seeing Stoke touch the sky, Constable reminds it, 'I am the man of clouds'. Seeing Rouen that early afternoon, Monet told his wife, 'Every day it is whiter; more and more it is blazing straight down . . .' Church towers, what are they really for if not to raise our sights?

Wild Places

They told me that the hunt would be coming through, but I had forgotten. All nature changes when the hunt comes through. Coming down from the study, I find the white cat shivering behind the ancient clock and thinking – the hunt! But you have a strong door and a moderately sized man to protect you, I tell her. This is no comfort, apparently; for she shakes the more. It is the hound 'music', wild and wicked. Exultant. It howls over the hill.

Now, when David the naturalist's collie bursts in on Saturday, yelling his head off, whacking the furniture with his tail, the cat doesn't shift. Simply looks down on him. Purrs, even. Thus the huntsman's hounds sound a very different note – that of terror. Creatures quake in setts, burrows, and nests, and the animal kingdom is frightened.

Terror is hard to communicate in literature. The more the terror writers try, the more unterrifying they are. Ronan Bennett's novel *Havoc in its Third Year* is a masterpiece about this emotion. Everything is understated – 'normal'. It is about a recusant Catholic family being hounded by keen Protestants in the seventeenth century. A quotation from Goethe prefaces it: 'Mistrust all in whom the desire to punish is imperative.' One remembers Saul/Paul. But the genius of the story lies in its terror.

The white cat stopped shaking eventually, as did all the creatures of the valley. The hound music died away. I thought of Christ's natural terror in Gethsemane. And of the Jews hearing the Nazis singing, their locked doors no safety, and their knowing this.

Lent once more. What shall my discipline be? Rather than fast I will say Compline before I sleep. Also feed on George Herbert. And recognise that the wilderness is not the wasteland. Naturalist friends have made this plain. Our East Anglian wilderness spread across the Norfolk–Suffolk border and was called the Breckland, but the Forestry Commission destroyed it a century ago. We still miss it. It is where they filmed *Dad's Army*. Prehistoric people dwelt there, as they did on most of our moors, preferring its openness.

I felt their presence when I walked on Rannoch Moor, Bodmin Moor, and many a wild place. Sometimes I saw their hearths. And I certainly saw their views, wide, unclouded, sometimes seaward. They liked an open life. The religious imagery of the desert conflicts with nature's realities. But then we come to Christ's privations and the prospect before him, and all is another matter.

The poet George Crabbe understood the botany of the Aldeburgh marshes, and found an intellectual and spiritual fulfilment in them. But he banished Peter Grimes there, a man who did not understand his own wickedness. Or could not. That was his tragedy.

Writers have been partial to deserts: Shakespeare with his blasted heath, Hardy with his Egdon Heath, now mostly ploughed up. But in *The Return of the Native* he allowed its furze to destroy all the best of the community that had settled there. Love, literature, beauty – all was gnawed away by grit, prickly plants and lizards. Long ago, the inhabitants of the Essex marshes and of the Fens were thought barely human. 'Then was Jesus led up of the Spirit into the wilderness.'

Mortality Among the Flowers

It is difficult to describe the atmosphere of rural life at this moment. Last week a poster was slapped onto the telegraph pole forbidding walkers and dogs to come down the track. There is a primitive fearfulness such as must have existed when coins were placed in vinegar instead of another person's hand and the word Plague was whispered. The world is arrested, still, holding its breath and wondering if it will happen here and not in some far off country of which we had never heard, such as Cumbria. It's then that I hear the spring birds singing and see the primrose profusion in the ditch, and recall how spring arrived at the Western Front, to the surprise and heartbreak of rural soldiers from many lands.

Natural death has darkened our small community. Laura's at six and a half, Albert's at ninety and a half. The latter in his Sunday suit, not a white hair in his head, clanged the bells for me at Mount Bures at 9.25 a.m. precisely every Sunday morning. And as a line of Alberts had done since the Wars of the Roses. Using every tactic I knew, I eventually persuaded him not to mow the harebells by the vestry by telling him that they were the origin of the bluebells of Scotland. After which he skirted round them. But old men like to keep 'the rubbish' down, knowing how incorrigible it is and how given a chance, it will grow up and bury you.

Once, giving a talk at the village school during Book Week, I found myself listening to the Albert of long ago in this selfsame classroom telling me how he slid down the mount of Mount Bures on his mother's old tea tray, flattening a path through the bluebells, the slimy stems of which speeded up his descent. It is strange not to count ten after Albert has stopped ringing before entering the chancel to begin the service, giving him time to loop the bell ropes and get back to his pew. And sad beyond measure not find him growing runner beans in his little Eden between the gravestones and the Norman fort. Thinking of Albert's grave, the neighbours are saying, 'Well, he won't have to go far!' But then he never did.

Isolated as I am by the foot-and-mouth restrictions, I miss my walkers whose dogs rush up for a pat, my unrecognisable riders in their helmets, my ramblers with their maps, my occasional mountain biker. This is what it must have been like in the Pest House, with everybody keeping their distance. But at least it could be the ill wind which might blow away some of the nonsense of the Countryside March. Townspeople and country folk alike are drawn into a common plight when the 'plumes' of disease are able to make vapour trails across every boundary invented by history, just as they did during the plagues of long ago, and will do forever. At Lenten Compline our breath spirals in the cold church, joining that of our ancestors as they muttered in the sacred quietness about the trouble *they* had with sheep.

The Watcher by the Beehive

The old friend takes up her position at the crossroads. Warmly wrapped, contemplative, familiar, she watches the world go by. One road leads to where General Fairfax stationed his troops during the Civil War, one to the little priory that a Saxon couple founded, one to Duncan's farm and to me, and one to the river.

57

Perched also at the crossroads are the Beehive pub and the letter box.

Not so very long ago the village – every village – peered out through lace curtains. Its patron saint was Miss Marple, Queen of Nosiness. But the TV has changed all this. Not only does it reveal far more interesting happenings than the window, but it has created an indifference to local morals.

Only twenty years ago, a landowner refused to let a cottage to an unmarried couple. Now, they could live any way they liked as long as they paid the rent. The Church, too, ceases to poke about in people's private lives. The old, rich, wicked, ruinous gossip that made life hell (and enthralling) is not so much silenced as given a more acceptable language.

But, in any case, say what you will, the gadgetry of the age – television, computers, cars, mobiles, not to mention the Freedom of Information Act – has turned parish scandal and eccentricity into something that one has to be adult about. These recent inventions have certainly wrecked rural fiction. Think of secrets like Lady Dedlock's or Mr Rochester's. *The Archers'* scriptwriters have their work cut out to keep Brian disgraceful. A love-child – gosh!

But the old lady sits by the crossroads, preserving, in the highest sense, the rural tradition of watching. It is good to see her. I sit out a great deal, and the horses, cat and birds watch me. And, at week-ends, the ramblers and the dog servants. 'There he was,' they will mention to their families when they get home, stamping my mud off, 'sitting outside with a book.'

Our ancestors were so eager to observe the world go by their dwelling-places that they built them as near to the highway as was safe. A cart, a young traveller, pilgrims, Gypsies, a bagman, a carriage, endless children, passers-by with whom to pass the time of day. If you lived in town, preferably in the busiest streets, bow windows like opera boxes would give full view of the drama of human existence.

Abraham was sitting outside his tent, an old man and deserving of simply 'looking', when he saw three walkers. It was hot. Company at last! He could not do enough for them. The scene always reminds me of James Boswell and Dr Johnson on their Scottish tour. How they would send their servant ahead of them to Lord Monboddo, for example, longing for guests in his castle, lonely, bored. Then, 'Dr Samuel Johnson is on his way!' And the joyful preparation. Nothing too much trouble for the passer-by.

Ancient Abraham ran to the approaching visitors. 'Let a little water be fetched and wash your feet, and rest yourselves under the tree', and to Sarah, 'Make cakes upon the hearth.' She was inside the tent when she heard the travellers tell her husband that she would have a son. She laughed. The things people said when they walked by one's door! When they sat under one's tree!

St Valentine

For the rain it raineth every day. Absurdly, I find myself, nose to pane, staring through sliding globules at the drenched exterior. I am a child again and the worst words in the world are being said: 'No, you cannot go out.' Neither could the farm labourers, as they were still called. They watched their tiny wages being washed away. Those who could had put a few bob by for a rainy day. So much of the rural background of the Gospels needed no explanation to the worshipping country people of only fifty years ago. The Septuagesima epistle is all about labourers' wages and its stark equalising and bleak conclusion would have caused some flinching in the pews. A penny if you toiled a full day, a penny if you toiled an hour. Farmer neighbours splosh in. Having been properly trained by their wives, they kick off their Wellingtons to reveal neat little liners over their socks in which they can pad around like Muslims. Outside, the field-drains are singing and with a good ear on a pouring morning it is possible to pick up all the cascading water music of the February land. In the city the damp white faces of the homeless glimmer in the underpasses.

St Valentine has come and gone. Poor martyr, how we take his name in vain. He had nothing to do with sweethearts. It was just that his feast coincides with the day on which the spring birds mate – 14 February. Little is known of him. The public mating on the Valentine pages of the newspapers makes gruesome reading, and for the press a nice annual earner. At least Margery Brews, writing to her 'Voluntyn' in 1477, kept it private: 'Myn herte me byddes ever more to love yowe truly over all erthely thing.' It was on a drear Sunday afternoon in February that the girl-farmer Bathsheba in Hardy's *Far from the Madding Crowd* amuses herself by sending the most tragic valentine in English literature. It breaks the heart of its recipient, Farmer Boldwood. It says, 'Marry me' – but it is a joke. To decide whether she will send it to a boy or to this ageing man, Bathsheba throws a hymnbook in the air – shut, Boldwood, open, Teddy. 'Of love as a spectacle Bathsheba had a fair knowledge; but of love subjectively she knew nothing.'

On Septuagesima I preach on God making something out of nothing. There was a void and he filled it. There was darkness and he lit it. This is what creation means. Below us, the Stour streams to the sea. Beside us the much rained-on tombs make clear reading. Some of their inscriptions are real valentines.

Speaking Likeness

Three invitations in a week to celebrate advanced birthdays, two octogenarian, one wittily inscribed 'for John's Coming of Age'. So far as one can actually see age hasn't reached him yet. On Peter's shelf a crowd of cards cry 'Happy 100th Birthday' – not his but his dad's. All this celebration reminds me that my own life tends not to rise to these party heights but jogs along in a fashion which for the most part ignores dates. Every now and then forms arrive to make me face up to the day, the month and the year.

The old friend who laid out the garden just after the last war also laid down the law on what to clear and when to clear. Thus the autumn sticks and mulch are only now being rolled back, leaving vivid grass and nourished beds. Bulbs reveal their presence, as does the butterbur with its nodules. I work until I cannot see, with Max enthroned on his usual apple stump, just gazing. I am this cat's servant. He meweth and I open doors, open tins and clasp him to my bosom for his reassurance, ton weight that he is. The top garden looks surprisingly neat in the half-light and the westering birds pass overhead in little groups. A thin oval moon spins among scudding clouds like a dud coin as I grope around collecting tools. Another day. Desk before noon, earth till nightfall. That's the way it usually is. The cathedral telephones about Lent. *Lent!* Yes, Lent is upon us, Lent and the desert wastes. The starkness before us. Returning in the blind hope of finding the secateurs, I observe the fox trotting over the corn looking this way and that, and not so much fearfully as appreciatively.

At Little Horkesley Matins I unravel the tale of the blacksmith and the carpenter in Isaiah 44. You will remember it. It is about these artisans going beyond their brief and becoming *artists*. They move from making useful things to making worshipful objects. To me their progression is admirable, though not to the great prophet. The Old Testament could not be more fierce about any activity than that involved with the making of graven images, whether they be of men, animals or plants. And the carpenter? Well let us hear his tale. He has nurtured an ash tree, chopped it down, and then used it to warm himself and to heat his bread oven. All well and good. He should then have gone on to make tables and chairs but instead uses his rule, plane, line and compass to create 'the beauty of a man' – a household god in effect. The one and only God of Isaiah will not have it and fumes against the vanity of 'delectable things', and the prophet himself puns on the foolishness of the carpenter turned artist. The man who carves his god from ash 'feedeth on ashes'. The early Christians put all the thunderous Old Testament denouncement of imagery behind them and painted Jesus and his friends on the walls of the catacombs.

The Word and The Worm

The Shrove Tuesday sun spun up between the ash tree and Duncan's generator, as bright as a button. It gilded my tea mug, and glorified the white cat who, as usual, was glaring through the window at the blackbirds.

The window contains an ancient IHS stained-glass medallion that Ian found in Framlingham. It is fixed to the pane with UHU glue. The morning sun, being as bright as it can be, burns through it. Henry, the Vicar, will be walking to our minute school – 13 pupils – to toss pancakes.

There are two figures on the hilltop: a girl leading a horse, and a young man descending from it with light steps, his face ablaze. He carries something under his arm which, when he opens it, is also golden and blinding. He tells us that it is something called the Word. He holds it above his head. He has yellow hair, and he came from the north. The Word glitters like sunshine.

In the afternoon, I rake up oak leaves, prior to the first mow. It is bitterly cold and wonderfully hot at the same time. The new grass is springy, and Wordsworth's wild daffodils make a fine patch in the orchard. Kate is walking her new puppy, a chocolate-coloured animal of unrestrained joy. She is training her, she says. An old joke comes into my head: 'I am a dog. My name is Sit.'

I pick a few primroses for the table. I think of Ash Wednesday and of Joel. 'Let the priest, the ministers of the Lord, weep between the porch and the altar.' Henry won't be weeping. He will be burning last year's palms to make ash for our foreheads. I re-read T. S. Eliot's 'Ash Wednesday'.

> If the lost word is lost, if the spent word is spent
> If the unheard, unspoken
> Word is unspoken, unheard;
> Still is the unspoken word, the Word unheard,
> The Word without a word, the Word within
> The world and for the world;
> And the light shone in darkness and
> Against the Word the unstilled world still whirled
> About the centre of the silent Word.

The fair young man with the Book walks through the land and opens its illuminated pages, calling out: 'Don't forget, you first heard it here!' Heaven knows what most of us made of it – this 'Word'.

Pip brings me our parish magazine, a monthly called *The Worm*, whose masthead is a dragon having a virgin for supper. Her white legs dangle from its jaws. But St George comes riding in; so maybe all is not lost.

Considering the inactivity of the village when I walk through it, its recorded activity is alarming. Somebody is going to line the bus shelter, free of charge. Should we keep the telephone box? The village-hall sign still has not arrived – 'The Recreation Trust has been asking for this for a very long time.'

Christopher writes about the Wormingford-to-Abberton pipeline and its funding. 'Eight years on, and we are still waiting.' Andrew, our archaeologist, tells us about Giles Barnardiston, the Quaker, who lived on our height above the Stour with his wife, Philippa, and who found the Word in quietness.

Bill and his dog, Cyrus, see a pair of otters in the river. As a boy, I witnessed an otter hunt – a disgusting business.

A Doleful Lent

Ash Wednesday, and ashes indeed, with the countryside closed down and pestilence free-ranging. It hitches a lift on the motorway and travels first class on the plane. Our feet carry it along. So does the wind. Indeed, as one farmer said, trying to stop it is like punching the wind. There is a difference between what is happening at the moment and what occurred in 1967. Although such a short time ago, the farms were smaller and more private then, less on the road, less cut down and open. Who now gave a thought to the fact that the chops in our supermarket trolley had already travelled the length of England? Rustling through my book of petitionary prayers, I cannot discover any which touch on the medieval reality of our disaster, and which will do for both our human and animal helplessness. Maligned grey squirrels swing innocently in the trees and among 'the first unfolding leaves' as John Clare called them. So all is well and all is ill. And what can we do? Little, it seems. Sickness must take its course. I recall an ancient petition – 'Have pity upon us, who are now visited with great sickness and mortality'. Although in those days it would not have been the illness of animals.

And so the fast begins. Michael the vicar presses ash from a small silver box on each of our brows as we kneel at the rail and I speak Joel's passionate language. His words echo through the arches. The tower clock crunches into action and claims another hour of our existence. Forty days and forty nights lie ahead. But who is counting! Are we not where the measurable and the immeasurable part company? Our penitence 'for all that is past' is signed on our foreheads. The altar candles gutter due to an untraceable wind which lives in the sanctuary. The coloured windows are blacked out by night and are best seen from the churchyard. Those who have given up whisky for Lent are already battling with their souls, it being a raw evening. Does anyone give up soaps for Lent? How hard that must be for the addicted. Preaching on George Herbert, I talk about his sensible latitude where fasting is concerned.

It's true, we cannot reach Christ's fortieth day;
Yet to go part of that religious way,
Is better than to rest.

Lent was Herbert's season. He was born in Lent, married in Lent and died in Lent. For him fasting was a method of 'starving sin'. But then he was an early dietician and nutritionist where both earthly and heavenly food were concerned. His feast day precedes Ash Wednesday and brings a kind of balance to what is expected of us in the days ahead.

Choir Man

A blowy wet wind for Fred's departure and for Ash Wednesday. The small horse pond which I cleaned out last week is filling up limpid and fresh. Buds are visibly fattening and the track is like the Somme. So all praise to the early spring rains. Michael picks me up from the top and we splash and swish to Little Horkesley for Fred's funeral, and listen on the car radio to an African version of *Messiah*. A pony-tailed head hails us from Fred's unfinished grave to show us what he has found – beautifully carved stones from the medieval church which the landmine destroyed in 1940. I had often wondered how so much decorated rubble could have utterly vanished. The youthful digger has made a circle of turfs and fragments and we don't inquire how on earth things will be ready in less than an hour's time, for they always are.

Fred's passing is special. He was nearly ninety-eight and had sung in choirs from the age of eight until within a few months of his death. He had sung with us a mere thirty years. He was a

Suffolk engine-driver who had driven hissing, whistling steam monsters from Mark's Tey to Cambridge, and then from Norwich to Liverpool Street. His condition for joining our choir had been that we must understand that he was a chancel man, and not a nave man, and since he had sung treble, then bass, in chancels before we were born, it was welcome, welcome! A late second marriage had produced a daughter who was still in her twenties, and this playing havoc with time had kept Fred from ever looking old in the expected sense. Listening to his phrasing as I stood next to him, it would occur to me that Fred would have been familiar with its pauses before the First World War.

We had some mutual memories of his first choir at St Gregory's, Sudbury, a most lovely church built by a local boy who became Archbishop of Canterbury, but also, alas, Chancellor of England, for Wat Tyler beheaded him for imposing the poll tax. Mrs Thatcher got off lightly. Archbishop Theobald's head was brought back to Sudbury and placed behind a glass in the vestry, where it made a mirror for generations of choirboys when they needed to fix their ruffs and comb their hair. Fred and I had as children stared out mortality, lost in our own reflections, eye to socket with the Archbishop. Fred, like all choirmen of his day, liked Stainer, and so at his funeral we sang from *The Crucifixion* and I read Thomas Hardy's

On afternoons of drowsy calm
  We stood in the panelled pew,
Singing one-voiced a Tate and Brady psalm
  To the tune of 'Cambridge New'.

Back home a strengthening wind carried the click-clack of the little diesel which runs along what remains of that Cambridge line.

Olney Hymns

A wild week. We battle through the hurtling darkness to say Compline at Mount Bures where gales hoot around the spire and have done some breaking and entering, blowing-in the vestry window. Will trees come down? Will slates fly off? Will there be a power cut? Keep us as the apple of your eye. On a further desperate evening we drive in the opposite direction to Little Horkesley to sing the Olney Hymns and as there are almost a hundred of us we are able to out-voice nature with their piety. First sung in 1779 in the tiny Buckinghamshire town where John Newton was curate and William Cowper was genius, the Church at large flinched from them. Such intimacy, such a touching of hands with the Saviour, such a keeping in step with him, it could not be decent. Also such an incongruity in the friendship which inspired them, that of an ex-slaver and a depressed poet. What did they have in common? The Olney Hymns give a full explanation, and when we sing them their pathology is so unclouded by the old religious language that it causes us to miss a heartbeat.

John Newton remained astounded that Christ would have anything to do with him, let alone be his close friend. He had gone to sea aged eleven and had both received and given every kind of abuse and degradation. He had done, and had done to him, unspeakable things – and yet at Olney Christ walked with him, a distinguished writer sought him as a confessor and the world respected him. He was clearly redeemed. Heaven assured him so. He was a strange man, very dominant. He had taught himself several languages, theology, morals, Euclid, often using the African sand as his exercise-book as he waited for the dockers of Sierra Leone to load his ship with the eighteenth century's most valuable cargo, black people. But he had been God-fearing and respectable, and would not allow his crew to swear. He said the offices on matins and evensong on deck every Sunday. It was a well conducted ship, all Anglican above, all hell below. But in 1764 he was sent to minister to the gentle lace-makers of Olney, the unlikeliest curate ever, and to become the companion of a famous but suicidal poet who likened himself to the most hunted of creatures, hares and deer.

Newton was certain, Cowper uncertain. Newton was Bunyan's Evangelist, 'pointing with his finger over a very wide field' and saying, 'Do you see yonder Wicket-gate?' Cowper was the man who said, 'No'. Then said the other, 'Do you see yonder shining light?' to which Cowper would have replied, 'I *think* I do ...' Between them, with certainty and uncertainty, they wrote and published the Olney Hymns, all 348 of them, as curious a partnership as will be found in English literature. 'O for a closer walk with God' we sing to the accompaniment of plaintive weather.

Dressing Down

I am ironing my gardening clothes, having scrubbed them, and should guests be present, to their derision. Life is divided between ironers and non-ironers. I am also attending Melvyn's morning class. This week – Archimedes. Where else in all the wide broadcasting universe could one listen to such a programme? Outside, a faint fall of snow is evaporating under the sun. The sun is throwing its golden weight about this winter. Birds sit in the snow in order to capture my concern. 'Look at us!' they squeak, 'in the deep midwinter, snow on snow'– that kind of thing. But even as they speak their warm bodies melt the few flakes and they are bobbing about on spring grass. I scatter it with crumbled cream crackers. They tell God about my charity. I listen to a woodpecker on a nearby dead elm, a fine drummer. The elms have returned, but only for about twenty feet, when they perish and turn a grey-silver in the field hedges. Grubs then take them over and they become woodpeckers' breakfast bars.

No actual holes in the gardening jersey and jeans, the cosy jacket, but some thinning where my joints are, some transparency about the knees. Some presence of seeds in the pockets. Melvyn's brilliant guests have got to the part where Archimedes has to examine the king's golden crown for authenticity. He has ordered it from the best goldsmith but there is something fishy about it, or rather silvery. Has he passed it off as 22 carat when in fact it is partly silver? Ask Archimedes. Then we come to the best bit, but the experts are somewhat cool about Archimedes jumping out of his bath and shouting, 'Eureka!' Why, anyway, was he worrying his head over such things as his body being an irregular solid? And why the volume of an irregular solid could be calculated by measuring the water it displaced when it was immersed? I tell my friends to be careful not to run big baths at the farmhouse. They are not in London now. Too much water and the pump starts up. Though what if it does? Isn't this what a pump is for? But ancient pump facts have been bred in me and although they are now obsolete I continue to honour them. I possess a kind of congenital austerity which is shocked when people wash up a few cups under a running tap or fill the bath. Melvyn's guests are undermining this. One thing the Eureka story proves is that Archimedes had a private tub and did not have to join the rest of the community at the Syracuse public baths. Imagine having to get all those bodies out before being able to shout, 'Eureka!'

The newspaper arrives and here is a bad-tempered youth modelling my gardening clothes, the coat costing £10,000, the trousers only £850. He wears an unironed shirt which has been designed to go straight from its maker to Oxfam. And here is Finance and Business with rows of lords with old faces and dividential thinking written on them, and of course one cannot stop thinking about the poor young man who was advised to give all his money away. And I wonder which section Archimedes would have been in, the Fitted Bathrooms or the Crime, his running

down the street naked and crying, 'Eureka!' Outside, the primroses are edged with snow, the hellebores, called thus because they
are of uncertain origin, like most of us, are magnificent, and the
hazel catkins are profuse. They said that Archimedes was so busy
inventing things that he didn't know what was happening. And
who does – exactly?

Plough Sunday

A residual devotion to, usually, some abandoned rite hangs
around in the village memory. Little that takes place in the
fields these days rings a bell in church. Barry the ringer told me
how he found himself in the real world at a Plough Sunday
service in Bures.

Bures bridges itself across both Suffolk and Essex, and is where,
traditionally, the fifteen-year-old Edmund was crowned King of
East Anglia. The Stour has been thinly flooded across its water
meadows since Christmas and glinting with birds.

Plough Sunday – it should have been Monday – comes after
Twelfth Night. Barry and I are old enough to find it normal
enough – only, as such things happen, progress, being the tractor,
displaced it. And this now long ago.

When I first came to live here, my neighbour William Brown,
who farmed above me, asked me how to take Plough Sunday
service. He was a Scot from Ayrshire, whose father had emigrated
from that stony ground to our rich but half-lost soil. So we found
a hand-plough among the iron litter, tied yellow ribbons to its
handles, and stood it on the chancel step of Little Horkesley
church.

A plough had for everlasting represented the very essence of
agriculture. When a rural congregation saw it just below the altar,
there was barely a need for office or sermon; while the hymn
itself sprang from the share. It would have been painted blue.

Ploughmen – called horsemen in our sliver of the world – made themselves obvious. And thus it had been for ever and ever, amen.

When it went, nobody brought a tractor into church. I can't recall what I said or what we sung, but the beautiful plough from the dead bindweed held our gaze.

Ploughmen, horsemen, walked hippity-hop, one foot in the furrow, one foot on its crest. Up and down, up and down, all winter's day, turning at the top, thinking of – what? Now there's a question.

W. B. Yeats wrote:

All things uncomely and broken, all things worn out and
    old,
The cry of a child by the roadway, the creek of a lumber-
    ing cart,
The heavy steps of the plowman, splashing the wintry
    mold,
Are wronging your image that blossoms a rose in the deeps
    of my heart.

The once most commonplace of country sights and sounds are eroding the poets' finer thoughts. John Clare preferred ploughing to gardening. Solitary in a vast field, there was no one to see that he was composing, no one to witness 'my muttering'. He made lines across Helpston's acres and, later on by the cottage fire, lines across paper, working double time. I possess a few ears of corn from a field where he ploughed, crisp, precious, though tractor-sown.

I have been shifting leaves by the million. Damp and dry, they leave new grass and yellowing grass, which will turn green. All in good time. My wood is delicately spiky with unopened snow-drops. It is hard to be inside. They are manuring up at the top, and the commuters' smart cars are spraying the muck, which is thoughtful of them.

Tracking

Proust's novels *Swann's Way* and *The Guermantes Way* were no more than the brief country walks which people had to take in order to get out of their towns and villages. Trodden countless times in a lifetime, they would eventually provide a kind of dream route for the local person who had to travel them. Bunyan, recognising that the Puritan work ethic had taken over the old spring pilgrimages, suggested that the daily way to toil could be a form of meditation, and I have no doubt that it was. Passing and re-passing the same objects for years often sets the imagination free, particularly when a compulsory tramp is done in solitude. He wrote a little book called *The Heavenly Footman* which had nothing to do with servitude.

Lent is when I do more than walk my track. To the top and back again is a mile and a half of flinty travel accompanied by birdsong. Also, should I be in my historical mood, by ghosts. Saxon farmers, medieval children, Georgian parsons, poor Victorian labourers and the youthful versions of some of the old friends who sit before me in church. Who planted the twelve tall oaks just after Trafalgar? Who climbed the vast split oak just after Marston Moor? Who picked the bluebells which are now just showing? Who lay in the hollows with whom? That would be telling. Footpaths lead to private experience, main roads to public happenings. Which is why we are advised to stick to the narrow way. Let the high banks enfold you, let the rain hollows splash you. Let the occasional fellow traveller give you no more than a nod, the pair of you being at your devotions.

The rivulet side of Bottengoms track would have been animated by hedgers and ditchers in February, but that was long ago. Now the elder twists and tumbles, the hazels make forests and the brambles impenetrable cages for rabbits. Arching trees make a stately entrance, after which there comes an airy humdrum scene of open cornfield and horse paddocks. Then often neglected but beseeching signs of 'Cars turn here' and 'MUD'. For the slough of despond stretches between me and Garnon's Farm, the dull brasses of whose medieval owners hang under the belfry. Optimistic young men in vans believe that they can get through but soon they are knocking on the door, contrite and amazed, and there are directions to the RAC on how to find the track. I see wagons and carts and maybe a smart gig containing a lady, all getting through with a bit of a slide here and there, and squelching hooves and a 'gittup!', and an all is well. And the ditchers glancing up at slivers of sky, and the February day dragging on, and their legs in sodden sacking, and what would now be done in an hour with a dredger, taking weeks. What is this? we might enquire, staring at this winter world. The answer is, a handmade landscape for us to wander in and contemplate our lot.

At weekends the young commuter families and their dogs walk it. They pause at the floods of snowdrops in my wood and look glad to have made the move. The footpath, they slowly realise, belongs to them. Wherever we stroll, the way belongs to us. At this moment it is our way. It converses with us at every step. It makes us fanciful and serious all at once. And then there is botany, of course. Who can miss it on a track? And there is perpetual skylark music from on high, and the postman coming down at a fair lick, and the old struggle and the old distances.

Walking the Tithe Map

A day of indescribably wonderful winter loveliness. I must say something about it, however, as the sun is hot on my neck. I am sitting, of course, with my back to the window, as this is the creative position. To face February full on, with the last snow being pulled from the grass like a rug, would be destructive to all other thought. Inseparable magpies will be bouncing around an old chopped up marrow.

A few miles away, in the Castle Park, snow is also being heat rolled from Roman mosaic floors and corporation pavements. A hare sits still on the exposed barn floor. The white cat roasts in the kitchen window. The postman arrives. Having read in the newspapers that there are icebergs, ten feet drifts, etc. once you get off the main road, he has walked down the track. I thank him profusely. Filmmakers then appear to get some snow shots to accompany my snow reading. Hurry, hurry! Winter is running away before your very eyes.

I telephone the hymns for matins. It is the feast of St Scholastica, but I keep them simple. She was St Benedict's twin sister. She wanted him to sit up all night to discuss the delights of heaven, but he refused. Thereupon she prayed for dreadful weather, and something even worse than any forecaster can invent roared around Monte Cassino, and he had to stay.

She had the brains; he had the organisation. They share a grave. A dreadful battle would one day shake their clever bones.

A pair of blanketed horses nose the snow away as they graze. My bamboo is Chinese, faintly rattling in the breeze and being intrusive as ever. A caller, dressed for a Captain Scott expedition, begs a bit of it. It would be a good time to walk the tithe map for a book I am writing, I decide. The map is signed 'Roger Kynaston'. It is May 1844 – the Hungry Forties – and no good time for tithes.

The poor would be gathering sticks to boil a pot; the better sort would be, well, hoping for the best. The village school would be intoning tables and collects. The vicar would be reading *The* (free to the clergy) *Times*. The church would possess its medieval clerestory for a few more years.

What did the Victorian restorers do with all that ancient building material? I expect to find fragments of it bodged into a farm wall, but I never do. How confident they were – to take down a clerestory and to put up a (very good) wooden roof. And all that glass . . . But I must not go on. That way lies madness.

I must live today. It is what February insists. It says: 'Make your own report on the winter.' Think of curates like Francis Kilvert. He didn't stay in. He strode across the Black Mountains, calling out to the housekeeper, 'I'll be back for supper!'

I am making this up in order to get myself into a proper frame of mind for attending the Friends of St Andrew's committee meeting tonight. For it will be bitter dark then, and nearly as bad as one is told by the weathermen. Tom's reservoir will be wearing its thin black skin of ice. Pheasants will scuttle sadly as I pass.

Perhaps, when the sun goes in, I will ring Tom and plead terrible illness. The time will come when the night will be as seductive as the day, and no one can stay in, and the telly will grow moss.

The Great Essex Earthquake

The earthquake woke me up just sufficiently for me to feel the ancient house dip a fraction, then recover its oaken equilibrium. It was as though its beams were boughs once more and bending to a pre-Reformation gale. An oak had to be centuries old before it could be part of a new house.

For ages, earthquakes were believed to be the fury of God or the gods, nobody having an inkling of plates shifting. It took prophets ages to realise that God was not in the earthquake, but in the silence.

We had a tremendous earthquake all round here in 1884. It was on 22 April at 22 minutes past nine in the morning. People were hard at work. It was a lovely spring day. Mercifully, Mr Damant the photographer was about to record it. Quite a lot of folk were at matins in Sudbury, Suffolk.

At Colchester railway station, Mr Blatch was personally seeing his first-class passengers into their seats as they set off for the City.

75

Just opposite, a workman was high up on a scaffold as he inscribed 'Eastern Counties Asylum for Idiots' on a building. At Wivenhoe, Mr Stebbing the grocer was piling up tins of lobster, and Lord Alfred Paget was being rowed out to his yacht the St Cecilia. At Wivenhoe Hall, young Jackson was still in his bath.

And then it happened, the Great Essex Earthquake. No deaths – but the property! How it fell to pieces! A thousand roofs slid to the ground; 20 churches were in ruins. Three entire villages went to wreckage.

Boats were thrown from the harbours onto the shore. There was a noise that nobody would ever forget. There was a blinding dust, and there was the pathos of what would later be the exposed interior, the wallpapered rooms hanging in the air, the fires blazing in the suspended grates, the unmade bed.

In all, 1,213 buildings were half-demolished and there were splinters, splinters everywhere. The famous Rose Inn at Peldon was made unsafe for smugglers, and the coastal churches, Langenhoe especially, were heaps of pulpits, ceramics, memorials, screens, etc.

Mr Damant hurried around with his fine plate camera. One of my favourite photos is his elegantly grouped picture of the Rector of Langenhoe and his friends standing in the ruins of his church clasping umbrellas and gently smiling.

They had curiously prophetic expressions, which would appear again and again during the next century, shaken looks that hid the shock, the automatic grin. And the strange stench of fallen architecture. All this would repeat itself – all over the world. And human beings would stand and stare at the swift demolition of their achievements as the dust settled, and would look so differently from how they felt.

On Saturday, the central heating gave up, and the farmhouse assumed its patchy warmth. Although I read the Instruction Book for all I was worth, there was no rush of oil, no oomph and flare. So the young mechanics arrived soon to emerge with faces of delight. What did I think?

'No, tell me.'

Triumphantly: 'A spider!'

The poor creature had crawled into the oomph-pipe and there it lodged, stopping the flow.

'It committed hara-kiri,' said the boy mechanic.

'Can I see it – the spider?'

They shook their heads sadly. It had done its worst and was no more. Or maybe its best.

Spectacles

I am at the optician's. We sit in a shop window, in various degrees of darkness and light. We are being framed at vast expense, or, in my case, being updated. We go to tiny rooms, and read the chart. The optician, who is about 25, won't have to do this for donkey's years. He has lustrous eyes, like a Gainsborough portrait.

The black discs drop in and out; the giant letters dwindle to nothingness. 'What do you see?' What a question. He cleans my old specs, to my shame. 'Your sight hasn't changed much.'

About four feet below us runs the road along which the Emperor Claudius was driven to his temple, where he would be made a god. But I am in the optician's chair, not the barber's chair, and I must not distract his attention with this kind of local information. So I sit, stock-still, as the letters diminish, tumble about, tell him things about me which I will never know.

I think of the Revd Patrick Brontë having his cataracts removed with a knife. Charlotte held his hand. The bandages were removed after a month's blindfold, and, glory to God, he could see. She began to write *Jane Eyre* in the lodgings, while all the time there lurked the terrible possibility of sightlessness for the rest of his days. The Manchester life clattered below. I wait for the bill. My expert sight-giver says, 'Next.'

The old high street is drab. The cuts are having their effect. Sale, sale, sale – but no customers. The bravura town hall is white in the afternoon sun. St Helena, clasping the True Cross, stands on top of it. She was Romano-British and the mother of Constantine. Is she the patron saint of archaeologists?

She would remember morning coffee in the restaurants below, the dressed shop windows, the departed elegance, the public library service – marvellous, this – and the gentlemen-only bar at the Red Lion, where a Manet-like lady kept a roaring fire. All gone, all gone.

Should the cuts come within a stone's throw of our public libraries, let us all cry out. Increasingly, the Government seems to have its eye so firmly fixed on the red that it can no longer see the wealth on the opposite page. The young never-employed – through no fault of their own – laugh in doorways. The regiment from the barracks is in Afghanistan.

I write in the mornings; that is, when I am not in one or other of my market towns, seeing economic sights and visiting their fine public libraries; and I pull the garden round after lunch, so that the bulbs won't be put to shame in a week or two.

Frost has broached one of the springs that everlastingly bubble beneath the Big Field, and a sparkling new stream finds its way to the Stour. Alas, this cannot go on. My head turns to hardcore, to fill-in, or whatever. This year and wherever, water thinks that it can do what it likes.

How the robins sing! How the catkins shake! How once more that vengeful man on the Damascus road hoves into view with his list of victims. And that 'Why are you doing this?' – a question we all might ask ourselves. And then that blinding stab of the Epiphany light, and the subsequent helplessness. Then the turnaround.

I de-mulch the snowdrops.

'Lord, this is a huge rain'

Many fields have pooled and many ditches have slopped over. We drive extra miles rather than dare Little Horkesley pond, now a lake. February fill-dyke is one thing, water pouring from headlands in wide, flashing scallops quite another. Nothing is running away. Lanes are navigable for the four-wheel drivers and for Wellingtons, but not for most cars. One almost expects fish to swim across the tarmac. Drains are blocked and rains fall on rains. Winter wheat looks like a paddyfield in China. Keith manages to drag the oil tanker from a slough of despond below Bottengoms. He and the oilman splosh about enjoyably. The gutters round the farmhouse brim over — everything everywhere has more water than it can deal with. And so it stays. It is what deluge means.

My text is taken from a cartoon in the *New Yorker*, now pinned up in the study. It shows a secretary opening the mail and talking to her boss on the telephone — 'Nothing important, nothing on fax, nothing on voicemail, nothing on internet. Just, you know, handwritten stuff'. I tell the damp congregation about the Apostles' secretaries, Epaphroditus, Tertius and Onesimus. They are not always used. Paul's letter to the 'foolish Galatians' comes direct. 'You see how large a letter I have written to you *with mine own hand*!' Outside, the rain will be drowning the dead, washing away the Christ and making the first snowdrops think that they have put to sea. Which is what Peter did in the first lesson, put out for a catch which could have sunk him. Nature does not know when to stop giving. Or sometimes when to start.

But I can smell spring. The Stour knows no bounds yet it has to admit a flooding greenness all about it. The footpaths squelch as much with plants as with water. They wait for dry winds to wring them out. I am reminded of the path from Treneague to Burlorne in Cornwall. It is past breakfast and my kind but ruthless (with guests) friends have shooed me from under their feet. 'Have a nice long walk' – i.e. don't come back until lunch. They have novels to write and other animals to feed. February in North Cornwall is what April will be in Suffolk. Rills trickle down the steep hedges – those slate walls which are now turning into hanging gardens – and the roaring black farm dog rushes out to eat me and turns to jelly when I pat his head. And the scent of St Breock Downs, plus the smell of sties and sheep-pens and rotting hay, and of bluebell and pines, makes a softness of territory which tells me that I am far from East Anglia. Three hours must I walk. I was reminded of my very first visit to Cornwall when I was nineteen and the drill at the Newlyn guest house was all out after breakfast and all back for high tea. In-between, I seem to recall, there were soaking drizzles, foghorns and melancholy, and always the sound of running water.

The Young Prisoners

Each morning, at about six, tea in hand, I sit for an hour looking out of the window, regular as clockwork. At first, there is nothing to see in winter, then shadowy shapes are 'laid in', as the artist who once lived here might put it. The window-framing of what was outside held a fascination for him. Especially when it snowed.

Christians used to have their window-songs: one for morning, one for bedtime. They say that George Herbert rose from his deathbed, seized his lute, and sang his morning window-song. My morning window-song is silent but tuneful, my being a 'morning person', and not very bright in the late evening, my metabolism tending to peter out. I take it as a great kindness on nature's part to come into view every day.

A long time ago, there was a natural-history essay competition that Richard Mabey, David Attenborough, John Fowles and I were asked to judge. The prize was £500, and publication in *The Sunday Times*. It was to honour the memory of Kenneth Allsop.

One year, a brilliant entry arrived from Dartmoor Prison. It was about bird-watching through a barred window, and we had to get permission from the prison governor for the caged naturalist to get his prize.

Windows have a way of limiting what one sees and, at the same time, intensifying the vision. I always try to get a window-seat on a plane, and do not always pull the little blind down at night. Vast cities briefly glitter below me. Night and day are on each other's heels, as in Genesis. Better not stare at the wings of the plane. They are flimsy, even patched. The Victorians raised classroom windows so that boys and girls could not see out, and would thus concentrate on their lessons. Although delighting in stained glass, such as the wonderful 1950s window in Little Horkesley Church in our benefice, I love churches where trees wave to me through clear glazing.

Poor Henry Howard, Earl of Surrey, could hear tennis being played below his prison window. Not quite thirty, Henry VIII had him executed for 'treason', a trumped-up charge for a wild genius who had quartered his arms with those of Edward the Confessor. Howard's immense gift to English literature was to invent blank verse, the patterns in which Shakespeare would write his plays.

Young Surrey lies in Framlingham Church, in a sublime tomb below tall windows. His window-song is a little collection of rueful poetry which I often take from the shelf to find him 'looking out' with clear youthful eyes at his world. It is a terrible thing for a state to silence its writers, to block out their views, as all twentieth-century tyrants did their best to do.

Renaissance artists like to give the Holy Family a room with a view. High above the group, there is often a glassless window filled in with scenery. A nearby hill, a blue stream, a ploughman, some birds, somewhere for the Child to play.

Once, in Burgundy, we found a small hotel at night, went to bed, and awoke to a maid throwing the shutters wide to the vineyards below. No glass, just scenery and a warm wind, swallows and shouts, church bells and life. Bonjour, monsieur! A glorious awakening, indeed.

I still find getting up, and sitting down opposite my window, pretty good, as does the white cat. Together we look.

MARCH

*A*pparently, there are more suicides in February than any other month. The colours of Christmas have been exterminated and New Year resolutions are seeping away in to grey and hopeless damp. No colour anywhere. Then to the sound of trumpets in thrusts March. Triumphant. Purple fields, the trees still black and naked, the green shoots of life piercing and rising-up through the earth. It is sexy, this surge of sap. Optimism is reborn. There is clear light and plenty of bracing air in which to walk. And mud to negotiate. Suffolk mud is a strange mixture of clod and water, making each step uncertain and exciting. The sky lowers darkly while clouds speed across. The sun suddenly appears. March contains the dark of winter and the light of summer almost simultaneously. After the hibernation of February, eyes closed, there is a shock awakening of all the senses, eyes open.

Ronnie's eyes, nose and ears are in full operation, creating the grand drama of March and the intimate immediacy of being alive. Not for nothing was his first ambition to be a painter: his writing is so intensely visual. As in Constable, you can smell the mud, breathe the air and hear the birdsong.

It's a long while since 1960, when I first met you in the garden of the East Anglian School of Painting and Drawing, but your beady-eyed pen hasn't drawn breath, or your heart missed a beat.

Maggi Hambling

Map-readings

A blissful spring in winter day. An hour of light snow and a morning of pale sunshine. Grey ice, thin as paper, on the puddles. Seed heads rattling against each other to keep themselves warm. Five pheasants in the dip. The church clock telling the hours piercingly. Wild daffodils, the ones which Dorothy Wordsworth noted for William, high up in the orchard mulch. The stream clear and hurrying. Gerald the shop dog bouncing through the goal-posts. The sky a pearly buff with sudden starlings darkening its edges. A walker's day, a wanderer's day. Thus bereft voices on the answerphone. 'We tried to get you.'

One thing leading to another, such as spring-cleaning, the climate being contrary, I turn out the map drawer, having already turned out the sock drawer. The latter is a great mystery. Eight single socks. How can that be? And some vast knitted socks from the Ice Age. And some nice tennis socks, very fetching. And no darned socks, these now being in the museum. But maps. It was a casual studying of John Speed's *Atlas of Wales* which led me to the map drawer. John Speed was a Cheshire tailor who died in 1629 but he was mad on maps and mapping. While acknowledging the great map-makers Norden and Saxton – 'I have put my sickle into other mens corne' – his marvellous *Theatre of the Empire of Great Britaine*, which is what he called his maps, is very much his own. He was often not very well as he got about, which may be why his Wales shows his exasperation with its 'uneavenness'. The air on Anglesey is 'reasonably grateful' and that is about all. But oh the maps drawn by John Sudbury and George Humbell, one could look at them for ever, with their grand cartouches and endless humps – 'the tops whereof, in the Summer time, are the harvestmen's Almanacks'. I look up Discoed, where I go every September, pop. sixty, or thereabouts, and there it is.

The map drawer doesn't stop here. Reading a map whilst in motion causes an acute anxiety. Reading one when one is still is sheer happiness. Some of my maps have been read to tatters. Some, being pre-motorway, would get you lost in no time. Each is a work of art, a dream, a reality, a will-o'-the-wisp, an essential need and a distraction. They whiff of ancient car-pockets, grass and destinations. See how they bend. See how Norfolk has fallen in the sea. But see too how beautiful the new ones are, how they make you want to set off this very minute to that village where there wasn't time to stop or that street with the bookshop. I have come a roundabout journey to the map drawer, one directed by my Sunday sermon about Jack Kerouac and Jesus being 'on the road', the writer discovering a by-path, the Saviour being a 'way' in himself. I hope that the congregation didn't get lost en route. We sang, of course, Cowper's 'God moves in a mysterious way'.

The maps, young and ancient, slither on to the table. What dear, crumpled old friends. What shiny new friends, the latest of *Ashford and Romney Marsh*, Land ranger 189, Ordnance Survey, with a view of Folkestone. There is the new *Cambridge Cycle Route Map*, Macpherson's *Fife, Kinross, Clackmannan and Perth* – last used by John Buchan? – and lovely maps with drawings of classy drivers and pipe-smoking walkers, and Bartholomew's *New Reduced Survey for Tourists*, one shilling. The magic when these are spread out, the endlessness of places!

Modelling

A wild goose is tacking against the wind, flying sideways in wide swerves. But the garden is calm, so it is books and lunch outside with a woodpecker hammering away overhead. Thousands of primroses and violets line the ditches and there is the distracting scent of buckthorn. I have just returned from Nayland where a roadman dressed for a part in one of those ecological disaster films rides a sprayer through the pretty streets and squirts weedkiller at the little plants which thrive in ancient walls. In the church John Constable's Maunday Thursday Jesus is blessing the Bread and Wine, his hands palm upwards, his face tilted towards his Father. The young local artist painted the altar-piece for his aunt Mrs Smith. I have seen it all my life and it is as familiar to me as the photos on the chimney-piece. 'Why', said his Uncle David, seeing it for the first time, 'that's Golding!' John's brother Golding had indeed sat for the Lord.

Finishing *The Cornfield* in London, Constable had to write home for a list of the wild flowers which were blooming at Flatford in July, when he had begun the picture. Henry Phillips the local botanist obliged. In July, 'all the tall grasses are in flower, bogrush, bulrush, teasel. The white bindweed now hangs its flowers over the branches of the hedge; the wild carrot and hemlock flower in banks of hedges, cow parsley, water plantain and ... the rose-coloured pesicaria in wet ditches is now very pretty; the catchfly graces the hedge-row, and also the ragged robin; bramble is now in flower, poppy, mallow, thistle, nop ...' And so Mr Phillips continues. Let Nayland pin his list on its noticeboard as a reproach to its spring spraying.

The mad tidiness of the current village, the fear of seasonal growth. However, we are much improved in other ways, heaven knows. When Constable needed a woodpecker to put in a picture, Captain Torin had to shoot him one and send it by stage coach to Percy Street. In Nayland I cross the road to the inn where Gainsborough's brother and Constable's father sat on the catchment board to run the River Stour.

The horrible war leaks into Lent, its sands which bred three world faiths accusing us all. The beautiful Iraqi faces on the screen are descended from the Middle Eastern people in Victorian stained glass. They are accompanied by our incomprehension of Iraq, of Islam. So I read the *Koran* just before reading Compline, then *The Sayings of Muhammad* – 'If you knew what I know, you would laugh a little and weep much'. And so Compline at Wormingford, the drenched tombs of Georgian farmers, the moon making a faint showing, the sticky buds bursting. It is almost All Fools.

To Colchester to model for an art class. This takes me back a bit. Am I sitting comfortably? Then they will begin. May I read – Calvino's novel *If on a Winter's Night a Traveller* – no, because then you will wear your glasses and hang your head. Did not Constable's brother have to roll his eyes towards heaven and allow his big workaday hands to lie heavy on the Lord's table? But his career as a model might have been more testing, for the original subject had been The Agony in the Garden until their mother had objected. 'Adoration was more becoming our Saviour than humiliation', she said. About twenty artists are drawing and painting me. I am not to look. I fall into a reverie. I must be careful in case this falls into slumber. The art teacher tells me, 'You may talk to us'. This is difficult as they know a lot about me and I nothing at all about them. I think what I will have for dinner, and about weed poisoners, and about an Islamic text which says, 'Angels will not enter a house in which there are dogs and pictures'.

Lent One: Our Airfield

'What I would like,' said the Australian guest, responding to my various offerings, 'is to hear a skylark.' Step right outside, I was about to answer, when I remembered our abandoned airfield. Although abandoned isn't quite the right adjective, since fanners and gliders have reclaimed it. However, if one wishes to hear skylarks at their zenith and creating what Marvell called 'the mosaic of the Air', then find a deserted World War Two airfield, or indeed any old battlefield, for they share the same exhilarating yet tragic ambience as well as a level earth and high heaven conjunction which larks themselves find particularly suitable for nests and songs. This week they were up over our ex-USAAF 362 Fighter Group Airfield, ecstatic specks making a glorious noise above the wet corn and oilseed rape, the latter about to burst into flat Van Gogh yellow. I entered the airfield near the glider base to listen to them. Fragile machines lay in snowy rows by the new clubhouse. On Sundays they are persuaded from their trailer-chrysalises to soar in pure silence over our church service.

The great runways were tom up years ago and have long joined the commonwealth of rubble. But the perimeter roads remain, curving into views which do not seem to belong to our or to any neighbouring parish. Coltsfoot and artefacts from the big band era are squeezed into their cracks. The Americans arrived in Wormingford on St Andrew's Day 1943, which happened to be the village's patronal day, although it is generally accepted that the Pentagon hadn't planned this. I gazed once more at the memorial by the hedge on which the names of the dead are engraved in close lists, like items in an old account-book. There are a few captains but mostly they are lieutenants – the Monument of the One Hundred Lieutenants. Some have names – Tray Dean – which flick against the consciousness like those among the credits of a B-movie, briefly reinstating a young smile.

I walked west all the afternoon, passing Mr Hodge's fine lambs. It has been a bad, sodden, deathly spring for lambs but these have come through. Impeccable fields and set-aside fields, military neatness and rusty tackle, sticky-buds and, of course, larks. The skies are one vast unending parade of cloud. At the saluting-base I face a rotting stack and a felled oak. There are grooves for the flagpoles. Miles away the orange wind-sock of the Essex and Suffolk Gliding Club billows happily.

Cloud Kingdoms

I am a chronic cloud-watcher, a condition which may have started when I was reading one of those hold-all philosophies such as Lin Yutang's *The Importance of Living*. I would have been about fourteen and, no doubt, should it have been a holiday, mother would have been calling in vain to where I lay hidden in the tall grass. Errands. Not that they were always avoidable and put my more or less reasonable shape to vast walks and bike rides to fetch this or that. William Hazlitt and John Clare were self-confessed skivers. There they were, flat on their backs on the good earth, their eyes travelling along cirro-cumulus routes, their heads filled with vaporous wonders whilst the world shouted for them to do this or do that. This morning the white cat and I cloud-watched together as the sun came up. What Dolomites, what Snowdons, what golden gates. She closed her jade green eyes against the glitter. I cancelled all rational thought. And we might have remained like this until kingdom-come had not the kettle boiled. 'O ye Clouds, bless ye the Lord.'

In the village we splosh about, for it is O ye rains with a vengeance. The subtle drainage system which kept us all dry for centuries is lost under tarmac and new housing and we don't know where to find it. But then water did always lie about in March, so as to make mirrors for budding trees. I have mended my ways and purchased King Edward seed potatoes and set them out in trays to 'strike'. Last spring I allowed the kitchen garden to go wild. Oh the shame of it. This year it shall bear, shall flourish. Digging it over where generations of farmers (or most likely their wives) have dug it is a treat, the rich soil falling from the spade, the robin helping. Looking down now, not up. Christmas roses are in bloom by the wall, and we shall sing, 'Once in Royal David's City' on Mothering Sunday, this to my mind being the best mother-hymn we know.

Back at the desk, back to the window so as not to be distracted by the rainy glories of the skies, I write about walking along the shingle beach from Aldeburgh to Orford and paying the boatman sixpence to row me across the river, and this too in springtime, though long ago when tides were 'neap' (a tide which occurs during the first or last quarter of the moon when sun and moon are in balance with each other). People sometimes talk about the tide of human existence and all things being equal, etc. The spring clouds say 'Phoo' to this. Moisture-laden yet weightless, they float across my retina with a suggestion of land masses, of marvellous journeys and dark destinations. I imagine Christ being received by them out of my sight. In a plane it is earth's geography which is taken from our sight.

Fetching letters from where the postman leaves them in a tumbledown shed, I send up a hundred rooks from an ivy-smothered ash. Their squawks drown out an harmonious bird orchestra. They whirl in all directions, black, crying, dreadfully upset. I beg their pardon. They wing away in a kind of furious diamond over Tom's farm, leaving behind the reasonable song of a thrush. Stephen arrives and we make our semi-amphibious way to the pub by the river. Travelling clouds race over its slow motion surface and are broken up by static swans. We hang our heads over the bridge and become dizzy with the conflict of reflection. John Constable would have stared up and down at this spot.

Doctor Nature

A green sequence of natural, rather than supernatural, meditations preoccupies my early Lent, each following the next in the way dreamings do, and stimulated by exquisite March days. First to arrive is Richard Mabey's *Nature Cure* with its echoes of John Clare's experience and of our years of talk. To be healed by skies and fens and flowers and the knowledge of these things, how wonderful. Of course, there is nothing new in these remedies. There they are, just being outside, and free for the taking. I took some big doses an hour ago as I wrenched up nettle stalks and bird-cherry suckers from the edges of the top lawn and listened to linnets. How well I felt – still feel. But it is marvellous to have this well-being all set out in chapters and set to music in words.

Alongside Richard's testimonial to nature, for there is always an alongside reading with me, I read another nature cure called *The House of Quiet* by A. C. Benson (1904). What good writers depressives are. I remember William Cowper. My love of his hymns sometimes creates grins in the choir. He was suicidal but nature in the form of vulnerable hares showed him a trembling world which his God sustained:

> Ye fearful saints, fresh courage take;
>   The clouds ye so much dread
> Are big with mercy, and shall break
>   In blessings on your head.

Cowper liked writing in his greenhouse where his current hare could play around in safety. He would be there when the frosts were over – 'When the plants go out, we come in' – and he preferred the natural history of Olney to smart resorts such as Margate which he likened to a Cheshire cheese full of mites. But A. C. Benson's *The House of Quiet*, the old book which fell out of the bookcase just when I was reading *Nature Cure* and murmured, 'Read me' turned out to be the work of a depressive at one remove. A great many confessions in those late Victorian years were at one or even two removes. Their authors invented scapegoats on which to pile their failings and feelings. Arthur Benson, the Archbishop of Canterbury's son, no less, and Master of Magdalen, Cambridge, was a depressive who used bicycle rides through nature to cast off the black dog. And they did. He and my friend Richard Mabey are healed by the same East Anglian flatlands, the one concealed by the etiquette of his day, the other gloriously open, but both beautifully descriptive of their regenerative property. Except that Benson is frightened by woods which for him can be 'near the confines of horror', also still water. He must have open country and running streams. All in all he reveals a large man with the terrors of a child still.

My third nature cure seeker has to be Richard Jefferies who is young but consumptive and far from depressive. He died aged thirty-nine in 1887, a Wiltshire farmer's son who, whilst not a Christian, possessed a vision of nature – which included his own body – which the poet Elizabeth Jennings believed matched that of Thomas Traherne. Richard Jefferies' *The Story of My Heart* is an exultant, unhidden paean to nature and one which accepts the naturalness of death. It is a hymn to joy and a dismissal of Time. Christ taught the disciples to live in the Now, to step out without a penny, to be alive – really alive. As does Richard Jefferies.

Stony Ground

Mid-lent. Stony imagery that contrasts with the spring. The Essene boys – the pious ones – make their way to the desert. 'Now don't overdo it,' their mothers say. Jesus is old for this kind of test. Nor will it end when he returns from the wilderness both of landscape and decision.

George Herbert, who is about his age, steps into a wrecked church. More wild behaviour. Paul reminds the Thessalonians that he has taught them 'how to walk'. Their difficulty could be that they live in a lovely plain, not on stony ground.

My Stour-side land is not conducive to harsh religious behaviour at this moment, being flooded with flowers and much visited by birds, and softened by low skies. I read of Christ's illness from that extreme self-testing in the Palestinian wastes with wonderment, as should we all.

Richard Mabey comes to lunch. I suppose we could count each other as the oldest of our friends. We have lamb's liver, onions, potatoes, baked parsnips, and a glass of champagne because it is his birthday. And sit by blazing willow logs, each having finished our latest books: his about Flora Thompson, mine about Benjamin Britten. The white cat sleeps on us in turn.

We talk about Roger Deakin, a marvellous writer who had been given a perpetual young man's view of the countryside, and who swam wherever there was water: in the sea, in his pond, in the river. He was somehow mature, although he had never quite grown up – a great achievement.

In church, I talk of St John of the Cross, someone I save up for Lent. If the South African poet Roy Campbell had not managed to save his papers during the carnage of the Spanish Civil War, this St John might have become nothing more than yet another vague person on the calendar. Instead, he is startlingly vivid on account of his Christ being the bridegroom of the Gospels.

When a woman told St John of the Cross that her prayer consisted of 'Considering the beauty of God and rejoicing that he had such beauty', he found the imagery he needed for his poetry. It was that of the seeking lover – the seeking lover on both sides. The scenes in which the Lord and his friend search for one another are in the wild landscape of Toledo. These craggy solitudes are filled with their love and desire for each other.

Cathedrals can be Toledos when the services die away, and especially when the doors close and the sightseers' footsteps fade away, and the arches speak their stony language. It is then that they might have something non-architectural to say.

St John of the Cross was not popular. He worked too hard. He was also, they complained, a crony of St Teresa of Avila. And he was, as some poets are, very accusatory at times. Like the desert. So they put him in prison to shut him up. But whether in prison, or in his cell, or by his favourite spot, the River Guadalimar, the blessed solitude was there, and he heard:

The music without sound,
The solitude that clamours,
The supper that revives us and enamours.

Who is Counting?

The spring arrived on Monday. Thousands of snowdrops in my wood, which had hung there in a closed, waiting state, opened up. Birdsong became loud and bell-like. There was an exultant calling from bare trees. Even the men prodding about in the squishy mess that was supposed to be the lower cart track, searching for a leakage, sounded joyful. They raised their voices in childlike delight when the water level began to rise around their wellies. 'We've found the spring!' they cried.

I turned off the radio. It has been running money, money, money without stop. I was born when farmers hadn't two pennies to rub together, as they said. This was bad. But isn't it equally bad to have millions of pounds to rub along with? To pile up this when one is old, as the rich men's faces on the screen frequently are? Who is counting? Everybody, it seems. Eventually, the total becomes astronomical, and pointless even to Mr Peston; for all I see are his wide eyes as the figures stretch them beyond comprehension.

In the old manor house on its Saxon mound (to prevent the Stour from seeping in) we discuss the parish's future. The young are dubious, the old philosophical. It was here before Domesday, and how can it not be here after Madoff, as it were?

Of course, the village bodger and not the diocesan architect kept the church more or less watertight. The books showed the care and expense. 'Mr Smith, for mending the tower, £3.'

Young men straight from the commuters' train and still in their smart suits tot up what we have and what may be required of us. Stone window frames made in 1450 need repairing. They must have accepted the lowest estimate. George Herbert used to say, 'Nothing lasts but the Church!' To his mother's horror, he paid for the rebuilding of Bemerton and Leighton Bromswold out of his own pocket, the latter as an architectural version of his poetry.

After the meeting, Tom and I talk about his herd of Lincolns and how very soon – well, April – he will open the shed doors, and, after a moment of disbelief at such good fortune, these cows will rush out of prison into the water meadows, leaping and bellowing with bliss.

Tom loves his animals too much for his own comfort. He gives them names, which they say is a mistake. A heifer to the slaughter is one thing; Kevin to the slaughter, another.

Me: 'You haven't got a bullock named Kevin?'

Tom's wife: 'Yes, he had.'

Alas, poor Kevin. Alas, poor Tom. I tell the white cat, 'Your name is Kitty.' She looks amazed.

At night, the ancient rooms say, 'It will soon be Lent.' All day, I write my tithe map book, only breaking off for reccies round what used to be my fields, getting cold and muddy.

Having to help judge a literary prize, I read, read and read. The authors are all strange to me, as indeed are some of their publishers. There was a time when it was all familiar, the names, the colophons on the spines, the puffs on the backs. In a way it is refreshing – and an education.

I read the obituary of Edward Upward, died aged 105, whose life contained all my youthful reading and all twentieth-century politics, all its ideals and rebellion. All of its excellent literary style.

Spring Arrives

It could be all over by the end of this page, that first touch of spring. The villagers will say, 'That was it!' in their triumphant way. They like to be accurate in their gloom. But I say that by the law of averages alone there has to be a fair number of these touches of spring, so, as somebody said, 'Rejoice! Rejoice!' They begin with steaming dawn fields and exhaling woodlands, with teeming birdsong and blissful atmospheric curtain-raisers before the hot sun is kicked into full view, and they end in glory. About nine (only commuters get up at the old country hour) a distant clatter and thunder, buzzing and whining can be heard. Oiled, cajoled, made ready to go, machinery from every barn and garden shed is at work. Everything from the lorry bringing red sand and brickage to fill in winter's ravages of the track to Len's Flymo is out, as am I. 'We have been trying to get you', callers complain about bedtime. No answerphone, no fax, no nothing. And 'No getting down there when it rains, and no getting out from there when it snows.'

It is my week for doing the ponds, beautiful portraits of which by John Nash hang in art galleries. Marsh marigolds smother their surface and the old plough horses for which they were dug would have had to nose their way through them to swig their mighty draughts. They would have been plain utilitarian then, deep watering holes for thirsty beasts. How decked out they are in my day! Stands of bamboo, sheltering quinces, dense ivies – and the marsh marigolds all set out on them like cups, so that they can remind one of their name, *Caltha* – 'goblet'. I have to bring some order without disturbing the goblets on their emerald saucers. Just above me something approaches which sounds like the army of young Fortinbras descending upon Elsinore, fresh from the Polack wars. Duncan or Hugh has managed to get one of their agricultural monsters 'on the goo', as they say in these parts. I wheel my lawnmower out for the first cut.

The Lenten Complines are coming to an end. How good they have been. Maybe we should all say Compline every night, Grace at meals and never 'supermarket' on the Sabbath. The American guest tells me all about Alcoholics Anonymous, which, he says, has become his church. How confessorial he is. There is nothing which he won't tell me. I think of the advice once given to whispering grass – 'The birds don't need to know.' During a ten-mile walk he recites a poem he wrote to a lover which throws him into a new light. As well as confessorial, Americans are ancestral.

This one takes flowers from the garden to a grave in a Cambridgeshire churchyard for a girl he had known thirty years ago, standing by it and cursing the man who had married her, just like a character from a Thomas Hardy novel. Then he leaves for Westminster Abbey to look up a forebear.

'When lilacs last in the dooryard bloom'd'

A pair of jays, dressed to the nines, swing warily from the holly bush – although the whole village knows that the white cat has never caught a thing in her life, being sloth incarnate. Yet the fine birds look down on my feast of crusts and old Christmas nuts with caution. The day is still, its light subdued. We have to read Jeremiah and John, both good authors.

At the Suffolk Poetry Society meeting we listened to an American woman reading from Walt Whitman's 'Leaves of Grass'. President Lincoln has been assassinated in the theatre, but the violence has been contained, and somehow robbed of its lasting evil. The quiet New England voice says: 'When lilacs last in the dooryard bloom'd . . . I mourn'd, and yet shall mourn with ever-returning spring.' It is one of those openings which capture the imagination.

The Connecticut reader asks: 'Have you been to Connecticut?'

'Yes, but long ago. Though not in the fall.'

When Lincoln's coffin continues on its way, it might well have been down my farm track:

Amid lanes and through old
woods, where lately the violets
peep'd from the ground,
spotting the gray debris,
Amid the grass in the fields each
side of the lanes, passing the

endless grass,
Passing the yellow-spear'd wheat,
every grain from its shroud in
the dark-brown fields uprisen ...

When the Suffolk farmers emigrated to New England in the seventeenth century, they took their seed corn with them, plus the seed of our wildflowers – or weeds, as we call them. Heartbreaking, it must have been. Did lilacs go, too? In order to bloom for a murdered president?

I tidy paths in warm sunshine. All the birds sing. Dutifully, I read Jeremiah and John, seeing what they have to say. Jeremiah despairs at our incorrigible nature: 'Can the leopard change his spots?' John records Jesus saying: 'I am the light of the world.'

It is Lent 4. Geese scream over to the river. Neighbours walk by. We tell each other the obvious: that the afternoon is warm and wonderful, that it is good to be out. In the evening, I read *Kilvert's Diary* for mid-March: 'This morning I received a nice letter from dear Louie Williams, who is barmaid at the Bell Hotel, Gloucester. She enclosed a piece of poetry entitled "Clyro Water" and signed Eos Gwynddwr which she had cut out of last week's *Hereford Times*, not knowing the verses were mine ...'

Poor Kilvert; when he asked his father, should he publish his poems, the answer was a definite no. What old Mr Kilvert would have made of the great diary, the Lord only knows. The Welsh border, to which, one way or another, I seem to become more and more attached, is haunted by the robust and yet short-lived Francis Kilvert. How hard he worked! How far he walked! How self-revealing he was.

When he walked to Credenhill on a 'lovely and cloudless' March day in 1879, he would not have known of the existence of Thomas Traherne. This amazes me – that the wonderful prose-poet who died in 1674 should not have been read until my lifetime.

The Unsheltered

Raw spring days. The wind whistles through the thin hedge. There is a profusion of birds and primroses. Duncan's fields have been polished by cold rains. I rake up ancient leaves, for the oilman cometh. The small tanker, bringing a year's warmth, will float to me on a bed of leaves, and the driver and I will fervently pray for a safe delivery, for the tractor not to be called on. He has a glass of milk. He has been a soldier, and has a way with enormous vehicles. I am safe until next April.

Writing is a static activity. Artists move about, shifting this way and that. My friend John Nash stood with his back to the north light from ten until four every day, regular as clockwork. Sandwiches arrived at one sharp; tea was by the fire, or in the garden. When he and his wife went to Cornwall or Scotland twice a year, he cleared a place in the studio for me to write. But I wrote outside in the garden when it was hot, and downstairs by the Rayburn when it was cold.

The great rural poet John Clare often wrote in hiding, lying low in a field or under a hedge, so that the neighbours could not see a ploughman engaged in matters which were none of his business. But he compared himself to the nightingale who 'hides and sings'. He led a double life in the village, although eventually it became a marvellous single existence of traditional labour, and the right words to describe it. Those who had previously written about the land and its seasonal demands had rarely put a hand to it; after Clare, it would be different.

Much of my writing is done on a rickety kitchen table under a fruit tree, although indoors I write with my back to the window, as the view is distracting. Somehow, this is no view when I am in it. And especially when digging and raking, keeping my eyes on the ground. Now I must make the sweet pea wigwam.

My friend Tony Venison is due. Learned and appreciative, for many years his gardening column in *Country Life* guided us all.

We met in the garden which Sir Cedric Morris created at Hadleigh, a few miles away, and Tony has inherited both its work-aday genius and its spell. We will sit in the pub and go over our past.

Mutuality is a marvellous thing, especially when it is controlled by a shared learning – although here I have to confess that mine has stopped somewhere at the elementary stage where gardening is concerned. But I am an expert and tireless, or uncomplaining, weeder. According to religion, Paradise, a sheltered garden, is where we should be. My first botany was in one of those Bibles which did not end with Revelation, but with a list of plants. And I sometimes hear God questioning us as we enter Paradise: 'My beautiful Earth; why didn't you enjoy it more, its trees and flowers?'

Lent is a kind of fertilisation of the spirit. It is the time when we have to find the space to let it grow. Its desert must bloom. I find that simplicity, not self-denial, is the better aid for this. It is what the Quakers tell us. I have just given a talk in their meeting house in Sudbury, Suffolk, my home town, and felt quietly blessed all the time.

Teachers

This delectable springtime continues. Lunch in the garden on Sunday after matins. All the birds operatic. The horses on the sloping meadows benign. The Wordsworthian daffodils under the budding fruit trees making a show. 'They make a show,' an elderly woman said as she planted asters. But no show in church. Lent is plain fare.

I must remember to see the hares' boxing match over my horizon. Sparring would be a better word to describe their activity. Meanwhile my badgers hump and trundle themselves through the orchard to the cold-running stream, leaving a highway through the shooting grass. As for daffodils, they have lost all sense of proportion, and wave everywhere, trumpeting their worth to the skies.

At the poetry society, Andrew and I pay homage to Mrs Girling, a Georgian lady who founded our school 100 years before the 1870 Education Act. Where would we have been without her? I think of John Clare being taught to read and write in the vestry, and of boys such as Thomas Bewick who were encouraged to draw on the smooth surfaces of the stone floor in church. Or, much earlier, the women who taught themselves to read from chained Bibles. I got the hang of the Holy Land as I pored over the maps at the back of Revelation during Canon Hughes's sermons.

William Hazlitt wrote tenderly about such things as he saw his old father, a man who had suffered greatly for his radical stance, 'withdrawn from the world of all of us'.

He goes on:

After being tossed about from congregation to congregation [he was an Irish Unitarian minister] ... he had been relegated to an obscure village, where he was to spend the last thirty years of his life, far from the only converse that he loved, the talk about disputed texts of Scripture, and the causes of civil and religious liberty.

Here he passed his days ... in the study of the Bible, and the perusal of the Commentators — huge folios, not easily got through, one of which would outlast a winter! ... glimmering notions of the patriarchal wanderings, with palm trees hovering in the horizon, and processions of camels at the distance of three thousand years ... questions as to the date of creation, predictions of the end of all things; the great lapses of time, the strange mutations of the globe were unfolded with the voluminous leaf, as it turned over ...

My father's life was comparatively a dream; but it was a dream of infinity and eternity, of death, the resurrection, and a judgement to come.

I have always loved this passage by Hazlitt, a young man who no longer believed what his father believed. The most honest and in its way shocking example of this dilemma is, of course, Edmund Gosse's *Father and Son*. One needs to be brave to read it.

Turning to the altar, I say 'I believe', thankful for the formula but never analysing it. *Credo*. Somewhat lost in it, like old Mr Hazlitt's camels, is my love of Christ as it journeys on from year to year, expanding, narrowing, leading ahead. Liturgy takes me over deserts. And then there is George Herbert's 'dear prayer', with or without words.

'Let us pray,' I say to the familiar faces which look towards me, and they gently acquiesce. The other Sunday I said Robert Louis Stevenson's prayers – the ones he said in Samoa – and they suited us very well, talking as they did to God and his 'household'.

Mothering Sunday

Mothering Sunday, and the days leading to it have been bliss-ful, bringing everything out, as they say. On a sudden impulse I clambered to the summit of the 'mount' of Mount Bures to get a Norman sentinel's view of things. Ten miles of springtime. Tributary streams, still very full because of all the rain, and the give-away humps and lines of a long-lost garden. Also a grey goose and a grey goat attended by a youth, all quite still. Hidden from him but plain to me are the graves of his brother and sister, who died in road accidents. Below, the moat is not much more than a damp saucer sprinkled with celandine. Which lord ordered this earth-castle to be piled up, Sackville ... de Vere? No one knows. Blackberries and bluebells have conquered it. The futility of so much of what we are made to do. Why do half the things we do, questioned Traherne, when one could sit under a tree?

But Maisie Pettican has been her ever-reliable hard-working self, and has made a great many small nosegays for the Mothering

Sunday service. I pile them on the altar and the delicate April scent permeates the interiór. During the last hymn – Stewart Cross's 'Father, Lord of all Creation' – boys and girls carry the yellow, green and white bunches to the singing women. 'But what if she isn't a mother?' – *sotto voce* once. 'Never you mind.' This year I reduce the folklore, which I reckon they must by now know by heart. Instead, I steer in the direction of today's Epistle and Gospel, which are full of intriguing undercurrents, the first being about 'children of promise' and the second about the boy who had his packed lunch miraculously turned into a huge picnic. His mother, I felt it safe to surmise, would have baked those five loaves. There are people present whose mothers would have been baking for them seventy years ago or more. I discover in an ante-diluvian guide which came with my mother's first gas-stove, a recipe for a simnel-cake but wisely do not give it out from the pulpit.

Francis Kilvert is the poet of church flowers. Some years ago I walked from Bronydd to Clyro to sit on the tombstone where on a March afternoon in 1871 he watched a spider 'scuttling over the sacred words and memories' and listened, unseen, to 'subdued village voices'. His flower-finder was Miss Sandell, 'who taught me more about them in ten minutes than I have learnt from books in all my life'.

The Best Thing Ever

I have moved my desk by as much as two feet to have the light fall better on the page. Why did I not do this before today? Before ten years ago, to be accurate? Furniture has a way of taking up a stance of its own, a moral or aesthetic position which says, 'Don't dare to shift me. I know where I belong.' I have friends whose rooms are tips, but move a chair to the window, and they are dreadfully put out. Writers can have an affair with their desks

– the poet Robert Bloomfield addressed his oak table quite passionately. Some do not have desks at all. Angus Wilson liked to write on the window-sill and D. H. Lawrence on rocks above the sea, under trees, in railway carriages, any old where. Penelope Mortimer wrote on her kitchen table, as did the Orkney poet George Mackay Brown, although he with his back to the window for fear of distraction. Ivy Compton-Burnett wrote in pencil whilst lying on her sofa, and Virginia Woolf wrote in ink whilst seated in a baggy armchair, the bottle strapped to a piece of board. But I write on a respectable Victorian writing-table, such as one would have found in a decent hotel at the time. Only work in progress is permitted on its top. Everything else is strewn around. And now it faces a different view, and so must I. And now, with the harsh March day full on the typewriter, I must prime the pump.

The primer this morning is Calvino's *If on a Winter's Night a Traveller* ... with, in the first chapter, perhaps the most alluring advice to a fellow writer ever given. It is about how to buy a new book, how to bring it home, and how to sit or lie as its pages take you prisoner. 'Yes', writes Calvino, 'you are in your room, calm; you open the book to page one, no, the last page, first you want to see how long it is. It's not too long, fortunately. Long novels written today are perhaps a contradiction: the dimension of time has been shattered, we cannot love or think except in fragments of time each of which goes off along its own trajectory and immediately disappears.'

But no sooner am I settled in the Calvino position for reading his amazing novel, and rejoicing in my added light, than a thought hurries into my head. Which is that it is Book Week at the village school and I have to be there to help celebrate it. The school is two miles away and the children, like the shepherds, will all be seated on the ground, or the library floor to be exact. No transport. The church clock says nine as I run past it. Alas, it is slow. Drawing breath – the local author must be dignified – I stroll in.

The children are on the floor and hoping that maybe I had come the field way and fallen over a cow or into the mere. I have to talk about Characters – the kind found in stories. There are characters in the Bible stories called 'types'. Types of angels shoot up their hands to ask questions, some leaving them wearily up in the air until Mags the Headteacher draws my attention to them. Alice, Mr Toad and William Brown fight for places next to Harry Potter, about whom I know nothing. I am a Potter virgin. A little girl tells me that she has an aunt who writes books with characters in them. She puts them onto the page with her pen and then onto the computer. Another William, just off to the Royal Grammar School, says that he is reading *Moby Dick*. The trouble with the bookwormship of children is that it makes grown-ups feel unsafe. I tell them that Beatrix Potter used to stay with *her* aunt just up the road from here. Well, at Long Melford. The other William takes me on an educational tour of the classrooms. They are miniscule Tates, artwork of every kind covering up the painted Victorian bricks. There are greedy paintings of pizzas and pancakes, the latter no doubt inspired by Michael the Vicar's cookery on Shrove Tuesday. And here are everyone's names in the Viking language. Kirk in runic script – it alters him somehow. 'Here,' says William severely, for I am not paying attention, 'is our wormery.' The poor things do what worms do but between glass plates. Outside in the playground I observe the return of the Hula-hoop. Nothing quite goes away in school.

Passio

A t twenty past eight precisely a watercolour sun comes into the farmhouse, picking out the gold picture frames and promising the earth. The cats hazard a paw or two into the icy garden, then retreat to a radiator. Birds de-moss the lawns and daffodils totter about in the new grass. It is England's famous spring, and not to be missed. The air is strong and sweet. Foot-and-mouth keep-out notices are in tatters on the telegraph poles. Ditch water pours away. The old men with their leaping dogs go by. I divorce La Reine Victoria from a blackberry bush. Easter is coming. 'Therefore let us keep the feast' we will soon be singing. Keeping feasts and Sabbaths, fasts and such likes, if only with words, keeps time itself in tune. Admirers of W. H. Auden were puzzled when he did so. Robert Craft found it surprising that he could refer quite readily to his religious conviction and practices, informing his New School audience that he will not be lecturing on Holy Saturday: When they told Auden Saturday wasn't a holiday. 'I told them it might not be for them, but it certainly was for me'. Passiontide reminded me of Auden's, bizarre to some, Christianity.

Passio = suffering. The road to Resurrection had to be trod with gravitas all the way. A few have trodden it for the many, which has been unfair but blessed. Faith's serious business has always been attended to by the saints. We have to make sure that faith's serious business is not reduced to pleasant customs. Christ's suffering and what we sometimes suffer because of it intensifies in the week before Holy Week. Julian of Norwich could not separate her suffering from our own. 'For the fundamental thing about the passion is to consider who he *is* who has suffered. I began to think about the majesty and the greatness of his glorious Godhead, now united with his tender body; I also remembered how we creatures loathe to suffer pain ...' And thus Passiontide, that sweeping into the calendar of all that we understand all too well, and from which God as man had no way of escape. For Julian the Passion was 'the greatest gesture our Lord God could make to the soul of man'.

A letter has arrived to ask if I would mind looking at one of the handsome eighteenth-century tombs in the churchyard to see if it is the writer's ancestor, who lived at the Grove. I get a chair from the vestry and *try* to make out its weathered lines. The letters are crammed with lichen. Moss makes fat fullstops. Here is the figure five, here a curlicue, here nothing at all. A gentleman lies below, but who is he? Sticky-buds wave over him. A honeysuckle feeds on him. His quarterings are smudged.

Country Matters

A crisp white world. Field edges have been trimmed-off by frost. The oaks are creaking. I am up early to write a new Introduction to George Herbert's *A Priest to the Temple or the Country Parson*, first published in 1652. He would have had the Bemerton windows wide in order to breathe – in order to live, indeed. I re-read his famous little book. What a nerve to write a rule for the rural clergy when one has only just joined them. And how did Mr Herbert come to such an understanding of his parish in such a few months? And, considering what a dandy he was at Cambridge, what a lot of ordinary common sense he has at his finger tips. By mid-morning the March sun is hot on the window and the ice is slipping. 'Immortal heat, O let thy greater flame attract the lesser to it.'

Commotion below – the hunt is in the garden. A river of hounds is flowing through it, one of them having the impertinence to gollop up the cats' leavings en route. Three huntsmen appear behind the hedge, though hoping that it hides them. One does a little bugling but the dogs stream on, soft muzzle to whipping tail. Then they have gone, all of them, men and animals. The cats! I tear down to save them. One is sitting many feet up in an old willow doing her famous Lewis Carroll act, the other ... Where is the other cat? I rush around calling, beseeching, composing in my head a letter to the Master of Foxhounds which will scare him stiff as I see pretty Kitty swallowed whole. The night comes and Bottengoms is in deep mourning for her. Look where she once lay, her favourite place, the imprint is there still. I put out, as usual, Whiskas for two and her sister eats the lot. Blinded with rage and grief, I fail to notice the sleeper in the piano. She stretches and makes a dissonance along the wires, a spangling of notes to accompany a greedy purr. Would Herbert, saint though he was, have put up with it?

Herbert told his country folk to 'think well – or better – of yourselves. But not without good cause.' The more tumbledown the circumstances, the better to make Christ's mark on them. What a privilege to be installed in neglect. And what a nuisance to have less than three years to reverse it. I climb the hill to have a word with the horses. Their nostrils steam and it makes them dragonish. No, they were not in the hunt, they tell me, just grazing. One of them rolls around on his back. Is it because he is happy or itchy? Gulls fly overhead, too high up to see anything to eat.

Wild Days

The brief cold violence of a March storm. All was as usual when a meteorological racket vented itself on our fields for all it was worth. Rain rushed down, winds cut the sky to pieces, lightning blackened and blinded the landscape in turn, thunder split our eardrums. Church towers rocked. Beasts cowered. And then – silence, after which the sound of all sorts of gutters and tracks doing their stuff.

Later, my eyes falling on a medieval gargoyle that now lies inside the church, I thought I saw a look of longing. What a come-down. Once, the March downpour gushed from that gaping mouth for centuries; now, only a concern for archaeology prevents us from stuffing it with our dripping brollies. Its stone lips are worn thin by historic waterfalls. Gargoyles have such sad features as they shoot the rain away from the walls and on to the dead. I give ours a little pat.

Deserts, not rains, are what we are to think about. Yet science has robbed us of their convenient Lenten aridity. No longer can we use them as geographical wastes; for now we know that they teem with life. The three great Abrahamic faiths are seeded in the same desert. Jews, Christians and Muslims entered human consciousness from the same gritty source. When we follow Christ as best we can into the desert, we enter his dilemma, his privation and terrible decision, and it is no longer a horrifying place.

But deserts do strange things to natural sounds. Voices are not what they seem. Reductive messages blow over the dunes, teasing the human ear. One day, a poet would call the desert's mocking bluff by seeing eternity in a grain of sand.

At the Lenten matins I wait for Christopher to come to Isaiah's prophecy, one that Jesus would have known: 'For the Lord shall comfort Zion: he will comfort all her waste places: and he will make her wilderness like Eden, and her desert like the garden of the Lord; joy and gladness shall be found therein, thanksgiving and the voice of melody.'

May we not now accept this ecologically as well as theologically? You know it makes sense. And of course we sing the 'Benedicite', clustering its praises. The village is chilly and draughty. 'I can't get warm,' says an old neighbour. There is a time when one cannot get warm. It is when one cannot get going as one used to.

But the March sun, once the March winds have stopped blowing it about, is enchanting. I feel it on the back of my neck as I clear the nut-walk, a surprising caress. And there are Easter lambs in Bowden's Lane as usual.

After the service, a visitor asks me to explain the *Agnus Dei* in the east window. Is it something to do with a coat of arms? Well, yes and no.

Gardening again; a lurid sky turns the earth blood-red. I toil right up to the first lashings of a second squall. The raindrops are huge and flatten my hair. Also the cat's. We enter the house in a dead heat.

The naked trees hurl themselves about; and can that Niagara roar be my downpipe – the one that props up the clematis? And is the roof safe? And the fat brick Tudor chimney that balances the TV aerial on its nose? And do the hosts of Midian prowl and prowl around? It sounds like it.

An Outing

'For, lo, the winter is past, the rain is over and gone; the flowers appear on the earth, the time of the singing of birds is come . . .' This is what I had had carved on the tomb of the artist John Nash. Lichen is gradually erasing it, but it is literally true at this moment. What a cold rainy winter it has been. What a singing of birds it is. What a sun pours into the garden and against the old walls, now that the hazel coppicing has been done.

And here is the Song of Solomon open on my desk. 'Make haste, my beloved' urges the last verse. 'How beautiful are thy feet . . .', but I mustn't go on. Scholars scratch their heads over its origin and say that if it is not read allegorically it has no business being included in the canon. But writers I love – St John of the Cross, Richard Rolle, St Teresa of Avila – loved it; so I love it too. And my singing birds break off to feed on chopped apples and mouldy Christmas cake. What a blessing it is when something cannot be certain.

To be correct, the singing of the chainsaw has come and gone. David brought down a mighty aspen bough which was drawing up the kitchen garden to fruitless heights. Its logs will dry out for a year, then burn well. But I will miss its dreamy voice, which said: 'Don't do a thing. Let me entrance you.'

Duncan has fished a hefty lump of iron from the horse pond. It was a wheel brake for a carriage, but now it is corroded into a kind of tuning fork from Mervyn Peake's *Gormenghast*. There would have been few steep enough hills around here to need it. Our lanes were notoriously dreadful, and shook carts and carriages to bits.

Lent plods on. I fill it with the humdrum: page proofs, and raking. I make plans, make unlikely dishes from the turned-out fridge, listen to Gerald Finzi, write kindly refusals, discuss Shakespeare with the white cat, give morning hymns to Meriel, feed the woodman, talk about the water supply with the council officer, and find primroses.

I hear the politicians shouting the odds, and the village football team distantly hollering. All noise is off. A dear friend goes to God at a mighty age, and on the radio Chopin at no age at all. On Saturday, we are off to Cambridge for the annual Readers' conference at Selwyn College.

For twenty or more years, Canon John Woods had drawn the East Anglian Readers there out of our isolation, because, although next door to each other in our clear landscape, we would not otherwise see each other. Writers who are Readers are doubly locked away, and so I find this jaunt doubly interesting. And I like this budding Cambridge, with the Victorian shrubberies about to burst, and the river damps promising glories along the Backs.

This year, I will say compline at teatime. And say to people I have met once a year for ages, 'I'm sorry, but I have forgotten your name.' And they will point to their badge, and I will get out my glasses. And George Selwyn will look down from his frame, and so will his son, John, and the undergraduates will look like children. And the drive back to the parish will not be without melancholy. Like a day at the seaside when we were ten.

Lectures are inclined to make me daydream. While some take notes, I take the opportunity to take stock of the days.

The Annunciation

A wild March afternoon at Little Henny, our neighbour village. It has its head in clouds and its feet in streams. Every kind of weather is chasing through it. We can see it coming in, the hail, the stiff rain, the surprising bursts of sunny warmth, the bouts of iciness. Having just sung the incomparable 'My song is love unknown' at the Lenten service (a *frisson* of delight when it was announced), Alan and I have gone in search of its author Samuel Crossman, rector here ages ago. We tramp through the March mud of what was not a happy living. The locals soon got rid of him. His church is now no more than a mark in a field. The deep lanes through which he would have walked only just take the car. Huge creamy bosses of primroses light the ditches, and magpies rush ahead of us. There is a scattering of houses, nothing more. If it is excitement you are after you must go to Great Henny. When I was a boy the Sudbury Boat Club would row down the Stour to Great Henny on Good Friday morning for beer and hot cross buns. But we, Alan and I, are at this moment elevated above such earthy sprees. We are where a dejected young seventeenth-century clergyman evidently sought solace in Herbert's *The Temple*, his querulous congregation having turned him out of theirs. Herbert's poems include one entitled 'Love Unknown' and his majestic meditation 'The Sacrifice' contains the line 'Never was grief like mine' which Crossman uses in his hymn.

Except it wasn't a hymn at the beginning. It was one of a handful of verses called *The Young Man's Meditation*, and as this little book was published soon after its author left Little Henny, one may presume that it took shape in its lanes and vanished church. It being such buffeting and exhilarating weather, with the puddles shining and the birds singing against a gale, I granted us licence to listen to Parson Crossman's words about the cruelty of the world and the love which overrides it. 'My Song' is a strong and uncomfortable statement about humanity's ability to turn on what is good, what is right. Priest–poets such as Crossman, fine minds in uncouth livings, would have been alarmed by the illumination they continue to shed.

Crossman departed from Little Henny in 1662 and had to bide his time. Shortly after the First World War, when the *English Hymnal* was being edited, Geoffrey Shaw took the composer John Ireland out to lunch. Halfway through it he handed a slip of paper across the table with 'I need a tune for this lovely poem.' Ireland read it and reread it, then wrote for a few minutes on the back of the menu. 'Here is your tune.' The words and the music now possess Henny's hilltop, homing there after three centuries.

New Grass

Now and then a casual remark introduces a lost vocabulary. Tom on the telephone from his farm down below says something about letting his Lincolns out onto the water meadows, and I experience the sight of that glorious rush of animals out of their shed and into the new grass. For minutes on end they are transfixed by the spring air, waving their heads about and caught up in an unimaginable bliss, then they thunder about and make gentle cries, and their beautiful eyes shine in the new sunlight. 'But I must keep them in for a couple of weeks more,' says Tom, 'until the pasture is established. Otherwise it will be Mud.' If I think about the old inhabitants of my ancient farm they tend to have two legs. Yet for centuries it would have been the home of beasts. There are the ponds where the Suffolks drew up their drink, there are the ghosts of pigsties, there is the hill where the freed cattle leaped. But where are the sounds? Where that clamour, those chompings, those raised voices, that restlessness of warm creatures, that clanking of pails and ringing of chains? At this moment if one stood out of doors all that one would hear is Mozart on the record player.

Yet, take a wet walk and wild animals betray their presence. 'We are with you still!' they say. Badgers have gone to a lot of trouble to undermine the track. Hares dance on the skyline, rabbits take cover. Owls call. Water birds sail on Mr Rix's new lake. Here is a fat dead rat and a thin dead mouse. Gaudy pheasants parade in the orchard. A stoat makes a dash for it. Rooks are patching up rookeries and soon the returning migrants will be building for all they're worth. But the grain store will not be a city of goldfinches. Frogspawn will look like grey tapioca beneath the marsh marigolds and, should I care to listen, I will hear eventually countless minute sounds, not to mention in early April the joyous blare of Tom's unimprisoned cows. Duncan's hens roam where they will but thousands of chickens scream unheard in an Orwellian gulag. I used to marvel at the obedience of farm creatures when I was a child. I mean, why didn't the cows jump over the hedge and walk to Bedford, say? Why didn't the sheep simply stroll away to some shepherdless hinterland? But no, they all stayed behind their hedges, terribly unsafe, terribly unadventurous, passive as those passengers on the Auschwitz railway – except that they could tell each other, 'We're in clover.' There are black lambs in the top meadow and dog-walkers in the green lane. The dogs are allowed to cover me with kisses. Some have swum in the lake and are soaking. Robins rustle. Pike stir below the bridge. But the animal army which made the farm work has long since trotted and galloped away into that animal heaven called Rest. Rest was the final word on many a tombstone too, for this was what its owner had had precious little of in this life. RIP. 'Come unto me and I will give you rest.' How people once laboured until, like John Clare's father, their bones gave way. But the resting animals became a kind of promise to labouring humanity who heard their breathing and saw their great bodies borne up by the earth. I have been explaining the lovely word 'mothering' to the children, and where best to watch it in action. In a stable, in a basket under one of those hooped houses where the pigs live, and very soon in the new pasture. Also, fathers do a lot of mothering these days.

The Bay Tree and the Desert

The vast bay tree (*Laurus nobilis*), some 50 feet high, which has stood scented sentinel for so long is dying – I think. Or it is having a spring autumn. Its leaves shrivel on the bough. 'I have seen the wicked in great power, spreading himself like a green bay tree.'

What is happening may not be terminal, however, and if Richard cuts it to the ground it will flourish all over again. Perfumed logs will spark in the grate for winters to come. Hissing and crackling through its fallen leaves, I remember that they should be crowning a poet's brow. This is no way to perish, and all over the primroses as well.

Lent jogs on. Lots of desert news. I am writing the foreword to a book about Virginia Woolf's holidays. Heavens, what undertakings! Half a train full of hefty luggage, bicycles and servants. Excursions in all weathers. And, most interestingly, a careful avoidance of all geographic, architectural, and 'general' facts.

Thus the tall novelist could move across England in a kind of personal haziness about this and that, particularly when it came to cathedrals or Stonehenge, or where one would expect a strong reaction, or at least a little wonder.

Sometimes, she is on her own, her bag filled with review copies for the *Times Literary Supplement*, for no Bloomsbury ever stops working, least of all during a holiday; and sometimes she is with Leonard and Vanessa, or five other people, and each day she gives the countryside attributions that one would never find in guidebooks, but which create such perfect settings for the talk in her novels.

Now and then she is ill and strange, and landscape comes to the rescue. There is a mighty discomfort in these travels, and a kind of pre-Betjeman anger towards those who are getting out of dreadful Victorian cities and in to red brick villas, which were

going up wherever their owners fancied; for there was little or
no planning.

All the same, it is odd for us highly factualised sightseers to find
Virginia's view of Stonehenge labelled, moodily, 'The singular &
intoxicating charm ... is that no one in the world can tell you
anything about it ... I felt as though I had run against the stark
remains of an age I cannot otherwise conceive ... a piece of
wreckage washed up from Oblivion.'

No one in our world is disallowed information on anything.
'Oblivion' won't do. But it does do in those perfect novels. In fact,
it has to. Indeed, it was sought for in that lonely walk to the river
in 1941.

At first, the desert did its utmost to obscure what Christ went
to it to find. Its sheer dullness robbed him of his intellect, when it
should have cleared it. It weakened his young body; it made
horrible sounds. And maybe it did so to the many other seekers
after enlightenment who came to it in springtime, as well as to
the Desert Fathers, who set up house in it later on.

What the Lord and his followers had to face was Oblivion, and
the desert maddeningly waved this possibility in their faces. It was
no help. Environmentalists now cause it to say wonderful things.
To which the sands can reply: 'Out of us grew the triple Abrahamic
faiths of your salvation.'

APRIL

We accompany Blythe through the month of April when the dead land reawakens with light and warmth, and water showers the earth. We share with him the seasons which are the seasons of God as well as nature; and can they be distinguished? The grace of God, for Blythe, permeates all nature, all things, all life.

Some say, since the Enlightenment, that we live in a disenchanted world, where what is sacred, if there at all, has been banished beyond, into ethereal transcendence, and so unobtainable to ordinary people, whose mundane lives just happen without value or meaning. Blythe's world is ordinary, yes, but suffused with Easter. Christ walks in the garden and light intensifies. Easter lilies trumpet in cold churches. The rubbish – the wild and lovely things – is filled with glory. The trees speak of bearing the body of Jesus, bluebells become the sky, the rain droppeth twice upon the earth, a blessing of mercy.

The days of April are laden with meaning, ancient meaning, found in hot cross buns which may only be eaten on Good Friday, baked, not shop-bought; and Christ's suffering is heart-breakingly beautiful. The days become years, as Blythe remembers, bringing the past to enchant the present, as a lark sings its way into art, and pigeon fanciers fill the Crown. The shadows stretch over the years, and Christ is in the dark places too – the tragedies of loss, the deaths of friends, ways of life long gone – the persisting grace as potatoes go into the fresh-dug earth.

Frances Ward

My Little Owls

Certain happiness. Pear blossom. Six a.m. tea. Matins for a dozen in the chancel. Making my sweet pea wigwam. Seeing strangers pass. Listening to the director of the British Museum on the radio. Watching the manes of the horses on the hill being caught in the wind. Reading Psalm 96.

Eating a miser's meal – pot d'jour, a curling crust, cheese ends, and a wizened apple. Loving my little cat. Not going to the party. Sploshing up the farm track. Remembering the Garretts in Cambridge. Listening to David Holt reading George Herbert. Seeing the boundary ditch full of water. A whisky at bedtime.

Silence. Oaks before ash promising a splash. Re-reading *Swann's Way*. Finding the nail scissors. Visiting the new bookshop in Stoke-by-Nayland. Watching the world greening. Remembering the Turners in Cornwall. Finishing a chapter. Choosing a page of *Kilvert's Diary* for a sermon. Hearing a climbing rose scratch against the window, like Catherine Earnshaw's escape-me-never hands.

Eating olives. The lawnmower starting at first pull. Feeding chaffinches. Watching Dan draw. The unbelievable scent of blue-bells. The kindness of strangers at the hospital. Ash log fires. New jerseys. Giving Vicky plants. Hearing bumble bees. Knowing that the summer spreads before me. Finding true sadness at the passing of Gerald, the village-shop dog.

Finding stitchwort and wild garlic in their accustomed spots. Touching the sun-warmed Roman bricks of the Saxon tower in Colchester and imagining the hands that formed them. Seeing beautiful girls lean on the thousand-year-old doorway. Myself seeing for the thousandth time the house of John Wilbye, the madrigalist, whose patron gave him a sheep farm for his services. Listening hard, what bliss to hear him singing among the shoppers.

Catching sight of my little owls in the blackthorn, where they have always been. The satisfaction when flowers and creatures know their places. Choosing hymns for Sunday – carefully, of course, as our three churches have three different books. Three parish magazines as well. Three of everything. One of the vicar; one of myself. I consider our oneness.

Rape will soon yellow everything. Its seeds will go to the crusher, and their oil to Waitrose. News from a foreign country comes. Owen has died in Wales. I hear his piano thundering Bach in his cold house. Also our talk as we climb the Black Mountain. How quiet it will be now. No loud voice, no confident keys. He was staunchly Chapel, and went on taking services until his congregation went to God before him. Then he followed. I took him to Shingle Street when he came to stay in Suffolk – as a treat. Was I having a joke? He had shown me mountains, wonders ... His bewilderment at this time-distance makes me joyful. It was quite something to disconcert Owen.

The April happiness of finding so much promising. To have it all before one. Though not to count the days, but to let them bud and open; the weather to try everything on from gale to serenity; the pages of the current book to fall into chapters; the man from the British Museum to show Shakespeare in a handful of artefacts; and George Herbert to show us the Church as only he can.

Thomas Ken, Bishop of Bath and Wells

It is the day of Mr Paddon's two-yearly visitation and those of us who are not on the mains have been pulling up our watery socks. He comes to sample our bacteria, to marvel that we are still alive and have not been washed into oblivion by our medieval supply. The Bottengoms water has never frozen in the coldest winters or dried up in the hottest summers. What is also remarkable is its ability to spring from the ground and then from my taps

– and then towards the river – all within a couple of hundred yards of its origin to its final disappearance in the valley. Thankfully, Mr Paddon is pleased with me for having carried out his last recommendations to the letter and we are able to resume our various water memories before he sets off on his bacterial mission to The Grange and to The Hall, both a mile from the mains and, like me, drinking from the same source which refreshed centuries of their inhabitants. As with these ancients, I have to share a stream with foxes, badgers and, I suspect, Max the cat, but it flows fast and constantly, so let us hope that it bears all their impurities away. My chief anxiety is that it shouldn't worry Mr Paddon once every two years. His exciting news is that he has found a Victorian well in his garden and, after he had cleared it of twenty feet of rubble, found four feet of pure water too. Does he drink it? He eyed me warily. He is on the mains.

The Gospels being so full of wells it was no wonder that hydrolatry became popular. Worshipping water seemed an obvious thing to do. Water was never simply water, it was different wherever one found it, especially holy if a saint lived near by, particularly medicinal if it coursed through certain rocks. The writer James Rattue adds another reminder: 'In pools of water the human being first saw his own face, and could see the world mirrored around him: and this is perhaps the most surprising and extraordinary power of water.' As I read this I thought of Thomas Traherne's magical poem 'Shadows in the Water' in which a boy staring into a puddle 'chanc'd another World to meet'.

. . . what can it mean?
But that below the purling Stream
  some unknown Joys there be
  Laid up in Store for me;
To which I shall, when that thin Skin
Is broken, be admitted in.

Wells which contained mineral properties which soothed sore eyes were called 'sunrising-water'. It is Passiontide, the days of suffering which precede the Redemptive Death, when Christ went down into the depths.

Digging

Holy week. A soft gale troubles the bare trees. But it will not rain. Gulls land among the horses. The stream pours unseen to the river. The garden calls.

I re-read Julian's revelations of divine love in which, for me, there is an unparalleled account of the crucifixion — one that could only have been written by someone who had witnessed official torture. Also a slow dying. It comes after Julian's enchanting comparison of God's love to a hazelnut. 'What is this? It is all that is made.'

She translates medieval Christianity in a way that makes it acceptable to us, all these centuries later, and never more so than when she describes what happened on Good Friday. Without writers like her, 'We do not know, we cannot tell, what pains he had to bear.'

And yet her Christ is a gardener sent by his master to plant love in his creation, digging and banking, toiling and sweating, turning and trenching the ground, watering the plants the while.

'And by keeping at this work he would make sweet streams to flow, fine abundant fruit to grow; he would bring them to his lord, and serve them to his taste.'

Although a young neighbour does most of the sweating and turning these days for me, I can look on the Bottengoms garden with some pride at the hard graft that created it, long ago.

In fact, I love digging, especially in the kitchen garden, where the soil fell off the spade in delectable clumps, and robins followed me up and down, up and down, and the mower made its neat mark; and the excitement of deciding where the runner beans should climb this summer could be intoxicating. So when a friend came to tell me about his London allotment, my heart went out to him.

And when I visited the Garden Museum in Lambeth, its relics spoke more of human happiness than mere toiling and sweating.

Anyway, I have made a start. The white cat looks down at me from a tree. Nesting birds watch anxiously from ivy grandstands. Bluebells, their buds still near to their roots, perilously close to the badger setts, promise a show in May; and, altogether, I have made a start. Making a start is the thing. One cannot do it often enough.

How terrible it was that Jesus had to suffer in a garden – probably one that he knew and delighted in; one in which ancient olives were rooted in Jewish history: Gethsemane.

He had walked there after the Last Supper, accompanied by his disciples. He would have crossed the brook, Kidron, and descended the little valley between Jerusalem and the Mount of Olives.

It was springtime, and Julian of Norwich walked with Christ in Gethsemane. She was a young woman of thirty, and was not well, but 'thought it a pity to die'. And rose from her bed because she had much to say.

It was 8 May 1373. It was then that she wrote her masterpiece. It became illegible with time, as we all do; but a modern scholar, Clifton Walters, brushed the grave-dirt from it so that we could find our way about in Holy Week, meeting the gardener and saviour, and be forced to comprehend his crucifixion, and attempts to uproot him, and then to arrive at his glorious flowering.

Creek Wood

Ben, seven, and Sam, five, have just been paying their yearly visit and each is roughly a foot taller than last time. Their grandparents haven't grown an inch. Sunday tea with homemade jam tarts, followed by dominoes, and the catching up of news. Cold April rain dashes down and, as we repeatedly tell each other, such scenes as this must have often filled the farmhouse kitchen over the generations. Visiting rituals are never more ardently and properly observed than by visiting children. They like to find things as they left them, though not empty plates, of course. Max, who shares W. C. Fields's opinion of children, flees from their caresses. The company gone, I hurry to St Andrew's to read even-song for just the five of us and the candles waver in the draught. Holy Week. I can hear the wind gusting against the tower and all the small sounds made by an ancient structure which is caught in a squall, the tappings and fidgetings, and above them our voices speaking Psalm 62: 'As a tottering wall shall ye be, and like a broken hedge.' Though only if we are mischief-makers.

Holy Week then advances. The nights become wilder, colder, the day skies bank up with unshed snow. Then from church to church we ride, Maundy here, Good Friday there, the Vigil by the Mount, Easter everywhere. Drifts of stitchwort along Old Barn Road are picked out by our headlights, at first suggesting that a few flakes have fallen, this and the staring white of blackthorn. One silent afternoon I walk in Creek Wood, and a glider passes through a dark mass of starlings. But my head is filled with Florentine artists, not oil-seed rape or an inspired sermon. I have been reading Vasari's *Lives* again, that crucial multi-biography in the long history of art.

Thus in Creek Wood musings on *c.*1500 Tuscany where whoever was not painting, sculpting, writing or composing to a previously unknown perfection was employing those who were. Like April flowers, Renaissance men came out of the ground. While they may not have known much about archaeology, they knew Art when they saw it, and here among the foundations of their new cities were exposed ancient marble and bronze works of such divinity that they had to surpass them in order to honour God. It was the age of the non-specialist. Call yourself an artist?

Then make me a dome, a clock, a poem, a tomb, a tune, a likeness so like myself that I will be immortalised. As for the popes, their prayers were as often in their commissions as in their religion. Frequently and metaphorically they were forever on their knees before some rascal with a paintbrush or chisel, begging for his genius. And what did these artists do with all the money they demanded? Nothing. One of them put his in a basket which hung from the workroom roof from which anyone needing some cash might take a dip. At Easter both the Resurrection and the Renaissance poured from all the churches into the exultant streets, hand in hand. 'In God is my health and my glory.' Psalm 62 again.

Art and Weather

'It was not always like this,' I admonish the white cat: 'tinned breakfast regularly at six, gorgeous radiators, blackbirds through the window, devoted old chap.' Sometimes I hear them, the skinny labourers clumping down from the bothy to feed the stock, the girls singing in the dairy, the barefoot children falling over the dogs, the mother shouting, the pot bubbling. All gone into the dark, says the poet. Or into the light, says somebody else.

Easter lilies are trumpeting in freezing churches, good for at least a month. Easter Anthems – 'page 165 in the green book' – are sung, have died away. We have trudged all the way to Emmaus for the feast. On the farm both the corn and the 'rubbish', i.e. all the wild and lovely things, are springing up. In the churchyard, a stone has been taken away to have Gordon's name carved on it. In the great ditch, there are wild garlic, dog's mercury, and bluebell stubs all over again.

Marina Warner and I have returned from shepherding some university students round the Constable country in a downpour. We stand and steam by the fire. In East Bergholt churchyard, we called on the artist's parents, his father Golding and his mother

Anne, Willy Lott, and the Dunthornes. It was Mr Dunthorne, plumber and glazier and house painter, who had shown the teen-age Constable how to mix his colours. And it was young Jonny Dunthorne who had set himself up as picture-cleaner, and who had scrubbed Rubens's mighty *Château du Steen*.

In Dedham Church, we peered up at Constable's beautiful Christ, who may have been modelled by the doorkeeper of the Royal Academy, an ex-soldier and ex-village choirboy, for whom the artist found a job after the Napoleonic wars.

The steep lane to Flatford Mill was a watercourse, an added river. My brother and I used to whizz down it on our bikes, John Nash in his Triumph Herald, on the way to the flower-painting class, with his model, a single bloom from the garden, leaping on the dashboard.

What with our dogs rushing about with joy and people stick-ing wet mobiles in their ears, and the sheer muddle that down-pours set up, nobody takes much notice of my lecture. I tell the wind: 'This is where *The Cornfield* is set; this is where he painted *Boat Building on the River Stour, The Hay Wain* ...' Dogs rejoice. No one complains. Marina sploshes along, staying wonderfully elegant in her long coat. 'John Constable was the most weathered of all the artists of his day. He could paint rain.'

It was Jesus who drew his friends' attention to the equality of rain. It fell on the just and the unjust. Shakespeare likened it to the inescapability of mercy. I am devoted to it, though not when I have to talk through it.

I think of the tramping Jesus in all weathers, him and his friends either scorched or soaked. I imagine them sheltering, their hair dripping, their robes clinging, the sandy mud squelching between 'those feet'. O for Bethany and one of Martha's meals!

And now it is Wednesday in Easter Week, and we must read Luke's last words. 'These are the words which I spake unto you while I was yet with you ...' So pay attention. Let them not be rained off.

As it Was, As it Is

Good Friday, but long ago. The early morning Suffolk town was barely awake when they sent us off to collect the hot cross buns. Other erranding boys and girls boasted how many they would eat for breakfast. Bakers' vans, like Arks of the Covenant, were being trundled through the waking streets, steaming with buns. Good Friday was half in mourning for Christ and half at play. The Boat Club rowed down river to devour hot cross buns and bitter at Henny 'Swan'. Henny means an island on river land which is frequented by wild birds. The Boat Club boys needed to be wild birds in order to stand the cold. They shook in caps and mufflers and were as pink as blancmange or as white as death. Their oars cut into the icy Stour as fast as they could as their crews lusted for buns. They would not have heard of the young rector of Little Henny, Samuel Crossman, who had written a book called *The Young Man's Meditation*, a little collection of poems which included 'My song is Love Unknown'. He had been reading George Herbert's 'Love unknown' and Herbert had been reading Psalm fifty-one. For this is what happens to divine love. It streams through the imagination of poets, rhyming up here and there, catching a tune, catching a congregation.

But back to small town Good Fridays. Should they be early, then it would be snowing, if late, the sticky buds were glistening on Miss Baker's vast horse chestnut and the first swallows would be whirling around the green copper spire on St Peter's. But whether early or late, the Three Hours would slowly pass in icebox conditions. The wan Welsh rector Canon Hughes would fidget in his miserere stall and the well-off old ladies would come and go in fat fur coats, their powdered cheeks turning blue. The truly saintly sat it out. Every little while Mark Fairhead the organist would play a verse from 'O Sacred Head' and we would stand and sing, 'Thy beauty, long desired, Hath vanished from our sight'.

Although where I was concerned this was not true. I found his beauty all too terribly present. It was heartbreaking. All around, Suffolk voices were pleading, 'I pray thee, Jesus, own me' and the tower clock would say another hour to go.

Good Friday these days, in the village, that is, amounts to ante-communion for the two or three, and one hour for the many. Stainer. No talking when we leave. Car doors going, clump, clump. Smiles through glass. Cries from the footballers. At teatime I look up the recipe for hot cross buns in *The Universal Cookery Book*, a very pre-Delia authority acquired by mother about the same time as I was sent to the baker's before breakfast. It said, 'Cassis, 3 tabl. yeast, mace' and a surprising number of other ingredients. The buns had to be brushed over with warm milk and 'baked a nice brown'. But as every child knows, hot cross buns must come from a shop, not from mother, and on Good Friday morning, not from the deep freeze. They must arrive plentifully, not just one for you and one for me, and they should never be eaten except on this tragic morning, then fillingly.

A Vigil at Mount Bures

As we find our way through the shadowy lanes of Easter Eve, it occurs to me that the first vigil kept at the Lord's tomb was there to prevent his leaving it. 'Watch it, seal it, makes it as sure as you can,' was Pilate's advice. Our watch takes place at Mount Bures, our height. There are the usual score of us and our ceremony is brief. We acknowledge the unutterable sadness of the night but we do not see in the happiness of the morning. The Saturday between 'It is finished' and 'He is not here' is a void, a poignant hole. Maybe this is what it should be, a gap in the otherwise high drama of the liturgy to bring us up short.

Joyce has laid a little fire just outside the church porch much as she would have laid her own grate before she got the central heating, and Michael has to use a cigarette lighter to ignite it because of the liturgical requirement of a flint. A tearing spring wind puts it out over and over again. Then a whoof! and a blaze from which I take fire for the Paschal candle and we all take fire from it.

Our ancestors were more direct and explicit concerning Christ's grave, more inclined to see it next to their own. More urgent for the morning, more candid about the night. The burial of God himself half-reconciled them to their own going down into the dark. Bitter, bitter it would be, like that hyssop forced against the dying tongue. For them, Easter Eve was the ultimate ante-feast, and the Lord's tomb and their own tombs that inescapable ante-room to all that would shortly open up before them, Heaven itself. During the Middle Ages, toy tombs consisting of wooden frames decked with funeral hangings would be placed in the north aisles of parish churches and the Host would leave its position at the sunrise window and disappear from sight into these model vaults.

When Counsellor Joseph came to plead for the corpse, the Roman governor was astonished to hear that Jesus was dead. So soon! The crucified were required to last longer than this, it was the object of such an execution. 'Take it,' he said. So the sympathetic Joseph had the dreadfully injured victim carried to a nearby garden in which his own cave-grave awaited an occupant and placed it inside with full Jewish rites. The 'cold hard stone' of it distressed George Herbert as he remembered the tender flesh so recently unmarked, so warm and living, so breathing and beautiful, and he thought guiltily of men's stoniness when it came to injuring others. Why, 'our hard hearts have took up stones to brain thee!' Julian too and other poets and artists could never target the physical Christ, that shocking sight on Easter Eve. They were haunted by his obsequies and by what I still contemplate – the terrible aloneness of the body on its first full day in the grave.

Care was taken not to blunt the distinction of Easter Eve.

Neither the horrors of Friday nor the joy of Sunday were allowed to overwhelm the pure sorrow of Saturday. He suffered and was buried. The Arimathean's rock tomb would have been sweet with fresh linen and the half-a-hundredweight of myrrh and aloes supplied by the reckless Nicodemus, and heavy with women's spices. When all was properly done they blocked its entrance against marauding animals. For them it was indeed finished, ended, all over. Joseph may even have been thinking that there would be anon space for him to lie alongside his young friend. They all went away, and the watch arrived – the vigilant.

Sepulture in a small room has since been regarded as superior burial. The great tend not to go into the earth but into stone boxes, although the crowds who saw and heard Christ would have all gone into the sand. As for him, without Joseph's hospitality he would have been left on the Golgotha tip for the scavenging creatures. Not that this would have affected the Resurrection. Many in the late twentieth century have but a moment of incandescent sepulture at the busy crematorium, and yet, like the old Mount Bures farmers in their big brick tombs, there is time there to wait until the day breaks. The burial of Christ helps to resign us to our mortality. Easter Saturday is the harsh pause between this life and another. So we believe.

Some years ago I had to write a critical Introduction to *The Death of Ivan Ilyich*, the novel which marked the ending of a crisis of faith which had preoccupied Tolstoy during the whole of the 1870s. I often think of it as *the* Holy Saturday tale. Up until writing this book Tolstoy had taken a rational look at death. Death on the battlefield, death on the scaffold, death of the muzhiks in their huts on the estate, the death even of his own small son. But when he reached the age of fifty this rationality left him, for his own death could not be far away. He wrote, 'It is time to die – that is not true. What *is* true is that there is nothing else to do in life but die. I feel it every instant. I am writing, I'm working hard . . . but there is no happiness for me in any of it.' This to his brother. *Death was* – and yet he had to stay sane and work and earn money and look forward to Easter and cut the hay! The result of all this activity was to make him nervous and imaginative, and so he concluded that only some mundane business, such as purchasing more acres, could stop death getting such a grip of him. Thus he set off to buy a forest hundreds of miles from home, taking with him, purposely, a high-spirited young servant with all his life before him.

It was while staying at an inn that Tolstoy had the classic nightmare of his bedroom becoming his tomb. All rooms were tombs! All talk was part of the everlasting silence; all movement was no more than a pathetic human twitching of the everlasting stillness; all horizons were walls. 'I tried to shake off my terror. I found the stump of a candle in a brass candlestick and lighted it. The reddish flame, the candle, the candlestick, all told me the same story: there is nothing in life, nothing exists but death – and death should not be!'

Thus was inspired one of literature's most brilliant explorations of death, or of Easter Saturday. Ilyich is a pushy provincial lawyer well on his way to being a Moscow judge, his and his equally thrusting wife's burning ambition, when cancer strikes him down in his mid-forties. His ambitious wife is furious, his friends are embarrassed. How unfeeling of Ilyich to show them death at their age! His sickroom would have been the terrible room of Tolstoy's nightmare, had it not been for Gerasim the peasant youth through whose healthy flesh and selflessness there operates the Christ of Easter Eve, the Lord who enters the tomb with us saying, 'I too was here.' Just before entering, the lawyer's eyes were opened to a 'dreadful deception that for him had shut out both life and death'.

I once took the poet James Turner to Little Easton church for the Good Friday music. It was where Thomas Ken had been rector – 'Teach me to live that I may dread/The grave as little as my bed.' On Easter Eve James wrote:

We have sealed the tomb,
High on the hill of Golgotha the scarred wood
Stands untenanted . . .
The trumpet sounds
Over the scandalous hill, distantly proclaiming
A whispered promise
Of the perfect Oblation.

I find Easter Saturday therapeutic. It makes darkness reasonable. As we carry our wavering lights into the grave it becomes once more our familiar nave heady with tomorrow's flowers. Wild primroses, hothouse arums. 'Vigil or not,' say the women sensibly, 'there won't be time to do them in the morning.' I think of Joseph getting his servant to chip away at the rock to make a tomb from which both Christ and himself would burst free.

My Trees

'How many trees have you got?' asks the little boy. One, an enormous willow, has tipped over, and he sees it split in three. A hundred, two hundred, I hazard. I planted a few broad-leaved ones a lifetime before he was born. To fill the spaces left by the elms. I live in a small wood, thus, tree-music is a constant.

The wood is greening at this moment — greening and whisper-ing. I have sent a postcard of John Constable's bark-study to Dan to tell him: 'Please come on Monday.' My trees enchant him. He has been to the David Hockney exhibition, and to Paris. The Hockney wood puzzles him, as it does me. The absence of botany, shall we say.

When Constable was a lad, and walking to see his Wormingford family — 'the Wormingford folk' — he had to pass an enticing medieval park, about five miles from here, and the baronet kindly gave him a pass which said: 'Pray permit Mr Constable to draw the trees.' This so that the gamekeepers did not drive him out.

Tom Gainsborough had painted *Cornard Wood* a few miles away. They say that there are more trees hereabouts now than in their day. Paul, our tree man, has to hold an inquest on my tumble-down willow – what to do? A standing tree inhabits the sky; a fallen one lives nowhere, and dies everywhere.

In the past, Christians called the Cross 'the Tree'. Fortunatus sang:

O Tree of beauty, Tree of light,
O Tree with royal purple dight,
Elect on whose triumphal breast
Those holy limbs should find their rest!

In the Saxon poem 'The Dream of the Rood', the writer is contemplating the crucifixion.

The finest of trees began to talk: 'I remember the morning, a long time ago That I was felled at the edge of the forest And severed from my roots. Strong enemies seized me And fashioned me for their sport, bade me hold up their felons on high ... I saw the Lord of Mankind courageously hasten to climb upon me.'

My trees certainly chatter away – best of all, the aspens in summer; *sotto voce*, enticingly, articulating tree happiness. I lie beneath them, book unread, seduced by their soft song, like John Clare or Thomas Traherne. So much occurred under trees in the Bible. They became markers for beginnings from Eden onwards. Scripture is a virtual forest and a simple shade, a bare wood and a glorious orchard.

Our churchyard trees were planted by a Victorian priest. Should one of them depart, we introduce another. Their dust and our dust have an arrangement that suits us both. I sit under them, waiting for the ringers to approach an end. They have to be pagan in spite of our poets, which is another kind of sacredness.

There are wayside oaks that are contemporary with Arden. And, down by the river, delicate, shivery cricket-bat plantations, which are harvested every fifteen or so years. An Easter full moon looked down on them.

Lark's Voice

A warm spring morning. I wheel the old newspapers up the farm track for the dustman, two-thirds of them unread. Helpless we are before the waste. But the larks! It is father's birthday. He would have been 110, an April boy.

Returning, the skylarks cover me with their song. Two of them? An entire lark quintet? The music is high and glorious. But the Big Field is used to it. Decade after decade, since Edmund or whoever it was, these dizzy birds in the blue air making a singing canopy for the early toilers. A pair of devoutly married magpies, tremendously handsome, add a couple of low notes. But chiefly it is larks. They are invisible to the admiring eye.

One thing I did read in the paper was that Vaughan Williams's *The Lark Ascending* remains our most popular piece of music. But it is now journalistically correct to bewail an absence of larks. Where do these people live? Poets strive against each other to sing the lark, Tennyson with his 'sightless song', and John Clare to his Jane, 'The lark's in the grass love, Building her nest'; so we know what is on his mind.

Lark's voice, says my bird conductor, 'A clear, liquid "chir-rup" song, a high-pitched, musical outpouring, very long sustained, in hovering and descending flight, and occasionally from the earth or a low perch.' So skylarks do not even need the sky. As feathered music, they can be grounded or ethereal. The trouble with skylarks is that they refuse to allow ornithology to cage them. Off they wing into human art the moment they open their mouths, theirs clearly being the song of songs, as the Psalmist puts it, 'in the house of our pilgrimage'. And so I loiter to listen to it all over again, the song of the Big Field larks as it fills the universe.

John Clare now and then put his Northamptonshire skylarks in their place – 'a bird that is of as much use in poetry as the night-ingale'. But then, being Clare and village naturalist-extraordinary, he writes as follows: 'The skylark is a slender light bird with a coppled crown on the head [and] builds its nest on the ground and lays five or six spotted eggs. This is the one celebrated by poets for the sweetness of its song. They gather in flocks after harvest and are caught in some parts by nets, thrown at nights in great quantities. A redcap lives about seven years in a cage, a skylark about fourteen. I knew of one kept tame by a publican at Tallington.'

It was on an April day like this that John Clare read in his local paper, the *Stamford Mercury*, that 'The Lingfield and Crowhurst choir sung several select pieces from Handel in the cavity of the Yew tree in the churchyard of the latter place. The tree is 36 feet in circumference and is now in a growing state – The hollow was fitted up like a room and sufficiently large to contain the perform-ers – On clearing out the interior of the tree some years ago a 7lb cannon ball was discovered which had no doubt been fired into it ...'

There is a vast oak in my track which would have been stand-ing then (1820), hollow in parts, though nowhere wide enough to hold even a flautist. But a great many creatures dwell in it. It drinks from a brook. I think of the Lord in springtime and his bird-music.

Hale-Bopp, the Easter Comet

A week of looking upwards. Sweet spring days with much going on overhead. Not a lot of work done, if one leaves out slave labour in the garden and talks and lectures. The emphasis has been on staring aloft at fleeting wonders. First there were the

jackdaws in the churchyard horse chestnuts with their chaka-
chaka sociability, bouncing around on the topmost twigs and
inviting any passing rook to join in. Then there was the second
sighting of the barn owl cruising low over the pasture in the half-
light on majestic wing, and then of course there was Hale-Bopp.
We were about to enter the Crown when the snowy comet
caught our eye. There it was, right over Little Henny. We sent the
landlady out to look at it. On Easter Saturday it will be only
twenty-three million miles away. Now there's a thought. It was
faintly veiled by cloud, like Jerusalem in Lamentations, a cloud
which the writer of this tragic dirge maintained was deliberately
created in order 'that our prayers should not pass through'.
Lamentations, a set book for Holy Week; I read it all through,
thrilled by the grandeur of its sadness. It has long had a dual liturgical purpose: for the Jews to remember the destruction of
Jerusalem, for Christians as an articulation of their sorrow as the
Redeemer sets his face towards a hill beyond the city. 'Is it nothing to you, all ye that pass by? Behold and see if there be any
sorrow like unto my sorrow' (Chapter 1).

The inconsequence of cosmic happenings. The Crown is
packed with guests for the annual dinner of the Pigeon Club and
the fanciers have come from far and wide. They are no less soci-
able than birds, and now and then I fix an ear in their direction,
hoping to pick up a prize example of their lore. But all I can hear
is a jolly roar, the human version of what is going on among the
churchyard trees. Back home I look up what was going on when
Hale-Bopp was last seen from Earth and discover that in 2700 BC
the emperor of China was classifying plants, which ones to eat,
which ones to put in the medicine chest. His subjects dubbed
him the 'Divine Husbandman', and one can hardly expect so
great a botanist to find time to gawp at the stars. Auden summed
up the way we manage to get on with our lives in spite of what
is occurring in the skies. When Icarus falls to his death it is not a
disaster for the ploughman toiling below, only a splash and a

forsaken cry. Suffering, says the poet, 'takes place/while someone else is eating or opening a window or just walking dully along'. And it is true, it does. But then so does human happiness. The barn owl, the comet and the jackdaws share our universe, and this is a comfort and a pleasure. To see them we have to look up.

Staying at Home

Fortunate the writer or artist whose parish is his universe. I dare say there were those who urged George Mackay Brown to get about a bit, to leave Orkney and see the world, but he famously never did. We were long-distance friends, the kind of writers who originally began to absorb each other's landscape by osmosis. He never saw mine, except on the page, but once I flew off to Kirkwall without saying that I was coming, and there was his exactly as he said it would be. I travelled from Kirkwall to Stromness on Mr Peace's bus, and there was George walking towards me along the granite street in a cutting wind. 'I was told someone had arrived,' he said. We had tea by a big coal fire using 'Mother's best cups' and with myself taking in as much as I could of his work-den of a house when he wasn't looking, the cliff of books, the curly lino, the single photograph, the kitchen table which was his desk and the rocking-chair which was where he 'interrogated silence', as he put it. 'What a mercy God had taught us how to write,' he observed. 'What else would we have been fit for?' We talked of Thomas Hardy and how, in the morning, I was to sail to Hoy. A few yards away the sea was churning in the harbour and I remember thinking, 'How amazing! I am in Hamnavoe!' This was the old name for Stromness which George used to give himself a kind of elbow-room in time.

He died a few days ago, and just in time to get himself buried on the feast of St Magnus in Kirkwall Cathedral, that rose-coloured shrine built all at once during the twelfth century in contrition for a murder. There are only three great works of architecture in Orkney, St Magnus Cathedral and the Rings of Brogar and Stenness, the latter over 4,000 years old, yet in their sharp-edged brightness not ancient at all, but like airy temples just awaiting a congregation. What strange hymns were sung here? Not far away was Skara Brae, a group of fully furnished cottages c.3000 BC. Stone cupboards, seats, tables – everything still as it would have been when the family set out for the service at Stenness. George himself moved from age to age, and from island to island at will, and as the fancy took him. His Orcadians were given a time-span plus a timelessness, so that they were never cut off from their past or denied their own kind of ruthless present. He was an astringent poet – story-teller. One could imagine him in a post-Viking monastery, not very useful except for prayer and words. St Magnus Cathedral has its own little poets' corner – Edwin Muir, Eric Linklater, the Saga writers – and now George. He was profoundly Christian, a writer who knew his place. His bones lie in the high kirkyard where I sat after we said farewell.

Brutal Realities

The great quandary of those who write about the countryside, or who paint it, is how to keep the euphoric vision, if not out of the general picture entirely, in its proper place. Such a vision of rural life is always in demand – always has been. When that peerless village poet John Clare wrote his *Shepherd's Calendar* his publishers demanded far less reality and much more charm. These thoughts occurred to me as, by coincidence, I wrote a fresh Introduction to Mary Russell Mitford's classic *Our Village* as the beef crisis deepened. This delightful book has acquired something of the reputation of being, like John Constable's paintings, the euphoric vision exemplified. Stick to such blissful scenes and you will never encounter the nasty woodshed, let alone be tempted to look inside it. No worse injustice to the writer and the artist could be offered. Each of them knew more than enough about village life to pretend that it was paradisiacal, but they also knew that the essential happiness of humanity should still be found there in some shape or form, and that their own glimpses of it should be revealed in their work. Constable painted against the agricultural ruin and distress which followed the Napoleonic wars, Mitford's horror during her flower-gathering walks was having to pass the workhouse.

April 1996 will always be remembered as the time when the modern management of 'all ye Beasts and Cattle' – for make no mistake, every creature which we eat, fish, fowl and cow, is ethically as well as medically involved – cracked. Whatever the politicians and farmers do, and it will take years of repair, things will never be quite the same again. Unlike Mitford, when I walk I do not have to skirt the poor folk rotting away in the workhouse, and unlike Constable, whose uncles and aunts lived in Wormingford, I do not have to watch desperate labourers firing ricks, but I do know enough about certain forms of today's farming that when I pass some spots I have to weigh the practice against the cost. Villages are intriguing because they combine the most free-ranging gossip with the utmost reticence. Some things are always talked about, some things never. They also contain many new inhabitants who wouldn't be able to tell wheat from barley, as the saying goes, and for whom nothing is going on so far as they can see, agriculturally speaking. Such incomers through no fault of their own will never be able to understand the farmer himself, and his unique suffering at this moment. Christianity's most tender imagery comes from sheep. Beatrix Potter, famous sheep farmer as well as immortal animal-image maker, observed that 'every lamb that is born, is born to have its throat cut'.

Our Shop

The retention of the village post-office-shop has of late become *the* rural essential. This vanished, and all is lost. Ours has been tottering on the brink of oblivion for some time and since it is the only store for several miles in all directions, we have been holding our breath, myself particularly as it has been a crucial part of the economy of Bottengoms Farm since the days when the order included paraffin oil. Now all is saved. Faithful Margaret has succeeded in passing on the business, and the familiar little place will continue to buzz with our wants. The news deserves a peal of bells. There are villages round here *sans* post-office-shop, *sans* school, *sans* pub, *sans* much going on in the church beyond a monthly Communion, *sans*, really, the right to style themselves 'village' any more. I preach, though not in the pulpit, the duty of us all to buy things in the village shop, to visit it weekly and to enjoy it for what it is when in good hands, a holiday from the supermarket.

The crisis brought to mind for the first time that the very first shop I entered was undoubtedly a classic village store, that of Mr Jacob. It was five minutes' pram journey along the lane and was not one of your ill-stocked little dens profiteering on fire-sticks and lemonade crystals, but an adequate grocer's and hardware supplier for those who couldn't get into the local market town. Silvery cake-tins, sides of bacon, boiled sweets in tall glass jars, cigarettes, ham on the bone, fish from Lowestoft on Fridays. And an urgent notice which said, 'You may telephone from here'. Returning to that Suffolk churchyard recently, I saw Mr and Mrs Jacob's matrimonial tomb and imagined their large, kind faces looming across the counter to see the new baby. A few years later we would visit their shop to buy celluloid windmills, gob-stoppers and to 'give the order'. At Bottengoms the order says simply 'tea', 'cheese', 'razor blades' or whatever, and the right brand always arrives, as though by magic.

There are no shops in scripture, only markets, as one would expect in the East. The five thousand were a long way from a market, hence their plight. They must have been spellbound to have followed their new teacher to where there wasn't a bite to eat and until hunger caused them to yearn for warm bread and delicacies and market-stalls. Listening to Easter reminiscences of Jerusalem, tourist after tourist confessed how the stones of the city overwhelmed them by their sacred association, and how the stoniness of the countryside shocked them. Aridity. It is something which even a green English village has to guard against.

At Tiger Hill

The white cat, who now spends the night in the study, is able to lean from a high bookcase and give my tangled mop a tug as I pass through the curtained rooms to where the Whiskas lives, just in case I might forget. After a ravenous breakfast she takes to the window to catch the dawn jogger at his rite, a watcher and a holy one without a doubt. And then, although I have provided an excellent cat flap, she stands at the door for me to let her out. Carefully, just in case there might be wolves, she looks in all directions, then heads off to goodness knows where, and I listen to Canon Noel Vincent talking about the growing distance between the book-led and the Internet-led man. This is a worthy observation and necessary to believe.

Organists have been in the ascendant. First Meriel, usually as indestructible as the service itself, isn't well enough to play for evensong, so what to do, the congregation seated? So I climb the tower to find Peter and whisper to him through the clamour, then read his lips. 'Yes.' Soon we are rollicking through Charles Wesley's happy 'And can it be', reminding me of a boyhood evening at Mousehole with the Methodist fishermen, pints in hand, singing it across Mounts Bay, and glow-worms lighting me along the cliff path. Organist number two was David Drinkell, whose parents arrived to tell me how he is doing at St John's Cathedral, Newfoundland. Wonderfully, they say, producing an e-mail to convince me. But then he was the organist of St Magnus, Orkney and is the disciple of far-flung church music. His wife Elspeth is Orcadian and he says that once you have lived there the call of the northlands gets into your soul. I see him at Wormingford, ringing bells, playing introits, lifting the worship. Then – there is no end to this organist business once it starts – David Kinsela arrives from Sydney via Paris, where he has been giving recitals. All this in seven days. And now I must ring Christopher with the hymns for Easter Six, that pre-Ascension day, for as Mrs. Alexander wrote, 'And ever on our earthly path, a gleam of glory lies.'

We have also held the annual bluebell party at Tiger Hill. It was warm, almost at times hot, and a nightingale sang half his song, breaking off midway as if rehearsing. About thirty of us, counting the children. I observed yet again how small children grow listless at picnics, lolling against father, longing to go home. 'But we've only just come! Sit up. Go and find the others!' The bluebells carpeted the woodland floor in their millions, a kind of electric blue which misted into a blueness which was beyond botanical description, verging as it did on the paradisal. We devoured egg sandwiches and wine, squishy cakes and tea, and now and then ventured into the bluebell ocean. Or sky. The picnic spot was guarded with banks of alkanet, a plant of absolute blue, though despised – 'You can't get rid of it!' I was sorrowful to hear this. It reminded me of the woman in Thomas Hardy's novel *A Pair of Blue Eyes* who complained how she hated a plant which neglect wouldn't kill. 'Look,' I said, turning to my fellow sandwich-eater, 'alkanet.' 'You can't get rid of it,' she replied. Alkanet is Arabic for henna. Would this abstruse information convert her to its delights? Hardly. There is no more severe sheep-and-goats ruling than that which defines the acceptable and non-acceptable flower. *Pentaglottis sempervirens*, how fair thou art in my beloved's bluebell wood.

Low Sunday

This was the day when those who received baptism at Easter put away their white clothes. The altar is heavy with the scent of lilies which are too full of life to be thrown out. Cold churches make flowers last, sometimes for weeks. They thrive in the sparse congregation, reminding it of crowded processions and rites. The tower flag has been lowered and folded. The graves suffer their first shearing and have their Easter tributes re-arranged. The mower is started up, as are the rooks. We ask God to put away from us the leaven of malice and wickedness, the thing which makes our tempers rise.

Duncan sits in the kitchen and foresees farming trouble ahead. Change anyway. More change than our fathers could ever have imagined. Contrary to what is popularly said of them, farmers have an opportunistic plus imaginative streak which comes into play when they are forced to alter their ways, and some of them find excitement in having to head in another direction. Part of their present trouble stems from their lives and work not being of the remotest interest these days to their neighbours – to the rural community at large. To most country people farmers are landscape-minders, not food producers, and they are praised more for their footpaths, etc. than for their crops. Duncan's dogs sit obediently on the doorstep, eyeing the cats. He sits in the chair in which his father sat when he paid me a visit. Many visits, and William approaching his hundredth birthday. His father, when things failed in Ayreshire, took a brave direction. He left his stoney Scottish fields for loamy Berkshire. Old farmhouse kitchens have always been debating chambers. Polite talk went on in the parlour. The fields used to be easier to respect than to love, so hard was the going. But what to do now? I say that, having had double our usual fall of rain, we could not have got on to the land at all, had it been 1890. We could have starved. As it is, Dave arrives to mop up the mud in the track with hoggin, and we go out to look at the corn. Every few yards it becomes waterlogged, peering from the flood like rice, and a moorhen is actually having a little swim in a furrow.

The Horses on the Hill

'No house should be *on* any hill or on anything', wrote Frank Lloyd Wright in his *An Autobiography*. 'It should be *of* the hill, belonging to it, so hill and house could live together each the happier for the other.' Bottengoms Farm is roughly contemporary with a book called *De Magnete*, written just up the road by William Gilbert in 1600 in which the terms 'electric attraction', 'electric force' and 'magnetic pole' were first to appear in the English language. Thus I see an author in his study and a farmer down by the river toiling away, the one letting in the light, the other keeping out the weather. 'Electric' is Greek for 'amber' which, when rubbed on the warm arm, sends a current through the conducting flesh. However, several centuries would pass before it illuminated my shadowy rooms. The old friends who inhabited them in my youth sadly put away the Aladdin oil lamps with their battered parchment shades and had a single bulb hung from a beam in each room, never loving this improvement. A generator in the garden linked up with Duncan's farm over the hill and the light would quiver when he switched on his grain-drier. 'There', they would complain, 'you never got that with the lamps!' Brought up as a child in subdued interiors, I still do not possess a torch and am an expert on the degrees of darkness, of which there are many.

The unknown house-builder set his farm due east. As everyone knew, death and sickness dwelt in the south. Summer poisoned the ponds, bred disease. Thus I am facing bright dawn all the year round. The new sun rolls along the hill like a hot penny 'fading the furniture' as they used to complain, not to mention the front door, over which a roll of beach canvas would be let down to prevent the paint from bubbling. Brown or green paint it would have been, not my Trafalgar Blue.

The commotion of the Easter services over, I am able to think at last. Morning tea, morning light, morning cat and the roll-penny sun hill – 'enough to blind you'. Or enlighten you. The hill mourns the pony which has been put down. He was thirty-six. The children rode him. Oh, sorrow, sorrow. Oh mortality. Oh hill of horses, some ploughing, some idling, some gathering for a horse chat, with my sunshine on their backs. How do horses grieve? One of the many meanings of 'put down' is to dethrone. The small pony was dethroned from his high hill, as we shall be, bodily speaking. But bees are about, bending the sloe blossom to their will. I sit in an old wooden chair which I have mended at great cost and drink tea, and give praises to God for the lawn-mower, and for being due east, and for still being enthroned of a sort. Seabirds, sniffing turned earth, whizz by. How well we sang the Easter Anthems. How patient I was this year when we came to the dreadful 'That were a *present* far too small' and not remotely murderous. How good I am this daybreak, facing up to things. I make a silent resolution where the hill is concerned. I will climb it and see what is going on all around it. I will give the stricken beasts a consolitary word and they will give me a cautious look through the electric fence. Their paradise is guarded by fiery currents. They will pity me for having to feed so low down, for dwelling in the vortex of the rape ocean. They think I have come up for air, but I have climbed the hill to give them the time of day.

My Workroom

I write each day with my back to the landscape, and especially these last few days because it has been extra distracting. The steep untypical East Anglian hill with its present April growth and its past hint of pre-history is usually diverting enough, but this week it has been given the Marc Chagall touch in the form of some escaped black pheasants and a freed black rabbit. Do not look out. Looking inwards I see what I have seen for decades as I settle to the firm Victorian writing-table, first to have a brief priming the pump little read, this morning it was Augustus Hare's *Biographical Sketches*, and then to write for three hours. The room is ancient beyond telling and was where the artist Christine Kühlenthal slept before it became my study. It is a house without corridors, a run-through where one passed in and out of private happenings without seeing them, such as Christine powdering her face by lamplight. Dead these thirty years, her simple make-up occasionally makes its presence known as I tread the wide floorboards from which not all the art of Dyson can draw the final dust.

Writers and artists are happiest when in their workrooms. Two journeys hang upon the walls of mine. One is taken by a sailing ship and the other by farm carts. The ship is an etching by Francis Unwin and the carts are a pencil drawing by his friend John Nash. Off they go, to the China Seas, to manure the fields. Books crowd around, all the poetry nearest to me. With my glasses on I can make out Betjeman, Blake, Browning, Byron, and through a haze many Lives. The big German press in which Christine kept her shoes now holds my manuscripts. Her forty pairs to my three pairs. Behind me and to hand is the holy bookcase, the three different hymnals for the three different village churches, the *Churchyards Handbook* – very exciting – some of the Prayer Books from Edward VI on, Julian, Rolle, Bunyan, Augustine, Sir Thomas

Browne, all the latest things. And Helen Gardner's *Faber Book of Religious Verse* and, naturally, *The Holy Grail: Its Origins, Secrets and Meaning Revealed* by Malcolm Godwin, for I must keep up.

Time evaporates here. Farmers' children, four in a bed, or shepherds snoring, or a young man packing his bag for Waterloo or Gallipoli, or Biggin Hill, or the tall Slade girl putting on her Dorelia John dress in the dark and scattering her powder into the floorboards, and now myself, tapping and scribbling, careful not to look out for fear of seduction by the lovely day which lies the other side of the pane, or by some wicked author who is bent on catching my eye from his shelf. It is the feast of St Mark, that 'Stay awake!' saint, that swift mover of words, that thrilling activist. Old Paul, having run the race, and who is unutterably weary, longs for Mark's quickness. He tells Timothy, 'Pick up Mark and bring him with you ... when you come, bring the cloak I left with Carpus, and the books, above all my notebooks.' In his 'The Eve of Saint Mark', John Keats seems to be looking from my study:

And, on the western window panes,
The chilly sunset faintly told
Of unmatured vallies cold ...

Except of course it is the chilly sunrise faintly told through an eastern windowpane. So he was a night writer in some small room where his habitation would be brief.

April is the Driest Month

The talk is all of drought. The radio talks of 1751, but Mr Chaplin of 1922, when such huge cracks appeared in the fields that they pulled the shoes off the horses and the crops withered on the land. Though not as ancient as Mr Chaplin, I too can recall extra-dry seasons when the village ponds showed their bottoms and people were seen far from home with slopping pails. No mains and, miles off, a well which never ran dry. My Bottengoms is a farm which never ran dry. It has always been moistly afloat, what with its spring-filled ponds and its being part of the water table of the river. 'It's another world down there!' they say, and so it is. No mains for one thing. No well, for that matter. Only a squelchy bubbling spring under the elders to guarantee no drought. 'He who trusts in the Lord,' says Jeremiah, 'shall not be full of cares in the year of drought.' A few miles east spread the mill shallows in which John Constable's *The Hay Wain* had been drawn so that the water could swell the felloes of its wheels and one can see in the painting both the wet and dry wood. He himself called this painting *Noon,* and it is permeated with the languor and panting of midday, man, dog and horse all listless as the river soaks into the spokes and the flies buzz.

Although only April, the lack of rain has created a certain somnolence such as might be expected in August. The fresh greens of trees and grass should drip and patter but they have a still and arrested quality. Each evening before supper we step outside to wonder at the marvellous comet which is eighty per cent water, a celestial river flowing through our universe and too sublime for our intellect to fathom. Each late afternoon I dig and sow, noting the whiteness of the clapboarding on Duncan's barn, the whiteness of Stoke-by-Nayland tower five miles off, the white horses and dead-nettles, and the distant whiteness of blackthorn which itself is a kind of firmament caught in the hedges. There was a Matins when 'something happened', only who can say what? Worship is like that, sometimes just a rite, now and then an extraordinary thing. I had preached on the pastoral image in Christianity and the shepherds being star watchers and poets, these activities being the offshoots of their calling, and we sang the post-Easter hymn 'The strife is o'er, the battle done', and all the happiness of the faith flooded the building and quietened our hearts. Or so it felt, and what is felt is. I had taken the petitions from George Appleton's *Jerusalem Prayers*: 'Cleanse and sweeten the springs of our being, that freedom, life and love may flow into both our conscious and hidden life.'

A distant figure cleaning a pasture is struggling into an anorak. It cannot be, but it is – the month's first good shower. The world is suddenly wet and shining. Blossom drenches us in scent and with a bit of luck there will be a bit of mud.

General Thanksgiving

Returning from Mary's funeral feast at the Thatcher's Arms, we see Mark drilling. Today's thin April rain and yesterday's warm April sun give a two-tone surface to the seed-bed. The drill doesn't have to miss Shoals, the saucer dip, which would have been a shallow pond when Mary was a girl; for it is now as dry as the rest of the field. No slough of despond in these days.

The machine makes a welcome clatter and drone. Nesting birds are noisy. At the funeral, we said the General Thanksgiving. 'This to be said when any that have been prayed for desire to return praise.'

A fervent rumble of 'We bless thee for our creation, preservation, and all the blessings of this life; but above all for thine inestimable love' had filled the old church, as we all stood, or rather crouched, proxy for Mary in gratitude. She had been a woman of beautiful language, of surprising words, who had very nearly seen her century out. The church had been heady with Easter flowers.

I change and drag the lawnmower out into the light for its first cut. The grass is rich and tall. A friend – a great gardener – deplored today's fashion of cutting it all the year. 'Don't forget it is a plant,' he would say, 'and it needs to grow.' To put down this year's roots. To wave a bit. What was Mark drilling, we wonder – sugar beet? His drill climbs up the hill, passes the badgers' sett, and wanders away into an inestimable distance, pencilling the spring earth.

It is a perfect moment for fecundity. We need not bother God with the prayer for plenty, or with thanks for it either, as Mark's seeds make themselves at home in their shallow rut. The garden has got a head start on them and is crowded with blooms, wild and tamed. Patches of new grass are spared the lawnmower as they are rich with celandine and violets.

The General Thanksgiving was written by Edward Reynolds in 1661, the year he became Bishop of Norwich, and was called thus to differentiate it from the particular thanksgivings for rain, fair weather, peace, etc. The thanksgiving for health is ignorant of medicine, and views sickness as a divine visitation 'for our sins' and takes us into a world of fear and retribution, superstition, and helplessness. But as someone associated with sensible Puritan Norwich, and an excellent writer, I like to think that corn-growing East Anglia entered Bishop Reynolds's mind when he created the General Thanksgiving, which remains adequate for our general awareness of being looked after by our creator.

Bottengoms Farm benefits from the February coppicing. The morning sun floods it. It is warm on my back as I sit at the desk. It – and the rain – hits the old house. One can easily get grown in. Half a dozen years, and the shadows fall. There are heavy spring dews, the kind that John Constable dared to paint with Chinese white, to the hilarity of the Royal Academy. It believed that green fields and trees were all right for the countryside but were not at all right for Art. Brown for framed grass. And when the great artist painted dew – 'Constable's snowstorm' – it didn't know whether to laugh or rage. But there it is, shining on every leaf, my April brilliance.

The Do-nothing Day

This is what the diary says. Let the world or the village – they are much the same thing – get on without you today. This is so novel an instruction that I have to ring up friends to confirm it. They look in their diaries and tell me that I am not wanted anywhere. 'Take a break,' they say. 'Make the most of it.' So I go to church on Radio 4. The service comes from Edinburgh with a certain severity, with fine metrical psalms and an accomplished sermon on the commissioning of Peter in Acts 21. Both language and chants forbid me to put my feet up. Just because for once in a while you have nothing whatever to do there is no excuse for sinking into Sunday squalor. Outside, I hear no bells. Surely the ringers should have something to do? Maybe the valley wind is up to its old tricks with bell music, blowing ours along the river to Bures or into the woods. Such a silent morning. I climb up the crest of Pea Hill, unshaven, going nowhere, and not a pleasant Sabbath sight, and there on either hand lie Garnons and Maltings, ancient farms which early this century were stirred into a little prosperity by those who had fled the stony fields of Ayrshire to try their luck with our ruined agriculture. I was told that they looked in vain for metrical psalms and plain ministers on a Sunday. 'So where did you worship?' 'Why, with the Countess of Huntingdon's Persuasion at Fordham.' Ruth, who came on her bike to help me in the house every Thursday, was one of the last worshippers there. She was married to a Scot, a Lanarkshire man, who could turn his hand to anything. Lady Huntingdon's chapel has turned into a desirable dwelling with a front garden flowering with headstones. When one sad day I took her funeral in the parish church, all the chapels having run out, I kept it simple to make her feel comfortable.

Meanwhile, this holiday. I license myself to dig and read. Nobody comes. The telephone will ring but who can hear it from the kitchen garden? I turn over the dark soil and plant pota-toes, carefully extracting the white roots of bindweed, my spade clinking against fragments of cups and saucers, plates and old nails, and much evidence of carelessness and accident. The hours take their time to wander past, the spring birds sing, as do at this moment the congregation, for it must not get it into its head that it is excused duty as a surrogate prayer-force for the community. 'Say one for me!' it cries to us churchgoers, a label I detest. On exceptional occasions the whole village crowds into the back seats to say one for itself. And sing! But not every week, that wouldn't do.

The holiday ends at Gordon's farmhouse, once Lady Huntingdon's, and he I am grateful to observe had supper in hand. I collapse in his chair. Doing nothing wears one out.

MAY

*T*he last time I saw Ronald Blythe I recall we were talking in his Bottengoms garden just near the hedge. With orange-and-yellow warning colours glowing vividly as they zipped past us, his local hornets were among the many topics of our conversation. These electrifying insects aren't typical pollinators in most gardens. For some, in fact, the sight of them triggers instant arm-waving or worse: spray cans filled with chemical sprays. 'For the children' is the usual hollow justification.

Here, in this uniquely peaceful place at the end of its long drive, it was entirely otherwise. 'Hornets,' I remember Ronnie saying to me, as we paused to enjoy the insects' thickly banded colours, 'they are so gentle.'

His response was not just against the grain, it reflected pin-sharp wildlife observation by Ronnie. Many is the time I've tried to photograph these beautiful, rather shy creatures, and during moments of nose-to-tail intimacy, never once have they shown aggression, but merely the indifference of a native intent on its own daily life.

I am so delighted to discover in Ronnie's account of May that he is as true to his judgement in the privacy of his home as he was on that autumn afternoon. Here you find him carrying hornets from the larder, one after the other, 'by means of the classic postcard and glass method', as he calls it. Because to this patron saint of the southern English countryside, each neighbour is treated according to their merits, and each individual life is uniquely precious.

Mark Cocker

May Day

' All good farmers go to Church' is among our wittier ads –
meaning of course Mr Church our seed-merchant. Jennie
Church sometimes plays for me at Mount Bures on an organ
which John, who works in the great seed sheds, pumped by hand
as a boy. I knew the triumphs and hazards myself. One could be
thinking of something very interesting, and there would be no
music. He and I go to the seed sheds to see a pollen mill, myself
in a state of disbelief. A *pollen* mill? It is a very special mill of
which he is the miller and it grinds pollen imported from China.
There was the silk-route and now there is the pollen-route, and
the latter ends at High Fen, which I can see through a haze of
bare trees from the garden. John shows me a small packet and we
muse on the countless Chinese bees and the thousands of Chinese
flowers which went into it, so to speak. Outside is a much-loved
lane of my childhood, a helter-skelter of a road which rushes one
through a water-splash. This was the way to the bluebell woods
and blackberrying. How strange if the pollen from our Arger Fen
bees sped to the pollen mills of Beijing.

We roam from dusty seed-temple to seed-temple. No windows,
otherwise they would be aviaries, and softly lit panels to catch the
moths. The separator for peas is the same as that used for diamonds.
A revolving drum lined with gramophone needles picks out the
peas with weevil holes. John and I climb ladders, walk planks,
journey through soft canyons of hessian and are in the realm of
embryo, whilst on the other side of the wall every wild and cultivated plant heads for its maturity. I tell John how our local pilgrim
fathers, hundreds of them, took their Suffolk and Essex seed-corn
with them when they sailed to Massachusetts. And, having no
sorting drums with gramophone needles, took lots of our wildflowers too. What a comfort to find some Arger Fen bluebells
blooming in embryonic Boston. John said that one of his duties

was to maintain the true vetch for our county. We emerged via cracked mustard, kibbled mace, salad rape, coriander, and sacks of exquisite linseed, each seed a polished jewel, to cold sunlight.

It was an American, Charles Warner, a friend of Mark Twain, who wrote, 'To own a bit of ground, to scratch it with a hoe, to plant seeds, and watch the renewal of life – this is the commonest delight of the race, the most satisfactory thing a man can do.' One can only hope that what one seeds will 'come true'. Like our vetch. Crop trials are held in the fields surrounding the great sheds in which the seeds find their perfection. Listening my way round the parishes, I find myself in a new country the moment someone draws me into the secrets of his work – John, for instance. His seedsman's philosophy has altered my geography.

Deaths of King David

May winds roar through the poplars and honk in the chimney. They raise the horses' manes, ruffle the cats' fur and bring down spirals of laburnum. Birds are flung about the sky. It is wind of an inspiring sort. It shakes but does not cut through the hollies, so I can read in their protection. I am reading the last words of David, 'the sweet psalmist of Israel'. A king, he said, had to be 'as the light of the morning, a morning without clouds, and as tender as rain-washed grass'. And I see the translator making his way through a sopping English meadow in May-time, his gown trailing through wet buttercups as he makes his way to the desk.

Paul arrives to have a drink before putting his sheep out, forty here, fifty there, only twenty in a little paddock which has not been munched these ten years. The sheep will eat down the roughage and, if they stay long enough, will leave behind flower-rich meadows. Shearing-time draws near, though shorn of its old wealth. Paul is sad. 'Nobody wants our fleeces anymore. They are rubbish.' The word is shocking in an old room which must have heard 'wool' as another name for money. I tell him about the magnificent chapter in Thomas Hardy's *Far From the Madding Crowd* where the shearing in the great barn is turned into a village equivalent to all the other human achievements, however mighty, and of which the Psalmist sang. Hardy's favourite Bible words were from Kings I, 19 in which Elijah, discovered cringing in a cave by God, is ordered out and to climb a mountain. Reaching the summit, Elijah waited for the Almighty to speak to him in Wagnerian language. But when at last it came the divine message was in a still small voice. These are the words written on the memorial window in Stinsford church, the epicentre of Hardy's imagination.

We are off to see what they are up to at Sutton Hoo. Container traffic from Felixstowe makes canyons for the little car to pass through. Heavy land turns to light land, Suffolk's sandlings with its conifers and seabirds. And how changed Sutton Hoo is. What we last saw was a group of rather battered humps above the Deben and some rabbit fences. Nothing more. You needed your wits to see the wild, grand funerals of East Anglia's royalty, the Wuffingas sailing away to heroic bliss in their treasure-laden boats, the cold gales filling the sail, the screaming, mourning gulls, the down-to-earth thud of burial. I shared this mixture of reality and dream in 1967 when I biked over to watch the British Museum re-dig out the now treasure-emptied ship. It was hot and breezy, and the young archaeologists had become a shirtless crew, and the plastic erected to protect their excavation had billowed into a huge cracking sail. One good blow, and they would be well on their voyage back to Sweden.

The original dig in 1939 was made by the local archaeologists plus two gardeners, Mr Jacobs and Mr Spooner. It was only when the amazing gold and garnets began to show themselves that Mr Kendrick from the British Museum was called in. To prove that so great a man had not been brought on a wild goose-chase, he was met at Woodbridge station by the leader of the local historians with one of the fabulous buckles in a tobacco tin and shown it in the waiting room. And now we come to English Heritage in, one must admit, as sensitive a mood as possible, confronted as it was by little more than humps and rabbit tracks. I carried Seamus Heaney's *Beowulf* with its uncanny account of what occurred here, although the unknown author was in another place altogether:

> Silver and jewels buried in the sandy
> ground, back in the earth again
> And forever hidden and useless to men.

The Flower Raiders

Two parishes are in pre-flower festival ferment and the click of secateurs is heard in the soaked gardens. Having beseeched heaven for rain, we now earnestly pray for sun. On the day, that is. Or over all three days of the three festivals which, of course, must not take place on the same weekend. And if all this sounds as complicated as fixing the date of Easter, well then it is. Flower festivals spell quota money (the sum which every parish pays to the diocese each year), also wild ambition and achievement. Drenched foliage is being snipped in my garden by neighbours-turned-Amazons in their pursuit of arrangement. Nothing daunts them. My silvery elaeagnus submits to their blade and the next time I see the shiny ivy it will be climbing up the aisle and, to misquote Robert Lowell, hanging in the oasis of lost connections. Of course, like every other male around, I am awed by what is being done. One minute a glorious jumble of blooms propped up in plastic buckets, the next pattern and high ornament. Pam arrives at the house to borrow my portable gramophone, a 1920s affair last wound up by Jeeves. Her flower festival theme is the September Club – our over-sixties group. I play her some Geraldo,

'Yours till the end of life's story, yours till the birds fail to sing . . .' On Thursday I take a furtive look at what is happening, and there in the late evening, and careful not to get in the way, stand Barry, David and the rest of the handbell ringers at their solemn practice, and all of them half-drunk with scent. Little St Alban looks down from his canopy on the reredos. They had killed him on a summer's day on Holmhurst Hill for sheltering a friend who happened to be Christian. Some say he exchanged clothes with a priest in order to save him. The future Hertfordshire would have been covered by June flowers.

At Tiger Hill I listen to botanists just back from Nepal, classic flower-hunting territory. Also the birthplace of the Buddha. Like Jesus he never wrote a book, like Him he began his ministry at the end of his twenties, like Him he said, 'By faith you shall be free and pass beyond the realm of death.' Like Him he 'went forth from my Home to the Homeless life, and became a searcher for what is good, what cannot be surpassed . . .' His title is *the* Buddha (Enlightened) to differentiate him from the lesser enlightened, just as Jesus is Christ (Anointed). Unlike the Lord, the Buddha had to endure old age, living until he was eighty. No one knows when he died; his life is all *circas*. But we know where he walked, where he sat, where his serenity still marks his resting stages. Like Jesus, what he taught was remembered and written down by others and his words spin along lines of the utmost simplicity, and also along lines which are hard to follow. The Buddhist nirvana is difficult for us. It means 'the stopping of becoming'. The plant hunters brought his flower, the lotus, to Britain from the foothills of tropical Asia. Given that it can be found in the village, should it enhance the lectern?

Old Ladies

Chilly May days. Lilacs cense the mown lawns. Blackbirds do their best. Horses stay still and converse. The church smells nice. I gaze anxiously at the ashes — will they escape the plague? The oaks are in full leaf, and the Stour Valley is wondrous to behold.

John and I go to the Thatchers for fish and chips, and to look at the immense view. We discuss the Etruscans to muzak, and the insatiable human need to be immemorially entombed. *The Churchyard Handbook* is not much help in this direction. It is generally believed that we will be remembered for 40 years after we are 'gone'. But the car park is full of comings and goings above the Iron Age bones. Fresh hedges are green walls, and Mount Bures' church spire thrusts into a low sky.

My existence straddles two dioceses: Chelmsford, and St Edmundsbury & Ipswich; but, since I can't drive, they are as unreachable as Rome for all practical purposes. Friends return from them with tales of wondrous singing and preaching. Long ago, I used to imagine what it must be like to live in a close where every day was a procession.

Down at the farmhouse, life is a procession of a writer and his cat. Today, the pair of us pause at the glorious sight of the vast laburnums in full bloom on the long walk. 'Look thy last on all things lovely,' Walter de la Mare said. Not that I feel the approach of Last Things — rather the reverse, but no one should miss May or its flowering shrubs.

I once carried an armful of lilac into my grandmother's cottage when I was a boy. Pandemonium. 'Take them out — take them out!' Then, 'Poor child, he doesn't know any better.' She was a Suffolk countrywoman born in the 1870s, and a lover of even-song, and her existence was rich with superstitions. When she saw television for the first time, she said: 'There is something I want to know: can they see us?'

Spring brings her near. It was less securely Christian than the winter, particularly May-time. But the bumble bee trapped in the window would give her unwanted messages. Now and then, Canon Hughes would sit with her of an afternoon, on his round of old ladies, his Welsh and her Suffolk voices winding in and out for the destined half an hour.

The Blythe graves tumble about in the village churchyard, their stones hardly legible. When I took an American cousin to see them, he was indignant at the wild scene. I explained that this was the wildflower bit of the churchyard, to do with saving the planet, or something. He was not appeased.

He stared at the humps and bumps of his relations, and I remembered a poem by Thomas Hardy, in which a London churchyard was destroyed to make way for a railway terminus.

Thus peasant dust from centuries past made way for our relations, and theirs would hold a name briefly — forty years, maybe — after which the faces of the dead would vanish from memory. The youthful cousin doubted this, too.

But the immortality of certain wildflower sites — bluebells, for instance — is something I cannot doubt or rationalize. The Tudor woman Joanna Sturdy, who cast two of our bells (she took on the business after her husband died), would have seen our Arger Fen bluebells, I am sure. Anyway, the May-time rite of going to see them is never neglected. There they are, in all their jazzy blueness and multitudinous splendour. Just where they were when we were ten.

The Reverend Francis Kilvert

May-time, when I like to read *Kilvert's Diary* to the congregation. It is not all that keen on readings, much preferring speakings without notes. I see the youthful Francis in his Clyro pulpit, trying not to see the girls. And I think of handsome Mr Elton eyeing Miss Woodhouse and her £30,000.

I look down on the same dear ones year after year, often seeing them in the places that they have vacated. The lasting enchantment of *Kilvert's Diary* is its lasting freshness. And particularly in May. It is dewy, and untouched by maturity. He would die suddenly at thirty-nine, never having quite grown up or grown out of his freshness. It was heaven's special gift to him. In May, he blooms like the plentiful flowers in this parish.

> Wednesday 13 May. This happy afternoon I went lilying in Hartham woods with sweet Georgie Gale . . . Today was the Bath Flower Show. But I would rather have gone lilying with sweet Georgie Gale in Hartham Woods than have gone to a hundred flower shows.

> A lily of a day
> Is fairer far in May

> . . . We were talking of Father Ignatius and his monastery in the Black Mountains.

Kilvert's happiness came and went like our May's downpours and sunshine. Witnessing young men in habits hacking away at the soil as if they lived in the Middle Ages made him miserable. No enlightened Church of England, no girls. And when all around them in the Welsh hills the spring was in full tilt, and when clearly Robert Browning's God was in his heaven, well, it was perverse. Yet he was touched by their holiness. And thankful that he had a gardener. Parish duties aside, he needed all his energy for walking, and all his confessions for writing.

As president of the Kilvert Society, I haven't enough energy to attend its meetings on the Welsh border, but my heart is often there. And, anyway, what would the white cat, let alone our three parishes, do if I followed Kilvert around?

Herefordshire in May is both near to and distant from East Anglia. At the moment, ignorant as much of distance as of time, the white cat slumbers on an old chest. She has pushed aside a pot of dried poppy heads and a dozen novels to make a polished bed.

Outside, soaked horses devour soaking grass. Down below, the Stour is high. The lanes are better paddled than walked. Every now and then, the skies are turned off to allow me to mow a lawn; for life in a village is concessionary. No sooner do I go in at the first spat than green woodpeckers, collared doves, pheasants and chaffinches come out.

And so have all the bluebells at Tiger Hill – maybe a million of them. We all paid court to them, treading slippery paths, intoxicated by their strangely beautiful scent, awed by their psychedelic blueness. Are there words for it? A new Wayfaring tree has been planted in their azure realm. Our ancestors set *Viburnum lantana* on pilgrim routes just for ornament.

Human cruelty often stops Kilvert in his tracks. Mindless cruelties born of ignorance were part of the old rural year. Walking to the Bronith, he finds a dead blackbird in a gin. It is a late Easter, and the creature reminds him of the Cross.

The Launch of the *John Nash*

Biblical rains for Rogation and for the launching of the *John Nash*, a multi-modal river punt. At first the downpour is playful, merely drenching us, but then the heavens tip it out and the willows thrash the surface of the Stour and the millrace makes white water. No organist at Mount Bures so we sing sweetly unaccompanied. The rain is no more than a dark threat at this moment. Rogation, *rogare*, ask. Ask, beg God not to flatten the May crops it would have been long ago. But who now worries about what goes on in the fields these days? Who in the village actually sees a field? Who looks at one? The birds of course, and I at this moment take them in as they threaten to become lakes. Dutifully with bowed heads we ask for nothing for ourselves, only that it may soon rain in Australia, that a lost child will be found, that the tent by the river won't blow across into Suffolk. As John Keble said – is not his College our patron? –

The former and the latter rain,
The summer sun and air,
The green ear, and the golden grain,
All thine, are ours by prayer.

How can my Rogation sermons cease being farming history, I ask myself? Is there a soul present with 'dearth' or 'plenty' on his mind? Yet the childlike persistence of this annual asking is at least a reminder of the Fatherhood of God. We snuff the altar candles, count the offering, seize our umbrellas and make for the *John Nash* where a lovely dark girl, who looks like a figure from an Etruscan frieze come to life, waits to pour a glass of champagne on its hull. In 1929 a young artist and his wife punted here during the August holidays, she lying back on cushions, he in his gaudy pyjamas poling their boat out of the reeds. I had shown the Box Brownie snaps of this idyll to Francis, with today's result, the multi-modal river punt awaiting its maiden voyage. The rain at this moment was no more than a pelting of coin-size drops. Would the young boat-builders finish their casual account of how they created this enchanting craft before we were all swept away by the torrent above?

But then, braving this, the *John Nash* was manned and passengered, unlooped and oared, steered and on its way. Wormingford millpool spread before it, as it had done for the artist perched on his decidedly non-multi-modal vessel.

He had come here via the Western Front, from the roar of Ypres to the crashing of this little stream on the banks of which both Tom Gainsborough and John Constable had set their sights.

And within walking distance of each other. During our long friendship I rarely heard John Nash refer to either of them. It puzzled me during my youth. Only gradually did I witness what he saw, the day-new river, the flashing of it, the immediacy of its climate, the pike stirring, the roach darting under the bridge. I would lie reading as he sketched, each of us lost for entire afternoons in some dateless present. And then his, 'Call it a day, old fellow!' But what day? And then gradually and in the nature of things, the vanishing and just the Stour flowing.

Lunch in the barn to 'Brittonic music by Twm Twm'. I quote. Wild stuff. And even wilder music as the rain proper, no longer restrained to mere drenchings, unleashes its possibilities. Will the cars and the multi-modal punt join forces and sail out to Harwich?

Blythe's Corner

Early Ascension, early Pentecost, and early heatwave. Such a May! Rosy apple-blossom, Van Gogh rape, blue-green wheat, diving swallows, psychedelic bluebells, and a kind of lively warmth that is unlike that of a hot August, and which caresses one in the lanes.

The Queenslanders arrive to check up on our common forebears. All Australia, they say, is mad about a BBC programme, *Who Do You Think You Are?*, and tracing families on the internet is all the rage.

Terry has traced ours back to the eighteenth century – not there, but here in Suffolk. If he could have his life over again (he is at least forty-five) he would be a genealogist. He unloads his findings: a fat packet of Blythes, only a few known to me via family gossip, and most safely at rest in the births, marriages and deaths registers until – in Queensland – Terry stirred their bones.

I am to take him where their dust lies. It is only just up the road – well, twelve miles. The sunshine polishes the hired car from

Heathrow. The ladies on the back seat cry 'Look, look!' as the yellow rape or a thatched house sizzles by.

I show them my birthplace, which was a thatched house until it burnt down just after the last war and is now a pair of neat bungalows. We glide on.

There is a shock — mine of delight, theirs of consternation — when we reach Blythe's corner in the churchyard, the resting spot of all those rustics on Terry's internet Domesday list; for, unlike most of the ancient graveyard, it is a waving meadow of cow parsley, bull daisies, summer grasses and lanky cowslips, the latter 'paigles' to us. 'Wildlife Area' says a card on a stick.

Through the wildlife, I can just see Uncle Fred's cross and Aunt Aggie's biscuit-coloured and shaped stone. Uncle Fred, who ploughed, fought on the Western Front, and fathered five children before he died at twenty-five. Aunt Aggie, who gave us falls from her orchard, rubbing them on her skirt and showing us the bit that was safest to eat, a large old woman in a little house straight out of a picture book.

Her house had a brick floor, an apple room and a fire that never went out. Speckled photos of young soldiers hung on the walls, and polished brass shell-cases stood on the mantelpiece. The house was full of silence. When I last came to her grave, a sycamore tree was growing out of it.

The Queenslanders took many pictures with their digital camera. A gentleman seated by the church door was reading a book, *How Jesus the Jew Became a Christian*. I stood by the Victorian font where I was baptised — the medieval one lay outside, split in two. A pair of marvellously dressed men lay on either side of sanctuary, Sir Robert de Bures in glorious armour and Mr Jennens in periwig and ruffles: one all in brass, the other all in marble.

And there, between them, the folk in the Wildlife Area sang Merbecke and hymns about rest. How they toiled! But less so in May. In May, there was comparatively little to do on a farm, except to feed stock. Suffolk sheep were still in the meadows, ancestors, like us, of a local breed. But the yellow rape, the thatch, the hired car slowed down before them.

At Pentecost

Rape has given way to flax as startling acres. Both crops attract handsome subsidies for the farmers – hence their successive colour dominance of the landscape. Each attracts bees in their pollen-seeking multitudes and they say that what gardens can offer is no match for these illimitable yellow and blue gathering grounds. They are universes of singing colour, eye-stopping, so that often for a whole minute or more one can see nothing else. Thus our dazed approach to the Brett valley in which, as well as the little Suffolk river, there lies the bluest ocean of flowers. The flax! The flax! In his witty essay 'On Being Blue', William Gass describes Kandinsky's colourful conclusions: 'Yellow cannot readily ingest grey. It clamours for white. But blue will swallow black like a bell swallows silence "to echo a grief that is hardly human". Because blue contracts, retreats, it is the colour of transcendence, leading us away in pursuit of the infinite.' The flax fields lead me away to the Cavendish–Glemsford farms of my childhood which in early June were blue to the hedge, as though the summer's sky had descended to the earth.

Charles telephones excitedly. He has something to show me. He has at last found the old well. Its concrete lid has been hacked off to reveal the deep and perfect shaft. We drop stones down as we did long ago, counting the feet and make it forty. We look with wonder at the brickwork, still rounded and faultless as it was when the well-makers had finished it.

Now Pat, who had never been put to a trade
But laboured away with a pick and a spade,

Got a job to perform which was no simple matter,
T'was to dig out a well, till he met with the watter.

James Thomson, 1824

As I leaned over to catch the glitter of this long-darkened water far below, the terrors of Ovens Green returned to haunt me. Ovens Green was a ruined cottage on the way home from grandmother's and we were as children implored, ordered, threatened not to go near it, and all because of its dangerous well. But we did of course, sickeningly thrilled by its clammy depths, counting the feet as our pebbles ricocheted from side to side, and estimating the number of disobedient boys and girls who had fallen in. Similarly, it was criminal to pick the garden flowers which continued to thrive at Ovens Green – 'They don't belong to anybody' – 'No, and they don't belong to you.' John Nash told me that in his youth he gathered cuttings from old and often nameless roses from deserted cottages in Buckinghamshire.

John Constable's *Ascension*

'It is getting on top of you', remark the friends as they wander through the garden. And this just before my one big spring weed. The beds shimmer with sweet cicely, buttercups and campion, and look not unlike Giverny. Trailing behind them, I think of the in- and out-nesss of existence, the weeds and the garden flowers, the wheat and the tares, the sheep and goats. What a lot of it there is in religion – in life. The chosen and the unchosen. The useful and the merely beautiful, the good sons and the bad sons, the listening sister and the bustling sister. My first dandelion clocks, each telling a different time, blow across the land.

On Ascension Day at Dedham Constable's painting of the ascending Christ is lifted up over the north door of the parish church in which he would have run wild, the grammar school

173

being a few yards to the east. He and the other boys climbed the mighty tower to try to glimpse 'Harwich Water'. Soon his relations were all for him painting altarpieces, a respectable trade and not badly paid. So he had painted *Christ Blessing the Elements* for Nayland, his brother Golding modelling for the Lord, and *Christ Receiving the Children* for Brantham down by the estuary. He had a sensuous–mystical love for the human body, calling it a kind of divine landscape, and drew it in the life-class at the Royal Academy School long after his student days. A favourite model was a discharged soldier from Wellington's army, a Suffolk lad whom Constable had helped get a job as porter at Somerset House, and who may have sat (soared) as the ascending Christ. There are many drawings of him. A distant relative of the artist, a Diss brewer named Edward Alston, had offered Constable £200 to paint the picture, some said to win favour with the Archdeacon of Colchester who licensed ale houses. But here it is, the Lord vanishing from our sight as we crane our necks.

Brother Abram who worked Flatford Mill down the road advised John: 'It would be certain *pay*, and now *you could knock it off*!' Trade was in the doldrums and money scarce. So, believed some of the family, was John's talent. Thus, find him what local jobs they could. 'Job' was to become Constable's most detested word. Abram reminded his brother, 'My floodgates at Dedham and Flatford must be repaired, several millwrighting bills coming in so that I cannot keep my money in my pocket'. Later, he never failed to send John his share of the Flatford profits, slender though they sometimes were. Christ, humanly beautiful, rises above their sums.

May for Proverbs

I write with the window wide, with a horseman passing, with a bumblebee furious against the pane. Last night, walking in the dark, I was startled by crashing and yelps in a ditch. Two badger snouts rose out of the crushed cow mumble to see what kind of creature was plodding by. They kept utter silence as I passed, then resumed their quarrel. Bluebells overpowered their musk.

In church we are to read proverbs and wise sayings. These Rogation month lessons are a favourite. The Book of Proverbs ends with two feasts, the Feast of Wisdom and the Feast of Folly. A proverb is a form of words which one cannot get out of one's head, and thus it constantly reinforces certain beliefs and actions. I check the lesson-readers' names. Who shall stand at the eagle-winged lectern and give us a feast of wisdom or folly? Oh, the power of the lesson-readers' master! I say unto Gordon, 'Read this', and he readeth it. He reads, 'There be three things which are too wonderful for me, yes, four which I know not. The way of an eagle in the air; the way of a serpent upon a rock; the way of a ship in the midst of the sea; and the way of a man with a maid.'

Later, nodding in the hot garden, made semi-conscious by a monotonous chiff-chaff, I come to with a start, remembering that 'a little slumber, a little folding of the hands to sleep' is all that Proverbs permits after lunch. I watch the horizon through my lashes. A pretty muntjac deer is trotting along it, taking care not to fall off. I had been reading *The Apocrypha*, my mother's copy, I see, with her name on the flyleaf. 'When I was born, I drew the common air, and fell upon the earth which is of like nature, and the first voice which I uttered was crying, as all others do.'

The Fairweather Visitors

Mid-May. I beg Paul the woodman to cut down an ancient willow which is doing breaking and entry. Now on its last legs, it is having a last sprawl. Should I wake during the small hours, and there is a faint breeze, I listen to it softly scraping against the window like a tree-Heathcliff begging to come in. Vast

willows put on a spur when they are falling to bits. Paul's felling
tools drone a dirge all afternoon.

Richard Mabey arrives and we do our nightingale and bluebell
stint. The day is dull and still. A kingfisher skims below the bridge
which links Essex with Suffolk. The river is aquamarine and
strong-flowing. We talk of Edward Thomas getting his glut of
England before Flanders when 'a bullet stopped his song'. We
have no idea what has stopped the Tiger Hill nightingales' song,
but silent they are. But there are a million compensations, scurrying deer and handsome colonies of yellow archangel, the most we
have ever seen, all along the stream. 'Why were dead nettles, deaf
nettles, dumb nettles, named *archangelus* in the Middle Ages, unless
from the angelic quality (which is hardly archangelic) of not
stinging?' asked Geoffrey Grigson. And there, on the far side of
the stream is the Long Acre. I think of the long acres in my life,
the one which we reached halfway to grandmother's, the one
which stretched behind my house at Debach, and the one I have
explored in London and which would have been mowed (long
acres appeared to have been more stately meadow than field)
where the monks of Westminster would have walked, especially
during Ascension-tide, their habits trailing in the rich spring grass.
The great poet William Langland took his name from his mother's long acre, a flat strip of earth under the Herefordshire Beacon.
The Lord left this world at its most transcendent moment, when
it was at its natural best. Were the Middle Eastern swallows wing-
ing it to Britain?

Fairweather visitors of another kind are on the wing, or more
accurately on the A12. 'We thought we would come and see you.
Don't do anything. We'll bring a picnic. What is the track like?'
The answer to the last is, 'Like a long, twisting and waving corri-
dor of flowers. Like a living wall. Like nothing you will see this
side of paradise. Call it cow parsley in excelsis. Only mind the
bend where the telephone pole totters, not to mention the weary
jogger.' On Saturday nights the village hall bursts with learning as

the Quiz tables are set up, or throbs with line-dancing, as we all make our escape from television. Not a visible stroke of work is done on the land. On the contracted-out farm it is like perpetual sabbath. Stillness mounts on stillness as weedless crops drink greedily from the sprayers. There is a lot of supermarket veg growing in immaculate rows, as is only right.

An in-any-weather visitor is Meredith. He is the quiet country-man who carries his reserve to the limit. Long ago I said something like, 'Meredith – a Welsh name?' and naturally received no answer. When the novelist Ronald Firbank was asked a direct question he would say, 'I wonder'. But Meredith was silent. He reminded me of Uncle Bill whose eyes were forerunners of my own and into which he would stare impersonally, as one might into the eyes of a portrait. We would sit opposite each other by the coal fire and let it do the talking. Meredith does jobs for me now and then. 'How are you, Meredith?' We are together, wordy me, wordless him.

The Passion of St Edmund

The may is browning, the rape rotting. A cuckoo and a night-ingale at Tiger Hill sing at once. And it rains for the first time since March. I hear it coursing through the guttering and see it writhing through the weeds on the track. How can I praise it, with what words? The white cat lets it thunder around her where she muses below a shrub. A daft weatherman on the radio apologises for 'a miserable day'. I allow it to soak me as I put the finishing touches to the tubs of sweet pea seedlings, with their tall cane wigwams. The once pallid earth darkens under the onslaught and buds open before my very eyes. Or almost.

We attend the Historical Society to listen to a lecture on Edmund, our local saint. The car park is packed. Who would have believed that he would have been such a draw? But it turns out that although we have a respectable audience it is the footballers who have swelled the spaces. Distantly, they run and shout by the Stour, leap and hug and holler, just like on the telly. The village hall curtains are drawn and the family tree of the Suffolk royal family glimmers on the screen. What a multitude of branches and tendrils there are as brief life follows brief life. These are the Wuffings from Sweden and Sutton Hoo, and the lecturer says that they can trace themselves back to nourishing wolves like the Roman emperors. Who was it that protected the decapitated head of the martyred King Edmund, but a wolf. This creature lurks under a miserere seat here and there, so watch out.

As we are in Bures we require learned confirmation that Edmund was crowned above our river, as our grandparents maintained, but the lecturer is not so sure. What is certain is that the poor young man, so brave, so holy, had to become the St Sebastian of England. When the lecturer showed his university students a medieval painting of this execution, with all the arrows in a vertical row, they cried, 'One hundred and thirty-six!' Maybe Edmund would have had a go at darts. Such frivolity over, we enter via the doubly illuminated manuscripts into his glory. The loop in the Stour would have been the same, the spring rains, the playful young men, the remorseless cruelties on the News, the churches with their talk of love, the ravens darkening the sky, the boats bobbing in the reeds. The captured King re-enacted the captured Christ. In *The Passion of St Edmund* the Dane says, 'Know you not that I have power to kill you?' and the King retorts in 'a weak but firm reply', 'Know you not that I know how to die?' And so it goes on, the idiot fighting, through the ages.

It is Rogation but, having so much, including this rain, what more dare we ask of God? At Little Horkesley Henry the vicar takes a procession through the rape and onions and corn, and we salve the asking question by asking for others.

The fields are wet, the air sweet and soggy. The Cross flashes like Edmund's spurs as he hid under Hoxne bridge, giving him away. It sways past lilacs and laburnums and eventually under the churchyard limes. The gravestones sparkle like jewels. Late rains have laid the human dust, put it to rest. St Edmund's was shut up in a gold box for centuries. Now and then they opened it, to music, and peered inside to see that it hadn't blown away. It was a cure-all for body and soul. I hope that there were days by the river when he could forget all this. Just lie in the wet grass without his crown and listen to Suffolk birds.

Matings – Boys, Girls and Birds

A John Constable morning. Cumulus clouds heap up on each other, then break to allow the blue to appear in a vast restlessness. He insisted that the sky was the keynote to the land, colourfully speaking.

I see him striding over the hill towards his uncle's farm in his white clothes, turning the women's eyes. Like the skies, his personality was one that chopped and changed, thrilled and meditated, to the rolling displays of the weather.

When young in the Stour Valley, he would carry a little palm-fitting sketchbook in which he would pencil the earth and the heavens. When no longer young, he would paint the racing clouds over Hampstead Heath on oiled paper, having to invent wild brushstrokes to keep up with them. Below Hampstead, London miasma denied the existence of the aerial mountains and cerulean apertures to the country of the hymn book.

Preparing something for Sunday, I let Matthias, Dunstan, Alcuin and Helena drift across my retina. Who will be the lucky one to get a mention? Dear great saints, bright unclouded creatures, shine on.

Nippy final frosts. As I drive with John from the Norfolk coast, the Saturday afternoon roads are all scrubbed up by heavy rain. We journey across country, knowledgeably below drenched trees, hardly meeting another car. Where is everybody? At the football.

Whitebait and Guinness in the Lavenham pub. Young lovers. Trumpets and other instruments dangling from the beams to remind us that Lavenham's Salvationists still play on the Market Square. And two Salvationists from Northumbria at our matins the following morning, singing well. Plus a party to hear the banns. New faces. How could we know of an impediment to their marriage or anything about them? Oh, the excitement of a *Jane Eyre* figure bursting in!

A century ago, the Church of England became disturbed by the number of village lovers marrying far from their home parish, fed up with nosiness, and Dean Hole of Rochester applauded the bicycle as a liberator of the rural male from local restrictions.

Banns is a medieval word for proclamation. It was sometimes used for the prologue of a play. The wedding could raise the curtain on a comedy or a tragedy, although usually something quite ordinary, as Philip Larkin saw on the station platform one Whitsun long ago.

My wood is restless with mating birds. Their voices are raised over belated bluebells, and indignantly, should I garden late in the evening. I have cast a bit of wire netting over the potato mounds, just in case the badgers heave into them, hungry for worms.

May is an enticing time, and I can hardly bear to be inside. But it is cold. No sitting about. Work, work, and no shedding a clout – i.e. a jersey. David arrives hotfoot from a meeting of the Cambridge Prayer Book Society and a lecture by Angela Tilby at St John's College. She is one of those people who make things believable. It is something they do without knowing it – this beautiful passing on of what they understand.

He has brought rhubarb from his London allotment, which you might think was coals to Newcastle. But mine needs a week or two more. It, too, is badger guarded. The badgers huff and puff in their setts at twilight.

The Fate of the Imagination

It is a late May afternoon and I am engaged in that form of meditation known as weeding. How the May birds sing! I am on my knees hoicking out the undesirables with a nice new silver fork, untwirling the everlasting sweet pea fronds from a nettle and sadly, for they always make me think of that Dürer drawing, piling up the dandelions. I cut fresh edges and smell pear blossom. A lean tomcat calls to pay court to Kitty, who eyes him sanguinely, safe in the knowledge that there is nothing doing. The sun is warm, the grass wet, the jeans muddy. It is great to be alive. 'Oh, the work, the work!' laments a caller. I think of Gilbert White peering from the rectory window at 'my weeding women' and most likely not believing that they could be at their prayers.

My meditations are random and ranging. For instance, I contemplate St James, the man from Bethsaida, which means the House of Fish (just as Bethlehem means the House of Bread) swimming away to Compostela in his silver box, and what a welcome he got! In her pilgrimage book *On Glory Roads*, Eleanor Munro says that 'It is the fate of the imagination sometimes to be trapped in the very structures it invents . . . the Lord, as a construct of thought, understood this natural condition. He who had been a wayfarer, coming out of the dark like a wind, standing over Sinai like a flame, travelling north in the Ark, in scriptural fact approached his installation in a Temple with a troubled mind. "Down to this day I have never dwelt in a house . . . I made my journey in a tent and a tabernacle . . . Did I ever ask any of the judges why they had not built me a house of cedar?" (Samuel 2, 7.5–9).'

All I can think of as I dig away is that nobody requires a house in Maytime. A mighty stand of cow-parsley three feet tall below the kitchen window, almost in flower, dares me to touch it and so like some petty deity I let it live. I will watch it whiten and sway

as I wash up, and become a lovely fragment of that glorious trans-
formation of the English roads, their ravishing take-over by
Anthriscus sylvestris in a week or two's time. I always cut tall stems
of it to place in big old pots by the brick bread oven so that I can
enjoy it inside and out, and where it kindly makes its own starry,
branchy perfect shape. This would have been anathema to the
men who built the oven for whom it was 'Devil's meat'. They
should have got out more and into that divine universe of flowers.

Late that evening I watch Muriel Spark seeking to define her
art in slowly accurate sentences, the Scottish rawness attractively
present. So broke was she in London that a stationer had to give
her the five quarto sheets on which to write her debut story 'The
Seraph and the Zambezi'. She has always written with a ballpoint
pen, three to each novel. I wrote my first books with a relief nib,
dipping and sliding it along the ruled foolscap, but these days it is
three to a card ballpoints. Recently in a rush I came away from
Smith's with red ballpoints and so there are entire chapters in
rubric. Hearing the recently dead speak is strangely moving.
Muriel Spark, maybe, has a slight cold. Her eyes are weary and
watery, and now and then she presses a tiny scrunched hanky to
her nose. She is in Tuscany and her study window frames vignettes
of the hilly landscape like those seen in the old masters' portraits
of the Virgin. At one point she describes bombed London, the
wallpapered rooms hanging in the air, the plants taking over, the
intimate interiors open to every gaze.

The Hornets' Nest

Bank Holiday rains could not drown our fixtures. Bells crashed
through them, cricketers played through them, visitors to the
Flower Festival splashed through them, and the diocese will be
solvent. Lakes appeared in the lanes. Ditches churned, boughs
tumbled from trees in sheer wateriness. The flag on the tower

wrung itself out time and time again. Tom brought his cows in. They who had only the other day run from their sheds in unutterable happiness now trotted to take thankful shelter from the wet outside world. But the sugar beet swelled. My farm track rippled like a river and the ancient horse-ponds shone like slate.

Whether the bees and hornets in the larder were taking shelter it was hard to say, but a furious murmur met me when I entered it in search of marmalade. It is a long brick-floored room in which the tall fridge-freezer is in constant battle with the iciness of the larder itself. It was as I thought, a poor fat bee was glassily imprisoned on the washed jam jars shelf, and I set it free by means of the classic postcard and glass method. When I returned the buzzing was still there, only now there was a great choir of it coming from all directions, a kind of orchestrated sibilance in which rage was being expressed symphonically. Thus, six times did I set both bees and hornets free, carrying them one by one into the garden, displaying immense courage. Meanwhile Henry our vicar was innocently laying a hand on an unseen hornet in the church, with dreadful result. Mercifully all he suffered was agony. Hornets provide a kind of first strike in the Pentateuch when God sends them before the Israeli forces to scare the enemy. They dwell peacefully in my vine, sunning themselves in the garden-lamp. No one knows a time when they were not there. But how could they not fly from a lidless jam jar? Why did they come so near to death in their glass gaol when the door was wide open?

During rain pauses I begin the May weeding, sloshing about. The washed world smelled delicious. I leave red campion and cow-parsley among the garden flowers in order to attain my 'Giverny' effect. That shimmer of legitimate and outsider bloom which ravishes the late spring gaze. The freshly seen earth is rich and dark and, like me, soaked to the skin. For on days like these one does not become dry just because the rain has stopped. Richard Mabey has sent me some of his morning glories through the post, and I plant them in scrubbed orange pots, stick them with bamboo, and line them up with my sweet peas. The white cat, who never minds a shower or two, paddles around.

All this done, having read a fine essay by Colm Tóibín entitled 'In Search of the Writers of Aran', I find J. M. Synge's plays in the bookcase, where they have lain unopened by me. With the rain returned, I read the amazing *Riders to the Sea* and *The Playboy of the Western World*, forgetting time. Synge said, 'In a good play every speech should be as fully flavoured as a nut or an apple' – though many of his are as bitter as almonds. He was writing in Aran a hundred years ago, yet as modernly as any writer at this moment. The early deaths of his Aran men chime sadly with those in Iraq, 'whose families have been informed'. Well, that is something. The politicians who caused this disaster fly about the world.

A May Night in the Belchamps

The birds cannot sleep and rattle around in the bay tree. It is light enough to watch flowers. My lilacs and honeysuckles tremble from the touch of some unseen creature. It has been quite a day, a return from old ground. It is where I biked as a boy, mother's school-prize Shakespeare in the saddlebag. The same scented May wind was blowing across the Belchamps, a secret and distinctive country of three linking villages, Belchamp Walter, Belchamp Otten and Belchamp St Paul's. I reminisce to Tony, who is driving. He is contending with a handsome jack hare which dashes ahead in the dead middle of the road. First an Olympic sprint of two hundred yards, then a standstill in perfect profile which says, 'Admire me'. And this for miles. Tony brakes, goes on, brakes. Hares being laden with our tomfooleries, such as being able to dance in time to our music, change sex when they feel like it, sleep with one eye open, love being coursed, and heaven knows what else, will now be said to like being chased by a car. 'Oh, why doesn't he jump into a field!' Tony wails. But the hare knows what he is doing, for when he comes to the signpost to Borley he takes the left fork, leaping along a cow-parsley avenue.

We are taking part in a dedication. Belchamp St Paul's is crowded and Bishop Edward preaches from a dizzy pulpit, as though heartening us from an upper storey. Arriving at the last minute, we have the last seats – those where the hymn books live – and we have to share a service sheet. All three Belchamps packed into one church, and singing, 'I was glad when they said unto me, we will go into the house of the Lord.' The chancel where I sat reading local history as a child is airy early Tudor with a clear glass east window through which the spring limes quaver in nervous re-patternings. Among their roots lies the dust of Arthur Golding, whose translation of Ovid Shakespeare borrowed for *The Tempest*, whole lines of it. Ted Hughes translated *The Metamorphoses* at the end of his life. Arthur Golding at the beginning of his. He called it 'Englishing'. He Englished Calvin and over forty Puritan authors, lived to be seventy and died in the bulky hall a few steps from the churchyard.

Our friend Richard Bawden has Englished St Edmund, St Andrew and Our Lady and the Child, and turned them into engraved glass Saxons for the new ringing-chamber screen, beautiful, wide-eyed holy ones with cross-gartered legs, wheeling haloes and mouths barely holding back their smiles. Life-size and confident, they are telling the Belchamps, 'We are still here!' The tall bishop throws dedicatory water at them as we sing, 'Ye watchers and ye Holy Ones'. Arthur Golding would not have approved. The stern old Puritan never lived down his youthful amorous Ovid, the bestseller which Shakespeare found so handy. Poets and artists, they must be watched.

Drifting

Trinity, and the garden flashing with secateurs and, across the fields, the church a-sway with ladders and ambitions, for the flower festival is upon us once more. Shirley has come for willow rods, which should have been simple enough, but we discover that these have become unreachable due to what the village calls 'your triffids', i.e. the forest of polygonum which defends willow from flower arrangers. The vicar and I attempt to reach the willow, only to come face to face in the polygonum jungle like Stanley and Livingstone. When we do find access, Shirley promptly cuts all the leaves off it and goes off with a bundle of sticks. 'You will see!' More flower arrangers arrive and I stand guard over my rarities, brave as anything before the secateurs. 'Just six of those,' they plead. 'Think of the Quota.' I assure them that I think of nothing else. I tell them that in the eighteenth century the tower of a Suffolk church was roped with garlands. They snip away. Him and his history.

Ian and I drive off to the sea and walk for miles along the shingle. Longshore fishermen, out of reach of all domesticity, loll beneath heroic umbrellas in perfect bliss. The waves thunder and clink a yard from their boots and fish swim where they know they cannot be caught. The longshoremen are grateful for this as they would find it very exhausting to have to reel them in. Idleness, who has sung thy praises? Few. It is hard to find a good word said for it. Cicero believed that we are never less idle than when we are wholly idle, nor less alone than when wholly alone, and I can vouch for the truth of this. If the longshoremen ever feel the need for a patron, they might try Cicero. The sky is in tumult, alps and castles and palaces pile across it, incessantly changing its glories. Now it looks like rain, now it looks as if there is no point in doing anything other than sprawling in the lee of a dune and dreaming. A little boy runs to a patch of sand and writes across it, pensively, like Jesus before his questioners, 'as though he heard them not'. Ian and I wander in the churchyard. It is full of bull daisies and lovely May grasses. The cloud architecture is seen through broken stone window frames and above roofless walls. Flax being the agricultural flavour of the month in Suffolk, we are soon in deep blue, acres and acres of it. We see a marsh harrier making low reconnaissances above it and with barely a flap of wing, though with no luck. Do birds see blue? I suddenly remember D. H. Lawrence and his wife having breakfast, with red-mauve petals on the tablecloth and his suddenly thinking, 'How lovely is the self this day discloses.' Together they watched the roses picked yesterday waiting to fall.

Letter-cutting and Barley-cutting

Great craftsmen share the attitude of saints, poets and philosophers who, early in life, set aside what most of us believe to be desirable and essential. They are often praised for this, although it puzzles them, they having no use for a thousand things which the world decides are a must. Whether one's craft is prayer or literature or thinking or letter-cutting, there isn't the space for much else. Craft of any kind is a spacious business. Donald the marvellous letter-cutter and carver generally has arrived on his flimsy drop-handled bike to talk about a headstone for our friend Cedric Morris. Just 'Sir Cedric Morris, Artist, Plantsman' we decided. Plus his dates, of course. And Welsh slate. Donald's craftsmanship in this particular memorial line stems from seventeenth- and eighteenth-century inscriptions cut all over our church floors. 'I can't keep my eye off them.' Neither could Eric Gill, whose legacy is Donald and – he reckons – about sixty letter-cutters like him. They once held a conference in London, all the letter-cutters of Britain, and Donald said, 'Hands up if you are left-handed.' Three left hands. Donald has a theory that the sculptor who first cut the Roman alphabet and Roman figures was left-handed. He is a defender of the left hand.

We talk of being lads among the artists of these parts and eat a not over-crafted supper.

Near midnight I leave Donald at the top of the lane and return to the house in what looks like an agricultural version of Jurassic Park. Keith and Bernard are thumping across the hill field baling barley straw. What is keeping them up so late? Is it some atavistic instinct or custom bred into them by their grandfathers that harvesting must mean sleeplessness? By the way in which the balers rock across the stubble, beaming their headlights at outraged pheasants and those creatures who believe the night to be their own, their drivers are like children who celebrate being allowed to stay up late. It is a light night, the far western sky still with its combings of sunset, and the summer air, discounting the barley dust, is delicious. Trees and hedges are one-dimensional cut-outs and have become different and unfamiliar. At midnight the late harvesters switch off and the huge machinery itself settles for a nap. 'I should think so!' say the birds.

On Sunday I talk about Nicodemus in all three churches and we sing Faber's 'Pilgrims of the Night'. Nicodemus is the Gospels' pilgrim of the night, a Sanhedrin councillor who, although enthralled by Jesus, found discretion the better part of valour. Later he would throw discretion to the winds and bring a mass of embalming spices for the poor mangled body of the young man who had privately assured him in the dark that 'God so loved the world, that he gave his only begotten Son'.

My Birthplace, Acton, Suffolk

'Here is the church' – a fat gooseberry; 'here is the steeple' – the tuft; and 'here come all the country people' – the juicy pips. It was always St Peter's, Sudbury, Suffolk, when I said this.

Yesterday, I walked in the small town, remembering this and that. Here is the north door, thinned to a biscuit by the centuries.

Here, on its left side, is the stoup – dry now, but medieval fingers once touched holy water in it. Here are a few church-hugging tombs, even if most of the Sudbury congregations are being run over regularly by buses.

It is a cold May morning, and the familiar borough could well have been Proust's Combray, somewhere where memory is put to work.

Quite a few people are sitting about – sitting, at ten in the morning! It would never have happened in my day. They cannot all have had a funny turn. Nice railings, to which Canon Hughes never chained his black bike. Gorgeous reredos, under a dust sheet. Wonderful bells, which Father listened to, standing out in the garden on practice night.

A writer's task is to make ordinariness extraordinary. This is not something that a writer can help doing. 'That boy's head!' they said. Whatever next!

I was looking for half a dozen butter-knives with bone handles. 'Bone handles, you say, sir? Try the charity shops.' Lots of these. Fat ladies, scrawny old chaps. The jewellers' where Father bought Mother's rings.

Andrew has loaned me a book that I have been searching for all my life, *The Claimants to the Estates of William Jennens late of Acton, near Long Melford, Suffolk*. Andrew and I were born in this village. Mr Jennens had been its squire, a bachelor who drowned in money. Birmingham iron channelled rivers of it to his Suffolk address. He filled vases with it, put it under the bed and in the cellars, gave it to anyone who would be good enough to take it, but still it flooded in his direction. A will was no use; it washed away wills. He went to church on Sundays, and sat below his marble father, and I hope some of his money came the Revd Mr Bickersteth's way. When, at last, Mr Jennens died, the litigants swarmed in. But the lawyers were too smart for them, and, during the next 40 years, took it all. The Jennens case entertained society and enthralled Charles Dickens, who put it to use in *Bleak House*.

I was less interested in this scandal, however, than in the author's description of Acton Church, where both Andrew and I were baptised, and where my father's name is on the Great War memorial. Not that anything happened to him: just there and back to the Dardanelles, the usual thing. Before this mishap, he sang in the choir.

The 1877 book never mentions Perp. and Dec. or the mighty de Bures brass – the finest, some say, in England. But it adores the varnished seating and the floor space, and that 'in the north-west corner of the churchyard a place of accommodation had been erected for those who during divine service may have to satisfy the calls of nature'.

The north-west corner is where my ancestors lie. It is now the wild plot. Our crosses will be floating in cow-parsley, one of the loveliest sights in England. But poor old Mr Jennens, drowning in Birmingham money and being dubbed a miser, which he never was. Just a lonely man who could not swim in it. Thirty or so years after his burial, they pulled his mansion down, brick by brick, and sold each one.

Early Haymaking

It comforts me somewhat that it is the youthful commuters who now talk about haymaking and cows, putting hedges back and seeing sugar beet leaves take a shine after a good rain, and not the old farmers. When the commuters arrived we all thought that they would put the acres which went with their fine houses out to foster-care. But no. A number of them dash home from the City to feed stock before settling to hear how wicked their children have been in their absence and what is for dinner. Occasionally, if one is lucky, it is just possible that an actual farmworker might be spied during the hours when they are away totting-up immense figures in Bishopsgate, but generally the farm waits patiently for its owner to return, put on his jeans and comfort his cattle. Tom said that he had spent the spring holiday cutting his hay and silage —some of it in the riverside pasture which is still called 'Constable's' on account of it being owned by the artist's uncle before the Napoleonic wars. This haymaking ended perfectly in heavy rain which penetrated the shorn ground, polished the blue-ish ears of corn and pounded the willows. Rushing through it, I glimpsed a drenched white cat quietly observing sporadic lightning from a drowning wall.

Later, in the post-storm stillness, I walked to Hugh's to hear the result of the Flower Festival. We do not put on this yearly show for nothing. No Flower Festival takings, no quota. To think that the diocese's economy rests on such arrangements. This time the theme – there has to be a theme – was islands. So during *Songs of Praise*, standing between the school's lusty Treasure Island and Pip's cool Iceland, I read 'No man is an island, entire of itself, everyman is a piece of the continent, a part of the main.' But when I came to 'if a clod be washed away by the sea, Europe is the less', President Chirac was the man who came into my head. St John the Divine on the Isle of Patmos dislodged him. We sang hymns which were clearly entire of themselves, their once immense messages half-lost in favourite tunes. Then we loaded up the takings, switched off the lights, locked in the scent and left all this floral ingenuity to get on as best it could with the grey severity of the pillars and the blackening painted windows. Waiting for the key to turn in the lock, I heard the clock go clunk. A kind of that's that. The table-tombs of the Georgian farmers and millers, so useful for the flower arrangers' sandwiches and wine, were resuming their well-lettered dignity, and the churchyard trees were all standing to attention and getting ready for their secret night-life.

As May crosses into June we are to read the Book of Ecclesiastes, that matchless confession of world-weariness, although how anyone can be world-weary when the days are at their best, heaven only knows. The Preacher wraps his gloom in such marvellous language that he somewhat undermines his conclusions. When he complains that there is no new thing under the sun, I – at this pre-summer moment – can only ask, 'Does there have to be?' Reading on, disillusioned or not, who can resist this enchanting writer? He is the man who had everything but who is now an old man for whom everything has turned to dross. He venerates sadness and makes it beautiful. Yet at the very end, just before the silver cord is loosed, he finds the light sweet and the sun 'pleasant'. As shall we all.

JUNE

*O*ther writers might notice young trees breaking through their rabbit-proof guards, but it's hard to imagine anyone but Ronald Blythe comparing the spectacle to Peter bursting his chains in prison. His June is St Barnabas and Trinity Sunday, the flower festival and the hymn-fest, St John at midsummer of course, and the feast of St Austol. Like his favourite poet, John Clare, Blythe is attentive and unsentimental in his observations, reaching his deepest raptures when faced with a meadow of fescue and rye. Clearing a ditch, he feels ashamed of his tidiness. 'Nature adores a muddle.' Admiring the 'gaudy' fields of borage, he knows it must be combined twice and also where it will be sold. A very Clare-like knowledge, this, obtained by the steady, perpetual listening that gave Akenfield its power.

His summer calendar contains its solemn stations, funerals for farmers' wives and mugs of tea drunk in mourning when a dying willow must be chopped down. Death is adjacent, not far away, and the past is always swimming into the present. Watching a solitary neighbour making hay, he recalls the crowded pre-war fields, the sweaty girls with their pitchforks, their shoulders bare and their bonnets on. All gone now, of course, and yet lingering still, like the Palestine and Rome of the early Christian martyrs. A gossipy, parochial fondness attends even the most exalted figures of the scriptures. Elijah and John are cousins, Blythe observes more than once, while Barnabas and Paul had a mysterious quarrel and no longer speak, like two parishioners in doggedly separate pews. Heaven certainly contains the sound of poplars clapping in a summer breeze, but this somehow perpetual past is not rose-lit. He still remembers chalked signs outside pubs: 'No peapickers, no gypsies'; the unmarried women who had to make do; further back, the Quaker boy martyr tormented to death by guards in Colchester prison.

Then *bends back into* now. *Ripe corn, ripe gooseberries, the click-clack of a train, the trees like cardboard cut-outs. In his ancient house full of spiders, Blythe reads Barbara Pym and Jean Rhys and St John of the Cross, feeds the white cat. He accounts for the hours, missing little. 'At the moment, the day is holding back its potential and seems uncommitted, but in a little while the sun will spin up in the east like a gold coin. Yesterday, the washing dried in an hour.'*

Olivia Laing

The Poet and the Woodman

What a day it was, yesterday that is. A shore wind took the burning edge off the June sun, the poplars hissed, the gliders floated angelically overhead, and I sowed two rows of Scarlet Emperor beans, one row of spinach beet and lots of cucumbers. I also sent the organists the Trinity hymns and wrote an introduction to John Clare's holy sonnets. And cooked a chicken. I thought of poor young Richard Heber in the fierce Bombay heat and his early in the morning song.

Clare's holy song was not the official one. He sang out of doors and rarely in church. Sundays found him as far away as he could get from his parish in order to find what he called 'the eternity of Nature'. He was the outside worshipper whose creed was, 'Nature, thou truth from Heaven'. His fellow worshippers in this outside aisle were the kind of people who never got a Sunday off, shepherds and herdboys. Thinking of that distant scene my great-grandfather Charles, a Suffolk shepherd born in 1830, comes to mind. Shepherds did at least work but John Clare, skiving off every Sunday goodness knew where, did not do a stroke, hiding away in the ling with his hard hat as a desk. Once he wrote a tender hymn about 'An outcast thrown in sorrow's way'. This tragic Christ contrasts with his magnificent God the Creator. As for the Comforter, there would be long years in the poet's existence when he was absent.

Paul the woodman returned to see what he could do about the tumbling willow, a vast tree whose six branches were opening out like an enormous daisy, two of them towards the ancient bread oven. He stood there, pondering, then said that he would come back. No sooner had he disappeared than more branches fell, cracking a tile or two and swishing helplessly against the studio window like the biggest wiper in the world. Paul was interested in this self-destruction but reckoned that one of the still-standing branches would be less beneficent and spoke of real damage. And so in five hours, his chainsaw moaning, the willow was slain. I gave him the ton or so of its wood and by teatime all that remained of a century-old tree was its hollow heart and sawdust. We mourned it in mugs of tea. 'How many cricket bats did I reckon they would get out of one of them bat willows down by the river? Guess.' Me – 'Twenty …?' Paul, satisfyingly, 'Sixty to a hundred!' There were hundreds of bat-willows growing in the marshy grass by the Stour. They were a crop felled every fifteen or so years, and beautiful beyond words, the hazy joy of the Impressionists. But all those cricket bats in the growing, all those springing boundaries in the making! The plantations have been there as long as I can remember. From minute saplings just pushed into the earth – only they must touch the water line – to Lord's in the time it takes a player to grow up. Well, as Paul said, 'It makes you think.' Woodmen make you think, being philosophical by trade.

We all go to Esme's ninetieth birthday party. She says, 'Don't think about the weather, I am having a marquee', and I imagine one of those elephant tents groaning from its ropes. But it is a canvas pavilion from the Field of the Cloth of Gold, open-sided and crowded. Half the congregation and half the part of Esme's life we knew nothing about. What would John Clare have made of this sabbath happiness and its scent of crushed lawn, herbacious flowers and wine? He lived a long time in his madhouse, writing, writing sane words to 'my creator God'.

Soaked to the Skin

The wily rain has caught us out, myself and Mr Death. We stand opposite each other with the lashed orchard between us, he and his sopping dog under the oaks, myself under the great Harden pear tree whose ivy-laden boughs, I thought, would keep me dry. All day it has rained but only in dribs and drabs. Having lured us out, it fell upon us. Soon the water-sheet is so dense that Mr Death becomes a vague shadow although only a hundred yards away. The deep ditch behind him will be yellow and swirling like old Father Tiber. I am only momentarily safe because the ivy suddenly tips from the pressure of the downfall and I couldn't be wetter than if I had jumped into the pond. Summer rain, which dismisses the roses. I wave to Mr Death in a kind of acceptance of our common predicament and I imagine a response from his side of the flood. All the birds raise their voices, not to be drowned out by a mere tempest, and Mr Death's labrador sploshes joyously towards me and we embrace. The mower and all the gardening tools glitter like diamonds in the beaten grass. After ten minutes we know it must stop, and probably as abruptly as it began, for no sky can empty itself at such a rate for long. But it doesn't stop. In fact, it trebles its downpour and then continues for ages. There being no such thing as shelter now, I wander through it as a weather experience, only to find my way blocked by sodden plants. There is no passing the St John's wort. Usually a green and fiery wall between the yuccas and the bay tree, it has swayed forward in a drenching arc, blocking the main path. St John's wort, *Hypericum perforatum*, is my favourite Christianised plant. Its blooms point to the Forerunner of Christ, that 'burning and shining light'. Every flower festival, though failingly, I try to persuade the Mount Bures arrangers to place hypericum around the little statue of the Baptist on the reredos but the old sacred language of flowers is now a lost language, and has given way to a language called Arrangement, whose grammar I have failed to master. However, I must admit that the worshippers are always kindly tolerant of my daft notions.

We have been saying farewell to Sawyers. The old friends who brought up their family in this remote and lovely farmhouse are moving to Hadleigh and a walled garden and shops round the corner. Juliet, who was born at Sawyers in 1920, sits beside me eating strawberries and we talk of her Uncle Martin (Shaw) who composed his tune 'Little Cornard' there long ago. The new Sawyers family lie on the lawn a few feet away, youthful, pretty people with a fat baby and all kinds of plans. Juliet doesn't know which room she was born in. Sawyers has honeycombed its accommodation for five centuries and upstairs it is an intimate warren of bedchambers, steps and passages. The goodbye picnic just manages to accommodate itself between light showers. We look up and tell ourselves, 'It won't be much.'

A Farmer's Wife

The passing of the farmer's wife – for as long as any of us can remember, a distinctive voice in the land. The rain holds off. The church fills with farmers' wives from all over; farmers, too, of course. I walk slowly before Geraldine under the churchyard limes, in the telling silence that precedes the Sentences, and think of them, these robust countrywomen who used to do 'the writing' and who still are an indispensable force in the management of a village.

Geraldine's life had been plain for all to see; for her farm adjoined the church, and her cows and other animals took part in Rogation. Her pretty grandchildren sing 'Yea, though I walk in death's dark vale, Yet will I feel none ill' in the front pew. And I talk about farmers' wives in general, a host of them making their no-nonsense motherly way through my head.

Barry tolls the bell, Tony reads what farmer John wants us to remember about his Geraldine, and then we sing, 'O, that old rugged cross, so despised by the world, Has a wondrous attraction for me', the neglected hymn surging through the church and out to the stockyard. And then everybody gets into big cars and drives them down into the valley for the funeral feast at the inn where Constable's barges had a rest.

Farmers' wives have not been left out of agricultural history, but their role has been somewhat taken for granted – though not by Thomas Hardy and George Eliot. Emma Woodhouse, of course, doubted whether it would be possible for her to meet one.

I like Dorothy Hartley's account of them in her wonderful book *Lost Country Life* (Pantheon, 1979). I told the congregation about it in my funeral address. It was women as well as men who made the English landscape, and who decidedly made the English country garden.

The farm labour-force has gone, but during its generations of existence it was the farmer's wife who nurtured it, patched up its hurts, fed it, and bossed it about. Often of an evening in my ancient farmhouse, I think I hear the dairying, the breadmaking, the calling, the singing, the never-ending toil. I hear the same bells and the same water-music from the stream. In the church-yard, the farmers have done their wives proud, and their names are spread out on handsome tombs.

Country deaths stir up a residual faith. It is not to be analysed, but accepted. We have to die in order to put on our immortality, I tell the understanding crowd.

The Psalmist was sad when he looked across the fields and realised that he was no more than a sojourner there, 'as all our fathers were'. He is rueful because his beauty is 'consumed away, like as it were a moth fretting a garment'.

And yet – I preach to this mourning, knowing assembly – farming people are lucky; for whether they followed the plough or now steer the combine, the marks they leave behind possess a certain indelible quality like no other on a local earth. This farm-er's wife and her husband John were unaware how intensely 'local' their lives were – how unlike even the lives of their farming neighbours. It endeared them to us.

I read them a poem by John Clare:

Love lives beyond the tomb,
And earth, which fades like dew!
I love the fond,
The faithful, and the true.

Honorary Ringer

There they stand, in the front row at evensong, the Past Masters and Present Master of the Essex Association of Change Ringers. For have not they achieved a peal of 5,040 doubles in two hours and forty-four minutes? A board goes up in the tower to say so. I, an honorary ringer whose only achievement is to have tolled for the service, am humbled before them. We sing of the sacred minster bell which peals o'er hill and dell, and have our photo taken. I am well-versed in peal-boards and do not like to see them skied where those who come after us cannot read their justified boastings. It is a soft pre-summer night and outside the limes are standing stock-still. Earlier on, I preached on Barnabas, Son of Consolation, whose real name was Joseph. He was the leader of the first missionary journey but was swiftly overtaken by Paul. They parted company over John Mark. Joseph-Barnabas and Saul-Paul were the first men to hear the word 'Christian'. It was said at Antioch, and noted by two Jews. Barnabas had led Paul by the hand and taken him to the Apostles. It was the day of introductions and departures, of definitions and confrontations, of new names and discoveries. Only camel-bells would have rung out over these vast events. Past and Present Masters do not stay at home. In the worldwide freemasonry of towers they are honoured guests. But there are numismatic limits, as an eighteenth-century writer proved. Had our ringers tried the twelve bells of St Paul's Cathedral, say? Of course, they had been welcomed there. Although to ring all the possible changes on twelve bells would taken seventy-five years, ten months, one week and three days, reckoned the old bell author. But what a peal-board!

Our bells spent their first four centuries in All Saints, Colchester, arriving at Little Horkesley in 1958. Those who listened to them most would have been the prisoners in Colchester Castle, a notorious hell-hole. Among them would have been the Quaker boy-martyr James Parnell, a hero of my own youth. I thought of him whilst watching *Songs of Praise* from the Norwich Meeting House. A remarkably successful evocation of the life of Elizabeth Fry in which the hymns had not had the worship wrung out of them, as must happen in many much-rehearsed programmes. Parnell was a tiny lad who had talked with Fox and Whitehead in their prisons, and who had come to grief with the law when he preached outside various East Anglian churches – 'steeple houses'. And thus hence to the terrible Colchester prison and from the road to which rang our five bells. A woman gaoler lodged him in a high-up recess in the wall and made him climb a rope to fetch his meals. He fell and died. The verdict was that he committed suicide. This was reversed. He was, like so many prisoners then, murdered by gaolers. They said that he would have been a great writer, another Bunyan, maybe. He was eighteen. But he heard our bells. All Saints, Colchester is now a natural history museum, and where James Parnell's grave was dug is now, on a summer's day, a corporation park for children, lovers, picnics, band music and meticulous flower beds. Aged fifteen, he had written an essay called 'The Watcher, or a Discovery of the Ground and End of all Forms' ... Were he living now he would have been following Bob Geldof around.

In the rose-crowded garden sometimes I hear the Horkesley bells and sometimes the Wormingford bells. But never at once, not due to the wind, but because the ringers cannot be in two towers at the same time.

On the Feast of St Barnabas

Hay continues to be cut and has been this past fortnight. All the great hill meadow opposite Bottengoms has had its grasses laid low, so have the beautiful Grange pastures, some of which would not have looked very different during Georgian Junes. I can walk to church that way, as must have done for generations the farmers who lived in my house. First down to Duncan's reservoir, my disturbance raising a mallard or two, then past Celia's plantation, the trunks of her new trees now so fat that they have burst their rabbit-guard chains, like Peter in prison, then along the Chase, and then over the new stile and into the rich swells of this hay country which tumbles from valley into valley along the Stour. I pass the house where the tree-surgeon's mate lives, and his dogs raise the roof. A green lane follows for a quarter of a mile, then there is a hay path to the village school and an over-sleeping-policeman-ed path up to St Andrew's, bumps so massive that you would think enemy tanks were about to invade the playground. Somebody will soon have to take a firm hand with the excessive car-focused litter which has invaded every English village these last few years, and usually without the slightest consultation of those who live in them. Count your signs and then estimate those which are truly necessary.

It is a good honeysuckle year. It decks the table-tombs and at Wood Hall clings to the roof. Harold has introduced it to the lane hedge, where it clambers along in its sweetness. Mine thinks it is a scented rope walk for possible monkeys and has swung itself from tree to tree in great style. My old friend Richard Mabey says that pollinating moths can detect a honeysuckle a quarter of a mile away and that it is a plant for bowers and arbours. It and lilacs made the natural shelters of the earth-closet when I was a child. Honeysuckles and lilacs outside, the *East Anglian Daily Times* cut into squares and strung to a nail inside, and fearsomely scrubbed white seats – two of them. Just for company.

I preach on St Barnabas, son of consolation, as Luke dubbed him, the Cypriot who introduced St Paul to the Apostles. Could there ever have been a more potent introduction, other than to the Lord himself? He and Paul came to some kind of grief over John Mark and some say that he wrote Hebrews. But I talk of world-altering encounters and of the Son of Consolation at Antioch and possibly Salamis, and of the extraordinary new teachings floating around the eastern Mediterranean and the Aegean. The reading for his day is from the Book of Job. 'When the ear heard me, then it blessed me; and when the eye saw me, it gave witness to me.' To console: to alleviate sorrow. At Pentecost Barnabas follows hard upon the heels of the Comforter.

Trinity Sunday: the Flower Festival

The flower festival is upon us. Blessed Gertrude, Constance, Anna, have mercy. Tantalising weather blows cold then hot, teacups rattle on the tombs, cuckoos call from Arger Fen, rooks debate in Philip's new-mown hay, commanding women cry 'Oasis! Stepladder! Leaves, more leaves'. Husbands are in need of special prayers. There are charming tents under the trees, garlanded perpendicular, an alabaster St Alban under a pergola, artful drifts of roses, our de-wormed Victorian hearse burdened with lilies, our font a pool of infant buds. The carboy is full of pounds (thank Heaven); and Harold's honey-bees, weighed down with loot, hum against the sanctuary window (1866) in which Mary, with a halo, listens, and Martha, without a halo, carries a huge pile of washing-up. There is intensive child labour – 'Fetch me some more water and see that you don't spill it' – and then comes the immortal moment, the flinging open to the world of our south door, the oohs and ahs, the wonder. Did we ever see anything like it? Only once a year. Billy and Pat, whose last Festival this is, beam modestly. O prosper thou our handy-work. Amen say their obedient husbands, dreaming of whisky.

In the evening I conduct the now immensely popular hymn-fest, standing in the pulpit like a jack-in-the-box. The village has chosen its ten favourite hymns, writing them on the church door like Luther's ninety-five theses. The church is crowded and I stare down on the myriad countenances of friends and flowers. To space our songs I give miniature talks on the words and the music, and everybody falls back into their seats with unconcealed self-indulgence. The publicly singing individual is never more privately devout. Fine poetry, adequate rhyme, adored tunes, confident doctrine, up it all soars. Who is to evaluate it? No one. Did they know that their beloved 'Dear Lord and Father of Mankind' is the last part of a poem called 'The brewing of Soma' in which Whittier denounces an ecstasy drink used in vedic worship? Of course not, but what's new? At the moment, everything. Parry, Bunyan, Canon Dearmer, the enchanting Bianco, Sir Henry Baker, Bishop Heber, Mr Chalmers-Smith from Scotland, St Clement, John Marriott, who as well as writing 'Thou, whose almighty word' composed 'Marriage is like a Devonshire Lane', all are new. Our children ring Cowper on silver hand-bells. Worn out, we wander home.

The Stream and the House

The great day, or rather the great afternoon, dawns. It is warm and still, and so exactly right for the yearly mudbath or the raking of the watercourse. Precious clothes of a quite dreadful nature exist for this task and I exhume them from where they were folded away safely just twelve months ago. Torn jeans, a jersey you can see the clouds through and the pompom hat knit-ted for me by the rector's wife ages ago. Dear spotless rags, how often you have soaked up the Bottengoms mire. I attire myself in them tenderly, and there it is, and not quite washed out, what Rupert Brooke called 'the thrilling-sweet and rotten/ Unforgettable, unforgotten/River-smell', still hanging around as I splosh my way upstream. For what water my house doesn't want runs on into the Stour. However, this time my way is barred. A big blackthorn, long dead, has crashed across the ditch, so back to collect gloves and the saw. The gaunt tree is oddly light. Were it not so tortuously prickly I could have lifted it bodily with one hand and cleared the bank.

Now I am at the source, the spring. It begins as a mere trembling of the earth but in six yards it is rushing over my feet on its tumultuous journey to the valley via the roof tank. I chop nettles and brambles and irritate nesting birds, and am ashamed of myself. Nature adores a muddle. So far so pleasant. The worst is yet to come, the bailing out of the brick sump which is the first stage of Bottengoms Farm's last word in hydraulics. This is no job for the effete. It requires a brave descent into the kind of mud which beauticians would pay a ransom for, and it is invariably at this point in the ditch-cleaning that visitors arrive. The Parceline man, for example, the most spotless person I know. 'Sign here,' he says, lowering me his snowy pad. 'You've got your work cut out all right,' he says. And, 'Rather you than me, ha ha!' After him come grand old country ladies out for a drive and a tea, who instantly recognise what is happening and are thrown into nostalgia. They tell me of wonderful girlhoods in manors when it took a hundred goes at the cellar pump to run a bath, and enviable heatwaves when the supply dried up entirely and nobody washed at all. And, best of all, times when *they* were allowed to climb into the mud sump and slop it out. How the world has changed, and never for the better. Now all they have are gold taps from an ad in the colour supplement.

I touch bottom. The spring which has flowed since farmers settled here in Saxon days washes the bricks. I sit on the edge listening to its music as it passes across sand and stones, along pipes and a miniature aqueduct, and then impossibly up into the roof and down into the kettle. It is very accomplished, this stream, contriving to be both domesticated and wild. Resolution: visit the water supply more frequently, make the mud clothes last for another season. My bare footsteps can be seen for a week. Man Friday has been around.

The Death of Miss Helen Booth

I am walking to Helen's funeral. The afternoon air is moist and still. Birds sing loudly. Where the lane twists the hedge grows invisible under a mat of wild rose and traveller's joy. Fine stands of agrimony and mallow rear on its banks. Cars whisper by. Helen's cars, beginning with a Bullnose Morris and continuing with Estates, make ghostly journeys. She ceased counting after the very public centenary and withdrew to her slip of a bedroom, and was comfortable enough. Her mind revisited where she had been, who she had been. We visited her, myself careful not to harp on her age, for the worst thing about being over a hundred is being told how wonderful it is. It is not wonderful at all – just the persisting heartbeat and life not knowing when to stop. Just another day announcing itself through the thin curtain and jumping into one's consciousness like a jack-in-the-box.

We were old, old friends and Helen and her sister hardly more than middle-aged when I took my manuscripts to the post office. They would place them on the scales, give a start, and tell me apologetically, 'I'm afraid it will be *Three and Six*.' Behind them rose shelves sparsely arrayed with balls of string, celluloid windmills, silvery baking tins, greaseproof paper and towering potplants. They were the last of the World War One entrepreneurial women whose smallholding skills – and failures – were plotted across the English countryside. In 1926, when they were in their twenties, their father had sensibly put them out to grass, so to speak, giving them seven acres and a couple of clapboard cottages, sure that they would make a go of it. And they did. Although never in any sense mean, they were mistresses of the stretched funds of the interwar years. There was no tragedy in their lives. They were not war-widows or war-bereaved fiancées but they did join the army of men-less women which, with few qualifications, had to make ends meet. Chicken-farms spread. It was a land of wire-netting and chirping huts. Ladies in breeches lived on shillings. They were the originators of today's farm-gate sales, with their trays of vegetables and eggs at the roadside.

Helen and her sister, Win, began with chickens and ended with cocker spaniels. In between there were ducks, geese and goats. But it was by their kennels that most of the world of country businesswomen knew them. They would show me their Box Brownie snaps. There they were, being tugged along traffic-less lanes by six dogs on a lead, their handsome faces turned upwards, coins in their bags, and maybe their lips learning lines for the current Dramatic Society play. For in those days one had to be artful to a degree to escape having a part in *Dear Octopus* or *The Mousetrap*. The world is divided between those who seek a part and those who pray to God every night not to be given one. Moreover, Wormingford in those immediate post-World War Two days contained two dazzling and more or less inescapable village hall theatre directors, Christine Nash, wife of the artist, and Guy Hickson, brother of 'Miss Marple'. He too had a market garden by the side of the road. And now Helen, dear friend and relic of vanished activities, lay in her bright coffin as we sang, 'We love the place, O God' and the young gravedigger and his dog waited in the wings, so to speak. And Win, long dead, waited for her sister in the clay. And of course somewhere else.

Grass

The great meadow is being mowed. Keith and Bernard clatter up and down its plunging acres on a machine which throws out burnt brown rectangular hay biscuits.

A voice says, 'Cry!'
'What shall I cry?'
'All flesh is grass.'

A tolerable image of transience. The washing bleaches on the lawn, the gooseberries are being gathered with the blackbirds looking on, thousands of old roses perfume the slight wind. Dark William Lob, delicate Celestine, rich Charles de Mille, susceptible Leda, modest John Clare, the latest to arrive in the garden. We have staggered home from yet one more flower festival at Mount Bures. Few in this high village have much notion of 'arrangement' in today's semi-professional terms and so we see something absolutely different, and flawless of its kind. Vicki read from the Song of Songs and John from the Lord's attack on materialism in Luke 12. Whilst Diana preached on a horticultural philosophy of life. Outside, the 'Mount', shaggy with brambles, cast long shadows over the graves of the congregation before the present one. If its flesh is indeed grass, then it is the best silky, tidy grass. We listen to the click-clack and whistle of the Sudbury train as it reaches our crossing but nobody glances at his watch. Nobody says, as they once did, 'What do you make it? I make it half a minute late.'

I have finished a book. A novel. And I do not feel as I am supposed to feel, that I have made and lost, or done with, a child. Rather I feel as some people do when the guests have gone, released. I think of all the things I shall do with no book to cry 'Write me!' as soon as I get up. I might read all the books which have been waiting for me to read this last year. Although I am not likely to be as deplorable as the late Jean Rhys and sit on the floor drinking gin at breakfast and browsing in old tales, smoking like a trooper and not giving a damn. But I might lie under the poplars to hear their summery clapping, one of the loveliest sounds in the world, and an immortal one I am sure. And I shall certainly consider the grasses as well as the lilies. If our flesh is to transmigrate, where better than to the rich greening of the world?

Lunch is Served

First the rain. It fell out of the sky in lasting douches, and was accompanied by sheet lightning which gave stagey glimpses of the surrounding hills. The farm track became as always a nice little river, the roses, Albertine, Cardinal Richelieu, Duchesse de Montebello, William Lobb, John Clare, etc. sopping wet balls. Old friends splashed their way across Suffolk for lunch, a semi-amphibious journey nobly undertaken. All went swimmingly until I turned on the electric oven to bake the fish-pie. I had been up since dawn making this. The guests were in the sitting room, Roy the wonderful Reader who has taught most of East Anglia what it is seeing when it comes to church, and our old friend Peggy who in a different sense has kept us in touch with our roots. Merry laughter in the next room. Then Gordon the church-warden arrives, having found my glasses in his car. These are the pair I cannot actually see through and which I take around for fear of losing my best spectacles. All is perfectly timed. Wine is served. Fragments of useful information thread through into the kitchen. The table is laid. The salad is 'fatigued'. What an improvement on Barbara Pym, I think, whose hosts offer even the higher clergy sardines on toast and Nescafé.

Then the disaster. The fine newish stove has lost a timing button, without which nothing happens. I see just an empty socket. I crawl on the floor, move the cat, see the huge fish-pie cold and white. From next door I hear the enjoyment rising and I know that it has to climax in this extravagant dish. It is a quarter to one. And I cannot even heat the plates. I think wildly. Bread and cheese? As Christians, I tell myself, they have no option but to accept such a meal with grace – although it may not stop them from dining out on it when they get back home. Since there is no way of finding the tiny button, I turn my attention to the top of the stove, which works. Soon there are mushroom omelettes, new potatoes, peas, and plates hotted over boiling water. Meanwhile, after the party, the vast fish-pie asks, 'What about me?' Well, half of you can go into the deep freeze and the other half can last me until Sunday. I then search for the lost button, going so far as to empty the Dyson tube and pulling out the stove from its alcove. But no luck. There is St Jude of course but he has to deal with lost love, lost rings, lost hopes, and I don't like to bother him. The next morning, early, boiling days stretching before me, glancing down at the scrubbed brick floor, bright as a button, there it lies, the all-important missing agent. Well, thank God!

It is Flower Festival at Mount Bures, the loveliest in all England – which is not to decry other such events. But at Mount Bures, any Thomas Hardy character can stroll in and be immediately at home. Also it honours its patron saint, St John the Baptist. Was the Lord recalling what they said of Elijah – 'Then stood up Elias the prophet as fire, and his word burned like a lamp' –when he gave that dazzlingly brief obituary of his cousin, 'He was a burning and a shining light'? I expect so. My annual role in the Flower Festival is to take a sprig of St John's wort from my garden and put it by his statue above the altar. This is the species *Hypericum perforatum* with its radiant light holes which are not perforations at all but little resinous glands. But how it burns like a lamp to our seeking feet.

Repent, Repent

Midsummer! The celebration of the sun and of St John the Baptist. An Edinburgh lady seated next to the Shah of Persia during a state visit said, 'They tell me, Sire, that in your country they worship the sun.' – 'So would you, madam, if you had ever seen it.' At Mount Bures, dedicated to the Baptist, we very nearly worship the annual hog roast, a quota-raising event which accompanies their flower festival. We eat gluttonously to music by Amadeus Boldwicket's Red Hot Peppers Jazz Band while in the golden evening light the semi-naked starveling saint stares across his cousin's altar. The birds are homing and calling above the cheerful racket, and the straw bales in Keith's barn creak under our weight. Midsummer. I steal back into the church for a moment or two and am met by a torrent of scent – and the austere gaze of John. The epistle on his day is about permanence and temporality, the latter epitomised as grass and flowers, and also about spiritual confidence. 'Lift up thy voice . . . be not afraid.'

One day this week I dared myself to do nothing and it proved to be the greatest activity. My metabolism fights against idleness and has to be fought back in return. Be still, I order myself, backing up this command with various well-known scriptural injunctions. But sitting in the garden at half-past eight in the morning! And the mind turning over at a pace. And forty bees rifling the nearest cranesbill, and Max the cat pausing on his ruthless way, aghast, and the look on the postman's face, and the enormous resolution on my own as I let the letters tumble where they may. How long can I keep it up, this unnatural sloth? I pretend that I am meditating or Thinking, though clearly I am not. I remind myself that as I am registered self-employed I can give myself time off. It is only logical. Yes, but where will it all end? Whole hours have now gone by and the bees have finished the cranesbill and are now on the phlomis. Pigeons are courting in the ash tree, clapping their grey and white wings and necking on a swaying bough. I feel wonderfully well – it is the inescapable result of conscious idleness to feel wonderfully well. But I can see some weeds and I can hear the telephone. And the new chapter fluttering on the lawn says, 'You will have to finish me one day, so why not now?' I begin to prime the pump. The pigeons reminding me of St John of the Cross's 'ring dove', I find his poems and read,

> The dove so snowy-white,
> Returning to the Ark, her frond bestows:
> And seeking to unite
> The mate of her delight
>
> Has found him where the shady river flows.

Occupations

Home from holidays to a rioting garden, my kind housesitter barely visible among straggling plants. What do they mean by growing like this in just over a week? I note a flycatcher's nest over the front door with father flycatcher on the wing above it. There is a grievous heap of post and an indignant cat, and Messages. Also Matins to be taken almost before I can sit down. Driving to Mount Bures with John, he calmly announces his retirement. The great seed shed over which he has reigned these last forty years will know him no more. We are passing gaudy fields of borage and flax as he says this, and what with their intensity and what with still not having my feet on the ground, I can only say 'When?' 'Two days' time.' *Two days' time!* This enormous statement fills the Land Rover. I mention the borage. 'Very profitable,' he says, 'you have to combine it twice. They sell it to the drug companies for arthritis.' We bump over the level crossing and he solemnly reviews his existence. 'When I applied for the job, I arrived at nine to the minute which, they told me, proved a lack of eagerness for it. "Come back tomorrow at *ten to*, then we'll see if we want you."' He was twenty-three. I preached on the calling of Peter while butterflies vied with the painted glass.

Tim has worked for the Catchment Board, which may not be its correct name, for thirty-five years, and thus has a decade to go. We have a breakfast meeting with him, Francis at the mill and the Colonel opposite. It is chilly and brilliant where the watermill stood until 1930, when it went up in flames. But the mill-race itself is roaring into the mill-pool, the more so since there is no wheel to turn, and shoots and hoppers to keep going. Tim gazes upstream at his winding empire, throws out his arms and cries, 'To be *paid* to do this!' His least enviable task is to set bliss against cost. Francis, the Colonel and myself are there to say, 'Hell to the cost, which won't be much anyway. Let there be Flow!' Every few miles for hundreds of years our Stour has been made noisy by millers as amber water becomes white water, and idling water becomes working water, lifting up its roaring voice. Tim's affair with the river began long before he became its official guardian. He has known its twists and turns since childhood, as indeed have I. We swop then and now anecdotes, and the morning warms up, and I slip in a plea for, perhaps, the most underestimated rivery delight, its ancient industrial noise. Pray let no cost silence what is left of it. This noise terrified me as a small boy having to cross the Floodgates. I saw drowned men going round with the wheel. Bird cries became human cries. Years later, when I followed the suicidal Henchard to the weir-hole of the river which flowed through Casterbridge, I knew only too well what he would see – himself. And here!

All Flesh is Grass

I must be the only person for miles around who has been naming his grass. Timothy, red canary, meadow brome, marsh foxtail, Nodding grass, Oat grass – I could go on for pages. It rises in the track to tickle the under-bellies of cars and in the set-aside to hide larks' nests. Wind and rain, and concealed infirmities, have brought an ancient crack willow crashing down, and Neil the woodman must be summoned. It always astonishes me how little space trees take up in the air, and how much room they take up when they collapse on the ground. There it lies, a Paul Nash tree, huge, horizontal, felled by circumstances. The cats stroll about on its tip with mockery, just as David strolled onto poor Goliath to cut off his head. I have always felt sorry for Goliath, a man exploited by his country because of his size. In a later age he would have been exploited by some boxing manager and ended up with brain damage. The fallen willow soon dies. Its silver leaves blacken. It wilts all over. Ben aged five balances himself on its trunk, shouting, triumphant.

The land goes its mute way. Not a celebratory sound unless one includes birdsong. Weedless fields, rocking hedges, contractors' corn, supermarket onions, unmolested wild animals, bone idle domestic animals, cattle (Lincolns) on the water meadows once more, Paul's sheep too by the river, all chomping their grass dinners. A hare prays on the hill, balancing on his back legs and crossing his front paws. Swaying, listening, one ear to catch what God is saying, one fearful of us.

Martin Bell Comes to Tea

The heatwave is felt every hour of the day. It says, 'Meet me at midnight, at four in the morning, at noon. Whatever time it is, I make all things different.' Thus I watch the indigo trees in the small hours. They are still and smoky with mist, and full of singing birds. The corn is static and blue, the new reservoir a silver line. The white cat stirs on the garden wall but the white horses, monumental beneath the may hedge, show not the slightest movement. William Cobbett *rose* every morning at four o'clock! I tell myself – got up and wrote. But I stand at the window doing no more than looking out, which is occupation enough at mid-summer, and the warmth of yesterday collects around my bare skin.

It is baking hot when Martin Bell arrives, he in his white suit, his sisters smiling, and all of us talking about their father Adrian Bell, that unique Suffolk writer. Their childhood farmhouse can just be made out through my willows. Adrian Bell was not so much a literary hero to me as a boy, but his being an author made me watch him. When I told him this – a confession of sorts – many years later, he laughed and asked, 'What did you see?' What do we see when we watch writers? Of course, we know all too well what writers see. Very strange things if one is to go by their books. Adrian set *The Times* crossword puzzles when he wasn't looking at Suffolk and putting down the likes of all of us between the wars. He was a loquacious man who missed very little and who wrote wonderful prose. He called his son Martin because of the martins in the eaves of his old house. Should we not borrow more bird names – Jay, Crane, Bunting, though of course not Cuckoo. After the Bells have left I re-read some of Adrian's *Silver Ley* and I am twelve again and biking on a blazing day to Arger Fen and there are chalked boards outside the pub which say, 'No peapickers, no gypsies'.

It is late June and we are to remember St John the Baptist. Not that I ever forget him. I am sure that if I had lived in Palestine then I would have looked at him as I once looked at our local author, somewhat sensationally, and would have deserved that divine reproach, 'What went ye out into the wilderness to see? A reed shaken with the wind?' Prophets were not to be stared at but to be listened to. But Christ's herald would have been a striking figure by the water's edge even to those too far off to hear what he said, day after day, month after month, until his voice became intolerable for some and they put a stop to it. He was, said his cousin, 'A burning and a shining light' – which must be the most beautiful of all epitaphs. They named the hypericums after him, those flowers which are each a golden speckled sun and whose juices are blood red. A tall hedge of them bends across my path as I cross the grass, half-blocking the way and telling me, 'Not so fast!'

Old chaps sit in the cricket pavilion, drink beer and observe their young selves in the photos. Cricket talk is the chamber music of sport, winding in and out, requiring all one's attention. The speakers are deputy patrons of the club and know just where to come in. There were great authors who actually wrote this cricket-talk music down and got it published. The pitch itself sizzles and dogs lie panting on the crease. You could cook bread in the scattered cars. I write the Sunday services. Do we know Percy Dearmer's 'Lo, in the wilderness'?

Trinity

The village bakes. Sudden winds fan the heat about and creamy plates of elderflower cense the hedges. Cars are ovens on wheels. Being told that we have only to lift the seed-drill for a few feet to double the skylarks, I examine the Great Field which was many fields when they were numerous. But there are still plenty of semi-bare patches. It is because its ancient dips continue to defy the density levels of seed, and they, plus the tramlines created by the sprayer, continue to provide feeding grounds for these birds. Only this year the crop is beans whose scent was a test for morality in the middle ages. It was thought that girls could not hold out against it, so boys were fined if they made love to them in it. Overhead, invisible now, the larks sing then drop like a stone.

Sunday ramblers swelter past, Sunday gliders cross themselves in the blue, Sunday ringers stay in cool towers where brass knights and their wives can keep an eye on them. I suddenly remember poor young Reginald Heber and his wife in broiling Calcutta, their thoughts on Shropshire. His see was virtually all British India, a land of endless deities and their marigold shrines, of natural excess, torrential rain, pitiless sun and exile. He had turned the bishopric down twice but India got him in the end. It drew him into its sacred chaos, into a life of all work, all duty, all brevity. He was a poet who had won the Newdigate Prize at Oxford so he wrote great Christian hymns in the heat. They liked them back home, saw the Church of England triumphing over the heathens, enjoyed their foreignness, their coral strands.

John, scanning the framed Victorian parsons on the vestry wall, wondered what they did all day. Well, there were 'the poor' for a start, those large labouring families which, like Reginald Heber, wore themselves out in the field. They said the Office, they wrote botanies, taught the choir to hold the note in his 'Holy, Holy, Holy' and lived, unlike him, for ages. Then they were laid to rest beneath a flat stone ringed with Latin and harebells. The people would talk of 'Mr Davies's day,' 'Canon Williams's day' as though they were reigns. And they were of a sort. But now we are looking for a 'House for Duty' priest. Whoever decides to live in our vicarage c.1955, rent free, no stipend, will have a famous view. So good that the job could have been advertised as 'View for Duty'. The Stour quavers in the heat-haze. This is the season for Anglican lassitude. As John Meade Falkner wrote:

We have done with dogma and divinity
    Easter and Whitsun past,

> The long, long Sundays after Trinity
>   Are with us at last;
> The passionless Sundays after Trinity,
>   Neither feast-day nor fast.

The Haymaker

The white cat worships water. It leans over the stream by the hour, looking in. Should it be indoors, washing-up water will do. 'In water face answers face', says the Book of Proverbs. What question does the white face with its green eyes ask? Both John Bunyan and Thomas Traherne would stare into puddles, Bunyan in the hope that they would miraculously dry up at his command, thus proving the existence of God, Traherne that, like Alice and the Looking-Glass, he could step into the reversed world which they showed. He believed that

> below the purling stream
> Some unknown joys there be
> Laid up in store for me:
> To which I shall, when that thin skin
> Is broken, be admitted in.

I advise the white cat to take care as she leans over water and remember what happened to Narcissus. But she never listens, being lost in reflections. Larks sing a hundred feet above us. The lawn steams after the downpour. Bernard makes damp hay. His machine drones all day on the top field, releasing scent, squelching on the turn, making geometry of the cut and the uncut.

As with almost everything on the farm these days, haymaking is a one-man rite. Whereas it used to be every able-bodied woman's rite, and old photographs show sweaty girls with huge wooden rakes and pitchforks tossing grass in blazing sunshine.

Bare arms and shoulders, but a bonnet of course. Bernard has finished when I take the field. Only a triangle of purple budding thistle is still standing, and harriers are wheeling over the blond stubble. Hay wisps hang in the hedge. Horses, their heads deep in still-growing grass, have their eye on them, and soon it will adorn their mouths like whiskers. Hay once had to be made when grass was full of growth, and sappy, then left and thrown about, and only when it was as dry as a bone made into stacks. Wet hay in a stack would heat up until it became an internal oven setting fire to the lot. The River Stour water meadows were hay-kingdoms when we were children, but now corn and potatoes flourish to the water's edge. The hay was as much wild flowers as grass and their chopped stems would scratch our legs and make painful walking. The air would be heavy and overpowering, and a feeling of lassitude would run through the landscape, causing it to droop. George Herbert, being a consumptive, avoided river valleys in summer, disliking their baked plants and aridity, and finding their water unrefreshing.

Midsummer Cushions

Today is summer. Summer proclaims itself. I feel it, hear it, smell it the moment I wake. Max wails like some implacable mendicant under the bedroom window. Food! I starve! O pity me, thy Cat! His tail whirls rose-dust. It being summer, he has stayed out all night. In half an hour I am climbing the hill to look down on Bottengoms in its valley and to see it reaching from its trees. Duncan has cut some of his hay, meadowsweet marks the waterways, hogweed towers, a late bat hurries home and everything is wringing wet but will soon be as dry as a bone. The wind is as hot as the sun and both scorch the flints in the lane. Fireweed is out, as is chicory, and the sky is an unlikely blue.

In church I am telling them all about St Benedict and Monte Cassino, when I suddenly realise that two old friends seated beneath me have far more reason to know about this great monastery than the rest of us. For the lesson-reader's brother and the organist's husband both died there during the Allied advance through Italy. Diana had been reading the final words of Acts, those which describe St Paul's arrival in Rome and his being allowed to live 'two whole years on his own in a hired house', although he was officially a prisoner of state. Had he lain low they might have forgotten about all that trouble in Palestine. Instead, he made his Roman home a halfway house for Jew and Gentile alike, 'receiving all that came to him', which was asking for trouble. The nave hums with summer, the monuments dance. We sing Cowper – 'I sought thee wandering, set thee right,/Turned thy darkness into light.' I can see the old brother and sister, several pews apart, in their Sunday clothes. 'Thank you for coming,' she always says at the door. He has been saving the harebells, staking out with orange markers where the mower must not go on their sward. How the mower will suffer. To leave part of the churchyard unmown – how unbearable. And what will the dead say?

And so on to Helpston to remember John Clare, which is my favourite day out in all the year. The schoolchildren have placed sixty midsummer cushions round his grave – a midsummer cushion is an oblong of turf stuck with wild flowers and the title of one of Clare's books, only now appearing. I am taken through blazing Rutland to where he worked at a limekiln and where the July plants have long drawn a rich botanical veil over what was in his day a ravaged landscape. There were limekiln men in Suffolk when I was a boy, ashen from cap to boots, and the limed fields did not look at all cleansed but somehow fouled by whiteness. John Clare was twenty here at Casterton, toiling hard in opposite directions, filling the kiln, filling a notebook, using his hat for a desk. Making love, getting wed, becoming famous, becoming lost.

The Day After Midsummer

Proofreading in the garden, the pages fluttering, the cat sisters rolling in a flower bed, alert now and again when they see the flycatchers. I am trying to forget some of the daft things I may have said during the great PCC debate on the lavatory. Should it be in the shed or should it be a Perp loo in the church itself? For eight hundred years we have gone to the bushes, I may have said.

Mr Sycamore arrives to slice off the rise in the track. Winter rains have run gullies on either side of it so that the middle has become the terror of drivers. Tall grass waves from it like a Cherokee's haircut. Mr Sycamore takes his horizontal knife to it. His machine sounds like one of those treadle dentist's drills. The ancient surface of the road is exposed and I think of all the women and children who picked these stones from the fields, generation after generation mending the parish tracks. Boys' work, girls' work, mothers' work, these flints once in their warm hands.

Travellers have made a camp on the wide green bend above Sandy Hill. Vans, dogs, brown children and a crowded clothes-line. They were there when I was a boy, when John Clare was at Epping.

'Tis thus they live – a picture to the place;
A quiet, pilfering, unprotected race.

I protect them from the slander of Clare's 'pilfering' whenever they are mentioned, even now. I remember their Colchester protector, Grattan Puxon, a solicitor's son who helped to legislate for Gypsies and travellers generally, helping to force the Caravan Sites Act through in 1970. Not that these freedom-loving folk cared much for concrete parking places and the adjacent loos, to be honest. But in a property-dominated society it pleases me to see their indifference to our now sacred bricks and mortar. Not

223

for them the first rung of the nightmare. A real Gypsy caravan appears at the flower show, a painted vardo with shafts and an enticing interior. I step inside for the first time. It is gaudily private.

Suffolk Writers

Early morning in the heatwave, the air still and sullen, the trees cardboard shapes, the birds silent. One can almost hear the dead rose petals falling. David's corn is a motionless bluey-green sea. At the moment, the day is holding back its potential and seems uncommitted, but in a little while the sun will spin up in the east like a gold coin. Yesterday, the washing dried in an hour.

The old house creaks a bit, and stays cool. Its pin-tiles cook. Strong eastern scents are burnt out of English roses. I watched a baby owl occupy one of those hedgerow elms that grow to 20 feet and then die. His baby feathers were as yet tumbled and unsettled. He looked down at me from on high. I mowed a bit, raked a bit, and heard a Wimbledon woman howling at every shot. I had left all the windows wide. The white cat, a Quietist, was sleeping the heatwave away under a bush.

On Friday, I went to the Aldeburgh Festival to talk about East Anglian writers. As usual, the North Sea was an immense wall about to fall on the borough. I met Martin Bell in the Jubilee Hall, and we sat on the stage, forsaking our notes, as we remembered his father, Adrian, the disturbing short story writer Mary Mann, Henry Williamson, and the youthful Julian Tennyson, whose *Suffolk Scene* lived in my bicycle basket throughout my teens.

Afterwards, Vicky and I called on Benjamin Britten, Peter Pears and Imogen Holst in their graves at the far end of the vast churchyard, then drove home, running into the weekenders. Soon, for we each lived down old farm tracks, there would be only animals and children to greet us. And this heat. Late at night, I watered the tomatoes from the stream, and listened to a grown-up owl.

The Armed Forces Service was somewhat a surprise. A bugler arrived, and four British Legions. And George, a little boy, to read the familiar lines about not growing old. We sang Charles Wesley's 'Soldiers of Christ, arise' for the processional … 'Leave no unguarded place, no weakness of the soul.' And I draped the flags against a statue of St Alban, a British soldier in Roman uniform who had changed clothes with a priest so that he could escape death during the Diocletian purge of Christianity. Was Alban executed in vestments?

Anyway, my history sermon over, I returned the standards to their bearers, one as young as Alban, one as old as the Second World War, and we sang our way out into the sunshine. The Colonel had read the Beatitudes, which I had lengthened to include, 'Ye are the salt of the earth … the light of the world.'

When we ritually gather at the Crown for a pint, however, it is to find half a dozen of the congregation smoking outside in a kind of purpose-built veranda, and looking like boys behind the bike-shed. Inside the bar, we virtuous ones, including an Air Chief Marshal, politely discuss 'belief'. It is 28 June, the feast day of St Austol, who most likely gave his name to St Austell. An absolutely idle afternoon, barring a few weeds, then evensong without bugles. The grit from the new road repairs flies up like hot deterrents.

The great bindweed is out and climbing the sloe bushes in the track, trumpeting summer. Its huge white bells peal from the ditch. It was called morning glory in Somerset, and may have given its name to the even more glorious Ipomoeas of New England.

Farmhouse Guests

Duncan and I agree: it is a growing year. Things grow every year, of course, but not as they do in a growing year. The garden has shot up, gone skyward. Roses look down at me, as indeed does the white cat, who is either under a hank of cool grass, or dizzily aloft in a pear tree, taking stock of the universe. A cuckoo is not far off, its cry not yet doubling.

Quiet, empty churches relax after strenuous attempts to define the Trinity. Once-a-week friends come out like birds from clocks, and we say more or less the same things. Wimbledon and atrocity take turns on the television. The one so perfect, the other so wicked. Humanity is an enigma, capable of the best and the worst. What Christ must have seen before it saw him!

We sing 'Holy, holy, holy', and, as always, I think of Reginald Heber, poet and bishop, who died young in India, after three years 'crowded with toil', nursing the sick soldiers who were on the ship. The Church seems to have insisted on this missionary enterprise when Heber would have rather stayed at home in Hodnet, Shropshire, described by Leyland as neither town nor village.

When Heber was there, it had a rectory at one end, and a prison at the other. He fulfilled the requirements of a Victorian cleric by being well-born, selfless, and a victim of work. His Trinity hymn distances God, places him beyond mortal comprehension. Our few voices rise and fall.

Later, the car creeps down the ancient farm track, caressed by overgrowth, disturbing bees, coming to a stop where the fruit trees begin. And now, as somebody wrote, the long, long Sundays of Trinity, neither feast day nor fast.

Twice this week, birds have flown into the house – a robin and a wren – and beat against the windows, rushing from one to the other, shocked by looking out of glass and not being able to fly through it. I cup them in my hands, and they tremble; I carry them to the door, and the release is nearly as wonderful for me as it is for them.

The white cat, who either through sloth or being well-fed, has never eaten anything which doesn't come out of a tin, adds to their terror by just gazing at them. Old houses in the middle of nowhere are open houses to butterflies, harvest mice and, once, a toad who liked a cool brick floor. At night, I sometimes hear a squirrel, but no rats. A man from the ministry did with these long ago.

But I have always been conscious of residents other than humanity who give this address, and whose claim for shelter is historic. Moths matriculate in undrawn curtains, and spiders make a new web where I have brushed down the old one. When I was a boy, I would lie in bed and listen to a spider on a route-march on wallpaper which had come adrift, tap-tap-tapping in the dark. And the beams would give a little groan, worn out with having to hold up tons of house.

The south wall, laden with grapes, is now three feet in the ground, its orange bricks and pale beams interlocked in a kind of supportive marriage. Ancient buildings are like this, out of kilter, and the stronger for it. There is a lesson here. But the wide floor-boards under the fitted carpet pine for bare feet.

To some creatures, these 'funny old places' are both home and trap.

Haymaking

Up at six these warm, blowy mornings, the prisoners to release. These are Charles's or Elspeth's or Harold's bees which have become trapped overnight in the double-glazing, plus a few moths and butterflies. The post arrives and is enough to break one's heart. A huge two-feet-square of a letter from British Telecom to say, 'We are cutting 10 per cent off your business calls' and a much re-used envelope from an old friend which reads 'Save the Trees'. Also a card from Richard Mabey whose whole life is given to environmental teaching, plus a big manila packet from a cathedral containing two lines on the date of a committee meeting. Taste, waste and ignorance make their customary bow between the tea and the toast. There is also a lovely fat book from the poet-philosopher William Anderson.

They are making hay at Maltings Farm, at the Grange and at the Hall. 'The hay appeareth, and the tender grass showeth itself, as the haymaker drones up and down across the pastures.' Green has bleached to near-white and the machine leaves the meadows looking like combed blond hair. It is the feast of grass, the festival of the Gramineae, that least individually recognised of plants. The many species tumble into polleny ranks whilst the blades cut on. To make hay is to make merry and also to make metaphors for our own impermanence. In scripture the rich and wasteful have their noses rubbed in it, so to speak. For hay is splendour laid low. We have proper hay-meadows and set-aside. The latter is a constant disappointment where I am concerned, for I always hope that it would produce a rare flower or two. But at Sawyers and below Tiger Hill the succulent hay-meadows of the past have been encouraged to return, and the machines rumble into an intoxication of grasses, clovers and bull daisies. When we were children certain flowers had 'to go with something' and bull daisies had to go with quaking-grass. It was a law. These still grow side by side in Boulge churchyard and close to the roses from Omar Khayyám's tomb which enclose the grave of Edward FitzGerald. Years ago I had to sit in FitzGerald's cottage at haymaking time to dole out the prizes for the local flower show, nearly every one of which went to two fearsomely competitive farmworkers. Where the poet was concerned, all flesh was less grass than rose petals. He has a line from the *Jubilate* on his tomb – 'It is He that hath made us, and not we ourselves', by which his family could have intended, 'Don't blame him for being so odd.'

Bliss – to sprawl on one's stomach in a haymeadow and give names to the grass family, the sweet-grasses, the fescues, the ryes.

JULY

*T*he idiom of modern cartography speaks of 'ground-truthing'. To 'ground-truth' is to verify in person, often on foot, information gathered by remote-sensing technologies such as aerial photography or satellite imagery; to test theory against thing, we might say. I've long thought of Ronnie Blythe as a ground-truther, in many senses. For decades, he has been fathoming place as deep rather than wide, and doing so by walking, talking, listening and watching. 'Off we go to walk again', he writes in one of these vividly sun-soaked, rain-soaked, thought-soaked entries from July; companionable, habitual, the phrase could be a motto for his work as a whole.

In July 2008, I went to see Ronald Blythe at Bottengoms Farm. He welcomed me warmly in for tea, we wandered the garden, and we spoke of our mutual friends, Roger Deakin and Richard Mabey (both of whom accompany Ronnie on a July walk to inspect the site of a future woodland, in one of the entries below). I remember how that day Ronnie spoke of John, Paul and Barbara Nash almost as if they were still alive, and I remember smiling at his brief aside that Ravilious's greenhouse lay collapsed somewhere in the undergrowth.

As I was leaving — rather starstruck by this encounter with giants of English landscape culture living and dead — Ronnie asked me to wait, then went and fossicked around in another room. He returned with two beautiful framed woodblock prints; one of a guinea fowl, one of a hoatzin. They were, Ronnie explained, by the engraver Eric Dalglish, who had given them to Barbara Nash in 1920. Barbara had given them in turn to Ronnie — and here was Ronnie giving them to me. I could hardly believe it; such a gift to me, a young writer, a stranger who had knocked on his door only a couple of hours ago. But that is Ronnie; like footpaths, he connects people to people, and places to places. The etchings have hung in

*my teaching room at college for twenty years, to remind me of the impor-
tance of generosity.*

*'Trinity Five', the first entry that follows here, is a miniature master-
piece. Ronnie has gone out for a night-walk, summoned into the midsummer dusk by the hooting of owls. The writing is extraordinary. The 'church
tower is a charcoal stump'; 'cats emerge from ditches with golden glances
at this late person', and the tawnies are 'mousing on the wing'. Reading
it, we move through several centuries at once; here with Coleridge and
Wordsworth, there in the decades after the Norman Conquest, now in the
late 1900s, as a 'blue flicker through thin curtains betrays the late film'. So
this passage moves on, deft, time-travelling and wise. 'Everywhere,' writes
Ronnie, 'it is all so perfectly interesting that one might never go to bed.'
This is his sensibility in a sentence; inquisitive, wandering, democratic,
giving us the truth on the ground.*

Robert Macfarlane

Trinity Five

A midsummer's night and the village all asleep. We are early birds. Commuters must drive off to the station from 5 a.m., farmworkers (few of these) must bump down the tracks an hour or two later, children must catch school buses at eight. Here and there a blue flicker through thin curtains betrays the late film. Standing at a high window, I am wooed by owls, tawny ones by the sound of their sumptuously deep, Melba-like *boos*. One is close to the house and preaching desolation. The haunting cry reminds me of Isaiah's description of the fall of Edom. Change the architecture and it might well be a description of the long-abandoned farm-buildings site which lies just below me. 'And thorns shall come up in palaces, nettles and brambles in the fortress ... and it shall be ... a court for owls.' But blackberries from last year's brambles fill the deep-freeze and bricks from the footings of tumbled pigsties will, this autumn, make fine paths. The nearest owl will have none of this; desolation it must be. His wild cry is answered far away with matching comfortlessness by an owl sailing through purple clouds to Bures. A small boy staring upwards: 'Birds don't know it's Friday.' Well, thank goodness for that. These midnight owls certainly would not consider them-selves to be lost in wastes and fit company for poor Job. They are mousing on the wing.

It is a night for a discreet wander – one must never forget the scandal caused by the Wordsworths and Coleridge at Nether Stowey by their nocturnal ramblings. That they were composing *Lyrical Ballads* was no excuse. I pray that Penny's dog is under lock and key. Wild roses festoon every hedge and cats emerge from ditches with golden glances at this late person. It is sultry and every window is wide. The church tower is a charcoal stump, just as it was during the summer nights which followed the Conquest. The clock face gives me its old-fashioned look. Gravestones are legible and there are dense scents. Young rabbits are dining off a wreath and other unidentifiable creatures rustle and fidget. Everywhere, it is all so perfectly interesting that one might never go to bed.

On the bridge which links Essex to Suffolk I lean over to observe the pull of the currents and the tiny shoals of perch and dench darting through the reed-mace. A sound from our neighbour church at Little Horkesley floats on the water. Bell-tongues and owls-songs join.

A Time to Wed

July. The hillside horses flash their tales, the white cat bakes on the wall, her eyes emerald slits. The oaks haven't the energy to rustle. All is burning and still. Using Roger Deakin's inestimable gift, a lightweight scythe, I have demolished a patch of rough before it seeds. The blue of the big field has turned a heavy green. Invisible larks sing without a stop.

It is Saturday – weddings day. The ancient church shimmers in the heat. The bells ring dizzily. The bride arrives. It is our Pam, on her brother's arm. They are neither young nor old. Just timeless. Ditto the groom. The choir, also neither young nor old, but comfortably settled in the space between these verities, sings 'Jesu, joy of man's desiring', and we all sing, 'Guard us, guide us, keep us, feed us'. It is heartfelt and unimaginably beautiful, with the interior sunshine playing on the bride's slender diadem.

Afterwards, some of us board her brother's restored 1947 bus. Next stop, the Crown. And then, late at night, with Japanese lanterns hanging in the trees and the thatched barns straight out of a Samuel Palmer, a Ruby Wedding party, and all the old friends from near and far at table.

On Sunday, I preach on Time. A scattering of dear ones. It is hardly a tactful subject, I realise, halfway through. But possibly they are thinking of sherry. One must hope for the best. Pam and her husband will now be in the Lake District in the rain. And may be watching it splashing down on Wordsworth's grave, the poet who was 'Surprised by joy – impatient as the wind'. At this moment, thousands of women priests are at their altars to the common sense of mankind and the glory of God.

But I must concentrate, although the heatwave plays tricks with worship. 'Are you listening at the back there?' Possibly you are in a summer dream that is acceptable to heaven. Who can tell? I think of the dragonflies helicoptering over my ponds, the blazing St John's wort, the children bumping down the farm track on their bikes.

However, Time. My notes look up at me, and in the fierce light are sometimes too bright to read. The cool nave is expectant; for this is its property, to hope for answers. But what is the question? Everyone – myself, the tall columns, the trapped insects, the hymn books – has forgotten.

The Preacher, who has seen it all, done it all, replies as best he can; that is, quite wonderfully. There is a time to make love, and a time not to make love, a time to gather stones, a time to throw them away. He said that, in the multitude of dreams, there are many vanities, and that it is a pleasant thing for the eyes to see the sun.

This beautiful book should be required for Anglican Synods and Vatican Councils – for each one of us. The Preacher had not only done it all, but read it all, and he, exhausted by, shall we say, theology, went in search of the truth or the words given 'by one shepherd'. 'Let us hear the conclusion of the whole matter: Fear God, and keep his commandments, for this is the whole duty of man.'

It is not yet midday when we drive off in glittering cars.

Thomas Hardy

Catching Thomas Hardy's name on the news – something about building opposite Max Gate – returned me to Dorchester. I had been helping to edit the New Wessex Edition of his works, and the kind woman who now lived in the great writer's house invited me to see it. Others, including Virginia Woolf, had seen fit to mock it, but I found it perfect.

Few houses had been so adequately designed to contain a literary spirit. Hardy's brother had built it for him, unearthing Roman graves in the process. *Tess* and all the other great novels drew sightseers to it from the very start; so a barrier of conifers was planted to hide it. Conifers, being what they are, did more than what was required of them, creating a sadness; and Hardy would sometimes stand at the iron gate in the evening, longing for a visitor.

But what particularly enthralled me, as I was taken from polished room to polished room, was the quiet contained time of their clocks. I was taken back to my childhood in Suffolk, where there were old houses without radios, only the tick-tock of a fine clock. No other sound. And, of course, in Hardy's case, and in such a modest dwelling, the chatter and singing of servants. He wrote *The Dynasts* to their merriment as they played ring-board below.

Bottengoms Farm is lucky to hear church bells, and fortunate to exist beyond traffic. The great heat has revved up the dawn chorus. With the windows wide at five in the morning, I listen to a full orchestra. Then, suddenly, it stops. There is silence except for the ticking of a clock, measured: a many-wheeled heartbeat to tell that the ancient interior still breathes. Now and then an old beam catches its breath, and there is a sharp retort. A momentarily trapped bird beats against the glass; a butterfly wanders on a wall.

Giving my annual lecture to the John Clare Society, I tell my favourite time chestnut. Dumas rushes from his study to cry, 'I have finished *The Three Musketeers*!'

'But dinner won't be ready for another hour,' his wife says.

So he goes back in and starts *The Black Tulip*.

But, as the Preacher says, there is a time for everything. How I love it when he tells me that 'a dream cometh through a multitude of business'. The heatwave will have them nodding in the City, and wilting in white shirts. The Wren churches will be cool, the Thames on the boil. The cars will be burning; the pigeons will seek fountains. My aspens, like Hardy's firs, present a forest to the sun. And a whispering concerto to me.

I lie below them, putting on a show of 'business', but dreaming away. I have to preach to the Readers at the Cathedral, but not until Saturday; and to the parish, but not until Sunday. For every service there is a season.

The white cat stirs in the cool grass. For every noon, there is Whiskas. For every late July, there is Jonathan to cut the track, to fell the tall grasses and thistles, and to slice off the rise between the ruts. In July, I ceaselessly let myself out, as it were.

Not that, like Hardy, I fenced myself in, for I have done little or no planting. My growth simply comes up of its own accord, and to its own luxurious timing. Every summer without fail for centuries, creating luxuriance, idleness, and this heavy silence. What business has work at such a moment? But I must prop the tomatoes up. I have to make what Solomon called a dinner of herbs.

Empire Christians

Trinity Five gone, and the July sun maintains its precedence. The windows are wide all night, and the old roses begin to fall. Rosa Mundi, York and Lancaster, and the species which have left my head are adrift. This is the week I fix the water. It is done for one more year. The springs will find their way to the tanks in the roof, and to kettles and baths, plus some expert help from the pump man. The overflow will go towards the dragonflies of August.

At lunch, a line comes up from Reginald Heber's hymn about the saints casting down their golden crowns around the glassy sea. Later, listening in bed to the summer, I think of him and his fate. And how refreshing a hot week in England would have been to him, compared with Calcutta.

He would rather have written poetry in rural England but, reluctantly accepting Calcutta at the third invitation, this see, being virtually all India, would kill him at the age of 43. We had the sense not to ask our friend why such a line should hang around in her Christian subconscious. Perhaps the glitter of the Stour Valley had further polished it up.

Heber had breakfast with Sir Walter Scott at Oxford. 'From Greenland's icy mountains', which we no longer sing, although Heber changed 'savage' to 'heathen', was written for a series of services for the Propagation of the Gospel in Wrexham Church in 1919, when his father-in-law commanded: 'Write something for them to sing in the evening.' Four years later, the youthful bishop was on his way to coral strands.

In his *Journal of a Voyage to India* he wrote: 'Though we were now too far off Ceylon to catch the odours of the land, yet it is, we are assured, perfectly true that such odours are perceptible to a very considerable distance. In the Straits of Malacca a smell like that of a hawthorn hedge is commonly experienced; and from Ceylon, at thirty or forty miles, under certain circumstances, a yet more agreeable scent is inhaled.' Almost a century later, E. M. Forster's wise Mrs Moore would smell trouble as her P&O liner reached the Raj.

India's faiths and Britain's faith would run into confusion. Though not so in Forster's autobiographical *The Hill of Devi*. I think he would have survived Heber's impossible task with a shaking of the head, yet we found him holy, holy. A completely brave young man in his struggle to overturn another holiness while dreaming of hawthorn hedges.

I remember my mother worshipping missionaries. Or shall we say giving them great honour. Some were her friends, and their return 'on furlough' for three months every three years was a thrilling time for her. The mission field was, to her, fertile ground, cultivated in some small way with her prayers, the collecting box, and her untroubled conviction that there were the heathen and there was us.

Her saint was Sister Joan, who ran a girls' mission school in Ceylon. I never saw this truly wonderful woman, but I don't doubt her goodness, her holy holiness. Her English scholarship and practicality. And the heat! More than that which makes the ancient farmhouse creak at this moment. More than for a week. Roll on the furlough!

Animal Matins

Twelve dogs, slumberous in the July heat, lie where the monks dug their patch. The dogs note each other's presence with heavy-lidded glances, and silver chains glitter from the soft folds of their throats. Two pretty goats, three fearful rabbits and four beetles also attend. No cats. It is the Blessing of Animals. The new electric piano has been lugged from the vestry and umbilically connected with the Priory mains. The piano is what is known as fast, sounding a note before Meriel's finger reports contact. The first hymn is 'Autumn days are here again', or something similar, and although I suggest that summer will fit, autumn is sung. It is the authority of the printed word. A small boy reads sonorously from *The Prelude* and I read Walt Whitman's 'I think I could turn and live with animals ... They do not make me sick discussing their duty to God ... Not one is demented with the mania of owning things.' Powerful stuff. The sky is a picture and the air is heavily scented with lime flowers. The metal stacking chairs become burning thrones. A little girl climbs a bank to conduct our petitions, after which I make a stately progress towards the animal kingdom where the dogs lie like mantelpiece dogs, one this way, one that. The goats startle, the rabbits hide, the beetles are gingerly revealed huddling together in their ring box. Pets – a Scottish term for any creature which is kept as a favourite and treated with fondness. I say the animal prayers which I have made up and there is much birdsong. Then coffee and Nice biscuits. Then the carrying of everything back to the church with 'Mind the grave.' This grave is artfully sited just where it can best bring one down, especially if one happens to be burdened with an electric piano. Strangers look surprised when we cry, 'Mind the grave!' Who doesn't? The animals return to their oven-cars and are transported away. Max lay panting in the orchard shade when I returned. Huge green-gold gaze, minimal purr. Who has he eaten this morning? Better not ask. 'I stand and look at him long and long', as Whitman said, and he goes to sleep.

A letter to the bereaved is one thing, a letter to the dying quite another. It would be far simpler if the dying had been more considerate and told one that they were ill. 'Oh, no, I am dying.' The voice on the telephone sounds lively enough, even if it has quite suddenly become a no-answer phone. I rack my brains as to what to say and the friend asks, 'Are you still there?' It is he who sounds anxious now. Yes, I am still here and most likely to be for years. I then listen to his treatment. It sounds awful. 'Not a bit.' His voice alters and is filled with concern for me. I would have told him about my strange sense of 'continuing' but he is on to the weather and 'Have you read?' and 'Did you see?' and 'What have you been up to?' The dying are so anxious not to worry us.

High Summer

Considering that the majority of churchyards are witness to 1,000 years of tears, it is strange that they are so pleasant to visit, to wander in, to sit in on a summer's day. 'Peaceful', the visitors book says over and over again. Peaceful inside and out. 'Do you remember when we threw a tablecloth over that table-tomb and had lunch?' I remind the lady doing the altar flowers.

The sky between the horse chestnuts is enamelled blue. Opaque. Unseen birds call. Mown or unmown, the English churchyards are green and lively. Georgian gravestones totter, Victorian memorials soar, today's slivers of slate don't know what to say. Albert 'Bert' in brackets. Rarely a biblical word.

I see them still coming up the path, the old ringers, the previous congregations. 'So you've mended the wall!' It loomed out into the lane, and had done so for donkey's years. 'It's the dead having a stretch.' An undefeated spring runs below it, freezing in the winter; so that we slip and slide to our cars.

But not now. It is high summer, the heat fanned by soft winds. Early Trinity, and we are to be clothed with humility. And then comes the scary bit from St Peter, 'because your adversary, the devil, as a roaring lion, walketh about seeking whom he may devour . . .' But the bees swimming in my balsam remind me of the poor dead lion on the treacle tin whose gaping carcass has turned into a honey-pot.

Neighbours move away. We say goodbye in the hospitable house. Already there are gaps where familiar things had stood. 'Oh, but we will often be back — you'll see.' But they won't. Their time with us has ended. They walk round the big room, taking photographs. But the marks on the walls where the pictures have been say everything.

I talk to a gentle, ill man, coming closer to hear his whispering words. Yet there is happiness rather than sadness. A kind of acceptance for things as they are. St Peter, whose week it is, asks God to make us perfect, and to 'stablish, strengthen, and settle us'. But it is unsettling when old friends move away. I mean, where will we go for Christmas-morning drinks? Have they thought of that?

Some have gone to Scotland, and there will be postcards from the white house above the loch to prove it. I see them opening the deer-gates to let the car through, and me waking up in the rare Highland air, and then driving to Ben Lyon.

Perhaps the young shepherd will bring his flock down from the hill, or the Edinburgh minister will be doing holiday duty at the kirk. The shelves of Scottish history will certainly be toppling in the drawing-room. Half a mile from the house, they will encounter Queen Victoria and Mr Brown having a picnic.

Perthshire amazes me — its scent, its indifference to human needs, its vast parishes, its blue ranges which should not have been clothed with pine forests, its stern nobility. Will the pine marten run along the wall? For we all like to think that the places which have become ours for a week or two possess a perpetuity for us alone.

The white cat has never been to the top of the track. 'Tell me what it is like up there.' Dangerous: bends, haywains with bales, sabbath cyclists, congregations going home, dogs getting lost. She has made her summer bed in the vast stone sink which once stood in the farm kitchen. There she sleeps her nine lives away.

Garrow at the Font

We baptise Garrow, that is Michael makes a watery cross on his brow and I read him a poem. The christening is wildly unpunctual due to there being Irish guests, including a Godfather who plays a tune on the flute. No, it is a tin whistle, and wildly musical it is. The church is cool and the churchyard is baking.

Garrow is a year old and sports a rosary. He lolls on Michael's arm like a Florentine Christ-child, serene, forgiving, turning his full gaze on us as we applaud the tin-whistler. An uncle passes him to me to hold. I am astonished, having no idea that Christ-childs weigh a ton, well a stone. He stares past me, looks past all of us to see what only babies see. We all drift outside to talk among the graves, and Garrow passes from strong man to strong man, bringing them a mite of his holiness in turn. Over the churchyard hedge the lane rustles where the graves stop.

Back home the farmhouse is locked into its four hundredth July or thereabouts according to those who list such buildings. Its inhabitants came and went. 'Every exit is an entrance somewhere', says Tom Stoppard. Trapped butterflies are shown the door via a glass and postcard. Having to work on a short story, I get the lawnmower out, a mechanical job being the best jolt to the imagination. Garrow has gone home to cake and wine. Traherne is the singer of Infancy, a favourite word and state of his. 'He in our Childhood with us walks, And with our Thoughts Mysteriously He Talks.'

Before the Coming of the Trees

I am in seigneurial mood, having just been made patron of what will eventually be one of the largest new woods in Britain by the Woodland Trust. Alas, I will have long been with God before its trees could cast their shade on me. Or on the five hundred acres of Essex farmland which it will cover. Richard Mabey, Roger Deakin and myself walk the wide-open site in the July sun, following dusty tracks between the last potatoes, the last rape. Over three hundred thousand trees, tonnes of wild flower seeds, new grass, old birds, all are on the way. We have lunch at the Thatchers' pub, sitting outside in the suddenly not quite warm enough afternoon, taking in the great view, a cool breeze fanning our fish and chips, and mull over maps. The new forest-village, Fordham, is at this moment a mixture of ancient Saxon settlement, Tudor farms, Poundbury commuters and lovely sweeps of Colne Valley meadows. Soon, i.e. half a century, it will once more be what it was, a forest community.

We wander through the already emerging wetlands to the river itself, where I promptly trip over a wire and fall flat at the brink. An extraordinary sensation, to fall and then go on falling. And to bury one's nose in a river bank. And to be heaved up and dusted down and to say that one is all right when one is not at all all right. And people go on talking about trees, but not how they fall, either in parts or altogether, one great plant simply coming down to earth. I surreptitiously examine my ribs and touch my nose, wobbling it about to see if it crunches, and wipe off a bit of mud. 'Are you all right?' asks Richard. 'Are you all right?' enquires Roger. They don't really care. They are saying, 'We hope that you aren't wanting to be taken home.' Victorian soldiers said, 'It is only a scratch, sir', to their colonels, before falling dead with a sabre cut. Then as fast as it took me to fall I am perfectly well again and we all three banish the horrid business from our minds. It will come back to me in bed, the dismissed ache, the nearly busted bone. But to get on.

The Colne is golden brown and studded with water lilies, and less than three yards across. And yet a dozen miles downsteam it is a tidal river which brought the Roman galleons up to Colchester. But here, marking the boundary of the forest to be, it is a stream waiting for Millais' Ophelia to spread herself in it. A blackcap sings in the medieval wood up the hill – Fiddler's Wood. Was there a Mr Fiddler? Or did the Fordham wives send their musician husbands to it to practice? Or did the fiddlers choose it for its nightingales, which like a bit of noise? Retracing our steps, we enter the ancient barn which has hoarded the hard-won crops from the forest clearings which we are about to plant with oak and ash. How dumbfounded the farmers would have been to know that one day the trees would be back, not stealthily in the form of suckers and natural seedlings, but with full ecological legitimacy. Nothing furtive. The corn barn is immense, still and weather-boarded, with seven bays. It is completely empty and the afternoon sun glitters through the knotholes and slats, turning the black walls into a kind of interior midnight with stars. There are chalk marks and scratchings where the last loads were totted up after the last harvest. Like so many East Anglian barns, it looks flimsy. Its doors are crumbling biscuits, its rafters are sticks. Yet it is woodland architecture at its most durable and will stand nobly in the new wood when it grows, maybe for five more centuries. All Saints Church stands companionably by, and Roger notes that the holiness of both buildings is enjoined. We may be living at a time when little is sacred but barns such as this speak of a time when everything was sacred. The latter was the time when patrons fell left, right and centre – if they didn't look out.

St Swithun

Mr Chaplin clangs two medieval bells. *Sancte Necolae Ora Pro Nobis* takes turns with *Sit Nomen Domini Benedictum*, a courtesy observed since 1460. It is all the bell-music there has ever been at Mount Bures. Mr Chaplin is eighty-five and without a white hair, and he has succeeded Jim who departed at eighty, which is no age at all. I wait unseen in the vestry until the ancient noise ceases and then, allowing a minute for Mr Chaplin to find his pew, descend steeply into the cool church. It smells of baked churchyard and has trapped within it some of the blue of the harebells which, in July, form a kind of cloudless sky at foot level. The heatwave devours the hilltop even at this hour of the morning and we can hear the drone of a barley-cutter. There are a dozen of us to be moved by scripture in this particular sundry place, and moved we are because Andrew has to read the Song of

Deborah and Barak, a terrible ballad all about a woman tricking a hunted captain into what he believes is a safe haven and then driving a tent-peg through his temple as he sleeps, nailing his head to her floor. Andrew does not stumble at this but approaches names such as 'Issachar' and 'Naphtali' warily. Jim used to plough through such verbal obstructions head-on, sending syllables flying in all directions. Surely the elderly women in their summery frocks are going to faint when Jael picks up 'the workman's hammer', but no. Andrew's ghastly words float over them because they have been seized by reverie and have been struck senseless by sunshine. Liturgy is playing its pranks in their devout heads and spinning holy daydreams around them. I try to take my mind off the tent-peg by concentrating on the kaleidoscopic colours which the east window casts upon a wall-tablet to children who perished during some Georgian epidemic. I hear Andrew conclude: 'And the land had rest forty years.' So maybe Deborah had something to sing about.

During the intercessions I read George Appleton's fine prayer for 'the casualties of history'. I can hear the UN troops digging-in above Sarajevo as I say it and human beings being turned out into meadows, and the everlasting racket of war. 'O God, my mind and spirit fail in the thought of all the casualties of history ... If thou art not a God of mercy, redemption and love, my pain is incurable. But I am comforted in the thought that the creature cannot rise higher than his Creator ...' The formularies of worship and of violence, how we hold to them. 'And the land had rest forty years' – what is that? We are not displeased to find it hotter than ever outside. Those who dwell in an equitable climate like its deviations to be extreme.

Captain Cardy Ploughing

What with weather, what with machinery, farmland soon becomes out of knowledge. I have two acres and all the other acres grow around me. The contours stay mainly unchanged yet at the same time mysterious. There is a slight amphitheatre-like rise above Lower Bottoms and what must have been a Slough of Despond in the Top Field for many a plough. The old Horseman (East Anglian for ploughman) tells me how it was when he drew his first furrow, setting it against a holly bush in the distant hedge. Hedgers never levelled a holly and I see them round the village still, many of them tall trees. 'It would have been about February', said the Horseman. And I see the Horseman as a slight youthful figure hip-hopping along behind his Punches, the plough tipping and reeling, its share striking sparks from the everlasting flints.

In the late nineteenth century, during that nadir of English agriculture, with even the horsemen, the princes of the fields, broken and half beaten, Henry Rider Haggard, who farmed in the Waveney Valley, watched the February ploughing with humility, familiar as he was with it. As with our present summer, it rained and rained although with less eventual ruination of rural life. He had spent his twenties in South Africa filling his head with the tales which would become *King Solomon's Mines* and *She* (who must be obeyed). Then it was back to Norfolk and this shocking sight of white men in the mud. His men, his demanding fields. It was 1898 when farmworkers, even the noble horsemen, were all lumped together in the popular mind as labourers, skill-less creatures whose duty it was to simply toil. While Haggard was shocked by their servitude, he began to see their art, for their work was nothing less. He wanted to destroy the huge social barriers which cut him off from his men but it was not only impossible but unthinkable. In an Egyptian pyramid he had seen a beautiful fresco of a king and his harvesters all rejoicing in a field together, the corn shining in their arms. If only Norfolk could be like this! If only his labourers would speak to him! He could afford to pay them twice their wage but it would put Norfolk's economy out, of course. So he told the world how they work, with what brilliance, with what strength.

'Ploughing is one of those things that look a great deal easier than they are, like the writing of romances. The observer, standing at a gate to watch a man with a pair of horses strolling up and down a hill for hours on end ... is apt to conclude that beyond the physical endurance involved the difficulties are small. Let him take the pair of horses, however, and plough for, say, forty minutes, and he will come away with a greatly increased respect for the ploughman.'

As boys we watched Captain Cardy's plough surge to the headland like a tall clomping horse-wave, wheel and flood back. He had fought on the Western Front and I always imagined to myself the jingling of the horse-brasses with the jingling of his medals. He did not call out to us. The irony was that when all the young men fled the collapsing farms for the glory of soldiering they were set to digging trenches, vast ditches made with spades by regimented labourers. The Horsemen rode. Nobody dared beat their bayonets into ploughshares. Everyone dreamed of their own church bells and forgot their own ditches and bush-draining. From no-man's-land they dreamed of someone's-land. When I went to see Passchendaele some years ago, it was drizzling but the mud was unlike the mud here. It was silvery in the trodden grass.

Henslow's Outing

Stephen and I are having one of our Suffolk meanderings when all at once a signpost waves to us. Hitcham, it says, come to where one of the mightiest of all village outings took place. The rain-filled skies are low and propped up by oaks and church towers, and the windscreen wipers click fretfully. But here, and all unplanned for, lies Hitcham. And here in my memory are dull Sundays in Cambridge marvellously enlightened the moment I open the gate of the Botanic Garden with the Sunday Key which has been loaned to me by my friend Denis Garrett the celebrated mycologist. Once created, the question arose whether it would be breaking the sabbath to visit it on a Sunday, and this key was given to people who could be trusted to do this without enjoyment.

But we are about to visit the parish of the wonderful John Stevens Henslow who practically single-handed removed a small physic garden in the middle of Cambridge to some forty acres of farmland along Trumpington Road and thus formed one of the world's finest botanic centres. He arrived at Hitcham in 1837 to discover a wretched village of warring farmers and child labour, and left it with a good school, allotments, cricket and athletic clubs and a history of railway excursions, the great one being that of Thursday 27 July 1854 when he took no fewer than 287 Hitchamites to Cambridge to see his Botanic Garden. He gave each one of them an eleven-page booklet which he had written and illustrated – he was a splendid botanical artist – and they all arrived at Cambridge Station at 9.20 a.m. They walked the Garden, had dinner at Downing College at 2 p.m. and in effect, due to their formidable and scholarly rector, had their lives changed.

As did an undergraduate named Charles Darwin. Henslow was only thirteen years Darwin's senior. Together they laid the foundations of the neglected science of botany and natural history as they explored the Fens, the college gardens and in the vacations further afield. When Henslow was asked to recommend a naturalist for a ship called the *Beagle*, he commended Charles Darwin. Unknown to both of them, the voyage of the *Beagle* would shake Christianity to its foundations. On Henslow's memorial in Hitcham church, by way of the usual flourish, we are required to look up Job 29. Which Stephen and I did in what we thought must have been John Henslow's own lectern Bible. It is the passage in which Job recalls his own honourable conduct: 'I delivered the poor ... and him that had none to help him ... I caused the widow's heart to sing for joy ... I was eyes to the blind, and feet was I to the lame ...' And no country clergyman could have done more for all his parishioners than this brilliant botanist. It took him out of Cambridge of course, and there were moanings at this. He died aged sixty-five and lies in the churchyard there in Hitcham, and under the nearly bursting rain clouds, a hero of mine.

In his *Autobiography* (1873), Darwin wrote of his old friend, 'His judgment was excellent and his whole mind well-balanced, but I do not suppose that anyone would say that he possessed much original genius.' But as a recent Director of the Cambridge Botanic Garden rightly observed, 'Without Henslows there are no Darwins.' Some time ago, recalling the Hitcham excursion, I took a dozen or so of our parishioners to walk in the lovely intellectual Garden, and must do so again.

Woodland Trust

Liz, the Regional Development Officer from the Woodland Trust, arrives and off we go to walk again the farm which will be a forest. The heatwave is blown blissfully around us by one of those southern winds which make heatwaves blissful. Pippen field, Silk Cobs, Ramson Pits, Muttone Meadow, Slatenways, all will soon disappear, along with many other fields and become Wrens' Wood. Wrens because the donor was in the WRNS. We lean on the new bridge over the Colne and watch sticklebacks and sand-dace darting across our reflected faces. The weed is the kind in which Thomas Hardy's victims drowned, their hair dragging in the current. We can just about make out Colchester on its far hill, the sunbaked buildings from this distance might be in

Eritrea. The Fordham acres are saying, 'What are you going to do with us?' So do some of the Fordham folk. Forests are not all trees we tell them. You will be able to see out. Already, left to their own devices, the only recently ploughed fields by the river are becoming marshland. Mace-reed is advancing across a once sugar beet field like a pike regiment.

'Swithun' comes and goes with not a drip of rain. In church I tell them about John Keble, who nudges St Swithun in the Lectionary. There they are, side by side, the Saxon rainmaker and the modest author of 'New every morning', which we sing commemoratively. The hymn echoes school assembly before we settled down to the common task of maths. Keble College, Oxford is the patron of Mount Bures, our, I like to think without any evidence, especially sacred little church which Keble would have fitted into. The locals like people to fit in. When newcomers arrive they are supposed to fit in. But now the parishes are full of people who don't make the least effort to fit in and who don't know what fitting in means. It is all very awkward, not to say bad mannered. And then there are those who are too odd to fit in but don't know it, which is a blessing. They are held up as examples of local tolerance, even sophistication. 'It wouldn't do for us all to be alike,' they say, bending understanding to the limit. Writers and artists are not supposed to even try to fit in, and are best when outside in some kind of celebrity. John Keble accomplished two things, one of them sensational, the other as quiet as could be, the Assize Sermon at Oxford which fired-off the Tractarians, and a book of gentle meditations entitled *The Christian Year*. A small shy priest, he did not like Swithun have a struggle avoiding preferment, because only one came his way – the Archdeaconry of Barbados, which shows how daft the Church of England can be when it tries. So he remained in his parish and wrote a handful of lasting hymns.

Untwining bindweed, I suddenly think how unpleasant it must be to be prayed for by the self-righteous. Though enough of this.

Irritants are a concomitant of religion. Perhaps my presence in the big field irritates the skylark, and is thus the source of its song. My irritation is sudden and then gone. Should I sting, I am metaphorically rubbing a dock leaf on the source of my irritability before he has had time to close a surprised mouth. All is forgiven before he has worked out what to forgive.

On the Way to School

Nervously filling in the time before seeing the dentist, I rewalk the way I went to school in the Suffolk country town. So much having changed, I imagined I would pass sites and developments, the usual thing. But there they still were, the cottages-turned-sweetshops, the modest terraces, the cuts and alleys, the pubs on the corners, the monkey-puzzle trees, the letter-boxes with V.R., the doorways, the coping stones where we sat and swung our legs. I could hear, though this time in my head, the clang of the shop bells on the C-springs which brought Miss Scott, haunted, silent, unwelcoming to serve us boiled sweets, or Mrs Gilder, a floury Juno, to hand us doughnuts. Miss Scott carried the exactitude of weights and measures to the limit and would, they said, have halved a toffee. Mrs Gilder knew nothing about weights and measures but everything there was to know about hungry children and sent us off with more than we durst expect or could have paid for. Both ladies in their neighbouring shops emerged from inmost shrines in their premises, the curtained rooms which Thomas Hardy described as 'penetralia'. How enormous they seemed as they leaned towards us over the tiny counters, huge Alices bearing down on their child customers, Miss Scott without a word, Mrs Gilder with her 'dears'. She had two floury sons and a kind heart, and is without a doubt in paradise.

And there is where the blacksmith's should have been but a new road has pushed it over, and there is the patty-man's shop, so small, however did he get into it. He had a double life as potato-cake seller and town crier. The handsome Suffolk white-brick terrace where the sweep lived, and the Miss Willises, 'Dressmakers' on a swinging card, did their expert business, has come up in the world, and would not be below the consideration of the local commuters. The Miss Willises were identical twins who wore seasonal weights of the same clothes, tweed in winter, silk and serge in summer, black woollen stockings and strap shoes. A single bow or raised hand did for the pair of them. They grew pansies and ferns and went to evensong, and would measure you up as soon as look at you. At home they wore pin and needle necklaces and knew the size of every woman for miles. Silent now their Singer, vanished their twinned decorum. The pity would be, they said, that one must outlast the other. But not for long. If a school cap was raised to them there would be a double Mona Lisa smile, fleeting, transforming. Not so Miss Baker at Pont's Palings – the artist Dupont, Gainsborough's handsome nephew, had lived there – she would croquet conkers at us through the iron rails with unbending skill but never a smile. For her the lovely horse chest-nut which dominated her street garden was an annual penance demanded of her by God. She shrank from boys and wondered why they had been made and turned her face from us as she batted us conkers. 'I hope you were polite to Miss Baker', our mothers would say. What else could we be? There was a time when every country town was an armistice of old women and cautious lads, with neither side caring to come too close.

The dentist is pleased with me and praises my brushwork, and I am grateful to him, for he has in the past worked mighty things for me, giving me, as he said, a good smile. We talk of his Scottish home. Then I continue my home-town tour by walking to the river, from which fifty or more swans have landed to sit on the Croft, waving their necks and fixing humanity with swivelling eyes. By the church wall, very upright, sits a Saxon bishop who died here in AD791. He is worn and lean. A mitre topples on his brow as he tugs a warm cloak around his slight frame. Just behind him in St Gregory's vestry, ghastly in its niche, is the decapitated head of Archbishop Simon Sudbury, murdered during the Peasants' Revolt. The Stour slides under the bridge, green, blue and glassy. And there we are, or were, ages ago, with our white feet in the water as we gorged on Mrs Gilder's buns.

Back to Wormingford. I have to choose ten pieces of music for Michael Berkeley's Radio 3 programme *Private Passions*. No easy matter. Some Bach, some Schubert, some Britten, a great hymn sung by a cathedral choir, some Belle Epoque songs, Butterworth, Couperin . . . John Wilbye . . . Ella Fitzgerald . . . my friend Peter-Paul Nash? Books and CDs pile up. The trouble is that I will have to enthusiastically justify these choices when I meet Michael. There is music which one can remember hearing for the very first time and there is music which seems to have got into one's head prior to memory itself. The music of the spheres, maybe. Totting-up my choice, it adds to twenty, so who to throw out? It is agonising. This is where the private passion comes in. Hildegard von Bingen's passion only for Christ fills the kitchen. *O ignis Spiritus Paracliti*, sing the Benedictine ladies, their voices winding like white swans' throats. 'The structure of Vespers is used in a plausible context' reads the label. In bed I listen to the stream splashing and the valley owls calling as they low-fly where the mice run for their lives.

The Summer Ploughman

Drenching days. Even when the rain stops the wind shakes torrents from the trees. Soaked animals are extra friendly so that they can share their sopping coats with me. Tall plants cannot hold up and the new ploughing shines with water. Having so often deplored farming inertia I am now suddenly quite excited by the ploughing of a field in July. It is the set-aside field which used to be Hilly Holt Land, Shoals, Ten Acres, Three Acres, Two Acres and so on to the hedge of Garnon's Chase. A vast multi-shared plough is lumbering up and down it and chopped hay is being folded into it like some pale addition to a rich dark mousse. It is real spectator stuff and the ploughman waves to his audience. But he must think me a lunatic to watch so.

At Diane's we eat bread and blackcurrant jam and watch about a dozen chaffinches flashing about in her briar roses. Then we are off to Bures to open the Carnival. I sit beside Colonel Probert in his 1928 Rolls and he drives it very slowly behind the boy band. 'The trouble is, it will boil if we go too slow.' I am now a grand version of the ploughman, cabbed and waving to familiar specta-tors. Over the bridge we go, from Essex to Suffolk in slow seconds. A mile away, the new bridge is for walkers only. Some young men are dancing on top of the church tower, and bunting is drying out. I make a speech in the Playing Field then do what openers have to do, become a big spender. I buy a Jubilee mug and Sylvia Townsend Warner's life of T. H. White for a pound, a jar of pick-led cabbage and a flutter of raffle tickets. Children shriek on the bouncy castle and a hopeful author nobbles me with his manuscript.

On Sunday a note left in the vestry by the vicar says, 'Bring large coloured umbrellas next Sunday as he intends to talk about St Swithun at the family service.' I preach on St Paul's inward voice telling him, 'First Jerusalem then Rome'. I imagine it rain-ing on the sea at Aldeburgh, 'prinking the waves', as Thomas Hardy put it. Paul has been shipwrecked on Malta where it too is being rained on, coming down for all it is worth in fact. The Maltese could not have been more welcoming. They rush around collecting sticks to make a nice fire, the apostle giving a hand. Only three days away lies the Italian coast which, of course, will be in bright sun. And gathering at Puteoli after walking the Appian Way will be the friends from Rome to meet him. 'Quo vadis, Paulus?' Whither indeed.

At Eventide

The conclusion of a Christian day. The still-fierce sun drains the light from the altar candles. They waver, pale and milky. The heavy presence of summer flowers. The giant oaken knight and his successive oaken wives raise imploring stumps. *Ora pro nobis.* The reformers lopped off their praying hands. Some 30 of us sing evensong: 'Lighten our darkness, we beseech thee, O Lord'.

The young priest who has been a prison chaplain all day is in the congregation. I should have said the prayer which asks God to pour upon him 'the continual dew of thy blessing'. But I say the evening prayer with which Robert Louis Stevenson ended the day in Samoa.

'Our guard is relieved, the service of the day is over, and the hour come to rest. We resign into thy hands our sleeping bodies, our cold hearths, and opened doors. Give us to awake with smiles . . . make bright this house of our habitation.'

Most days this week, I have sat outside this house of my habitation, listening to the late birds, pondering the reduction of a wild garden. For, as the Preacher did not say, there is a time for cutting beds and a time for the grassing-in of beds. But what a business it is. The deed is partly done, however, and I have the aches to prove it. Also, it looks surprisingly nice.

Which is why I am sitting where generations of farmers rested in July. Their hay was in, their corn stood high. And they ached and ached and ached, and it was somehow blissful to be seated in the fading light with a blackbird calling. To rest. It was warm, it would soon be dark. Just over the wall, the animals rustled themselves into sleeping positions; just over the hill, the flock faded from sight. It was Abrahamic.

I give myself a little drink, having no idea what a unit is. The white cat looks down from a column. St John's wort blazes away, having, it was said, been given a double dose of the sun. When, as

I usually do, I used a sprig of it to lighten my Baptist sermon, the churchwarden told me that it was a weed, and what a bother it was to dig it out. The saint, said his bereaved cousin, 'Was light – a burning and a shining light.'

Friends telephone, and trust that they are not disturbing me. Once, having to supply an address and gone to the study, I lose the phone itself until I hear it crying from a flowerpot. 'What are you doing?' ask the friends. Nothing. I am seated at the entrance to my tent, waiting for angels to come over the hill.

'What? Are you all right? Did you watch Wimbledon?' How can one say on the phone that one is praying? It is so unreasonable. Or that one is wonderfully worn-out with gardening. George Herbert was wonderfully worn-out with music and words and God and just being alive, and with singing his evening window-hymn, because so much had to be compressed into so few years. Ditto Robert Louis Stevenson.

Theirs was the same fate, the consumption. The sickness which consumed you. Not long to sit by the door watching the sun sink into the glorious west. Yet long enough to achieve immortality.

On the radio, a woman who is almost 100 years old worries about her future and her possessions.

Village School

Our village school is about to shut its doors after 170 years. It is a strange event. Thirteen children. Glowing OFSTEDs. Glorious scenery. Reluctant parents. Victorian Gothic. I was a governor for ages, and an occasional storyteller. Cars bumped their way to it over the sleeping policemen. Head teachers came and went. Lovely new classrooms were built on a meadow. Now, silence and stillness, for ever and ever.

I am reminded of Laurie Lee's wild farewell to his village school in Gloucestershire, as he walked away with his fiddle and his future. Our school had its crowded past, but no tomorrow. Somebody will live in it and hear, if they are quiet, the farmworkers' boys and girls singing the assembly hymn. This would have been a long time ago.

Back once more from the John Clare Festival at Helpston. Our Society has outgrown the school named after him, and has to fill a marquee. Rows and rows of familiar faces. The village has wide Enclosure roads and handsome Barnack-stone houses, toppling hollyhocks, and bird-filled skies. As always, I see the poet running over the fields to Glinton, to be taught to read and write for a penny a week, and to do his arithmetic in the dust of the threshing barn, and to lie hidden with a book in a deserted quarry.

What a good education he got, one that was perfect for our greatest rural voice. Clare, too, had a violin. The Gypsies showed him how to play it. We had lunch in the Blue Bell, where he would be found with his beer and his finds – wild flowers. They would straggle from his velvet pockets. Have you read John Clare? If not, do so at once. His life was bitter-sweet with a vengeance. Poor Clare. Great Clare.

Visitors bump down my farm track, where there are no sleeping policemen: only ruts and rabbit holes, loppity verges, rises and brief levels. But there are baby owls and white throats, cascades of July bindweed hanging from the sloes, where the parched wheat has recovered from a dry season.

Having mown all the grass, I sit outside, reading that curious book *The Cloud of Unknowing*, which I take to every now and then in order to feed my uncertainties. Its author, Richard Rolle, died in 1395, and, as he contemplates God in his short lifetime, he – as his editor, the wonderful Clifton Wolters, reminds us – explains what contemplation is.

That 'it is not the pleasant reaction to a celestial sunset, nor is it the perpetual twitter of heavenly birdsong. It is not even an emotion. It is the awareness of God, known and loved at the core of one's being. In this awareness there may be no overtone of beauty, nor indeed any sort of pleasurable response at all.'

While this may be so, I remain enchanted by Rolle's 'asides'; for, my goodness, how he can write! As I read him, I hear the cathedrals going up, and the faith with them. He knows that few are able to reach such heights, however, either in stone or belief. So he says: 'Not all those who read this book, or hear it read or spoken of, and as a result think it is a good and pleasant thing, are therefore called by God to engage in this work because of the pleasant sensation they get when they read it.'

He is a teacher who does not seek recruits. He certainly enjoyed the Middle Ages.

John Clare with Herdboys and Girls

A clear day. Not empty day. The difference should be, well, clear. Nobody is coming, the diary says. Give yourself a break from the new book, my head says. The skies concur. Venus having wandered across the sun, cloud Alps promise downpours as contrition. Even planets should know their place.

All this rain. The garden grows a foot an hour. I cut bamboo poles for the runner bean wigwam, trim their tops, and arrange them in a circle. Bamboo is a kind of grass. A huge stand of it gives monumental importance to a little lawn. The July birds sing their heads off. They, too, celebrate a clear day.

What did John Clare do on a clear day? Slip from sight of his nosey neighbours, for one thing. Steal away to the open-cast quarry down the road, where no one in his right mind would want to go, there to lie flat and let his imagination do all the work. Out of sight, out of mind. Why were they all so interested in him?

The father of an Ipswich Town footballer told me how his son could not go out because of the staring. His boy would have to drive to some foreign city, like Norwich, if he wanted to avoid all those eyes. Touches, even.

John Clare walked away to the wilds to converse 'with shepherds and herdboys', to learn the fiddle from Gypsies, and to find a clear day. William Hazlitt, when he was a boy, heard them calling from the Manse, but laid low in the long grass, not answering. There was reading to be done. I did this when I was twelve, feeling wicked.

The rain-growth of the past few days reminds me of all this, the shelter, the English countryside out of control, the kitchen garden pleading to be sticked, the grey puddles, the clouds sailing over their surface. A nervous green woodpecker has just stopped its dipping flight to rest for seconds, a yard from the window. Hares are about, they say.

'When are you going to get Jonathan to cut the sides of your track?' they say. 'When it stops,' I say. The rain. Every now and then it drops like a curtain on the scene. The white cat trots in like a walking dishcloth to dry herself on my jersey. It is murky for a clear day. But soft, I'll give it that. And sweetly scented, like Shakespeare's bank. Church-tower flints look like crown jewels from so much wet polishing, and last week's bunting like sad rags.

It was on such a day as this that the youthful John Clare went out hoping to see some girls' legs. But they had lengthened their skirts to hide their muddy stockings. Such is life. He noted 'signs of the weather in animals'.

Cats eat grass and their eyes lose their brightness. Swallows gather in company. Quails make more chirpings. Fowls go to roost more early. Dogs turn sick. Frogs turn black, and gather round their homes. Horses play around the yard. Hogs champ . . . cattle toss molehills. Animals sport and play before a storm. Cows bellow.

And poets who see that it is far too wet to work in the fields cry hurrah! Now for a dry spot in the Hills and Holes, the abandoned quarry, where one can read and write, dream and fade from sight.

Summer Cleaning – and Vikram Seth

A home and away week. Without thought and minus planning I turn out the larder. It is one of those rambling rooms tacked on to the farmhouse proper in the eighteenth century. It is also temptingly accommodating so that eventually it will contain a great many un-larderish items whose mouldy breath brings a whiff of mortality to the true inhabitants of this space, jams, wines, strings of onions and a nice bit of cheese. Thus, with the combine harvester passing and re-passing the north window, I bravely lift the lids of ancient preserves, amass old tins which will never see the oven again and, eventually, scrub the dipping brick floor with spring water – the kind which people so strangely glug from bottles on trains. It is late July. The combine trundles into view every few minutes in a haze of wheat dust. It puts on airs, pretending to be a cornucopia, the grain shooting out with cries of Plenty. It leaves blond streaks across the landscape as it appears and disappears between my toppling willows. A delicious new scent, one I haven't sniffed for years, fills the larder, the smell of scrubbed boards and bricks. As for the hot summer's day, it has passed, as has the harvesting man for the last time. I take my decidedly unwashed self to the edge of the field to gaze forth in weariness, having carted all the junk which a larder should not shelter to a shed, where it can go on mouldering with impunity. A startled green woodpecker gives a loud ringing 'laugh' as it zooms from its cover and undulates into the open. 'What a fuss,' says the white cat. This week's bed is an old stone sink lined with stonecrop.

Away to Salisbury. Only the green woodpecker's flight is faster. The Waterloo train is air conditioned and blissful. Basingstoke,

Whitchurch, more mown fields, great heat the other side of the glass, then the start of the chalk cuts, then the glimpse of the cathedral spire. I walk to Sarum College, make sure that my notes and readings are the right ones, then stroll across the languid grass to the West Door. What Mrs Proudie would have said one would not like to imagine. The lazing populace, the supine blokes, the abandoned ladies, the tentative lovers, the toppled children, the dogs doing what they liked, the correct describer of this sun-filled scene would not of course have been Trollope but Traherne, the poet of Christian delight, the master of enjoyment, the commender of summer sloth. But also the insister of intellectual awareness. 'To think well is to serve God in the Interior Court.'

Wandering through the cathedral I think of John Constable painting it and George Herbert singing in it. I hear the stops and starts of choir practice. I gape at the amazing, unbelievable vaulting, I peer at Magna Carta, the thirteenth-century thickly written piece of A4 vellum in its glass case, then take a seat. I allow architecture to exclude the sun. A young tourist asks me about cadavers and I explain. As I am so shalt thou be. He and I – so clearly everlasting? The choir continues its broken psalm. 'Try again, "With long life will I *satisfy* him" – once more.'

After the reading in Sarum College Vikram Seth and Judy Rees carry me off to Bemerton. We cross Herbert's garden and walk rather perilously – it is getting dark – over the unrailed bridge which spans the Nadder. The air is heavy with meadowsweet. We come to a second, safer bridge and pause, breathing in the night-time. I can hear nesting birds talking to each other. Vikram talks about the pike which lurk in the black water. He himself is full of light. Indoors he reads to us from Izaak Walton.

The Barley Harvest

Late July, the time of tall flowers, convolvulus tangles, strong southerlies and first harvests. People say, 'They are cutting at Langham' – or wherever. Combines, whose active life is on a par with that of the dragonfly, are being lured from their huge sheds. They put me in mind of May Days in Padstow when the ''Oss' would be tempted from its hiding-place to sway and dance through the ecstatic town. The 'Oss's coming to life, albeit for just a day, brings tears to Cornish eyes. Where the combine is concerned, it would be its failure to start or cut which would make the farmer weep. It groans its way into the barley leaving not so much as an ear for Ruth, whilst Boaz sways aloft. Translating such harvests into festivals is no easy task. Some unmasticated barley stalks are rescued for decorating the church. Strolling through the undoubtedly bounteous fields, the parched cereal scratches my legs and hands as it did when I was a boy, and there is the same revelling in the dip and sway of ripened landscape as the wind passes over it. At night I can hear the heart-stoppingly wild cries of foxes. I rescue a bat from Max, who can't think what to do with it, having caught it, and is bewildered by its very existence. I place the bat on a ledge of the tumbledown granary, where it palpitates like a scrap of velvet caught in a draught. I can see what the cat is thinking – 'More inedible even than a shrew'.

A young couple arrives. Can they be baptised, confirmed and wed? Next year will do. Far from youthful friends with the mark of sickness and hospitals visible, talk bravely under the limes. An ancient lady tells me that she has *two* bottles of whisky in her cupboard. I reel back in horror. 'They were from my wedding, dear [at least sixty years ago]. But I've never tasted Drink, dear. No never.' She says that she doesn't know what she would do 'without my God'. I know nothing of her past, only her present, which has a kind of rough radiance. I find myself thinking of her

as I give the annual John Clare Lecture at Helpston, and of the
poet's liking to work beside motherly women as they weeded the
crops because he could listen to their stories. It was Clare who
identified himself with the vagrant Christ, a fugitive Lord who,
although 'the blind met daylight in his eye', encountered inhospitality. In the lecture I call Clare the July man – it is his birth
month – and I connect his countryside as best I can with our
own. His hymn is painfully direct – 'The sick found health in his
reply . . . yet he with troubles did remain.'

The Worshipper

A stonishing heat, greater than any since 1976, when my old
pond completely dried up, the first time in living memory,
and revealed its Victorian litter, muddy lamps, horse-chains,
cracked crocks. The winds are like those on the African coast and
carry a resinous air which coats everything with a kind of black
honey. The grey churches are coolly welcoming and stand open
for walkers and bikers. On Sundays a single holiday-maker adds
conspicuously to the congregation. Xenophon, quoting Apollo,
said that everyone's true worship was that which he found in use
in the place where he chanced to be. This may have been all right
for sacred groves and mountains, no doubt, but it would be
putting one's charity to the test in some of today's churches.

I am moved by our small worshipping congregations, by the
privacy of their public prayer, and by the impossibility of my ever
knowing what is actually going on as they kneel, sit, stand, sing,
say, dream. In service terms worship is that ultimate reverence
which a community and an individual has to reactivate week after
week. It must be familiar, even commonplace, and yet at the same
time elevated and inspired. 'Wonder is the basis of worship,' said
Carlyle. Wonder is unlikely to fill the entire act of worship, but I
notice it creeping in here and there. Should it not, alas, alas.

'Religion ... will glide out of mind,' warned Doctor Johnson, 'unless it be invigorated and re-impressed ... by stated calls to worship.' I preach and teach on the text, 'The hour cometh, and now is, when the true worshippers shall worship the Father in spirit and truth.'

I remember once sitting in R. S. Thomas's church in North Wales with his poems in my head and his pulpit in my sight, the visitor from afar. I never confessed to it when we met in Ipswich to read our work in the Town Hall because I knew he hated prying. The God of the Old Testament never spoke once to poor old Eli, the saddest priest in scripture, the consecrated one who had never been granted 'the vision' nor understood silent prayer when a woman truly worshipped in his church. Church-going nowadays can be a traditional or pop concert *sans* worship. Yet who can prove its absence? No one – least of all myself as I too kneel, sit, stand, sing, say, dream in these ancient colonnades. One cannot always tell when something wonderful is going on.

AUGUST

*O*ne sweltering August morning, I walked down a far Stour Valley farm track, seeking a foreword for my first book. The journey ended at an ancient longhouse and a magical garden loud with bird chatter and typewriter clatter.

Inside and outside merged here, the house door wide open to a garden room with a robin sentinel among spades, plant pots and cat food. And then the upstairs clatter stopped and a figure in shorts appeared: Ronald Blythe in his sixties and perhaps not yet in his writerly prime; a historian praising the present.

When Christine Nash found this abandoned place, on a bright day in 1943, a stream poured across the floor in the Tudor idea of a desirable residence with running water. Later the flow had been diverted outdoors but still filled the kettle.

Ronnie and I began our friendship mid-conversation. My grandmother, Elsie Hearn, had been postmistress for Charsfield – now known to Blythe fans as Akenfield. We had centuries of Suffolk between us and decades of closeness to come.

Over many visits – house-sitting; weekending; twenty shared Christmases with my partner Joachim, landscape architect and Berlin synagogue elder – I got to know Bottengoms and its celebrant through all seasons.

But my warmest thoughts go back to August, and the years of golden essays like these. A time of butterflies, dragonflies, fetes, flower shows, scything the orchard, harvesting, stubble-walks; and of lyrical and philosophical prose written in summer air.

Ian Collins

The Transfiguration and Mr Rix's Onions

The August butterflies are at their nectar feastings all over the garden, but I dare not name them, for when I have done so in the past, lepidopterists have pounced on me without mercy. Birdsong, butterflies, moths, one can go so wrong. However, white and brown and tortoiseshell butterflies are at this moment all over the place, and a green woodpecker screams ahead of me whenever I go out. And I have preached on the Transfiguration of Jesus nearly a week before the sixth, so what will become of me, heaven only knows. This feast entered the calendar in 1457 to celebrate the victory of the Christians over the Muslims at Belgrade. History makes one despair. Brush it aside. Return to the mountain and that dazzling sight, that eternal and that homely vision, that little praying circle. A brownish-red butterfly beats its wings inside the pane. It beats against my hollowed hands, then soars into the sky.

Boyhood friends complain that I never mention our Suffolk hometown, Sudbury, so I will. I visit a shrine there at least once a month. It is called Waitrose. And I cannot fail to see the three huge wool churches and the statue to Thomas Gainsborough on the Market Hill, and the Croft with its hundred swans, and the Stour with its near-fatal memories (getting half-drowned in it when I was eight), and the farmers' pubs, and the not now quite recognisable faces, for Time insists on re-introductions. As for ghosts, they are now the main population, Canon Hughes on his big black bike, girls who are now old ladies, boys who are old chaps under the grass, music from long-locked organs. Plenty of butterflies in Sudbury, fluttering about the stalls without saying who they are. Ovid would have recognised them as classmates. The country buses come and go, shuddering through the ancient streets, a procession all of its own. I imagine Tom Gainsborough aged eighteen, easel on back, striding to Cornard Wood. I have lunch in the White Horse where his uncle was landlord and watch and watch, which is what writers chiefly do. 'Watch out!' they used to say as the harvest vehicles creaked through the town about this time of the year, squeezing the tarry roads. I cool off in St Gregory's where I worshipped as a young man and heard Canon Hughes thundering the Litany in his Welsh accent, his bald head sparkling with the effort of it. I hear the choir rendering Marbecke and the congregation rising to the occasion. Services, services, 'Shall we see you on Sunday?' What a question! I'm told that people are surprised, or intrigued, to hear that John Updike goes to church every Sunday. He used to write about me in the *New Yorker*, a 'me' I have never quite known, but I never wrote back, of course.

Wormingford is being cut, just fragments of it, not the full harvest. There is a rumbling introit which could only be the trailers in Mr Rix's onions. They are like long boxes with not quite wide enough sides, so the onions leave a nice trail which we are allowed to gather up. It is a kind of onion gleaning. The village school has broken up and some torpor can be expected. Holidays have scattered the congregation to the uttermost parts of the Earth, including Newmarket. There is lull and absence, there is dead-heading and ringing, there is nobody about. But then there rarely is these curious country days when the land is tidy to a T without a worker in sight. Yet, to transpose a glorious acknowledgment, 'It is good, Lord, to be here.'

Markings

They are laying Aleksandr Solzhenitsyn to rest in a monastery as I write, and I think of him, and of his two deportations: one to the Gulag Archipelago, the other to the West. His ingratitude for the second banishment amazed us. The West's vulgarity and consumerism appalled him. It was as though a Desert Father

had been found a nice home in Las Vegas. He will be lying unlid-
ded amid the sumptuous singing.

In *Cancer Ward*, he wrote: 'Nowadays we don't think much of a
man's love for an animal: we laugh at people who are attached to
cats. But if we stop loving animals, aren't we bound to stop loving
humans, too?' Last evening I watched two deer put down on a
venison farm. I also saw my barking muntjac dancing around
Jean's horses.

Yesterday afternoon, I suddenly remembered some unplanted
daffodil bulbs in the larder, and found a place for them by the
stream. It wasn't so much raining as damping, the trees dripping,
the air filled with soft wet flurries. Some cucumber seeds followed.
I was now warmly soaked. But how pleasant it was to be out.

I marked willow logs for sawing, and a forest of nettles for their
comeuppance. The contract man in his combine who had been
cutting the first rings of harvest gave up, and there was a sudden
silence.

I had walked all round this huge field last week, and had heard
it sizzle with dryness. Now all is moist. Bees rock in the tender
boat-shaped balsam flowers whose resurrection name is *Impatiens
noli-tangere* – touch-me-not. Because if you do, my seed will leap
into the universe. This beautiful water-plant has shot all the way
from a Shropshire riverbank to the Stour Valley since 1632. And
everywhere else besides.

The post-lady brings me news of *A Cropmark Landscape in
Three Dimensions*, i.e. a report on what lies beneath the onions and
sugar beet, unseen until aerial photography. Barrow cemeteries,
concentric ring ditches, long mortuary enclosures and cursus
monuments, some of them in Wormingford. Indeed, a line of
them wall off a loop of the river.

Intensive cultivation to its meandering banks – to their very
edge these days, with the price of agricultural land going sky-
high – has become the single biggest risk to our Neolithic and
Bronze-Age farmers' scene. I sometimes take my Christmas Day

walk through these invisible sites that one must go heavenward to see, and sometimes carrying the thrilling photographs. The camera can look inside you, and, outside, can see humanity's timeless scratchings on the significance of death.

Thus to evensong for six, the rain-smirched light looking for the altar through the lancet of the infant Saxon tower, and Barry holding the hymns together, and the prayer felt. Now and then I worry about this monthly service. Is it minimal? Is it 'all', as Julian would say?

Well, tonight it is everything. Forget numbers: think of validity. I read Isaiah. 'And the glory of the Lord shall be revealed, and all flesh shall see it together.' We half-dozen, and the ring-makers down by the Stour, and the Reverend Mr Cox, and the saintly Solzhenitsyn, and George Herbert, and Gordon the churchwarden.

Ninety in the Shade

Distant combines mutter across the fields, efficient yellow monsters biting down the corn. The harvest itself is a shifting dust cloud which forbids approach. Gone for good is the communal toil and the communal relief and joy which naturally succeeded it. Other than the farmer and his couple of men, no one any longer feels a thing about harvest, if the truth were told. Some old hymns and decorations a few weeks hence will do their best to resurrect some of the old emotion. And then no aching arms and backs in the pews – unless one happens to have been ringing bells. Never again that hard corporate way of experiencing what, still within living memory, had been the common fate of any village, which was at this time to be made to work all hours so as to have bread.

For the best part of a fortnight the temperature has made the heatwave mark, thus making the grade in classic English-summer terms. Blue dawns, blue dusks, and in between a scorcher. 'How do you like this?' we say in passing, instead of Good morning. 'Chalk it up,' we say, 'a summer at last!' The horizon wavers and such creatures as stand in meadows pant gratefully in one another's shadows. Not so mankind. For us a proper summer demands appropriate events and these, unlike harvests, are far from being left to a handful of participants. Thus through the August lanes we meander through the hot Saturday afternoon to Little Tey, where I am to open the church fete in the rectory garden. Accompanying us is Joachim from Berlin. It is his first fete and, although none of us know it as yet, following it will be his first cricket match. At two o'clock sharp Lady Laurie takes me to a familiar looking prop left over from the open-air performance of *Romeo and Juliet* a few days ago, the balcony no less, and at once I give sincere voice to the glories of the English fete which, even were it pouring cats and dogs, is never called off, never any different, indeed always gaining when in adversity. But to have a fete on a day like this, well what could be more perfect! Who could ask for more? Joachim, as yet innocent of fete drill and with a charitable amount of money burning a hole in his pocket, is pointed towards the cake stall. An unseemly rush to the cake stall always follows the opening speech, we advise him. Whereas, at a cricket match, whether on a burning or a freezing wicket, rush is not a word which applies.

We come across this idyll unexpectedly and even hardened rustics such as Ian and myself are momentarily stunned by the perfection which stretches before us. We meant no more than to show Joachim the wall paintings in Copford church but our way is blocked by the kind of unconsciously formed masterpiece which all comes together when a heatwave wills it. Living figures almost still in their whites on a living green, a long lime avenue coolly leading to a great house and in the churchyard the grave of Eric Ravilious, a fine artist killed in 1942.

Trinity Ten

Summer lightning. It throws the trip-switch and the old rooms resume their darkness. Or rather an intermittent brilliance. Enormously brave or daft, I stroll up the track to where it rises and I can see, miles off, Stoke-by-Nayland tower which Marjorie has had floodlit especially for her grandson's birthday. As boys, my brother and I would climb its cold stairs to confirm whether indeed a waggon-and-horses could be turned on its leads, or whether you could see Harwich Water. Now here it is, framed in ash trees, a still flame among the on–off agitation of the universe.

Such vividness set by, the village at this moment can only be described as being in a state of pause. Lots of people are 'away' – they don't call it holiday. 'We shall be away', and the dates. An elaborate silence announces that the school is away. The combines are certainly away, having done the barley and not being able to cut the corn for another fortnight at least. Rain falls across the latter in sheets, in torrents, hissing as it hits the dry ears and rock-soil. I am solicitous about this when I meet Mr William Brown who, approaching his century, sits in his car looking out, both motionless. Won't it harm the harvest? Not a bit. It will fatten it up. Just what was wanted. I tell him about the lit tower because he can now not see that far.

It has been a week of much ecclesiastical hissing one way or another. Such drama and reporters having to brush-up their Anglicanism. I remember once reading about the nation-shaking religious debates of Victorian Britain, and the writer saying that we would never see their like again. Well this one is very like and the papers are full of it, the more popular the fuller. I myself have heard Voices saying 'Have you considered your position?' Do seekers have a position, I mean a leg to stand on? Or only finders? Where do seekers stand? Should they seek out the finders or someone else? It is an interesting question to put to summer lightning. Duncan's sheep cluster on the rim of the hill, alternately seen and unseen, and I hope not frightened by drum-rolls of distant thunder. Pheasants crash about uneasily although every other kind of bird seems to be 'away'. Travelling through this neon-sign of a night, I think of that great scriptural word 'seek'. Discovering Christ in a secret place they told him 'All men seek for thee.' Shakespeare says, 'Light seeking light doth light of light beguile.' Young George Fox stood on Pendle and saw stretching before him the country of the Seekers. It was there that he – and they – found what they were searching for.

Walkers, Wanderers, Vagrants . . .

A pale but warm sun lightens the wet fields. The lawns are soggy and too rain-laden to cut, and the old roses look like old mops. But the runner beans are away. Tomorrow we are due to explore the hills and holes at Barnack, the open-cast quarry near Peterborough where the poet John Clare hid from prying village eyes to write. The weather forecasts are watery, but we'll go all the same.

Like those of all nineteenth-century – and earlier – folk, the accounts of his rambles usually mention the people he encountered, although they took second place to the birds and flowers. Stephen's do not. He is my best 'walking' friend. The descriptions of his walks are for me alone, although sometimes for his sister.

One has just arrived. It is beautiful, and as fresh as the hour when he started out – 4 a.m., at first driving a little way. 'Two things hit me as I got out of the car: the cold air, and a wall of birdsong, the last part of the dawn chorus.'

From then on, he takes me, his sole reader, into the lovely hidden Essex of 'the flat coastal plain towards Maldon, Bradwell, and the sea'. St Cedd's territory in fact.

But should Stephen pass another walker or worker, he will not mention him.

Nearly all foot-travellers of previous times say a great deal more about fellow walkers than they do about Nature – Nature in scientific terms, that is, although their descriptive handling of scenery can be superb. George Borrow (*Wild Wales*) actually walked so that he could run into characters for his books. And Francis Kilvert's *Diary* is an unconscious social history of the poor as they moved about: penniless lads, old soldiers and vagrant workers, each of whom would catch his kind attention for an hour or so. Wordsworth made such briefly met tramps immortal. Ancient laws were fierce about vagrancy, but in summer countless 'travellers' descended on our East Anglian fields to pick the peas, hops and fruit. All have gone. No longer do the village pubs display chalked disgust – 'No Gypsies, no Irish, no Tramps'. Such essential labour was paid, but not thanked.

This vanishing of itinerants, this now complete absence of the seasonal strangers, has played havoc with the rural short story. Masters of this literary genre, one of the most difficult and among the most entrancing forms of fiction, are robbed of the dramatic disturbance caused by the stranger on the road.

Read A. E. Coppard, H. E. Bates, and many of the other great twentieth-century writers, and you will see how rich and strange – and dangerous – the market towns and villages were when the old lanes were being tramped down even further by a travelling mixture of workforce and idling force, as they had been for centuries. All gone; all disappeared over the hill.

The Sunday newspapers have a section on Walks. They give maps and mileage and historical information. Little is left to chance. But 'chance' should be the pearl of any walk. The chance for Stephen on his 4 a.m. walk was that the world would give him its 'early showing', and it did.

Walking to church, or to the village shop, I hope for nothing in particular, but not once have I reached the half-lost farmhouse without the award of some kind of tramp-prize. Although it can never be of the curious quality that a 1930s walk, say, would almost certainly give, it will add something to the day. Someone I do not know has greeted me by my Christian name.

Death of a Young Farmer

Getting the balance right might be thought admirable, though not in every quarter. Balance is too equable, too lacking in drama. Many in the countryside prefer it when things are way out or at rock bottom. We have our doomsayers, both male and female. A new enterprise starts up in the village – 'I give it till Christmas.' A long time ago, after I had written about the great agricultural depression, an old farmer's wife beckoned me; 'My dear, you should have come to me. I could have told you much worse than that!' I delight in our doomsayers and would never think of attempting to balance their blackness with a spot of rational light. The pleasures of misery, let them not be denied.

But real darkness hangs in our little firmament as still-young people die. Friends who were seen in the fields until just the other day. We say their names formally in church and tenderly to ourselves every day of the week. Have we ever been more medical and less philosophical about death? How I detest the neologism 'terminal illness' and hope that when my time comes and they ask after me, the reply will be, 'He is dying.' These serious thoughts arise when one has to balance the rural idyll with sad realities common to us all. We are some 800 souls all told in the united benefice – the smallest in the diocese – and small changes and profound departures cast a kind of universal shadow across the valley. At the Bell-Sunday service I reminded them of the passing-bell – the one which John Donne mentions – and which was heard in the village until 1914, when the farmworkers in the fields would straighten up and count the strokes. Seventy-two, seventy-three . . . 'He had a good innings.' Or twenty-five, twenty-six, then silence.

I meet the ringers in the Crown, David, Bernard, Christopher, Evelyn, all brown as berries and clearly immortal. Their cars glitter in the yard. Ringers are masters of continuity. No sooner do old hands leave hold of the ropes than young hands catch on. We talk of Cecil Pipe the great Suffolk ringer, now with God. He once told me that it was 'the parson's daughters who started me off'. He had watched them raise the bell and when they had disappeared, tried it himself. He was twelve. He said, 'You must bring these two things together in your mind and let them rest there for ever, bells and time, and bells and tittle . . .'

A tunicked St Alban looks down from his position on the reredos. Suffered c. 209 on a hilltop in June, a young Romano-Briton. The children like him and are sad for him. 'What was the hill called?' 'Holmhurst Hill.'

Rain, Rain

Wet Augusts raise terrors in the farming mind. It is now over a century since the great rains washed away British agriculture, flooding its poor labourers into the towns and out to the Empire, reducing the fields to what the land agents called 'sporting interests'. Yet the memory of this disaster floats into the consciousness of rural England whenever it 'comes down', as they say. As it is doing at this moment, coming down for all it is worth. The papers call it climate change now.

My neighbour John who has the loveliest fields in Wormingford, with their surprising heights in what is popularly known as a flat country, has given me the obituary of a farmer who died in 1930. This obituary is in the form of one of his fields saying farewell as the cortège passed, the coffin on a flowery wagon, the Suffolk punches be-plumed.

'I have been a field for nigh on a thousand years, and I know men. Some are clever, some are kind, but very few are clever and kind, but he was, and I am sorry that all the other fields of England – who need him so much in these days – will have to go on without him.'

Sunday afternoon was visiting time for a field. I have no idea how to introduce our many newcomers to a neighbouring field. 'Swallings, Stony Hollow, meet Mr and Mrs Commuter. Have a word with them about your long life. Tell them not to mind the water in the ruts. Let them on a better day find a fresh view from your headlands.'

Contrary to what might be expected, the cat likes a bit of rain. She is in fact a weather cat and given to long spells of contemplation by the waterfall of a blocked gutter, watching it for hours, enjoying its sound. I find her now and then drinking from the brook like a lion, delicately poised on a stone, lapping deliciously, looking sideways for elephants. Should it bucket down she will often prefer a rainproof shrub to a dash inside the house, somewhere where she can smell and taste the downpour without being soaked. The horses too, one of them in genteel retirement from Newmarket, allow the rain to shoot from their shiny backs. I was about to find time for the Apostle Bartholomew but he was rained out. Bartholomew, son of Tolmai, what can you tell us?

Bird Garden

Bumping down the track, we are stopped by a pair of frowning little owls. They study us for all of a minute, before vanishing into a ditch. As they go, the afternoon light passes through their feathers.

We are returning from Hadleigh, where we bought new secateurs in Partridges, one of those wonderful hardware shops that sell everything from a pin to a suit of armour. And, of course, we went to see the vast church where the Marian martyr Rowland Taylor taught the Reformation, and Fr Hugh Rose founded the

Oxford Movement. No surprise that it is an archiepiscopal peculiar.

Some lads with a white dog, which is being hushed, loll on old sofas. Have they seen the wolf with St Edmund's head in the distant southern chapel? A bench end shows it being carried by the hair to the saint's body, to which it is united before the funeral, which the wolf attends before returning to his wood.

I have always loved this wide church and wide town with its endless timber-framed houses and terrible beautiful history. They were harvesting all round. The sun hit the fields with a kind of mockery of our earlier drought commotion, their yield being not half bad.

Back home, it is opening time. I open a bird garden for the Royal Society for the Protection of Birds at Flatford, and also our Royal British Legion vegetable and flower show in the village hall, where the silver cups wait for the winners. Two elderly sisters, the Misses Richardson, now with God, gave the Flatford Wildlife Garden to us. It is within feet of the Stour, and ready for public enlightenment.

I had ridden past it on my bike since boyhood, with no suspicion that these ladies existed, although they sold teas. It would have been close to here that Golding Constable, the artist's brother, who never went out without a gun, shot the 'woodspite' (woodpecker). John Constable needed to have one for the painting he was working on in Charlotte Street.

He was for ever writing home to check flowers and birds for his pictures, to get them right. But he would have been puzzled by a bird garden. Paul Nash called his father's tennis courts and elms at Iver a bird garden, creating these pale and enchanting visions of them. He was by the Stour just before the First World War, painting in moonlight.

At matins and evensong, I turn the Bible birds into a sermon. Ornithologically, they are not at all helpful, having human habits rather than their own. It is as though these prophets and poets had never seen a bird for what it is. And the dreadful sacrificial slaughter, at the Temple, of sparrows and doves. And the tenderness of the Lord. How it continues to break one's heart, this fearful approach to God via blood. How barbaric it was. And did nobody actually watch birds? Surely they must have done. Who could not watch a bird?

I remember John Clare and his birdwatching poems, the greatest in the language, and remember Ted Hughes reading Clare's 'The Nightingale's Nest' in Westminster Abbey, a masterpiece of bird observation written at a time when 'nesting' by boys of his age was a popular sport, like Golding Constable's potshotting as he wandered by the river.

Yet the poetry of poor Job's description of himself as 'a brother to dragons and a companion to owls', how lonely it is. Like my owls calling at night.

Gordon's Last Party

Northerly winds rage above and the sound is Wagnerian. Oaks and ashes clash, clouds race, rain flurries, and summer flowers take a thrashing. Now and then, having put on my gardening rags, I venture forth to renew my wall-scraping, these having lost all definition. The white cat watches from her favourite throne, the ancient stone sink in which generations of farm children were scrubbed. I can hear their protest above the tempest.

Tomorrow – Aldeburgh! Will the uproar last? I half-hope that it will. Already I can hear its mighty slap on the shingle and see its hurling darkness. I am going to Britten's old house where, ages ago, I walked with him in the garden. There were walls there, high and protective, above which the coastal gales raged.

How does one listen to the radio without hearing all this news? It is a problem. Now, they even hang *Thought for the Day* on a news item, so I try not to listen to that. Unless, of course, it is a

Sikh thought or a Rabbi Blue thought. And further footling grumbles. Why do TV newscasters straddle? The only worthwhile straddler is Evan Davies, whose gleeful conveyance of dreadful economics is a treat. There he stands, rocking and grinning away, every figure to hand. It is almost worth having one's bank balance take a dip.

Presenters may have to watch the thin line which exists between youthful informality and vulgarity. Summing up the wonderful Elgar concert at the Proms, Aled Jones cries: 'Not bad for the son of a piano-tuner!' But enough of this quibbling. There are Victorias to pick and branches to sweep from lawns.

We all go to Gordon's party. It is a highlight of the Wormingford season. The field has been harvested to make a car park. The garden has been weeded. Henry, the Vicar, has raised his beautiful tent which, clearly, has come straight from the Field of the Cloth of Gold. It billows fretfully and inhospitably, for the Northerlies are no respecter of garden parties.

Thus we crowd the farmhouse itself, and are cheerful whilst intermittent showers rattle the conservatory glass like lover's pebbles against a bedroom window. Talking to Tom about his herd of Lincolns, I find myself remembering Parson Woodforde sending his 'saucy' man Scurle to Norwich to gather some news and bring it back to the rectory, and of the yearly tithe party when – well, I had better not say what happened during this great spree. It was the eighteenth century, after all.

The *Ipomoea* which Richard Mabey gave me – sent in a wet parcel through the post – doles out its morning glory a flower or two at a time. Its name means 'similar to bindweed'. There are hundreds of species of it. Mine has bright purple flowers which bloom and wither in a day.

There is a kind of infallible succession of them, and their credo is clearly 'less is more'. They climb a bamboo stick by the front door, but unambitiously, staring beautifully out east and not up at the rose giddily waving above them. Their huge cousins trumpet along the track and wind themselves up in the telegraph wires, and make mats in the ditch, and are altogether glorious in themselves, though you would have to preach a sermon to make the neighbours admit it. In hedge-bindweed's case, less is obviously not more. Although nothing can be whiter than white, it makes a good try. Children used to love it.

David's Community Orchard

The remarkable day has arrived, at last, at last. I am allowed to see the Community Orchard. It was planted as long ago as February, in two acres of Woodland Trust. And its originator was, of course, my remarkable friend David Baker.

For ages he has talked to me about it, a Community Orchard, one in which local folk can devour local fruit. In our case, Coe's Golden Drop plums, Polstead Black cherries, Johnny Mount pears from Colchester, Sturmer Pippins, D'Arcy Spice apples and Grey Pippin apples from Mount Bures, one of our parishes.

There they stand, belted to poles. No longer can they escape into obscurity. We will observe them from blossom to fruit, and taste their ancient sweetness. Below them, my wild daffodils – the ones which Dorothy Wordsworth saw, and her brother immortalised – are taking root. Above them, the swallows haphazardly fly about in the cold August evening.

David leads me from tree to tree, making introductions in his eager voice: 'St Edmund's Russet, raised by Mr Harvey at Bury St Edmund's, Suffolk in about 1875. Sweet, juicy, rich, and densely textured, pale cream flesh. When really ripe, tastes like pear-flavoured vanilla ice cream. Disappointing if picked too early. Light russet with silvery sheen over with greenish yellow gold ground colour.'

He has driven all over England in his van to track down candidates for the Community Orchard, haggling with nurserymen, seeking advice from our next-door apple guru, the wonderful Andrew Tann, picking up clues about Twining's Pippin. Thomas Twining was the Curate of his parish church in the eighteenth century, a keen pomologist, and the grandson of the founder of the Twinings tea company. Oh, for more pomologist curates. Oh, for a curate of any apple persuasion – but we must not go into that. Let us be thankful for our David Bakers, naturalists who, with their dogs, leave the beaten path to discover a second countryside, with its stray fruit, forgotten flowers and neglected glories.

The Community Orchard – it deserves to be named after him, but he sweeps the suggestion away – is six months old, but in three years it will fruit. Wild tulips and rare grasses will carpet its roots. Wheatears will take a rest in it on their journey to Africa.

'Here,' David says in a grave voice, 'is the Isaac Newton tree.' Not the ... 'Yes,' David says, 'the very one.' It stands stiffly in its rabbit guard, and is far too short to fall on anyone's head. It has descended from Newton's garden in Woolsthorpe Manor, near Grantham. 'Cooks to a sweet delicately flavoured purée. Large, heavily ribbed.'

David breaks into my worship with, 'I must knock down some of your Victoria plums when we get home, to make some jam.' Here are the Black Polstead cherries. They rose high on Sudbury market hill when I was a boy; dark, dull, delicious.

Polstead cherries, Polstead cherries,
Red as Maria Marten's blood!

It is astonishingly chill for late August. The hedgerow trees are stock still. We march on. There are fifty-nine members of the Community Orchard, and I must say hello to every one of them. Some would have perished in childbirth had not David nourished them with pond water during the desert spring. No likelihood of death now, only of constant fruitings. Plus some allowable worship.

The Caretakers

M id August. Mr Cousins's bees are rifling my flowers in the late afternoons of hot days. Distant throbs betray a combine harvester, the first machine in the field. Barely a bird. Just this still warmth and motionless skies. Bell-ringing practice to go with so many bell-shaped blooms. I imagine Barry calling the tune.

Just a handful of neighbours maintain the three churches, change their frontals, Hoover their carpets, polish their brass, unlock, lock up, count the candles, turn the pages of the visitors' books. Turn the pages, too, of the dead.

Immensely grand folk sleep here and there, nodding away until Kingdom come. Here is Jane Austen's cousin or aunt from Chawton. How did she get to Little Horkesley? Someone will know. Here are John Constable's uncles from Wormingford mill, with a confident Esq.

Here is the poor young man who apologised to me for wearing a hat in church, cancer having robbed him of his hair. Here is beloved Gordon, who survived the Western desert and was photographed with Monty. Here is John Nash, who painted the Stour valley all his days. Here, making sharp corners for the tower, are Roman bricks, warm to the touch still. Here are noticeboards naming a vanished vicar, or rector. Here is summer weather. I sit on a burning bench and thank God for it.

In *Swann's Way* an old man tells a young man:

In my heart of hearts, I care for nothing in the world now but a few churches, books – two or three, pictures – rather more, perhaps, and the light of the moon when the fresh breeze of youth (such as yours) wafts to my nostrils the scent of gardens whose flowers my old eyes are not sharp enough, now, to distinguish.

Mercifully, I see not only the confident bell-shaped blooms of August, but the insects that rock them. How active the month is! Although, personally speaking, I have to admit that torpor reigns. Only those whose names on tombs remind me of their old busyness are less active than I.

Squinting through my lashes, I think I can pick out the blue smudge of hill on which they crowned Edmund, king and martyr, on Christmas Day, long ago. What else happened round about 860? Well, the convolvulus would have rioted in August, sure as fate. And the mother of the Lord would be high in the sacred firmament. And the husbandmen would be sharpening their sickles, or just lolling about in the sun.

And the mindless taking of life by the raiders, just like that by the Cairo authorities at the moment, would have been going on here and there in the name of government. Or possibly not. And possibly some enchanting seasonal sloth, with the August sun on one's neck, and a slowdown in one's heart, it being too soon to gather anything except pollen.

They say that Edmund would have been about thirty – which is far too soon to die. Morons stripped him, tied him to a tree, and made him into a target. This mindless taking of life and rattling of weapons – in August!

I think that my *Garrya elliptica* is on its last legs. Named after Michael Garry, of the Hudson Bay Company, it is propping up yards of grapevine. But if you chop it down it will rise again. A neighbouring holly says: 'Yes, yes! Give me more light.' But the white cat says: 'Let it be.'

The Way to Akenfield

Barefoot at dawn during the heatwave. The garden is seeding and tall. I water the cucumbers then the onions, carrying pails from the stream's overflow. How the Israelites lusted after these vegetables, and so would I have done given their parched land and diet. All the same, I am one with God in his dislike of complainings and whinings. He had given his people manna and they longed for — cucumbers. Mine are doing well. They glisten on the earth and are gathered with a gentle severing twist. I weed them after breakfast, take up new potatoes and listen to the old battery Hacker. Moist dirt and grass clippings pack my toes. The pigeons call to Mozart. Overhead, silver crosses steer to Stansted with only a faint noise when they approach my trees. Bernard's harvester begins to thump and the horizon to shake.

Later, we drive to Charsfield. How could it have got so hot in four hours? It is an auction of promises outing and I have promised to lead half a dozen parishioners round the scrap of Suffolk which I called 'Akenfield'. Here is my old farmhouse by the edge of the Roman road, there is my study window squinting over my hedge. Alas, all the elms have gone, the elms that made it so beautiful, which gave it a little grandeur. The house looks depleted, less than it was. We cannot slow down because of all the traffic behind us, so seventeen years of habitation are over before one can say knife. We visit Peggy Cole, the doyenne of our village life, in her famous garden where fruit and veg and flowers and grass flourish in the old cottage order. We walk her ruler-straight paths and see that everything is better than anything we can do. Her husband Ernie Cole and myself were churchwardens at St Peter's several heatwaves ago. 'Several' in Suffolk-ese is a non-committal number. 'Were there many there?' — 'Several.' The church has a fiery-red Tudor brick tower on a medieval flint and stone base on which the Virgin's monogram is let in, an elegant crowned M.R. I slip away to call on the dead, Ocean the Gipsy woman, Peter who helped me with the hay. Across the lane the children buzz in the school like bees, and the playground bakes.

On we tour to Hoo, for me the simplest, most sacred building in my personal guidebook, rubble walls, Early English windows, more Tudor bricks, an altar like an hospitable tea-table, a brick floor like a larder. I take a look (as he would have said) at Mr Buckles' grave. He was a devout farmworker who 'lost himself' in scripture and who would suddenly pause as he read the Lesson, looking up to explain, 'That was very fine, I'll read that again'. His wife would pack half a dozen eggs into my bicycle basket and say, 'Well, come again but not too soon'. And so on to ducal Framlingham Castle from which Mary I rode to unseat poor Lady Jane Grey, to stroll round the walls between the candy-twist chimneys and stare down at the deep dry moat. I am accompanied, not only by the promise-winners, but also twenty years of residency in these parts and people they would never know.

It is the weekend of the Transfiguration, enchanting, inexplicable, convincing. All these things. Upon the mountain the full glory of Christ. Down below the complete humiliation of some of his followers as they attempted to miracle-heal an epileptic lad. Alongside Jesus, the sharers of his vision. And the word itself, Transfiguration, how perfect. How disturbing that this feast was entered in the calendar to celebrate the victory of Christians over Muslims at Belgrade on 6 August 1456.

In the New Testament the Transfiguration story is told by three men who were not present but with agreement if not with the same similes, which somehow increases belief in what happened. Each agrees that Jesus' face shone like the sun. Matthew writes, 'His clothes became white as light', Mark that 'they were whiter than snow' adding, 'as no fuller on earth can white them', and Luke that 'they were white and glistering'. So Peter, James and John, who were there, had provided incandescent accounts of this marvellous event in spite of Christ's order that they should tell no one. Diana Collins, who has just died, told me that she climbed to the traditional site of the Transfiguration to discover a little plateau covered with spring flowers. It was where the three closest disciples had fallen to the ground in terror, not of the whiteness but of hearing God's voice. Jesus had asked them, 'Who do men say I am?' and God had given the answer. No wonder they collapsed.

When they stood up 'they saw Jesus only'. Herman itself is snow-capped, rising nine thousand feet between Palestine and Syria. I find the story mystical and at the same time rational. Life is a grubby business, half-lit, unclear, yet it should shine, if only now and then. 'Anoint and cheer our soiléd face with the abundance of thy grace.'

Richard Bawden has come to paint the garden. I see him shifting around to find the right spot. He is one of that host of artists who prop up easels in flower beds, who put August into frames, whose beards tousle the summer growth and who hope that soon I will be making coffee or popping a cork. The garden seat is covered with resting butterflies, satiated after their business with the buddleia, a bush named after a Mr A. Buddle, a botanist who died in 1715. Let us give thanks for him and other men who domesticate enchantment. Later, I watch Richard painting far below as I cut ivy from the roof where it likes to weave in and out the pantiles, dislodging them, heaving them up and bringing them down. I remove it from the brick bread oven and clip it in a neat line. Ivy dust smothers me and the silver ladder burns in the sun. The radio says that it is the hottest day.

Late in the evening Joachim telephones from Berlin to tell me that the Constable in the National Gallery there looks just like Wormingford. He sounds excited and happy. His voice is infectious and I catch his delight in things, this time a Constable landscape which has been behind the Wall for most of his life and which now spreads a familiar view before him, the Stour Valley where he has walked with me. He is an East Anglianophile. 'I am washing-off ivy dust', I tell him. 'Ivy dust . . .?' he repeats, suddenly lost.

Woodcuts

Because of the pattern of farmwork, even now farmers are bound to fall into certain timeless attitudes. Take Duncan watching Lower Bottom meadow being mowed at this moment. He, the man on the mower and his setters, and a scuttling rabbit or two, have all assumed the attitudes of figures in a Bewick woodcut, the machine notwithstanding. Dogs and humans are engrossed by the circling cutter and are even correctly turned-out for black-and-white illustration, Duncan in his white shirt, dark braces and cap, the abstract man in the cab, the glossy creatures bounding in the foreground. Falling thistles provide most of the action. Like children who will eat all round what they dislike, the horses have grazed up to the thistles and left them standing in small forests here and there. The stream which wriggles through the pasture has been wired-off to prevent sheep and horses getting stuck in it. Should I shout 'Duncan!' and shatter the woodcut? Better not. Let one man labour and another stare. Let dogs not look up. So I go inside to remind myself about Thomas Bewick, founder of the modern school of wood engraving. A Northumbrian boy, he taught himself to draw by chalking pictures on the church flagstones. His sketches were made with pen and blackberry ink. His woodcut books have a skill and fidelity to the countryside such as had never been seen before, and here are Duncan and the haymaker and their beasts in the Georgian meadow, just as I imagined.

Until he married, when his wife put a stop to it, Tom Bewick slept naked throughout the year, wrapped in a single blanket with the bedroom wind and the snow sometimes providing an extra covering. He walked in all weathers, waded across rivers without drying his clothes afterwards, and believed that boys and girls were 'harassed with education before their minds were fit for it' and would have liked their early years spent 'running wild by burns'. How he would have spurned today's test after test, or central heating for that matter. His *Memoir* is a printed burst of fresh air, cheerful, funny, accusative and with some breezy notions of the Church.

Will rain hold off? is what we are asking. Because harvest will have to be held off if it does not. The wheat is dry enough to scratch my bare legs, yet the ears still hold moisture, I notice – are quite heavy with it in fact. So the combine stays in its den. At midnight the first quarter of the harvest moon rocks in the oaks. At matins we read from that master of dryness, Ezekiel, whom God addresses as 'Son of man, can these dry bones live?' Jesus called himself Son of man. 'Son of man', God instructed the Temple priests, 'these are the ordinances of the altar.'

Bewick surveyed Georgian Christianity with conventional respect. But 'Wagon loads of sermons have been published ... of no importance either to religion or morality ... How could they stem from the 'beauty and simplicity' of what Christ taught? How could these teachings have become 'distorted and disfigured' by the various sects? They should be 'compared to a mathematical point, a point of perfection for all men to aim at, but to which none can fully attain ... As far as I am able to judge, all we can do is to commune with and reverence and adore the Creator ... I know of no better of which is called serving God than that of being good to his creatures.' Bewick's Franciscanism had begun when he was a schoolboy. He had caught a hare in his arms, had stoned a bullfinch. 'Struck with its beauty I instantly ran into the house with it. It was alive, and looked me piteously in the face; and, as I thought, could it have spoken, it would have asked me why I had taken away its life. I felt greatly hurt at what I had done and did not quit it all the afternoon. I turned it over and over, admiring its plumage, its feet, its bill ... This was the last bird I killed.' Let the hunter reach the fox before the hounds get at it and hold it in his/her arms and read from its dying eyes, 'Why have you taken away my life?' For fun, is their answer.

The Big Green at Mellis

The weather breaks. I can hear its change of tune as I pick the broad beans. From listless summer to soft turmoil. The trees which have stood stock-still like leaden trees in one of those farmyard sets we had as children are thrashing about, and shaking the collared doves out of them. Harvesting continues to throb in the fields like heartbeat and in the lanes the commuters are amazed to be held up by monster machines. I sit in the doorway waiting for the downpour. If the clouds get any lower the spire will puncture them.

Death 'the ruffian on the stair' is hanging around, upsetting the holiday plans, and maybe he will give us a miss. When he does arrive the Church will pull out all the stops for him. 'Death', it says, 'meet Life'. Although its language, so perfect for the occasion, will make us all cry. Friends under sentence of death talk to me on the telephone. How strange it is. Could I do with some plums? Theirs are so weighty that they have broken the bough and they must prop it up next year.

To Mellis to see Roger Deakin's moat. Roger swam up and down in his moat before setting off to swim round Britain. There is Mellis church. Pevsner, prying into it, saw 'no indication of the Renaissance'. That's Mellis for you. It has a vast green still governed by Anglo-Saxon rights and with old houses all round it, so that for generations the natives have been able to sit comfortable of an evening and watch what was going on, games, goats, courting, somebody going into Mrs Smith's, somebody sneaking out of Lizzie Brown's, young Fred coming home after midnight. Ancient folk going mad. And animals chomping up and down and boys being wicked. The usual thing. Mellis hasn't quite done with summer, I notice, and the splattering of rain will do no more than make the roach rise. This is de la Pole country, that romantic north-western Suffolk family whose castles and manors lie scattered around, and whose shields are fixed to flint walls.

May we go to Eye, to Wingfield to meet the de la Poles and look at their leopard's head badge and see their possessions now the corn has been cut? No, we are here to see what Roger has been up to, which is writing a book about wood – wood as material, which is what medieval Suffolk saw it as. Everybody went around keeping an eye on the growing trees and marking a future shaft here, a house-beam there. Everybody walked with a pocketful of acorns to push into the damp earth wherever there happened to be a space. Carpenters made wooden angels so that when you looked up in church you thought you were in heaven. Woodland hides Roger's farmhouse and, should his neighbours look up from television, they will not be able to watch him naked in his moat. We lunch on its bank and hear the invisible Norwich train scream by.

Compostings

Three old friends have been grave-hunting, returning jubilant. They have purchased three neighbouring graves, at £400 apiece, in one of those woodlands which cover you up in a nature burial spot not far from the Suffolk coast. They talk headily of silver birches and broom, of whispering grasses and humming bees. Twice have I laid to rest bodies in such places, one of a young farmer, one of an ancient historian, his in Essex, hers in Cambridgeshire, and each time the funeral was extraordinarily beautiful and sacred. God being its Creator, can there exist an inch of unconsecrated ground? Defiled ground, certainly, but who is to blame for that? However, being a chronic churchyard walker and tomb-taster extraordinary, I can see that this nature burial business is going to deprive me of my recreation. Last Sunday, for instance, I discovered in a churchyard near here, 'Nathaniel aged 17 and his wife Ann . . .' Now there's a story. And yesterday we laid my neighbour Leonard between a babble of local headstones, all of them communicating the village, and strolling past his house his nice dog gave me its customary bark.

These serious matters completed, the white cat and I lie on the grass and read a French novel, the summer having returned. Oh, how blissful to be on top of the earth, to feel the sun hot on one's skin, to see the pages flutter in the warm wind, to hear the squirrels scurrying for nuts and to watch the cloud Himalayas through one's lashes. I had read John Donne's 'Bring us, O God, at our last awakening/into the house and gate of heaven,/to enter into that gate and dwell in that house,/where there shall be no darkness nor dazzling, but one equal light' and now I smelled something so paradisal as to make me sit up and lose my place. My head had been touching the wild pea which David had brought from Tuscany years ago, and whose seed I religiously gather every autumn. Twenty or more purple flowers and their marvellous scent were suddenly 'out', and for all their worth. I imagined the Florentine artists, in search of pigments in August, having a rest against a rock and drawing up this same perfume, and feeling immortal.

The rain gone, the harvest arrives. Mr Bradshaw has taken his oil-seed rape, harrowed-in its hull and left a fine emptiness, acres and acres of light brown soil all neat and tidy-like, as they say. Soon the combines will be let out of their dark barns to gnaw wide paths through the wheat. A month of rain, and now the fields look as though they wouldn't mind a little drink. People are on holiday or toiling unsociable hours. Organists are at a premium. Sometimes we sing the hymns unaccompanied and say the liturgy alternately. I rather like these spare matins and evensongs. They are like interior retreats.

I must weed, not the garden but the bookcases. They bulge and sway, topple and protest. Not another volume. And I hate a tight shelf. So a hard-hearted sheep and goats business is called for. Or of course some more bookcases. And it takes such an age, this sorting, what with the reading and the absence of ruthlessness. Here is a fascinating edition of Helene Hanff's (*84 Charing Cross*

Road) *Apple of my Eye* . . . And now it is lunchtime for man and beast, the latter jumping up and down with greed.

Roger Dying

We sit by Roger's deathbed, Alison, Vicki and I. It is late Sunday afternoon with the heatwave fading, and Roger lies against a white mountain of pillows. The little window opens on to the mite of grass and the cool moat in which Roger swam all the year round, writing the Preface, as it were, for his strenuous masterpiece *Waterlog*. Now he whispers, his famliar voice a kind of human susurration in tune with aspen leaves, and we listen hard to catch his words. He looks if anything rather astonished, as do we in our different ways. When he drove from his ancient farmhouse to mine he would bring a present, a fine cup, a fine grapefruit sapling he had grown from a pip, and once a wonderful new scythe from Stowmarket. Now and then we were made to stand side by side at literature festivals and talk about the country-side and he would laugh because, he said, I used complete sentences, 'the kind you read'. And now his light flickers, every now and then flaring into his old self, every now and then on the verge of going out. The rough draft for the jacket of his last book slips on the coverlet. It is called *Wildwood: A Walk through Trees*.

I have brought John Clare's poems with me. I read the one which Ted Hughes read in Poets' Corner when we put up a memorial to him. It is called 'The Nightingale's Nest' and it describes Clare being torn between his need to come close to the sitting bird and his longing not to scare it. How can he communicate his not being like other men, or rather boys? It is a long poem and Roger's ears, I realise, are not at all dying at this moment. He is listening to Clare as keenly as we listened together to the nightingales at Tiger Hill. Both John Clare and John Keats – they knew of each other and shared the same publisher – believed that the nightingale 'lived on song'. Clare was the greater naturalist and knew all about those physical things which produced the music, the dense coverage below the trees in Royce Wood, the secret nest:

> ... no other bird
> Uses such loose materials or weaves
> Their dwellings in such spots – dead oaken leaves
> Are placed without and velvet moss within.
> And little scraps of grass – and scant and spare
> Of what seems scarce materials, down and hair ...

Walnut Tree Farm, the home which Roger re-created from abandoned materials, has always reminded me of how men long ago, and maybe even today, had a nest in mind when they looked around for a house. It hides away in foliage which brings secrecy to a vast open common, and going to see him there has often made me think of centuries of spun-out villagers as anxious as Clare to discover what is going on in nests not their own as he was when creeping towards his revered nightingale, terrified that she will hear him and her song be cut short by 'choking fear'. Only a year or two ago I had heard Roger Deakin recording the creaks and bumps of Walnut Tree Farm on the radio, and the rivery sounds of the Waveney, perfect scraps of nature's conversation. Could we hear John Donne's prayer? The one about the house in which there will be 'no noise nor silence, but one equal music ... no ends nor beginnings, but one equal eternity'? And thus we kiss and leave.

August for the Gadabouts

Torrential summer rains, though they fail to batter down today's short-stemmed corn, which doesn't even look wet. About half the harvest is in and what is still to be cut can happily wait until the showers and thunder and lightning have stopped.

Less than a generation ago the village would have watched such downpours with apprehension. The flattened wheat would be beaten to the earth and then shoot. A poor harvest was ruinous, absolutely miserable. The heavy rainfall is getting its own back on human hopes in another way by making lakes along the lane where new houses have ignored the old water table. The cornfields themselves dry out in an hour.

August for the insects. Lunch in the garden during a bright interval and a dragonfly helicopters on to my knee and turns his battery of eyes on to this strange landing stage of skin and bone. Dragonflies come in three sizes: hawkers because they hawk around ponds, darters because they come at you like javelins, though without a sting, and damsels a.k.a. demoiselles. My knee-struck darter is jewelled gauze. Bees swing in the balsam flowers and one of my cherished hornets dozes on a Miss Wilmott's Ghost. As for butterflies, it is like the old days, they are everywhere.

August for fair-weather friends who telephone to announce they are on their way. *Now?* 'We should be with you by lunchtime.' There is a pause while my brain races through the contents of the fridge. The telephone babbles on. 'We know you are always there in August.' Food vaguely settled, I panic over the state of the garden. These are the friends who say things like, 'We don't suppose you have a lot of time for gardening, what with your writing and everything.' Their garden wins all the prizes. They will take themselves off to the lovely wilderness where the old farm buildings once stood and shout, 'You'll have your work cut out here!' Then I realise how these things worried me once and now they worry me not at all. Where August is concerned, it is the towering month when plants reach for the stars and then fall flat. Having been taught that all this reaching upward and seeding and tumbling about is part of horticultural life, I do not cut the stalking forest down but allow it its fling. Rock and rot, dear blooms, it is your perennial due. The friends will go home to their immaculate beds and tell each other, charitably, 'He's managing all right but he should have some help.'

As everyone is on holiday there are few at church, so we sit in the chancel. We are serene, thoughtful, modest in our liturgical requirements. I preach on the City of God and ask, why are we bound thither and not for the Village of God? No answer.

The August Dragonfly

The dragonfly returns again and again to the open page, alighting as though it was a helicopter-pad, sometimes at the top, then at the foot, as the book rests on my lap. I clasp it stockstill. The dragonfly's wings are colourless and translucent, and I can read Binchester and Yatterdon through them, so no prizes for guessing what this book is. It shifts to *O qua juval*. It is a darter, a creature of speed and pause. I am a creature of sloth, and thus a scandal to Harold's bees as they assault the balsam. My garden-chair is like Cleopatra's burning throne and very soon I must muster enough energy to carry it into the shade. The stream is at its mightiest flow because of all the rain in the night, providing delicious fresh water for both darters and honeybees to sip. Over my head a green woodpecker knocks monotonously on the willow to see if the grubs are in. 'Yatterdon,' asks the dragonfly, 'isn't that in Berkshire?' It reminds me of Fanny Burney and her aristocratic husband, M. D'Arblay sitting on the lawn at Camilla Cottage waiting for the second Napoleonic wars to begin. They were in 'retirement'. It meant something quite different in their day, an exquisite withdrawal from the fray, just as I am at this moment pleasantly withdrawn from the goings-on in Wormingford. Dragonflies are Odanata, carnivorous creatures who begin as maids and end up as darters or hawkers or damsels or demoiselles. I must brush up my Odanata.

It often takes a late August afternoon to hear the minimal voice of nature, the sultry popping of seed, the whisper of dried petals, the scuttle in the vine. Such energy. I gently kick Conrad's *Letters* into the shade with a bare toe so that the cover doesn't curl. When the telephone rings from the sitting room I think how foolish of whoever it is to imagine that I would have the strength to get up and answer it. Over the hedge, a girl is talking to her horse under a tree. A hundred years ago Conrad was writing *Lord Jim* at Pent Farm, just off Romney Marsh and giving his literary agent Mr Pinker what for, reminding him that 'there are other virtues than punctuality'. Photographs of Conrad at work reveal that he would also give me a piece of his mind if he could see me in nothing but a torn shirt and shorts writing in a garden. He wore, even in August, a splendid suit, cravat and polished boots at isolated Pent Farm, as befitted a Polish gentleman. Moreover, inside, there was Mrs Conrad who could type, that marvellous style of his curling from the keys. My ballpoint does its best and now and then the dragonfly makes a sudden landing on a line. 'O English summer day,' it pleads, 'as it is my only day, last as long as you can.'

A Voyage

John Constable when a boy would have taken rides on his father's barges. I am riding in James's skiff, a pretty little Edwardian boat straight off a Tissot painting. When it sailed the Thames at Henley its name was *Speedwell* but now that it is sailing the Stour it has no name, I cannot remember why. It rides low in the evening water. The air is suddenly cool, the sky banking up to hide Mars, the swans fretful at being disturbed. We lie back on cushions whilst James rows and the willows trail across our bodies. Not another soul about except the young fisherman who is throwing bits of bread where he hopes to land a chub. Chubs are first cousins to dace and much sought after by coarse fishermen. We exchange river pleasantries as we pass through the tunnel and out of Nayland. Wissington ahead. Delicious watercress which nobody eats festoons the oars. I nibble a bit. It is peppery and good. It is not gathered these days, I have forgotten why. It is the same as swimming in the river, or not harnessing its power. Nobody does any of the things which river dwellers used to do any more. How powerful the Stour is. I can feel its pull, muscular and surprising. It is saying, 'I am not just a pretty face'. Rivers are disconcerting in the way that they present their own version of landscape. Walk along the banks, and it is the familiar account of the local landscape, get into a boat and foreign country is floating by. As well as patches of cress and weed, the surface is dimmed with combine-dust from the harvest until we reach the stony shallows which herald the millrace, then all is flashing brilliance. The water falls in a continuous glass sheet and is roaring with all its might. Ahead is the white clapboard skyscraper which is Wissington Mill and some of the tallest riverside trees I have ever seen. We debate as to whether we should let the friends who live in the Mill know that we are bumping about outside. No, we must return. An argosy of three watery miles has to be made if we are to be home by supper, and so more cross swans, more trailing alders to ruffle our hair, more corn-dust, then the chub-fancier, then the exposed gardens with their fashionable decking, then the currents into which we must not plunge and, all the way, 'the scenes which made me a painter' – John Constable. Although for him it was a toilscape, work all the way for men and boys and horses.

It is sad to disembark, to gather up the cushions and oars, and to walk the few steps to what was the miller's fine house, to feel our land feet. No bankside trees and bushes in Constable's day. The towing-path must be kept clear. But dozens of skiffs and scores of rods belonging to the Stour boys, the artist's 'young Waltonians'. And the familiar drama of 'The Leaping Horse' when a whistle would make a great Suffolk Punch jump over the little fences which kept the cattle from straying. Commuters cars are homing-in on the village. Showers and dinners and soaps await. Overhead the passengers will be buckling their belts for the Stansted landing. In the church Constable's 'Christ presides at the Last Supper'. James's arms ache from so much rowing, ours with idleness.

In the Vestry

Never so many waiting starlings. Were there five wires linking my transformer to Maltings Farm they would have sat there like some opening movement of a great piece of music. The mood is one of impending profligacy. Notices are being fixed to the roadside to warn drivers where the grain-wagons will turn in or emerge. It is very still. They are waiting to cut. Any day now the towering machines will, with a bit of luck, clank from the dens in which they have been sleeping these last fifty weeks and the wheat-dust will fly.

I have always loved waiting. Not too long, of course. Waiting for the friend to appear and who should be neither late nor early, so as not to spoil the waiting with anxiety or prevent there being a wait at all. Ditto with trains. Not to catch them by the skin of one's teeth or to have to stand on the platform for an hour, losing patience and losing heart. Just a nice wait so that one can look through the waiting-room window at the familiar meadows which cover King Cymbeline's city. Every priest will know about that special wait before the service begins. The bell is going, the cars are still arriving, the clock is ticking, the vestry prayer has been whispered, the church door has opened and closed heaven knows how many times, and still he must wait. And how pleasant it is. Another four minutes to read the framed Table of Fees, or to muse on the Victorian clergy in the framed photographs, with their huge snowy collars and resting hands – to think of them standing where he is standing, just waiting for the service to begin. 'Prepare us, O God, for the worship of Thine house.'

Our three vestries are distinctive where waiting is concerned. Little Horkesley's is ebullient, lots of choir finding lots of music and waiting for even more choir to finish ringing, and for the last-minuter to rush in at the penultimate moment. 'Don't hurry, plenty of time!' This is not so, but one has to be Christian in the circumstances. My mother was always late for church, something she always denied, declaring 'They started early.' Which was one way of looking at it. At Wormingford the waiting is for the congregation *en masse*. A minute to eleven and the church is empty and then, just as the clock is about to strike, there they all are in their proper places. It is a miracle. They are last-minuters, a special race, and by every law of rush they should be out of puff, but they are unhurried. They kneel and sit and exchange little leisurely greetings. And there is still a full thirty seconds to go. Alone in Mount Bures vestry, the waiting is an enchantment. I have often had a good mind to ask God to let old Mr Chaplin toll on for ever, or to the end of our days, whichever is the longest.

Wide Views

Stubble-walking begins. The great fields are cleared and bone dry, the harvest dust has settled and the lapwings are gleaning what they can, which is not much in these efficient farming days. Stubble-walking produces views which can only be seen in late August and the landscape becomes unfamiliar and vast. Here and there are black patches where the corn caught fire, a poor charred oak and a burnt hedge. This was tinder country until the weather broke, and the firemen were kept busy. The clamour of their engines intensified the sun's heat as they rushed to douse some flaming crop. But now the annual clearance and the parched earth between the wheat needles is full of finds for those with keen eyes, tin buttons, a worked flint and modest aftermath flowers which have escaped the spray. It is all so interesting that one hardly knows on which to concentrate most, the enormous reaped acres or the minutiae at one's feet. I am stomping and crunching to Dida's to use her photocopier, though mostly tramping through the lanes because they promise a storm. But it never comes; just a few penny-sized raindrops and an indigo sky.

It is the season of misinformation. Nathanael, who may have been Bartholomew, could not believe his ears when Philip told him where the Lord came from. 'Can any good thing come out of Nazareth?' Scripture is as unforthcoming on this apparently bad address as it is on the apostle himself – unless, of course, he is Nathanael, when the sharp interchange with Christ plainly reveals a man of bright perception. There was a St Bartholomew's Chapel in a farmyard near our childhood home. It stood on a slope and was full of carts and tractors, and hens sat in its medieval window frames. It took some getting to through the fields but now a motorway has managed to resite it, bringing it to the verge of constant traffic. The Benedictines built it at the same time as the Augustinians built their St Bartholomew's Priory in the Smooth Field, London, so the apostle for all his obscurity was real enough then. My own untheological conviction is that we are allowed the name only of certain men and women close to Christ in order for us to 'recreate' them as best we can. He frequently retorted, 'Do I have to spell it out to you?' Meaning in the case of Bartholomew/ Nathanael, 'He was of my inner circle – go on from there.'

SEPTEMBER

*I*n September 1977 John Nash died and Ronnie inherited Bottengoms, where John and Christine had lived since the 1940s. I had first met Ronnie in 1964, and thereafter often stayed with him in his rented house outside Debach while he was writing Akenfield. Bottengoms was a revelation. The enchanted hollow in which the old farm lay hidden had the feel not only of a lost world but of a lost era. At first Ronnie treated the house somewhat like a shrine to its recently departed ghosts, so imbued was it with fond and formative memories. To me, his junior by nineteen years to the day, the place had the aura of a museum of Bloomsburyana.

One day I insisted it was time to purge the house of sacred Nash clutter and supplant it with Blythe stuff. He reluctantly agreed and together we hauled a lot of decrepit things outside and made a bonfire of them. They included a motheaten and wonky chaise-longue. Its stuffing caught fire with acrid smoke accompanied by Ronnie's belated cries of misgiving. 'But that belonged to Dora Carrington! Virginia Woolf would have sat on that. And Lytton Strachey, Maynard Keynes, E. M. Forster . . .' 'They're all dead,' I said briskly, 'so they won't be needing it and neither do you. Come on — it was a frightful old thing.' By the end of that day the ashes of it all had made Ronnie extremely cheerful. Bottengoms was finally his, updated to the here and now.

James Hamilton-Paterson

Flying Seeds

One of my childhood autumn sounds was to hear a big spider negotiating the ancient bedroom wallpaper where it had become loose on the uneven wall. September spiders now appear in the bath, and have to be carried to the garden by the glass and postcard method. In fact, the latter spider transport is an essential September fitting, by the soap.

In the beds below, Himalayan balsam – *Impatiens glandulifera* – fires off all guns as I brush past it. It should be by the stream. If one has to have a pest, then have *Impatiens*, with its pink–purple flowers, sculptural stems, and happy bees rocking in its petal boats. I give it its head. Let it flourish where it will.

It was first discovered in the Looe Valley in 1900 and called 'a cumbersome weedy thing'. Well, so it is. But something infinitely more. It is undeniably grand and extraordinarily beautiful. When it is over, when it has aimed its last seeds and there is a hint of rot, how easy it is to pull up the shallow plate of its roots and carry it off to where it can speedily perish, its seeds popping all the way.

'Squeeze the pod gently,' I tell the little girl. The life between her fingers shocks her.

My garden is watery. Springs in all directions. And this morning, moles building an Underground, mercifully where it doesn't make me wild. So much going on, including the Vicar's departure. We were given good notice when this would happen. In September. But September has a curious habit of being distant until it is 'here'.

Priests look down from the incumbents board. Some stayed five years, others fifty. In a village, their ministries were like rural reigns. 'In Mr Tufnell's time,' we say. Our diocese, too, has shifted about. As for deaneries – we have been here, there and everywhere. Yet the parish itself is immovable. The same Stour-side confidence in itself, the same views – and not only the geographical ones. And now Henry is off to where he and his wife will have to work hard doing nothing. Or filling 'nothing' in with this strange commodity known as retirement. And what of us?

The Bishop is coming to see him off. He – Henry, that is – must have his last word in three separate pulpits, and in three magazines. Christian unity is all very well, but a benefice must be disunited, now and then. I met a previous incumbent the other day, and was astonished to find him well and sane after twenty years without us.

Mr Rix is irrigating his vegetable acres. A Versailles of fountains swivel in all directions. Wet sugar beet look almost pretty. But summer is leaving us, and the early mornings are sharp. Late roses are profuse. And such cloud formations! The light in East Anglia is said to be like that of the Low Countries, and the making of Thomas Gainsborough and John Constable, and especially the Norwich school of artists. This month, it has the clarity of cut glass. Orange and grey mountains journey above our heads.

Shaking hands in the churchyard, an old friend complains of 'those halls of Sion being conjubilant with song' – 'all jubilant' would have been enough. Yet it would not, although a leaving congregation is not the moment to defend J. M. Neale.

Not a fallen leaf on the graves.

The Freshness of Repeated Actions

Blessed routine. No appointments in the diary, thus a full day. Blessed Lord, grant thy servants the inestimable joys of routine. Blackberries for breakfast. They have to be eaten up before it's October and they get spitted. I wander about in the soaking orchard, a bedraggled sight. Pale hay where I have begun to scythe, brittle seeding-plants everywhere else. No fruit to squash in the long grass this year. But blackberries galore. My badgers have made a highway from the field edge to the stream. The stream has cut Wormingford off from Little Horkesley for ever and ever.

'But it is a united benefice,' I tell it.

'Whoever heard of such a thing?' the stream replies.

The Bishop is coming to see the Vicar off, routinely but lovingly. I shall hold his crosier and hand him his mitre. Each of them has mastered the art of routine — of retaining the freshness of repeated actions. Now what shall we do? Interregnums may be routine, but each one of them is a space that is not at all like its predecessors.

Henry's leaving present is a hefty garden seat that our village joiner has made from the immense old fir tree that swayed dangerously near the tower. It was planted by a priest in the 1890s. The remainder of it is blazing on our hearths. Simon, our woodman, brought it down.

All around, the Suffolk–Essex fields are in different stages of clearance, full cultivation — for the supermarkets — and rest. They are also full of birds, and are lit morning and evening by glaringly beautiful suns. The sky becomes an aerial goldmine of exposed seams, and a vision of the insubstantial. Our vicarage is the grandstand for all this. But my old farmhouse knows only golden mornings, and has never in all its centuries witnessed sunset. All its routines have taken place in broad daylight. And at dead of night.

There is no more compulsive routine than that followed by the true diarist. Diarists are frank about this. James Boswell admitted that he could live no more than he could record. And the self-indulgent Anaïs Nin declared: 'The period without the diary remains an ordeal. Every evening I want my diary as one wants opium.'

For me, the diary of diaries was written by a young curate on the Welsh border, Francis Kilvert. So what a marvel that they found the family photograph album to illustrate it. As president of the Kilvert Society, I give myself leave to pore over this black-and-white Victorian Church of England heyday. To identify the serious faces, the 'caught' tennis matches, the assembled college students, and the handsome person of Kilvert himself before death carried him out of sight, aged 39.

'Why do I keep this voluminous journal?' he asked himself. 'I can hardly tell. Partly because life appears to me such a curious and wonderful thing that it almost seems a pity that such a humble and uneventful life as mine should pass altogether away without some such record as this.'

The routine of uneventfulness, this is what I praise in the early morning orchard. Of Jamie the postman bumping down the track. Of the swerving flight of the green woodpecker. Of the white cat cleaning her chops on the wall.

The Seedsman's Celebration

It is getting on for six, and still I lie abed, automatically listening to *Farming Today*. I feel that it is my duty to report any cheerfulness that might break into its professional misery.

This morning, the programme tells me how the rain has caused the combines to get stuck in the mud. Well, I want to retort, are there not still thousands of people alive who harvested with their feet stuck in it? The Prophet Muhammad prayed: 'O God, make it rain round us, and not on us.'

The pastoral imagery of the world's religions is most in evidence at this time of the year. Heard, but not felt, not seen. Machinery alone bears the pain and gains the glory.

The dual depression caused by the puddled field, Bunyan's Slough of Despond, which squelched away both yield and joy, is virtually unknown to the present harvester. I see them on my Victorian tithe map, those sinks in the soil which the binder skirted if it had any sense. Theologically, they represented the ups and downs of village life, though never its *De Profundis*. One would have to plunge far deeper to experience this.

Tess was en-route to this god forsaken void when Thomas Hardy demoted her from the lush pastures to take a turn at trimming swedes.

> How it rained
> When we worked at Flintcomb-Ash
> And could not stand upon the hill
> Trimming swedes for the slicing-mill,
> The wet washed through us — plash, plash, plash!
> How it rained!

After breakfast, clad in my thistledown-light waterproof and wellies, I walked to the depressions on the tithe map. The combine had scooped the corn out of them, and the harrow had combed them into shiny ridges. I thought of the soaking plough-horses being geed round their perimeter, and the ploughman with wet sacking up to his thighs, and the little indented pond glinting evilly.

As John the seedman and his wife, Sheila, are fifty years wed, we join them at the golf club restaurant to celebrate. Their 1958 wedding album invites our glance. How can people be half a century younger and yet just the same?

The electronic equipment thumps out the 'Anniversary Waltz', and they dance. In the photograph, they smile in front of the church porch, c. the Armada. Guests take to the floor and hop about. Grace has been said. We eat rather a lot. We feel a unity of spirit. The golf club has grown out of the strawberry fields; the strawberry fields out of the aerodrome; the aerodrome out of the cornfields; and all in a lifetime.

Through the broad window, I watch a watery sunset, the runny colours, the blackening of the day. I think of a trip round the great seed sheds with John, and listening to his amazing facts.

He has been, all his working life, custodian of our seed temple. A million million separate entities of plant existence were there in the dust and dusk, just waiting. To think that Paul and John Nash painted their Western Front pictures in a seed shed.

I give the Golden Weddingers a book, and they say, 'We will read it in the winter.'

Saturday Afternoon

Like failing health, we sense rather than experience the first signs of decline in our institutions. To put it brutally, our annual horticultural show has not been what it was. One of the reasons was – for we have put this decline behind us – that we have long been intimidated from the grave by that pair of first-prize grasping professionals Pipkin and Drew, who, at another time and in another place, hogged the trestles, causing the rest of us not to compete. They were veg- and flower-raising farmworkers whose competitiveness was on a par with that of the bidders for Harrods and who now, one must presume, are scowling at each other across that great marquee in the sky. Their legacy remained earthy enough. It was that nobody who could not grow their kind of epic produce had any right to 'show'. This year Gordon put a stop to all that, and thus put a stop to decline. Brushing aside our offers to buy raffle tickets, etc., he commanded us to *exhibit*. In vain we pleaded the unworthiness of our blooms, our plums, our onions. Standing over us, he made us fill up the entry form, dismissing our protests as he pointed to our trees and beds. 'What's wrong with those? Lovely apples. Put them in.' Under these dire orders, I lugged to the village hall a massive plant for the Succulents section, six runner beans, some Victoria plums which deserved no apology and, something which I really did believe would be a knockout, a jar of quince jam, c.1996. However, it soon became apparent that where showing is concerned I did not know the rules. I was still reeling from the joy of hearing the flower judge say, 'Oh, I do like that! First prize!' when she came to my succulent, when I observed the jam judge when she came to my quince summoning up the kind of courage which a bomb disposal unit requires. First she set it a little aside so that it did not contaminate the other entries, and then she unscrewed it and tasted it. How was I to know that a metal-topped jam jar is a horrible sight to a judge, possibly the worst she has ever seen? Or that boomerang-shaped runners are equally *de trop*, though young Mr Tokely the veg judge holds back his shock. The big room fills with the special redolence of September, a classic biblical fruitfulness, as well as with cries of amazement as Gordon's bullied exhibitors find First Class propped up on their apologetic entries. Donald, whose task the yearly creating of the show is, smells recovery from decline and takes us to the pub to celebrate.

It rains like the opening of *Rashomon*, sheeting down, and the footballers play through it. Double glazing mutes their shouts. The ball itself is a watery meteorite slapping through the air. The soaked teams run with their mouths wide, yelling and laughing and drenched. The referee does those little backward steps which you see on television, spitting rain from his whistle. What a day.

Dwindling Landworkers

A vociferous week in the countryside, although it always amuses me when farmers bewail the remoteness of government when half of Whitehall seems to commute from farmhouses, barn-houses and restored cottages. The popular image of the farmer is that of a stolid man not easily stirred to wrath, whereas the truth is that he is likely to be an emotional and somewhat lonely chap now having to involve himself with many things which go against the grain. He lives on a hundred acres or six hundred acres with only beasts for company, all his men gone, and without the old sociability of market-day in the neighbouring town and scores of other things which came to a halt in the 1960s, never to start up again. A contractor zooms up and down his fields twice a year and his sons can't tell a coulter from a shovel. Hodge and his master have at long last parted company.

We pore over the old photograph albums, picking out faces, fashions, machines, wide views of small expectations. Here is the wrathful grandfather who threatened to hang the government during those huge farmers' rallies on Newmarket Heath in the Thirties when things could not have been worse. Here he is fighting the Church during the Tithe War. Here are Brownie snaps of quite unbelievable poverty in the tied cottages, the tin bath dangling on a wall, the arrested faces of the children, the bike against the woodpile, brief views of quite amazing poverty, of rural beauty not quite masking rural collapse. The history of agriculture is a roller coaster of heart-stopping plunges and brief peaks. Apart from wartime subsidies, no government has been able to steady it. But one triumph over what used to happen is that although plagues continue to sweep through the cows, pigs and chickens just as they used to from time immemorial, for the first time in farming history there is never corn failure.

At harvest festival the new commuters sit in the ancient pews and the old farmers walk to the lectern to read about Ruth gleaning and then temptingly resting at the foot of young Boaz's bed, and about Christ's seed parables, nodding comfortably to the altar en route. There is a home-made loaf on the altar and some especially grown long-stalked wheat to make a proper sheaf. And a positive supermarket display of fruit and veg for the churchwardens to take to St Saviour's, Hackney for the, to us, puzzlingly homeless. In the pulpit I do my best to reconcile agribusiness, as they now describe it, with yesterday's reaping, binding and stooking. There are still quite a few folk present, widows of horsemen, daughters and sons of the last classic harvesters who ran around the crowded fields to watch the poor rabbits and hares trying to escape the dogs as the binder reduced their cover, to see that I get the facts right. We sing the 65th psalm in which God 'providest for the earth' and crowns the year with his goodness, and its elemental language strips away all the agritech, if only for a moment.

Then a walk to the river, to see how it is getting on, as they say. It is swollen with rain. Later, a waning harvest moon casts its watery light on dripping tombstones. Grain-dryers thud in the barn, so not to worry.

Old Money-bags

Tawny gold days with chilly showers. Shrivelled oak leaves on the long lawn. The white cat in her winter chair. Financial mayhem on the kitchen radio. I have been dibbing bulbs in and clearing beds.

The first day of autumn being St Matthew's day, I preach on this reformed taxman at matins. 'Old Money-bags' our ancestors called him, because of his attributes in the stained-glass picture.

The entire village smells of Mr Rix's onions, acres and acres of them, grown for the supermarket. It is beautiful. I am still finishing up those that fell from his trucks last year, tugging them from the strings in the larder. Tonight I will pull the popping balsam from the stream, and the water will gather speed. Last night, there were loud owls.

Old friends have celebrated their birthdays: Duncan his eightieth, Dodo her hundredth – Duncan's in a snowy marquee, Dodo's in a mock-manorial hall at Hadleigh, which, as everybody knows, is an archiepiscopal peculiar. These two gatherings might be said to represent my world: one, farming and the Church; the other, the arts.

They were tremendous feasts, and attended by guests of all generations. Folk from near and far. There were wry speeches, and, at Dodo's party, the candles set off the smoke alarm. How various were their lives. She a girl at St Petersburg, he a boy from Ayrshire.

She walked round the tables on the arm of a tall youth. She wore a rich orange dress and the family garnets, and was her imperious self. We passed a photo of her parents' wedding from hand to hand — a terrace full of prosperous Edwardians with several years to enjoy before the Western Front. Dodo retains their confidence. We sit up when she telephones, never announcing who it is. 'Dodo!' we exclaim. Who else?

An entire universe of cousins etc. have arrived. The one I faced was Jean-Claude, a Protestant lay canon from France. We shout at each other over the plates. At Duncan's lunch, I say an agricultural grace and talk to a dear old man from the fields. He spoke of stooking the sheaves. His face was pale with Time — as was Dodo's — for the years have a way of quietly draining us as the months drain the leaves.

On Thursday, I went to Bury St Edmunds for the cathedral chapter meeting, the country bus wandering extravagantly through parish after parish, my nose pressed to the window to see as much as I could.

Then Bishop Nigel and Dean Neil in the chapter house, then tea, then an extraordinary confession from the Polish taxi-driver on the last phase home. Glancing at me, summing up whether I could take it, young, and, I thought, rather sad, he asked if I was 'religious'. Adding that he could tell that I was 'a gentleman'. What next?

Swerving past some cyclists, summoning up his courage, he said that he had seen an angel. Did I believe him? I told him about a great English poet called Blake, who saw angels in Golden Square in London. He told me that he was married and had a little daughter. I praised his English. He was, I thought, about twenty-two and rather lost. Or maybe found. He was certainly an adventurous driver. There are times when one must be an adventurous listener.

William Blake wrote:

And we are put on earth a little space,
That we may learn to bear the beams of love.

Becoming Old

We have two evensongs, one every Sunday at Little Horkesley, one each month at Wormingford, one with the biggest attendance, one with the smallest, and both stemming from traditions that are largely forgotten.

Churchgoing rules and figures in the countryside were created more by the timing of the main meal on the sabbath than by its prayer pattern. To enable their army of servants to have time off for God, the middle classes had dinner at two instead of eight. They went to matins (and holy communion about four times a year), and their staff, having washed up, laid the table for supper and dressed up, went to evensong.

There was much singing and, afterwards, long walks, then home again strictly by ten. And, of course, it was pre-eminently the service for the farmworkers and their families. Usually the best television of the week, plus, I used to suspect, some connivance by the clergy to rid themselves of this service, has resulted in the actual oddity of evensong in many minds.

It is, of course, liturgically most beautiful and spiritually entirely satisfying. Just to read it at home at about four o'clock sets the day right. If our three churches were nearer, I would read it in one of them, but they are miles away. So, I sing it alternately with Henry, the Vicar at Little Horkesley, along with this surprising-to-some large attendance; and every first Sunday in the month here at

Wormingford, with the Colonel, the bell-ringers and the church-wardens, the two candles wavering, the four hymns, too.

And I think to myself how good I am at Quiet control. Not even the wild goings-on of Jonah disturb us, or the lukewarm antics of Laodicea. All is submerged in ancient prayer. But for sermon I read both the great and small evensong folk something I have written about the sea-routes of the early faith, and I think I imagine its sound like the entrancing noise in a shell when it is clasped to the ear and entirely listened to.

To Norwich to talk to the annual general meeting of Age Concern. It is convened in one of those hotels that have conference suites, and I am met with a stand which says, 'How to arrange your funeral'. We are far from evensong.

In my late forties, I began to write a book about old age, feeling Time pressing on me. It was a philosophical riposte to Simone de Beauvoir's brilliant Marxist tirade against the dying of the light, and also a kind of stand against some of the ideas that have created today's old-age management.

An old lady was telling someone, 'And when she saw me she said, "Why, you keep on looking younger!"' But what an incomparably better world it is for the old, with its dentistry, hygiene, pretty clothes, disposable income – and long, long years. Four-score-years-and-ten are becoming the norm. Christ raised only the young from their death, those like the governor's daughter, or the widow's son, or his friend Lazarus, who deserved a life to live, not those who had already lived it.

And so to King Street in Norwich, the city's first entrance, by the side of which a very old woman went on living long after she had written a book called her *Revelations of Divine Love*. She said that 'We need love, longing and pity', curious necessities, some now would think. When she was thirty, she thought it 'a pity to die'; so she got better in order to be a writer, among other things.

Insect Thinking

Settling below the tomatoes on the east wall, I experience the usual futility of reading when the sun glitters through leaves and time itself takes a break. I might have sunk into torpor had it not been for the dragonfly on my knee. Gradually, landing and taking off several times, it became an object for meditation. It flew a few yards, then walked on bare skin with an adventurous uncertainty like a man on the moon. I could see cyclamen through its translucent wings. Invisible behind a hedge, someone set up a mighty clanging like a wild call to arms as the horses' water-trough was mended, and I turned a page, but still the dragonfly did not alter its course of brief flights and short stays. I assumed it was a Darter, being at that September moment deficient in Odonata knowledge and not liking to deprive it of its living pad as I searched for a natural history book. And thus we continued for an hour or more, the motionless man and the sensational insect, the banging in the meadow and the delectable autumn day.

Later, I read my favourite insect-contemplation essay, 'The Death of the Moth' by Virginia Woolf: 'It was a pleasant morning, mid-September, mild, benignant, yet with a keener breath than that of the summer months ... Such vigour came rolling in from the fields [when] the same energy which inspired the rooks, the ploughmen, the horses ... sent the moth fluttering from side to side of his square of the windowpane.' She should have opened the window and let it out, but she went on working and the moth danced his way to death. Soon she would fill her pockets with stones and walk to the river. The Kentish poet Sidney Keyes wrote her Elegy.

Unfortunate lady, where white crow foot binds
Unheeded garlands starred with crumpled flowers,
Lie low, sleep well, safe from the rabid winds
Of war and argument, our hierarchies and powers.

The Old Testament writers had a sharp eye for insects, as one would expect in the Middle East. Samson's riddle about the bees hiving in a dead lion is delightful. Tate and Lyle printed the answer, 'Out of the strong came forth sweetness', on their treacle tins. The Lord hisses up flies and bees and young David calls poor old Saul a flea. Judges spin webs as wiley snares, and enemies such as the Amorites chase one as bees do. But on the whole, Bible insects area plague and ages would pass before a country clergyman would observe dispassionately, 'After the servants are gone to bed, the kitchen hearth swarms with minute crickets not so large as fleas, which must have been lately hatched. So that these domestic creatures, cherished by the influence of a constant large fire, regard not the season of their year, but produce their young at a time when their congeners are either dead, or laid up for the winter, to pass away the uncomfortable months in the profoundest slumbers ...' Why did Virginia Woolf not open the window, then her moth would have lived? Why am I sitting here in the faintly rotting autumn garden long past elevenses so that a dragonfly can do whatever it is that dragonflies do on a nice quiet leg? Its pond shimmers through the nettles but it is me it is eyeing with all its eyes.

Any Other Business?

Autumn. 'The harvest is past, the summer is ended, and we are not saved.' Jeremiah the poet at his most poignant. Autumn. Two spiders in the bath, three harvest festivals and four committee meetings, and these before September is out. It has always been part of my fantasy life to believe that the last committee meeting would be the last. But what a hope. Warm voices on the telephone and a cold agenda in the post wheedle and demand further attendance. In vain my pointing out that I have done my stint or lost a leg. 'Put the 28th in your diary – eight o'clock as

323

usual.' There are those among our rustic bureaucrats who have never been known to say anything more than 'Please pass the sugar' when the coffee is served. I myself look back on an aeon of holy wrangles, doubtful decisions and inspired conclusions, and on big wall clocks in village halls ticking supper and my favourite programmes away, at merciful or cruel or hopeless chairmen, and at gifted doodlings – 'You should have been an artist' – round the edges of the financial statement. I am the wryly inattentive person in Henry Reed's 'The Naming of Parts', who balances the sublimity of the blossom seen outside the window against the regulations which must be enforced within the room. 'Any against?' asks Michael the vicar. ('Pay a little more attention that boy at the back. And sit up straight!') Quiet, unsung ministries. His – Michael's – is to the sick. There are others, some towards the running of our affairs.

But it is autumn and the fruit falls into the long grass. I press bagfuls of William pears on everyone who comes to the house. They don't keep. But the Victoria plums are stoned and put into the freezer. The sun is delectable and at bedtime the harvest moon is hung in the trees to show the foxes where to go. I lie listening to *The Great Gatsby*, wide awake and extremely attentive. At one of the harvest festivals I retold the enchanting tale of Ruth, and how it is that her romance has to come between the last words of Judges, when the young Benjaminites ambushed the dancing girls of Shiloh 'catching you every man his wife', and the first words of Samuel, when the trusting Hannah prays in the disgraced temple at Shiloh for a son. All this at Mount Bures where, somehow, I have to tactfully get faithful old Mr Chaplin to set the mower blades high so that he doesn't destroy the harebells. These are a rare and lovely sight in summer in that high churchyard. They are witch flowers, of course, also the bluebells of Scotland, and never to be picked once upon a time. They turn the ancient sward azure. Mr Chaplin is back to his cottage and into his gardening clothes by the time I have signed the register. 'Mr Chaplin, er . . .'

Blackberrying at Southwold

I was trying to remember when I first came here, as Vicki steered us through the holiday traffic. It would have been when little houses on South Green cost £400 and were not called The Bolt Hole.

The North Sea is a steady azure until it is within sight of the horizon, when it turns to skimmed-milk blue. The day is fair. The cannon point towards the invaders. The visitors are semi-dressed in pretty clothes, and there are some fine dogs. How delicious it is to be here after the A12 crawl. How could George Orwell have detested it? We park the car in a meadow, and go in search of Ian and Joachim, who are, we trust, cooking.

Southwold is having one of its white and gold 'Nelson' days, with whipping flags and well-scrubbed humanity, and the white lighthouse standing idle. I imagine English Impressionist girls crowding the bridge and holding on to their hats. After lunch in the harbourmaster's cottage, we wander across the common and pick each other the first blackberries. The public benches are deserted, as everyone is on the beach.

'See that house?' says Ian. 'It was built for retired servants.'

Authorship has taken a hold every few steps. See that house? It is where Agnes Strickland and her sister Elizabeth, whose name never appears, wrote *The Lives of the Queens of England*. I look her up. 'Her somewhat flat writings were extremely popular, perhaps because of their use in teaching.' I see these Victorian ladies putting down their pens for an hour for a gusty stroll to Walberswick, their maid banking up the fire for their return.

There is a kind of concealed strenuousness about the Suffolk coast. Maybe it was about keeping warm – not to mention solvent. Or possibly it was the wind perking one up. But a lot got done – although at this Bank Holiday moment, nothing whatever is being done, and the ambulating sloth, the prostrate bodies, the faint calls create a lovely watercolour rest. It is as though the Mayor of Southwold has appeared in all her golden glory at a window and decreed, 'Do nothing!'

Naturally, there are shrieks when a brave soul enters the sea, although Ian does so without a cry. But then he comes from Norfolk. Mostly, people sit outside pubs, deep in conversation. I thought that I would like to sit in an ocean-fronting window for a week, turning the pages of a novel, looking up, looking out, with a good cat for company. But the evening comes, and the Bank Holiday ends, and a few homing gulls wail their way along the River Blyth, and Vicki says, 'Wouldn't it be nice to live here! What do you think?' It is a question we all ask after a day out.

Meanwhile, back at the ranch, the grass needs cutting, and the white cat needs adoration. And something has to be said at matins next Sunday, Trinity 15. St Paul is in Corinth, staying with some fellow tentmakers, a man and his wife. They were Jews who had been driven out of Rome by the Emperor Claudius, and, having suffered for their faith, they were in no mood to change it for that being preached by their lodger, no matter that he belonged to their trade. Eventually, all three of them sailed away to Ephesus.

What would have been happening on the Suffolk coast then? Well, the sea would have been baring its claws to scratch at the land, and no one would have been swimming, that's for sure.

Moveable Feastings

Feeling around in the dark for the garden tools which I should have brought in when it was light, I am confronted by the huge orange stare of the harvest moon. It is the astral version of the pumpkin I have just cut for harvest festival. It weighs a ton, more by the looks of it than the moon. The harvest loaf itself has been baked at Coggeshall in the correct sheaf shape and will journey from St John's altar to St Andrew's altar. It is the old kind of bread which atrophies rather than moulders, and could well do another year.

Years ago, when the moon and its harvest were in kilter, father would take me to festal evensong at the Suffolk church on the hill where we had both been baptised, All Saints, Acton. There was stubble in the September fields in those days. Few cars, thus a tramping, talking congregation. 'Is that you, George?' someone would call, knowing perfectly well that it was. Up the lime avenue we would process, affecting surprise and delight at seeing friends we knew quite well would be there. The beloved interior had more to do with amplitude than taste. Thickets of michaelmas daisy, mountains of fruit and vegetables, the pulpit festooned with hops and grapes, the way to the lectern perilous with what was always politely called garden produce, and the indescribably holy smell of paraffin, starch and plants. A low sun blazed in from the west and mortified the oil lamps. Having walked three miles through stubble fields in short trousers – 'Sunday best' – my legs were scratched and slightly bloody. From where we sat I could view the stupendous glory of Squire Jennens, who died in 1722, dressed elegantly in lace and silk, and propped up on a marble mattress. He regarded our peasant thankfulness with a kind of tolerant disdain from behind his iron screen. He had been adjutant to the Duke of Marlborough and had retired to a mansion in the village. On the other side of the chancel was the equally wonderful monument to Sir Robert de Bures, who died in 1302, the year in which Pope Boniface issued a bull saying, 'Men live on two levels, one spiritual, the other temporal. If the temporal power should go astray, it must be judged by the spiritual power' – i.e. Pope Boniface. Sir Robert, who was six and a half feet tall, lay under one of the finest of English brasses. I knew him from top to toe, every chink in his armour, from rubbing him with kitchen paper and heelball bought from Mrs Diaper, who mended our shoes. Many years later, visiting my brother in New South Wales, I was touched to see Sir Robert's brass-rubbing hanging majestically in the hall, his surcoat flapping in its familiar way, his lion hassock comforting his feet and his long hands at prayer. 'Is that you, Sir Robert?'

He would have been alive when Covent Garden market was first set up, though he could scarcely have imagined marrows on his tomb.

The Mad and the Sane

I am handling Victoria plums, slitting them on the breadboard to let the stones tumble out. It is a plump sexy fruit, nice to touch, firm and soft and juicy. The greengages simply burst on their own account, the blackberries stain everything. The freezer swells. Mr Bradshaw has kindly tamed my tall wild hedge, made it into a come-to-attention straight line, taking care not to lop the lilacs, wielding 'the murderer' skilfully. We have quite forgiven this hedge-trimmer for the wounds it incurs. My only criticism of its use nowadays is that farmers tidy up too quickly after harvest and forget that they destroy all the hips and haws and other bird foods. Once it was the scythe which was death to the leveller, now it is this crashing knife which slides along the lanes like a cut-throat razor over whiskers. I barrow ash logs into the chimney corner and pile them artistically, leaving the sawn ends showing.

I am working on an essay about the World War One poet Ivor Gurney, the singer of Gloucestershire who, after the horrors of the trenches, like many another poor soldier, ended up in a madhouse, or to be exact Dartford City of London Mental Asylum, a dreadful place. Fourteen years after the Armistice Edward Thomas's widow found him there and gradually 'returned' the shambolic man in pyjamas to who he really was by means of spreading out her husband's maps to the Cotswolds on Gurney's bed. 'I spent the whole time I was with him tracing with our fingers the lanes and byways and villages of which Ivor Gurney knew every step and over which Edward had also walked. He spent that hour (strict visiting times) in revisiting his home ... he trod, in a way we who were sane could not emulate, the lanes and fields he knew so well, his guide being his finger tracing the way on the map. It was most deeply moving, and I knew that I had hit on the idea that gave him more pleasure than anything else I could have thought of. For he had Edward as companion in this strange perambulation and he was utterly happy.'

When one reads the rules of institutions, prisons, workhouses, asylums, some schools even, certain religious orders, one can only question the sanity of society itself. What of the present culture of the old peoples' home? What will posterity make of that?

To the village to call on Phil and his wife in a garden which is the size of four tablecloths. He is stringing onions, she is tidying-up after the hedgehogs. She feeds them each evening with Phil's fish bait maggots, all four of them as they creep on to the lawn, and she agrees that if it was the seventeenth century Matthew Hopkins, our local witch-finder, would be knocking on her door. Joan also feeds some forty sparrows. Later, Phil brings me two great strings of onions to hang in, first a tree, and then in the larder. Like everything else, they must ripen.

Fordham Wood

It was the kind of weather one reads about more than sees. First an uncanny build-up of meteorological emotion, then the declared helplessness of animals as they sensed it, and then the scramble to collect the garden chairs, the washing, the everything which had been taken outside and left in the sun's safekeeping for what seemed months. It caught me on the last lap, a sheet of rain which soaked me to the skin in one drenching minute. It ran in scallops over the bone-dry earth and rivered its way down the track to where it knew the river was. It churned in the guttering and spouted from rooftops. I let it beat on me, having nothing more to lose and it shot in an arc from my nose. Summer rain *in excelsis.* I had read outside all day and although the sky got lower and lower and the warm breeze stirred into a warm gale, and there was the sound of something or other on the march, still I read on the grass, having just done the watering as usual. The windows were wide as they had been for weeks.

And to think that only two days before the rain I and some of the strongest men the Woodland Trust could muster had nearly killed ourselves planting a dozen oaks in the new wood at Fordham, with a photographer from the local paper capturing our exhaustion. The ground was like concrete. It called for a pick-axe and all we had were beautiful silver spades. So we were reduced to scratching holes for oaklings, and saying sorry to the delicate plants as we introduced them to the home they would have for the following five hundred years. Will they when we are long gone tell each other of their dry starts? The following day about sixty of us walked the wood to be, men, women and chil-dren, and assorted dogs, tramping the hot land which is to become Wrens' Wood and listening to Geoff from the Woodland Trust, a Scot, telling us a thousand things we never knew about our own trees. Colchester was a Girtin or Cozens watercolour in the distance. The river on which it stood was a small stream at our feet. Here was a Stone Age farm, here a Roman farm, here the roots of the final wheat to be grown on these acres before a forest reclaimed it.

'Your old population is on its way back. Your barn owls, otters, nightingales, butterflies, wild flowers, your stag beetles, water voles, foxes, plus – Geoff estimates – some 213,000 trees.' I have been made Patron of Wrens' Wood and my pride knows no bounds. The humbling point is, how much of it will I live to see? The downpour will be feeding the ground, my tiny oaks, washing away my scratchings in the sand.

Mending the House

The autumn crocuses are out. Naked ladies. They stand in immaculate clusters here and there, but where I do not recall seeing them before, flowers of the utmost purity. And the ash leaves are flying, and geese, too. Will anyone remember if I preach last year's harvest-festival sermon? Since it was so good, I mean. And when will the rain stop?

It blows thinly through the garden, and Keith, who is replacing the Second World War soft-wood windows with hardier stuff, has to work from the inside. Scotland seems a world away. The afternoon sun will be splintering Glen Lyon; the surface of Loch Rannoch will be gunmetal grey.

I am trundling off to bookshops to sign copies of my new book, *Aftermath*, alongside Peter the publisher. How did book launches go in the '30s, say? Were there such things? I know that you were not a 'popular novelist' until you were chauffeur-driven, or retained a suite at the Ritz. Things have come to a pretty pass – one that the Government will applaud.

I make some tea for Keith and myself. I have watched artists paint, but rarely with the admiration I have for Keith as he saws and glazes, sizes and fits. In the spring, his window will fly open, and birds will take over its creamy sill. People will look out of it long after my sight has gone.

He has filled in all the cracks in the wall, and he will crown his labours with a new brass door-knocker. 'It must be ten years since I last done your house,' he tells me. Must it? Oh, golly! (I have been reading a post-war novel.)

I put out some five hornets per morning, including one from my hair. But mostly the beautiful creatures beat against a sash window in the guest room, where one should have been able to boast about them as a gift, though apparently not. Releasing them from the glass, they zoom off like Spitfires, all go. Soon, the frosts will make them take cover, and the old room will not hear their organ music.

I make sharp fruit salad with green grapes, the final plums, some miscellaneous apples, and some wrinkled mandarins. Waste not, want not. Spare me your economies, says the white cat, tasting my bare feet. No, I reprimand myself, at the benefice harvest service it shall be the story of Ruth and her return to Bethlehem, the house of bread, none other. The ancestors of Jesus were wed from its cornfield.

We shall send our produce to St Saviour's, Hoxton, where those holy women will turn it into soup and I don't know what for poor lads on the streets. What is harder and harder to get across to modern congregations is that harvest festival is not about charity but gratitude for what grows, what flows, what climaxes in the autumn. While the earth remaineth, seedtime and harvest shall never cease. So, say 'Thank you.' The newly authorised Druids have something to tell us on this point. So grateful was Egypt for the Nile harvest that the divine Pharaoh himself helped to cut it and bring it in.

We are to read Nehemiah, one of my favourites. It is he who inspired the rebuilding of Jerusalem, and the reestablishment of its government, and the purification of its customs. Its ruined towers stood up in the sand like autumn crocuses once more, and there was singing in the Temple.

The Little Horkesley Farm Walk

Peggy and Roy come to lunch. Walking through the orchard, as they must, she sees the Victorian plums nidnoddering on the bough, pulling it to the grass. 'They aren't quite ready,' I tell her, meanly. She says that when she went to the fruit farm to buy 'half a stone', the man told her: 'They're a pound a pound, Peggy.'

'A pound of plums a pound?'

'That's what they are paying, Peggy.'

She picked plums on this farm during the war for a shilling a cart-load, let us say. I relent, and pick her a pound. She is a great gardener, and will notice the hulms of my devoured runner beans straggling still by the door, and that the tomatoes are blighted. But late roses do me proud.

Roy, who knows more about churches and parish life in East Anglia than anyone else, talks about the Churches Conservation Trust, which is handy, as I have just visited St Mary's Old Church at West Bergholt. It has a beautiful 'arrested' feeling of being untouched by any of the late twentieth-century changes. Airy and sacred, rather scrubbed-looking, and with rows of hat-pegs here and there, and a Saxon north wall doing sturdy service still, it breathed afresh.

I could have sat there for hours, but we – about thirty of us – were on the annual Farm Walk on a Sunday afternoon. A lane without a destination – well, a sugar beet field – allowed us to divert to the wood from which the village probably derived its name. Coppiced ash and oak reached for the sky, and weedy green ponds watered the brambles.

The children, released from their computer dens (I am probably doing them an injustice), swarmed up trees, and the congregation, dressed for the part, shed decades. Then tea and open-air evensong, where I preached on 'Walk while you have the light', and a donkey from over the fence accompanied our hymns. And all the time the curiously affecting atmosphere of the Conservation Trust's church up the road hung around me, as it were.

There, at the west end, was the gallery where the farm labourers sang Merbecke to fiddles. There, in the impossibly ancient bell-turret, dangled a Victorian bell, its clapper dully visible, its cage nicely slapdashed with whitewash. And, strangely, over the chancel arch, were the arms of James I, only partly peeled away like one of those transfers we stuck on the back of our hands when we were boys.

Although under the arms was not the royal motto, but the first line of glorious Psalm 68 in Latin, maybe as a compliment to the king's famous learning. *Exurgat Deus Dissipenter Inimici* – 'Let God arise and let his enemies be scattered.' And it ends, 'O God, wonderful art thou in thy holy places.'

Why are not the West Bergholtians in this holy place? Because, in 1904, as it had become remote from the heart of the village, everyone saved up to commission Sir Arthur Blomfield and Sons, the firm that employed Thomas Hardy, to build St Mary (New) in their midst. Thus releasing St Mary (Old) to dwell in immense silence after near-on 1000 years of parochial clamour.

Hang your sun hat on a peg and sit there. Read Psalm 68, in which 'thousands of angels' take a holiday from Sinai, and singers and minstrels, and damsels with timbrels, and 'little Benjamin', and the princes of Zabulon, and goodness knows who else kindly deputise for a vanished Essex choir.

Trinity Seventeen

Crack of dawn. Remove harvest spiders from bath and sink by the renowned postcard and glass method. From glacial porcelain to dewy earth in a second, what arachnidal bliss. Howls from a starving Max who hasn't seen a square meal for at least six hours. Switch off after headlines for the great creative silence of the day. Walk through the sopping grass eating cornflakes and Thinking. Thinking in fact that this is just the day for stubble-walking. Hugh the farmer and I had just been comparing our early experiences of this activity: how, after playing on the reaped fields, we would come home with blood thrillingly seeping through our socks. Corn stalks were sharper then, we reckoned. Other hardships came to mind – the dust! The threshers would tie three-cornered hankies over their mouths and looked like pirates. Mind you, this year's dust had been terrible. So much of it that from a distance it looked as though a field was on fire. I thought of little John Clare in the threshing barn at Helpston forming his first letters in harvest dust.

The stubble-walk is to the mill from which a young friend will soon be setting off for the Arctic. I am bringing him Barry Lopez's exquisite *Arctic Dreams: Imagination and Desire in a Northern Landscape,* one of my favourite travel books. Its chilly jacket burns in the September sun. One field has been rough-harrowed and makes tough going. Another is greening with aftermath. But most of the way is a silvery crunch at every step. And in any case, stubble-walking is not for looking down but for looking out at views which you cannot see from roads, vistas which carry the eye towards such unfamiliar horizons that one sometimes needs to concentrate on a distant tower to get one's bearing. The nearest men get to larks – in their heady exultation, that is – is when they go 'cross-country', whether moorland, desert or just a sequence of harvested fields. The mill-race is like an eternally falling curtain and the Stour itself like an exercise in rivery modesty, hidden and exposed by turns, willows and alders marking its passage. It used to be full of punts and canoes, cries and bodies, but now its undisturbed surface flows under our bridge like brown glass. The rail is hot, the river colder than you might think.

During the service at Little Horkesley I read Binyon's 'The Burning of the Leaves', a trifle prematurely, maybe, but it is my object to keep the congregation up to scratch, poetry-wise.

Now is the time for stripping the spirit bare,
Time for the burning of days ended and done.

And now is the time for the annual church bike ride, so thank heaven the combines are out of the lanes. What chance would they stand if they met with these scores of holy pedallers? The tower captains have flung open their belfries in the hope of enticing new ringers. I pick plums.

John Constable

Noon. A serene hour. I celebrate it in a garden chair. Intending to pull a fast one on the forecast on the rain, I have been mowing since six – or from very early, at any rate. Yet the sun still shines in open disobedience to what was foretold. Over my head, in the old ash, invisible birds are kicking up a racket. Otherwise, all is silent; although I still have in my head the devouring crackle and roar of Jonathan's yellow monster as it eats its way down the farm track, doubling its width. From a blackberry-bound footpath, it has become a Chaucerian highway.

Jonathan enquires if my and his old houses were built with ships' timbers, and I say that England would have had navies unparalleled to provide all the beams attributed to them. No, looking up as we both did, that wood was cut from the hedgerows and forests. And when it was already centuries old. Now it is iron-wood.

But noon. Mountainous clouds apologise for briefly hiding the noonday sun, and the rain-drenched flowers are doubly scented. Pleasantly aching from my labours, I nurse the lazy white cat.

Were it 200 years ago, John Constable would have walked by on his way to Uncle Abram at Garnon's. There is a riverside pasture there still called Constable's meadow. When the artist made a bid to capture the attention of the Royal Academy with his work – 'my six-footers', as he called his greatest landscapes – he named one of them *Noon*. It showed a wagon having its axles cooled in the Stour at midday. It would become the proto vision of the countryside, *The Hay Wain*. His friend Archdeacon Fisher gave it this title, although the vehicle is more likely to have been a timber wagon than a hay cart. Such a vehicle would have carried the oak beams to my and Jonathan's farm sites.

While the Royal Academy remained tepid and near-blind about Constable's work, it was praised in Paris, where it laid the foundations of Impressionism. Almost the only recognition of it here was by the *Examiner*, which thought that it 'approaches nearer the actual look of nature than any modern landscape whatever'. Which is why, as somebody remarked, *The Hay Wain* is now the English countryside of every English mind.

Would the artist's *Noon* have been a better title? It has all the listlessness of midday: its reverie of summer heat, flies and drinking horses, of not much more to do. Of the wagoner calling it a day. I spent my boyhood by such water, wading in a bit, bare toes squeezing the mud. It provided my first sense of ennui. The smell of the river remained until bedtime. It held the torpor of the valley in July, signing it off on my skin with insect bites. How amazing to have been able to paint all this.

Constable sold *The Hay Wain*, *The View on the Stour* and another picture to a dealer for 250 guineas. Recently, another of his six-footers, *The Lock*, sold for £20 million. But today's art prices have more to do with investment than painting, with having somewhere to put one's money. Somewhere safer than the banks. Constable told Fisher how worried he was that the mockery of critics would injure his children. They played by this pool.

President of the Kilvert Society

At eight o'clock in the morning, I go to the orchard in search of breakfast, where the white cat stares at me from a sagging branch. I discover twenty unpecked, or ungnawed, pears. I also discover the following in Francis Kilvert's *Diary*. (As president of his Society, I have to keep up with him.) Alas, the Welsh border is too far away for me to accompany it on its neo-Victorian outings, much as I would like to. But this is what appears in the *Diary* for Tuesday 6 September 1870:

We went into the green orchard where beautiful waxen looking August apples lay in the grass, under the heavily loaded trees. Williams gave me a pocket full of apples. The postman came in with the latest news, the *Evening Standard*. Williams tore the paper open and we saw the reports of Saturday confirmed and that a Republic had been proclaimed in Paris under General Trocher.

Crichton sent me 1½ brace of partridges. Really people are very kind in sending me game.

Our postman, Jamie, bumps down the farm track, thin as a rake, infinitely kind, and puts the letters in a glass-covered box which will soon be lost in the undergrowth. Soon, we are to have one of those mailboxes on a pole which one sees in American films. All this to save Jamie a trek to the house.

Listening to Trollope's *The American Senator* on Radio 4 on Sunday afternoon, this visitor to England – at about the same time as Kilvert was writing his *Diary* – deplores the absurdity of the House of Lords, but delights in 'your pillar boxes'. The letter box on the church yard wall says V.R.

It was probably on New Year's Day 1870 that Kilvert, Curate of Clyro, walked to Hay-on-Wye to purchase his first notebook at Horden's, the stationer's, thus to create one of the most brilliant records of the rural Church of England. Even now, all these years later, no country parish should be without it. It greens the Incumbents Board and sets the registers alive.

Kilvert was thirty when he began his *Diary*. 'Why do I keep this voluminous journal? I can hardly tell. Partly because life appears to me such a curious and wonderful thing, that it almost seems a pity that even such a humble and uneventful life as mine should pass altogether away without some such record as this, and partly because I think the record may amuse and interest some who come after me.'

He was a tall, strong, glossy-haired young priest, who could not be further from the curates who were mocked in *Punch*. He would die, suddenly, at thirty-nine.

Kilvert spent a lot of his time at what he called 'villaging', that is, calling. This is what the *Hereford Times* said about his first harvest festival at Clyro: 'Upon the walls between the windows hung St Andrew's crosses of barley sheaves, the butts looped across with wild hop sprays. The chancel wall and west wall were adorned with texts of white letters on a scarlet ground, "Thou visiteth the earth and blesseth it."'

The service was short and hearty. Rare and magnificent ferns lined the altar steps . . . In the font 'a cross of white flowers floated in the water'. The choir sang an anthem by Mr Evans, the school-master, 'with great power, sweetness, and precision'. What more could one ask? My grandparents would have been in their Suffolk village church then.

Angels Unawares

Having done a respectable stint and being advised by Keith that some unusual plants are flourishing in the set-aside field, I make a trudge of discovery. It is Michaelmas eve, with a touch of chill in the air, the day ending in mauve and pink and torrential gold through which homing rooks clatter and squawk. Stumbling along in the failing light, I find thirty-five species of wild flowers in bloom, none of them at all rare but the fact that they are all out impressive. It is the old gang making a comeback to where they flourished before the sprays: rosebay, hawkbit, feverfew, persicaria, mallow, corn buttercup, centaury, etc. As I wander up and down unsteadily over the ruts and flints and humps, I sense that old malignity of the land towards those who mean to cultivate it. It is saying, 'You shall have your harvest – but at a price!' Countless ploughmen, their shoulders wrenching, their feet slipping one in the furrow, one on top, their horses steaming, would have confronted the earth's obstinacy on this brow of the hill as the share forced itself through it. These men would have known to a yard where it would be hard-going, and where the blade would 'sing'. Eighty acres of 'rubbish', i.e. wild flowers, at Michaelmas would not have been a pretty sight to them. Neighbouring farms bob in and out of sight as I plod on, eyes to the ground, just as they would have done for the generations who worked it.

Gordon and Peter, old friends from the Western Desert, have packed all the harvest festival produce into their car and taken it to Hackney for the hungry, plus a retiring collection. The church looks pillaged, though a strong scent of what has gone remains. I talk of angels. I take Michaelmas out of its legal context of school terms and farm quarter days and open its door, imaginatively speaking, to the angels. Their appearance has long overtaken their purpose in the Christian imagination. Three angel hymns fill the nave with wings – pinions – and Michael, Gabriel and Raphael come gloriously into view. They carry me back to another church, Blythburgh, where, the better to see these feathered marvels of the medieval mind, one has to lie on a bench looking up at message-bearing beings looking down. Angel, Greek for messenger. Purpose, not just appearance. I am also back at school assembly where a hundred high voices demand 'Ye holy angels bright' to assist their song.

Scripture teams with angels, as it must, being all message. The writer of Hebrews says that Christ had to be made a little lower than the angels in order to die for us. The writer is severe and tells us to give more earnest heed to the things which we have heard, 'lest at any time we should let them slip'. Stephen, preaching his fatal sermon, 'had the face of an angel'. In iconography he has more beauty than message.

Taking the Botanist for a Walk

The haunting nature of old religious words: 'habitation'. In one of the songs which the psalmist sent to 'the chief Musician' he differentiates between the habitations of God and man. Seeing the brick pinnacles of the church breaking through the turning leaves and wide panorama of Stour Valley farms, I note how the distinction has been preserved. Fumbling around in my head for a new walk for Richard Mabey, one which I haven't taken him on a dozen times before, I remember the hilly path to what the village calls Christmas-tree land, a pine-clad height which reveals our local habitations from the year dot. Flowers are scarce but special. Scarlet pimpernel in the furrows and the bluest of blue musk thistles. A heron flies up, its legs gradually drawing to its body like the undercarriage of a jet, for below us glints the Mere, a decidedly uninhabitable region, and the source of our chief fairy tale. Isaiah saw an abandoned palace as 'an habitation of dragons and a court for owls', and our deep and secret Mere is not unlived in, for we have stocked it suitably with legend. You won't believe it, but a crocodile which Saladin gave to Richard the Lionheart, and which he brought back from the Crusades and placed in the Tower of London zoo, escaped, swam down the Thames and up our river to our Mere, where it became a dragon and ate our virgins. There is a George V window in the north aisle showing it at dinner with two pretty legs dangling from its jaws just as St George rides in, so it must be true. Worm – dragon, hence worm's ford. The actual derivation of our habitation's name in Eilert Ekwall's *Dictionary of English Place Names*, that luminous work, is given short shrift. Who would swop a dragon for such stuff and nonsense. Green woodpeckers call from the towering chestnuts and gleaming white poplars which ring this hidden lake. From an escarpment Richard and I take a grandstand view of the habitation of a Tudor knight. It drops below us, each detail of it clear as daylight still, the broad deer park, the moated house, the straight avenue down which Elizabeth I rode in August for an expensive visit, and to be told about the dragon, no doubt.

I confess to Richard that high ground, high cliffs, particularly in brilliant weather, give me a heady feeling of immortality, and that once, lying above the roaring water at Land's End when I was nineteen, it seemed perfectly logical to stay there for ever and do nothing more with my life, an emotion which I thought no one else shared until I read Thomas Traherne, who describes it to perfection. Did Richard share it? I asked. 'No, I do not.' There's naturalists for you.

My farmer neighbour's birthday, Michaelmas Day, and he is a hundred years old. Although he has been with us for half a century, his Ayrshire origins are plain enough. He carries his habitation with him, as do all Scots. The stony acres which he left as a boy lie just below our rich soil, just as they would if he had sailed to the colonies.

A Late Harvest

By the moss rose, a baby hare scarcely big enough to warrant the name leveret trembles. It seems unconscious of my presence and is immobile. Transparent ears through which the morning shines. The white cat approaches, so what to do? A single clap of my hands sends the leveret to safety and the cat to sulks. It is my Cowper good deed for the day. The air is still dusty from yesterday's harvesting. There is a wheat powdering of oak and ash. The ponds area delicate grey but the shorn field, an enormous one, is as gold as you can get. Also – car-bound churchwardens rejoice and be glad – my track has received its annual pre-harvest haircut, and never a better one. 'Track!' it protests, 'look at me. I am a Saxon highway! Mr Sycamore and Farmer Tom Bradshaw have had their way with me.' Tom has even gone so far as to reply to the usual harvesting groans, in his village newsletter, with 'If you see the combine going to the field please take the opportunity to shut all your windows and take your washing off the line.' Down by St Andrew's, the onion wagons scrape past worshippers' cars with just an inch to spare. Why people have to go to church just when the harvest tackle takes to the lanes beats the drivers. The bells, which once heard the excited shouts of 'They're cutting at Garnons!' now ignore the whole business. Turning my John Clare lectures into a book, I don't have to wonder what happened in his day. For there it is, every exhausting moment of it, every custom, every ritual joy and pain. And I can just see a Helpston farmer apologising for the inconvenience. Those who brought the harvest home would have swayed across their own thresholds at moonlit midnight, scratched to bits, and a little drunk, as they deserved to be.

Upon the waggon now, with eager bound,
The luster picker whirls the rustling sheaves;
Or, resting ponderous creaking fork aground,
Boastful at once whole shocks of barley heaves:
The loading boy revengeful inly grieves
To find his unmatched strength and power decay;
The barley horn his garments interweaves;
Smarting and sweating 'neath the sultry day,
With muttering curses stung, he mauls the heaps away.

Houses are taking a long time to sell, they say. The agents' signboards wave rather desperately from trim hedges for months on end. Yet those searching for something of character, as they call it, still have to search wide and hard. Having never bought a house it is all a mystery to me. It is clear that there are folk who just like a nice change and who move the mortgage on. The young are offered jobs they can't refuse, and off they go, like birds to a better bush, like Mark and his wife, who have only just got the curtains up and the garden right. But there it is. Walking to the post office, I bid good-day to the latest strangers. But my hornets return time and time again to delight me and terrify the guests. One is reading my dictionary at this moment, buzzing across the page like a tiny tractor. If it could turn the page it would see that it is our largest wasp, a tawny yellow social wasp more than an inch long, which uses its fearsome sting on man only if attacked. 'Wasp,' I say, 'I am a man of peace.'

OCTOBER

*W*henever I sat facing Ronnie at his elegant little table in the corner of the room, close to the crammed bookcases, I was always startled by the way his face changed. At one moment I saw a fragile man growing older year by year, and in the next I saw a boy, filled with the laughter and energy of youth.

And now as I read of him as a night walker I suddenly know him better, because in a few brief sentences he manages to encapsulate something of the transient delicacy of his presence in the world and the way he is able to move as seamlessly as a ghost between time past, time present and even time future.

The text is deceptively simple. He describes walking home on a moonless night and how, as his eyes adjust to the dark, he is absorbed into the darkness that surrounds him. Once he has relinquished all sense of self, the cultivated fields become the earth of their first beginning and a clump of flowers close to the path becomes the original flowers of paradise.

It is a journey of some two miles, down familiar lanes, across a ditch, and into the soft bowl of landscape that surrounds his home. He catches the house 'unawares' and 'wide awake in its hollow' and the house asks him how anyone can own anything at night: a question that has no need of an answer.

Julia Blackburn

The Damascus Light

Every season has its day, its epitome. And this is autumn's apotheosis. It began at dawn, with haphazard yellow streaks which announced sunrise, and it will conclude in rich gold. This much I prophesy.

Ash leaves fall like the Albert Hall poppies, sadly and significantly, alighting on my hair and braking their descent. Huge birds, too, although, only when I go in, a bouncing hen pheasant and a sprawling green woodpecker who has lost his balance. It is warm, almost sultry, and quite still. Some fields are greening, some doing nothing at all. Just waiting.

Harvest festivals roll into one another. Annette, the Archdeacon, preaches about parched lands while my brook falls musically into my pond.

David and I unearth a crushed granary, get a good fire going, and burn sodden timbers, mats of ivy and some very strange things that have been mouldering away since Suez. And all the time the blessed autumn day caresses us, calls us, spreads itself out decadently.

We smell of rot, become imprisoned in chicken wire and, now and then, hold up our finds. A coalscuttle, good as new, and things that are barely recognisable; for such is existence below a departed shed. Its interior was limewashed against dampness, maybe, for seeds. There are no end of jam jars.

Spiders peer through them. And then the October sun bursts in where it cannot have been for a hundred years. We talk divinity.

A stranger calls to bring me a lamp from – Damascus. It seems to be constructed of splintered glass which becomes kaleidoscopic when it is switched on, and very gorgeous, like when one sees through one's eyelids. The white cat stares at it uncertainly. Damascus! Imagine it.

I think of Paul's blindness at the gate, and that demanding voice. It is all I know about Damascus.

I look it up in one of those know-all books. No mention of lamps, but people lived there 1,600 years before Paul arrived with his warrants and was guided to the street called Straight.

Wasps come in after the lamp, game for anything gorgeous. It always takes me a week to like a new thing, and longer than that to love it. What would David like to drink – he having toiled so hard? 'Port,' he says. Port! After supper, we return to the old stack-yard to watch the ashes glow. Owls are calling up and down the river. Through the distant window the Damascene lamp is shining like Christmas.

The first lesson for the next evensong is Proverbs 4: 'Wisdom is the principal thing; therefore get Wisdom; and with all thy getting get understanding.' Quite. 'Exalt her, and she shall promote thee.'

The news is dreadfully unwise at the moment – very unexalting. But then, it was unwise of me to stand on a wasps' nest and receive three stings. 'Vinegar,' David says. The stings fade into an itch. More wasps on the wrong side of my bedroom window. I let them out into the smoky darkness.

The owls are hard at it now, and the valley has become a kind of trumpet, funnelling their melancholy hoots into two counties. I dream of poor Captain Naaman of Damascus, being given sick leave to go to wash away his leprosy in the Jordan, and travelling Paul's road in reverse, and the prophet not even bothering to come out to meet him, and what a ditch compared with the Abana, the Pharpar . . . And most likely owl ridden.

White Cat Stylites

What an early October! I have given myself up to it. Let Robert and Stephanie, the Angels of Mammon, pour out their dire warnings, I cannot understand what they are saying anyway.

I have sat in the sun. I have read poems and books about butterflies. David rang to say that he has been haymaking in

Buckinghamshire, and I have crunched over the warm dry mast from my oak trees, picked quinces, and seen the 7.40 flight of the Stour Valley geese.

Harvest festivals loom. Phyllida will have saved a sheaf from the dusty threshed field to focus our gratitude. Archdeacon Annette will mount our pulpit. There will be an anthem. And God will 'restore the voice of joy and health unto our dwellings'. Thus 'We offer unto thy Divine Majesty the sacrifice of praise and thanksgiving, lauding and magnifying thy glorious Name for such thy preservation and providence over us.'

When the Essex and Suffolk Hunt ran through Bottengoms like a horse-and-hound river, ecstatic, noisy, the white cat took to the trees. Since when she has dozed on a brick pier, gazing down on me with green eyes as I tidy the dying beds, a kind of feline Simeon Stylites, or pillar ascetic.

Simeon started low, but gradually built his pillar up to 40 cubits, and there he sat for years and years, preoccupied with adoration, and looking down on lesser beings. All this in the cause of Chalcedonian orthodoxy. The white cat descends fast at the mere hint of food. Or love. Late roses act as censors.

Friends are terribly ill as their time runs out. They buy plots and choose hymns. The autumn warmth creeps into their rooms. 'It must be nice outside.' Fresh flowers and unread books on the table. 'How about a nice little drink?' Oh, yes. When to arrive, when to leave.

I have been listening to Hildegard of Bingen, her voice as soaring as ever it was after close on a thousand years. We heard it in an ancient church where it climbed around the Norman brickwork and out into the evening air, the girl singing it rapt and beautiful. Nothing dies, the song says. I was actually sitting below a plaque I had unveiled years ago – but to whom? I have to read it to find out.

Joachim telephones from Berlin. He is preparing for Yom Kippur, the Day of Atonement. There will be crowds in the synagogue, and fasting, and thrilling singing by the cantor. He sounds happy and busy. He designs gardens and rides a motorbike. What is the weather like? 'Gorgeous.'

I imagine the late sun on the face of the Lord, as he picks and nibbles corn. Corn is instantly understood, but manna means 'What is it?' We walked through prickly harvest fields when we were children in Suffolk. The heat and rough going wore us out. We were not tall enough to walk in this way. 'Catch up!' the grown-ups would cry. We disturbed larks, and the dog crashed ahead.

The church was like a greengrocer's. Nothing merely symbolic. Just 'Plenty'. Grapes swinging from the oil-lamp brackets, apples tumbling, marrows like airships. Brown eggs in hay nests. Home-made wine, elderberry – very heady. And the last congregations to be aching with toil. There was this rich smell of produce, of locality.

The Death of Children

October mornings are doubly black as rivery mists and sunlessness gradually part company, creating degrees of opacity. At first, or at 5 a.m. say, nothing is visible from the north windows – the same north windows whose light fell on John Nash's easel – and I am unable to make out as much as a great tree. Then comes the soft unveiling of the familiar view. Daylight forces the mist to take colour, to thin itself, to let me see through it at actualities beyond it, just as George Herbert said we should see beyond the unsubstantial artistry of coloured glass in churches and recognise the glorious realities which they can only suggest. Landscape artists begin a work by blocking in the major objects which stretch before them. October dawns work this way. First the featureless void, then the murky outlines of what this particular view must contain, then, gradually, gradually, all that exists on

NEXT TO NATURE

the other side of the pane. The birds, those that have not decamped
to Africa, call out. It is a new day. A beam wavers and sweeps along
Garnon's Chase, stripping oak after oak of its remnant cover as
Tom's car twists towards the station. If I stood in the drenched
grass outside I might hear, faraway like moneyed sirens, the faint
screams of the commuter trains.

A scholar has sent me his take on a John Clare poem 'Graves of
Infants'. Simultaneously in the press I read about the Pope's having
to deal with Limbo. Look up Limbo. Oh my goodness. 'Those in
limbo are excluded from supernatural beatitude, but according to
St Thomas Aquinas enjoy full natural happiness. The existence of
limbo is a matter of theological opinion on which the Church
has never pronounced definitely either way.' But then we come to
limbus infantium – unbaptised babies who although born in original sin are innocent of personal guilt. In fact, although many a
child was too ill to make the font, it would have had the midwife's
sign of the cross on its forehead and her speedy, 'In the name of
the Father ...' the minute it emerged, infant mortality and her
grubby hands being what they were. 'Limbo ... mumbo-
jumbo ...' murmured a voice on the radio. I suppose that the
Church does have to now and then turn out its medieval attic.
However, here comes John Clare, father of nine, survivor of twins
and sanest of poets where children and what we now dub ecology
are concerned. Rural religion and economics have frequently
shown their madness when we compare them to what he believed.

In 'Graves of Infants' he enters the vast sadness of nineteenth-
century child mortality. You raised some, you lost some, they said.
Victorian literature is full of what most families experienced, the
deathbeds of boys and girls. Country churchyards are full of children – city ones too, of course. Should a child die now it shakes
the entire parish. By disease or accident, it is unnatural to us. But
not long ago it was entirely natural, for nature itself was tragic, as
Clare knew all too terribly. In June 1844, from Northampton
Asylum – his 'Mad House' – came his reconciling conclusion to

the common fate of many children. It was the only answer which he could make sense of. Brief life or long life, it was no more than aspects of nature:

God is their parent, they need no tear . . .
A bud their life-time, and a flower their close . . .
All prayers are needless – beads they need not tell;
White flowers their mourners are, nature their passing bell.

Lancelot Andrewes † 1626

Warm, blustering winds and tumbling fruit. The river's surface crinkles under the attack and weathervanes spin around. Crows and gulls are blown into each other's air-space, and there is all the usual October exultation. The wildness and a procession of harvest festivals remind me of visits to Morwenstow, Parson Hawker's autocratic kingdom, and watching the Cornish sea dashing itself against his limits. They said he commanded his parishioners to attend the funerals of every drowned sailor thrown up on his shore, and some of them plainly black and heathen. There was a little wood nearby where he wrote *Trelawny*, a ballad we thundered out at school. At nineteen he married a lady of forty-one and was perfectly happy. And of course he brought harvest parties out of the barn and into the church. Those barn-releases after the incredible toil of reaping by hand have been heavily expurgated. Hardy himself could not describe them. What Robert Hawker did – in 1843 – was to revive the medieval Lammas (loaf-mass) during which bread made from the first corn of the year was consecrated at the altar.

Our harvest festivals are somewhat incoherent attempts to revive an agricultural economy which flourished before combines and supermarkets, post-Spry flower arranging and the minimalising of the landworkers. One could truthfully say that there is not an aching back in the nave – at least not from gathering-in. The dark side of the hymns, 'the Angel-reaping o'er', we take in our stride, although I sometimes find myself glancing at a Victorian window to an old couple, the Nottidges, who are being cut down in the field by a bent figure with a sombre halo. Poor Nottidges from the big house opposite, the angel reaping o'er had, long since, gathered their teenage children. To outlive one's children, 'that's not right', as we say in Suffolk. The rightness of things, of festivals particularly, cannot be taken as said; it has to be retaught. Farmer Amos, an earthy young man (and a marvellous poet), denounced religious feasts which left the people spiritually hungry. Beautiful children bring up tokens of today's plenty, tinned soup, baskets of carrots, sweetcorn, Cox's apples – and an oak tree in a pot. Has a potted oak been stood on an altar before – I mean since the Druids? I describe how the farmers on their Sunday walks always took pockets of acorns during October and pressed them into the moist hedgerow soil. 'Where shall we plant your oak?' The little boy is at a loss, half smiles, says nothing. His gift is out of his hands. Back home, plenty in the shape of pears thuds into the long grass.

Trinity Eighteen

Gathering – one of those ample words which accommodates a whole range of meaning from beneficent collecting-up to ruthless taking. All this because I have been gathering the plums, tugging the laden branches towards me with a rake and stripping the firm purple-yellow fruits one at a time. The cat has slept in a mouse-brown bed of hay under the plum tree for the past fort-night, watching the stars through its leaves and just using the house as a restaurant. I have gathered the nuts, the blackberries, the tomatoes, the huge prickly seed heads of the artichokes with their silvery bracts and the runner beans. The apples say, 'us next'.

The mechanical hedger, known to Grandfather Brown the farmer as 'the murderer', has done its grim duty and left the lane-sides nice and tidy.

Hebrew law forbade total gathering in the fields and orchards. Something had to be left in the corners for the poor to pick up. Friends arrive for the late-summer loot, knowing just where it lies. Some make for the bay tree, of which it hardly seems grateful to remark that it spreads itself in great power like the wicked. But it is certainly taking over. The cadences of the season are those of Tyndale. His immortal language hangs in the sharp air. I have been hearing what the scholars have been saying about him as his half-millennium approaches, William Tyndale the gentleman-scholar from a Gloucestershire village who remains more influential than any other English writer, Shakespeare included. At first there was a demented rushing around to gather and incinerate every telling sentence. Imagine attempting to burn out 'In the beginning was the Word . . .' Most of the Authorized Version was essentially Tyndale's version. They strangled and burnt him at Vilvorde. He was aged about forty-two. He came to mind again as I gathered falls, rock-hard Warden pears once thought, when baked, suitable pudding for the higher clergy, and the first-down apples. How did an apple get into the Fall? Tyndale says nothing about an apple, just the 'fruit of the tree' which was 'to be desired to make one wise'. Yet the carol-singers will soon insist that it was 'all for an appil'. How did an apple get into the Fall? Because in St Jerome's Latin Genesis *malum* is the word for both apple and evil.

I have been to visit a sad husband whose wife has been gathered. The emptiness of the small house opposite the cropped field. He takes a paper from behind the clock, the traditional place for letters and instructions, reminders and lists. 'This is what she wanted.' They are the hymns for her funeral, written just three days before. The words tumble about. We have tea. It is the first day of his inadequacy.

Weather

The classic rainy day: the sky a liquid colourlessness, the trees drenching sieves, the farm track a river, the fields just dull and wet. The old labourers 'saved' for such a day because, unable to work, they would not be paid. Four horses soak it up, the streaming day; whether indifferent to it or enjoying it, who knows?

Cocooned in the old house, I have to settle down to it as it rattles the windows and surges through the guttering. Field-wise, it could not have come at a better time. October was dry as a biscuit, and the dusty winter wheat had been aching for a shower; but this downpour! It is not unlike Australian rain. One minute I was baking, the next drowning. No point in running for shelter. In any case, it had been thrilling: the heat suddenly all washed away, and oneself as wet as a surfer.

The Duke of Norfolk's magnificent tomb in Framlingham Church has a Genesis frieze that includes Noah's Ark. Benjamin Britten liked to take children to see it. He turned it into one of his Church Parables, *Noyes Fludde*, with a marvellous setting of 'Eternal Father, strong to save'. I remember singing it for the first time in Orford Church, long ago. William Whiting wrote it for *Hymns Ancient and Modern*, in 1860. Britten's version is heart-breakingly plaintive, slow and sumptuous.

He would have seen the memorial to a Victorian crew in Aldeburgh churchyard, and would have more than once witnessed the lifeboatmen launching their new boat to rescue some vessel, maybe some holiday yacht that had not understood the North Sea's power: from being leisurely, it had become imperious, throwing craft and men about like toys. We lesser mortals watched. Watching is a coastal profession. Also a Christian imperative.

St Matthew reports Jesus as saying: 'When it is evening, you say, "It will be fair weather; for the sky is red." And, in the morning,

"It will be stormy today; for the sky is red and threatening." You know how to interpret the appearance of the sky, but you cannot interpret the signs of the times. An evil and adulterous generation seeks for a sign, but no sign shall be given it except the sign of Jonah.'

Jesus refers to this sign more than once; so what is it? That he will be returned to life and not swallowed up? The island nature of Britain has given its Christianity a flood-based imagery. They say that our coast may have lost three miles in a thousand years. Certainly, its dwellers spent much of that time keeping the sea out. But the inlanders would not have noticed, or minded – and in many cases would never have seen the sea.

Those who lived by it were farmers and fishermen by turn. Some were marshmen, and a different breed altogether. Think of Peter Grimes. There cannot be many sea views framed in a Gothic arch as at Aldeburgh. It is how it first presents itself to the traveller to this town. The road to it once ran through the arch like a grand canopy. Or saw it as a divine approach to sea wealth or sea desolation. The great sea poet George Crabbe's severe parents lie beside it.

Like St Luke, Crabbe was a medical man and a voyager. Or, rather, the voice of those whose business was in deep waters. Both scientifically and spiritually, he took its measure. Luke's Acts of the Apostles set the lakeside faith sailing through the centuries, finding harbour here and there, but then restlessly taking to open water. The Aldeburgh fishermen meditate (chat) by their boats by the hour.

Impossible Money

An autumn morning, very early. The white cat washes herself on one end of the ironing board as I press shirts on the other. The ash leaves have all fallen; so now it is time for the hawthorns to follow suit. Not a mite of wind.

On the radio, Evan Davis, Mammon's angel, is talking to a Mr Warren Buffett, of Oklahoma, who is the world's second-richest man. Mr Buffett lives in a nondescript house with a nondescript car, and there is no computer in his nondescript office. He likes Evan, with his sweet, crocodile grin. Why does Mr Buffett do it, make impossible amounts of money? Evan does not ask. He knows that Mr Buffett does not know why.

I walk in the dank, after-breakfast garden, and smell the lovely rot. Nothing can be done until the trees are bare. A waste of time. Blackbirds scuttle out of berries, geese whoop overhead. I gather some Warden pears for the oven, but let the last roses stay on the wall.

It is the feast day of St Frumentius (I looked him up), a youth who took Christianity to Ethiopia in the fourth century. All true. He and his friend Aedesius got permission for Greek businessmen to set up chapels all over this kingdom. When Frumentius asked for a bishop, St Athanasius made him the bishop. He and Aedesius were most likely teenagers. Mortal spans were brief then, and one did not hang about.

The faith they took to Ethiopia was that of Christian Egypt – the Copts. I see them frescoed on walls, tall elegant young men in classy robes who were taken seriously.

On Bible Sunday, I prayed for translators. And I suggested that it would be a good thing if we each read the Bible at home, as well as from the lectern. Have I not seen them riffling desperately through the pages in search of Amos? Mother would have found him like a shot. What a lot of sacred things there are, what a lot of wicked things! And the travels! Everyone walking miles, like Frumentius and his friend. And the poetry – how divine! Here is St James on money in William Tyndale's translation: 'Go to now ye rich men. Weep, and howl on your wretchedness that shall come upon you. Your riches is corrupt, your garments are moth-eaten. Your gold and your silver are cankered, and the rust of them shall be a witness unto you, and shall eat your flesh as it were fire.'

Today we touch coin only for small things, when once it was touched for everything – although I dare say that Mr Buffett still understands the need for small change, embarrassing though it can be: nothing rolls as far as a penny in church.

Like everyone else, I sit in luxury to observe the naked and the hungry, while the banks we have saved with public money give huge presents to themselves. Where Christ went on about materialism, the Church goes on about sex and gender – things that little interested him.

Outside, the golden time is here, each yellow leaf a payment for the summer. 'Let us go into such a city and continue there a year and buy and sell, and win: and yet cannot tell what shall happen tomorrow. For what thing is your life?' Tyndale after St James.

Just two more days of October for me. Then all the saints, most of them broke. And the lovely autumn passing.

The Cornfield Ancestors

Ash leaves fall first. They sail down from the mother tree and spatter the grass. It is moist and mild. A delectable October day. I have come in from sorting out the yuccas whose 'Spanish sabres' stand guard against guests. But how handsome they are as they give grandeur to the garden! When I saw the dead heads from the main stem, it is like cutting through a pineapple, juicy and soft. Blessed rain is in the offing, they say.

Harvest festivals succeed each other in the three parishes, which means variations on the same sermon, as some people attend each one. Thus I try to change the theme of the book of Ruth, which was obviously written by Thomas Hardy. It proves that Jesus's family originated in a cornfield.

Ruth's declaration to her mother-in-law is a perfect way for anyone to state his fidelity to Christ, and, I would like to think, prophetic. '"Whither thou goest, I will go, and where thou lodgest, I will lodge: thy people shall be my people, and thy God, my God" . . . So they two went until they came to Bethlehem.' Which means 'house of bread'.

'Do not forget to put a loaf on the altar,' I unnecessarily instruct the harvest festival ladies; for they forget nothing. Our harvest is, of course, long past, and next year's wheat is in. The Big Field darkens in the rain. Snowy gulls quarrel over it. The white cat sits in the hedge, keeping dry.

Judith arrives to interview me for her magazine *Waves*, because I helped to judge East Anglia's version of the Booker. She is late, Bottengoms being notoriously hard to find. When she asked a van man the way to Wormingford, he said: 'Who could tell you?' Or something like that.

She filled up minute pages, took photos, and sipped hot water and lemon, as I tried to say something original about my life. We walked round the bedraggled grounds, and I remembered how, long ago, I had helped judge the Booker Prize itself. William Golding had won it – £10,000 in those days – with his sailing ship novel *Rights of Passage*. I remembered how he had looked rather like an old ship's captain, with his whiskers and blue eyes.

It was about an 1830s voyage to Australia, and a passenger list that should not have been investigated. When it was – well! Not the least wonderful thing about his novel was Golding's ability to stay in period where the seamanship was concerned. Never a task, never an order, that was informed by modern navigation. When I praised him for this as we stood at the bar, he twinkled. His wife shook her head. Novelists' wives, or husbands, often shake their heads. It is among their necessary functions.

As for ships, a number of them voyage about in my imagination. One was a fishing boat on Galilee in a very bad painting that held my attention in Sunday school. Another is in a marvellous etching by Francis Unwin which hangs before me at this minute, a clipper in full sail; another in R. L. Stevenson's *Letters*.

I have been, in a way, a passenger on these vessels. I still am. Flight has destroyed travel. We must pass through climates and time zones that touch our flesh if we are to travel. Flight does not allow this.

'I have you in my heart'

It is too beautiful to work. They said that the sun would shine, but not like this. Deciduous shapes wander down, palmate, cusped, linear, ovate, pinnatifid, and settle on my hair. The warm October sun touches each one. The white cat sits on me, rumbling like a tractor.

'But,' my head reminds me, 'you have to go to Wales to tell them about George Borrow and his *Wild Wales*. And join in the celebrations for the mended church. And meet old friends, some of whom have been dreadfully ill. And take stock of Offa's Dyke.' Time enough. Luke has seduced me with his warm spell.

Only last night it was heavy rain, so that the vicar had to splash down the track to take me to the PCC, though not cold. As ever, I was amazed by the mixed abilities of its members, their expertise on practically everything. Wild weather beat on the windows. Future services stretched away to kingdom come.

But now, this golden day, with the blackened seed heads popping and the horses wearing their bright blankets, and the dog-walkers waving. I imagine Commander Aurelius Bassus, from Camulodunum up the road, collecting his wife and children and saying: 'Come on: tie on your sandals. Let's walk west to that nice humpy valley up the road. It is far too nice to rule Britain.'

I see them now and then, the old idlers in my fields, cutting a hazel switch, shouting at crows, or just spread out in the year's final heat, never for one moment realising that they are historical. No one does. We can accept wars and commerce and dates, but it takes an effort to see a ploughman's autumn face in, say, 1638, and find it to be our own face in the present sunshine.

The arborist has been called in to give, we hope, a clean bill to our churchyard trees. They were planted by a clergyman in the 1890s, and lend splendour to the river approach to the village. Hedgerow oaks of great antiquity add to the fine scene. We await the verdict with bated breath. If all is not totally well, all is far from hopeless. The acer leaning towards the tower has to be watched; the glorious horse chestnuts have dark patches – but not to worry.

Removing a great tree can leave the kind of space caused by demolishing a house. One of lost habitation. A buddleia perched on the north wall, however, cannot stay. And we have a water butt instead of a tap for the grave flowers, although bottles of spring water in the vestry for sacred purposes, of course. The Stour flashes below. A little girl's grave is a toybox, and is animated with plastic windmills.

On Trinity 22, I preach on glimpses of the Spirit, how people show them without knowing it. We are to ask God to keep his household the Church in continual godliness. The epistle has Paul telling the Philippians: 'I thank my God upon every remembrance of you', and that 'I have you in my heart.' How grateful this is; how moving.

What happened to him in Philippi, his first European church, to draw such affection from him? He and they exchange 'joy'. In the practical sense, they helped him during his imprisonment. In every other way, he and these proto 'Christians', like the friends in Antioch, have lifted one another's spirits, and a great love travels between them.

The Spirit is common among us, but never commonplace. We see him on televised faces, their owners having no idea that he shows himself. On the sleeping face in the train. Or on Rembrandt's many faces.

Roger Deakin

It is before dawn, and dark. Very soon, the masses of hazel which I have let grow will filter-in the day. Each winter, I wave my saw at them, then see their stumpy catkins, and reprieve them for another year. I tell them: 'Coppicing is good for you' – and their boughs shine.

It is St Luke's little summer, and he is doing us proud with his warm sunshine and soft winds. I imagine him carrying his Gospel scrolls to the most excellent Theophilus, his publisher, saying: 'Make a good job of it.'

Roger's *Notes From Walnut Tree Farm* arrives in the post, and there we both are, setting off to Tiger Hill, he in his big boots and big black coat, tall and bursting with health. Although not so. His dust and the brown-red dusty bark of the old pears in the orchard are one.

He would arrive unexpectedly, looming into my low rooms, happy and expectant like a dog. Where shall we go? What shall we do? His *Notes* answers these questions. Reading them, I feel more deserted than at his funeral. He was so dead there, and he is so alive on the page.

Here is what I said. Here is what we did. Here is the white cat listening. All this week, she has opted to make a bed in the rope-box, purring thunderously on the uncomfortable, one would think, coils. Maybe she has ancestors who joined the Navy: ships' cats who mucked in with sailors and saw the world. Roger's cats are all over the place in his book, on the Aga, by the moat.

Thinking of him reminds me of the scythe that he brought from Stowmarket. And this reminds me that it is a good day to cut the tall seeding plants in the orchard, the frail horsetail and tall hogweed. I have to keep the scythe high enough to avoid the primroses and cowslips. I am writing about Thomas Traherne.

Every now and then, thinking of a good bit, I hurry indoors to put it down.

How Traherne adored being outside! He said that he would have liked to lie under a tree all day – all his days – wearing a leather suit, and doing absolutely nothing except thank God for letting him see the earth. As he was the rector, however, he had work to do. And, as it was in the seventeenth century, there was theology to rail about. But, like Roger, he had to put himself on to the page.

I have always suspected that much of Traherne's immortal *Centuries of Meditations* was scribbled in the open air. He is the singer of human happiness. His prose is so intoxicating that it makes one unsteady on one's feet.

We are off to Felixstowe to have lunch with Ina. Old Felixstowe is the scene of the most frightening ghost story in the language, M. R. James's 'O whistle and I'll come to you, my lad'. New Felixstowe was the seaside for gentlefolk. The crunchy shingle will make the waves hiss as they slap their way through it, and possibly St Luke's sun will take the chill off it.

St Felix sailed from Burgundy to Suffolk to convert us. In 631, he was made Bishop of Dunwich, setting up a fine school for boys. Dunwich has been washed away but its bishopric is undrowned – is as dry and bright as a bone.

Will we have time after lunch to see Dunwich crumbling away? No. Roger would have said yes. He said yes to everything.

Saxons Ploughing

It is not quite warm enough to sit outside, although here I am, reluctant to admit this. The afternoon sun appears five minutes each hour. There is no wind, just an October stillness trapped and waiting. Ash leaves sail down like perished hands. Bells ring, although from what direction it is hard to say, the river being in one of its oblique moods and carrying sounds from confused directions.

Peter-Paul the composer is on his way. The mysterious satchel will be riding on his shoulders. Sustenance for a three-mile tramp? The latest score? I must not ask. He will be passing Wiston Mill, passing Garnons, looking about him as he does. The homeward commuters are fuming on the A12 but as yet I do not know this, living as I do in another world. A gas tanker leaky, they think – blocks their weary way. The white cat teeters along a wall, piteously calling for food, anything will do – smoked salmon, cream; heaven knows that it never asks for much in exchange for being so beautiful. I finish reviewing new books about trees for the TLS, adding up the words and fixing the pages together.

Peter-Paul appears. He has a satchel on his back and big clumping shoes. He has been surprised by a heron and gratified by a buzzard. I give him cake and tea. He can't sit on the garden chair because it has collapsed; so he squats on the doorstep and talks about music in novels, rather disapprovingly. 'Why do they do it, these fiction writers, tell stories about musicians when music itself is rather beyond them?'

I say that the characters in a quartet or a quintet, or an entire orchestra, if it comes to that, offer the novelist an enclosed group on which to work. Think of *The Archers*, I nearly add, but think better of it.

The first novel about music I ever read – in my teens – was *Maurice Guest* by the Australian writer Henry Handel Richardson, who was a woman. It was about a love affair at the Leipzig Music Academy. Suddenly remembering it, my heart stands still, as they say, and I have a huge longing to read it all over again. Is it in the house? Unfortunately, Peter-Paul has left before I can stun him with this wonderful tale. Next time.

Gordon the churchwarden arrives to collect thankful items for harvest festival. I supply baking pears and honey, plus the usual instructions that he, great servant of Christ, does not need. Have

I any time? No. Should I turn some of my Discoed-Presteigne lecture on ploughing into a harvest sermon? Why not?

I imagine the Wormingford fields being ploughed with Saxon bullocks, the poor animals plunging up and down our hills, the ploughmen, their legs cross-gartered, singing lost songs. Or simply swearing, the share splitting the amaranthine flints. The latter now and then edge their way up in the track, sharp as razors.

And – now I am in a fanciful mood – I see a Roman from Colchester, half a dozen miles south, and not cooped up in his wall, taking a nice walk on what was once my land, and seeing what I see: the swerve and dip of it, the unchanged contours of it, the same nip in the autumn air of it, and, of course, the pencillings made by the plough across it. And in his temple a thankful pile of sheaves to Ceres from it. His Celtic predecessors went further. They put an ear of corn on their pennies.

So now to the thankful pulpit.

Plenty

Delectable days. St Luke's little summer approaches. Mornings at seven are wreathed in soaking mist and enormous webs supply a kind of white darkness. Mornings at ten are ablaze. The village struggles with 'plenty', or the opposite of enough. Neighbours say that they have never seen anything like it – although they have, of course – but such amazement does at least make us take stock of orchards running over and weather which is bliss beyond compare. After breakfast I hustle through desk-work so as to get out and make the best of it. After supper a story-book moon hangs in the skeiny ultramarine sky as bell practice subsides and the ringers make their way to the Crown. 'More tomorrow!' they promise, meaning not peals but days like this.

I take the last of the harvest festivals, omitting the thanksgiving for Plenty but taking care to include the General Thanksgiving because Phillida loves it. Worshippers have their special devotions. Edward Reynolds wrote it in 1661, the year they made him Bishop of Norwich. His language – 'We bless thee for our creation, preservation, and all the blessings of this life' – and now spoken by us just once a year, excite a quiet but noticeable fervour. They rumble forth. The truth is, this year's plenty is giving us a bit of a headache. What do you give the postman when his van is already bursting with Bramleys? There are plastic bags full of falls at gates saying, 'Take me'. And yet in the supermarkets Golden Delicious, a misnomer if ever there was one, can only be had at a price.

As children we inhabited a universe of gathered or fallen fruit, of jams and kilner-jars, of cookers and eaters, of apples laid out in the larder like regiments, and of waste and rot in the long wet grass. There were days when an apple would be a welcome gift, and days when you let it lie. Vans would take the falls to Debenham to be squeezed into cider. The prodigiousness of nature and the measured-ness of nature, by turn, used to be a yearly hazard. The cry went up, 'They won't keep!' Keep me as the apple of the eye. Meanwhile, fat birds sing opportunely in the groaning hedges and I see that even the rhubarb is having a final flourish. But the deep-freeze implores 'No more!' We must certainly keep our heads. Sensible Bishop Reynolds tells us to ask God to 'give us that due sense of all thy mercies, that our hearts may be unfeignedly thankful . . .'

One of his mercies, or October miracles, is that my fairy-ring champignon have survived the mower. They bloom, if that is the word, in their circle, concentric, untouched, as they have done since my boyhood.

Wuffingas

St Luke's golden days. The trees burn, the air is alternately ice and fire. Hard pears thud down into dying butterbur whose tottering leaves are no longer strong enough to preserve them from bruises. A score of small birds quarrel for leg room on the electricity grid marked 'Death' and 'Keep Off', which suggests some exaggeration on the company's part. I sit in the garden having a drink and listen to the radio. Somebody mentions Sutton Hoo, that magic place which for many years was an hour's bike ride from another garden. I would ride there to watch its re-exhumation during the great heat of that summer and see the sunburnt archaeologists, shirtless and dusty, and the plastic sheets bellying out from their poles, looking as though the sand ship was off to Sweden once more. The fabulous boat with a glittering king at the helm would be sliding into the Deben, or whatever he called his river then, and off to Europe for, as his regalia proved, there were no limits as to how far he would go to add to his finery.

My old friends Rhoisia and Bridget would be making tea for the young scrapers and diggers just behind the dig. All three of us felt a faintly hereditary interest in what was being dug up and some ownership of the king's glorious chattels. Thus we would bump down Mrs Pretty's field track with the same ease as Lord Tollemache would bump over his drawbridge a few miles south. The Anglo-Saxon burial site was our family grave. Rhoisia and Bridget's family had in some mysterious fashion known only to the Church of England occupied the living of Buxhall for centuries. To them the discoveries of Sutton Hoo were being made by workmen – and women – employed to delve into their inheritance. To make tea for them was a similar Christian kindness to making tea for their gardener. I was devoted to them. They were elderly twins. What I loved was their version of history. By the time I should have taken it down they had disappeared into timelessness. It would have been a masterpiece like Jane Austen's *History of England*.

'Who did they say was buried here?'

'The Wuffingas.'

They would exchange a doubtful look, a kind of, 'If you say so, though *we* have never heard of them.'

And now, another life on, the king of Suffolk is on the *Today* programme, which says that the National Trust is about to take care of him. There will be a viewing platform, a car park and a restaurant. In 1939 Mrs Pretty, a friend of 'the girls', as we called Rhoisia and Bridget, paid Mr Brown 35 shillings a week and lent him two of her gardeners to dig up the Sutton Hoo treasure. For the best inventory of what they found, read *Beowulf*, perhaps in the new Seamus Heaney translation. I can hear the harp being played in the hall and the ancestral shouts and the whirling gulls.

Fire Frost

Bottengoms is a frost pocket. Hard winters make a bee-line to it. It crumps and crunches with cold, and holds on to its frosts even when the sun hits it. Proust once described a Paris frost cutting its way through the walls of his apartment with 'a silver knife' and I too can hear a really great frost doing something to the pintiles which gives me the shivers. And it used to be uncanny how Jack Frost drew his pictures on the inside of the panes, proving that nothing can keep him out. That is, until the central heating arrived. I quite miss his cold art. As children we heard the house being warmed up from scratch every morning, the tinkle of the kindling, the lighting of oil-stoves, the stamping of feet as logs and coals were fetched, and then miraculously porridge steaming in a hot kitchen. Keeping the fire in overnight was an expert business but some managed it. It was an art, the finding the flame, the puffing it into a blaze, the laying of the wood in a kind of wigwam above it and the knowing when to stop. And it was heroic to take off one's pyjamas in the bathroom which was a kind of interior frost pocket especially fitted to our nakedness.

In Suffolk a good man always rose before his wife to make a good fire. But there were good wives who boasted that 'he' never did a hand's turn in the house and who said that 'he' always got out of bed to a good fire, bacon and eggs and a warm shirt. Women at that time were nervous about male domesticity and even where their husbands helped, going so far as doing the washing when babies were born, would brag of their uselessness in the home in order to preserve their masculinity. In winter washing would hang above the frosted grass like crystal boards.

To Essex University to give the third of my seminars. Its grey towers soar above Wivenhoe Park like rookeries for students. My dozen or so drift into our classroom with their stories and poems. Behind the lines being read are the intentions to write. Their ages run from twenty to maybe forty, and their nationalities from here to China. They are each to read me something in their own language. The Jewish girl from Exeter reads something from Exodus in Hebrew, the French student gallops through Rimbaud's *Le Bateau ivre,* the boy from Epping reads me some pages from a novel he is writing about love in Essex. I read them a short story. The evening cold cuts my ears off as I run through the campus to the bus.

Swarming in the Nave

We walked to Nayland for supper, carefully picking our way through the sodden grass by the darkening river, and the occasional pockets of trapped heat astonished us. Heifers parted to let us through, sweet-breathed, trusting. I have wet feet. The willow plantation has already lost half its foliage. A boy and a girl and their dog cross our path, strangers, but there is a flurry of goodnights. It is indeed as good a night as St Luke can rustle up. We stopped to take it all in on Wiston Bridge, the full river, the homing rooks, the now impassable banks where the Constables' barge horses softly clumped along, elder branches tucked into their harness to keep the midges off. Leaning over the rail Peter-Paul announces that he will be off to Vienna next week to compose and teach. We have stood on this bridge since we were boys to watch the Stour moving seawards. It smells just like it did then. We push on. The wood is already black and night-filled. It says, 'Watch out! Take nothing for granted'. Its old trees lean out to give us a fright, just as they did long ago.

And here comes Nayland with its hugger-mugger houses which were built for looms but are now prized by retired gentle-folk and young commuters. The latter will be taking off their suits and putting on their jeans and shouting, 'Dinner!' as their children struggle over homework. The ancient streets and courts are blocked with cars. My toes are floating around in my socks. The sensation is private, wicked and perversely enjoyable, so I won't borrow dry ones from Peter-Paul. It is what happens when one arrives the river way.

Whilst preaching on St Luke I catch a faint distraction below, a mild hitting about, and dodging. Of what? If flies have got into the church maybe we should try elder boughs. 'No, no', they explain at the door, 'it's *bees*'. Bees are in the nave and buzzing around. I can see them now, a great many of them, angry creatures zooming through the pointed arches as they seek escape. Who will get them out? Harold, of course. And he does, being a friend of theirs. 'They take their hook', as we say.

Stephen telephones from his Bury St Edmund's bookshop to tell me that he has sold out of *Korans*. 'Everything Islamic has gone.' Good news. Christians should read the Koran and Muslims should read the *New Testament*. How else can we enter the debate? The editor of my Penguin *Koran* says that it is the earliest and finest work of Arabic prose. It has a whole chapter on The Bee. 'Your Lord inspired the bee, saying, "Make your homes in the mountains, in the trees, and in the hives which men shall build for you. Feed on every kind of fruit, and follow the trodden paths of the Lord."'

The Meaning of Plenty

Amiable southwesterlies and alternate stillnesses. Tumbling fruit in the orchard, small thuds from the drenched grass and part-gnawed Williams from the foxes' and rabbits' breakfast. Alf searches for what they have left to make pear wine. Later I listen to the singing and groaning of his saw as it turns dead willow boughs into nice stove-size logs. Crows are tossed around like scraps of burnt paper by the turbulence, abandoned and giving themselves up to disorder. Three small grandsons are running wild in Alf's house. His dark eyes shine with approval. David telephones to say that his granddaughter must write an essay about local abbeys and priories 'by the morning'. She is twelve. I look up half a dozen and give dates and places. He receives this expert information somewhat doubtfully. 'Austin Canons' – are you sure?' I recommend her to go and have a look at a nearby ruin. 'Oh, she hasn't got time for that.' I spell Cistercian. It is now elevenses and Alf and I break for philosophy.

Harvest festival piles upon harvest festival and I am severe on relevance. Let not the theme park enter thy head, and decidedly not thy parish church. Let not the flower arrangers leave no room for the harvest loaf on thine altar, O Lord. Let there be Plenty in the shape of corn and marrows and plums and all that is edible. Let there be no doubt about the realities of this cele-bration. Parson Hawker of Morwenstow is said to have started all this in order to rescue his flock from the unmentionable goings-on in the barns after the last field had been cleared. Those old hand-gathered harvests, who now has any idea of the labour involved? Is it any wonder that Victorian gravestones harp on 'rest'? Thomas Hardy noted the new boots purchased with harvest money striking sparks from the floor tombs in Stinsford church. I preach one of my harvest sermons in the private chapel of the man who murdered the princes in the Tower – 'allegedly', of course, though true, I believe. The chapel is exquisite. I imagine this gentleman at Mass, explaining to God that he was only carrying out orders. Somebody has scratched *Groyne que vodroy* on a buttress ('Let him complain who will'). The Suffolk congregation has eaten its Sunday lunch and will soon be eating its Sunday tea. But the harvest is sandwiched in between and the response is sweet and genuine. I sense as in so many other places Christian people doing their best to discover relevance – doing all they can not to be present at a thanksgiving but *as* a thanksgiving. It is often the ecologist, rather than the priest, who these days is able to teach the relevance of a pastoral vision. We shall starve physically and spiritually without it.

Night-walking

The night-walker. Not an approved activity, but a rewarding one all the same, and whether in town or country. In either place one has the world to oneself. In cities the architecture takes on an ethereal gravity and in the village all occupancy appears on a short lease. Having to slip away early from the harvest supper to finish a review, I mention that I shall walk. Apprehension, solicitude. Have I a torch? But the night-walker has night eyes. A torch would ruin his vision. The lane twists and turns until it comes to the pair of old railway sleepers which bridge the ditch, by which time I can see for miles. The horses are paired like statues, and as still. The grass is wet and scented. I won't wake Duncan and Jean up because they are at the party but I hope their dog will remember me as a friend. Their old farmhouse looks like a fort and their cropped fields have ceased to belong to anybody and are just earth. A great clump of paradisal flowers bursts from the path into the moonless light. Red campion. The Suffolk hills roll up from the Stour and are temptingly scattered with secret woods. Alas, it is only two miles home, and I am in the mood to night-walk five. 'You can stay out till breakfast – you're not a child,' says an eccentric voice. But the review. I dawdle the last distance, making it last like a sucked sweet. The house comes suddenly into view. I have taken it unawares. It is wide awake in its hollow and dazzlingly illuminated by a single bulb. It too has slipped owner-ship as the workhorses once slipped their traces and I might be running towards it in 1696. 'You – those people – those to come, how can you own anything at night?' it is saying. Max, night-walker extraordinary, sees me and shows off joyously, dashing up a tree and dancing about.

Some years ago I sat in Coleridge's house in Nether Stowey in the very cottage room in which the young poet wrote 'The Rime of the Ancient Mariner' with one hand, so to speak, while rocking his son to sleep with the other. The Wordsworths were nearby at Alfoxden and it was the custom of the three to night-walk in the Quantocks. Oh, the scandal! Three folk, and none of them married to each other, out all night! They were composing *Lyrical Ballads* on the hoof. 'The moving Moon went up the sky, And nowhere did abide.' The Old Testament more than once speaks of 'the vision of the night'. Job was an insomniac and couldn't bear the vision of the night – 'Desire not the night.' Just before St Luke's tide I stood in the enchantingly lit church at Long Melford with the rector Christopher Sansbury and saw what its builders could never have imagined, an interior revealed from without – by floodlights. A glass gallery of medieval gran-dees shone as bright as day.

A Nip in the Air

The first frost. It reminded me of being allowed to write about Coleridge in that same little room in which he had written 'Frost at Midnight' at Nether Stowey. 'The secret ministry of frost', he called it, that sudden dropping of air temperature below freezing point and the icing of October vegetation. Smelling it on its way, Max takes up his winter position by the stove. But something else brings Coleridge's poem to mind, it is the friend with his baby son on one arm and his pen doing its best to compose music at the same time, although not at midnight. But at least both young fathers have this in common, that the hand that rocks the cradle needs to stay awake. Coleridge's fire is nearly out. It is no more than a blue film of flame, which in his day announced a stranger. How people used to meditate on burning coal! My grandmother would sit up late in order not to waste the fire. The art was to coordinate its dying down with one's regular bedtime. But at Nether Stowey father has to stay up in order to get some work done. He is twenty-five and his thoughts seesaw between 'My babe so beautiful!' and having to make a living, as do those of my friend. Both men are manfully coping with dual forms of creation, their hard-working wives abed. The first frost at Bottengoms crisps the trees and nips many a rash flower in the bud. The grass crumps, the stars are silvery bright and the pheasants are indignant. It is amazingly cold. I think I could see my breath if there was a moon.

The agricultural malaise begins to be felt. Had we been dairy country or sheep land, its effect would by now have been blatant. But we are corn country and the set-aside fields have for some years now rather drearily broken us in to reduction. My first thought when such acres were left unploughed was that (*a*) this was a return to the old tradition of letting part of the farm lie fallow and (*b*) that marvellous old flowers would appear. I was mistaken. To lie fallow was to be ploughed and harrowed but unsown for a twelve-month, a kind of sabbatical which both rested and enriched. Set-aside is a subsidised way of doing nothing so as not to overwhelm the European granaries. As for finding plants which have lain dormant, one would do better to investigate the banks of the new motorways and the beautifully revived flora of ancient lanes now that the local council ceases to spray them. Farming, historically, has always been a thing of lean and fat years, of golden years and dearth, as the Prayer Book puts it. So far has the village moved from this, its once central task, that it takes all one's service-taking strength to put back any sense of harvest into the harvest festival and the harvest supper. Were this any other century, we would be tightening our belts. Instead, following the accountant's advice, we are drawing in our horns. Two girls are tending horses on the slope which has been farmed since Saxon times. The October sunshine flashes on their spades. It is hot. In a few hours this pasture, a frost pocket, will glitter with cold and the horses' breath will melt the ground as they feed.

The World is One Big Field

The single field which was nine fields has been ploughed and rolled. Only a man with a knowing eye could detect where Shoals ended and the Hilly Holt Lands began, for the ploughing is seamless, and ignorant of the old boundaries. All week long the village has droned with tractors as some half a dozen ploughmen turned over its huge acreage. And as if this was not enough, a handful of further soil disturbers have carved a red path all along the lane in which to lay bright blue water pipes. I made my post-harvest survey of the one field which was once nine and thought of the relentless labour they once demanded. Many an ancient ploughman walked lipperty-lop from having trod all his life one foot in the furrow, one foot on top. Human strength and horse strength were pitted against the never-defeated enemies of weeds and mires, and usually came off worst.

During the thoughtful lull following the Black Death, when a third of the clergy died and the social order generally broke down, the poet William Langland made Christ a ploughman, that is, the essential lord of the land and community provider, and his cathedral a barn. Revolutionary stuff. There is a touching and perhaps little-known reference to the world's wrongful low regard of those whose entire lives are spent in what were all too often killing fields so that bread could be eaten. The sharp-tongued Jesus is the speaker: 'Suppose one of you has a servant ploughing ... When he comes back from the fields, will the master say, "Come along at once and sit down"? Will he not rather say, "Prepare my supper, fasten your belt, then wait on me while I have my meal; you can have yours afterwards"?' So it always was. All the great rural writers deplore the low esteem in which, historically, the field workers were held. I watch Keith and Bernard and John ploughing with the latest machinery, high above the ruts, yet still with an innate artistry which says, 'I leave my mark on this land, so it must witness to my skill.'

'Go out and look at fields,' I shall tell the harvest festival congregations for the umpteenth time. What a hope. 'You do our looking for us,' they reply. 'That is what artists and writers are for. We've got to dash to Sainsbury's. Can we get you anything?'

It is the sixtieth anniversary of the Massey Harris 21 Combine Harvester, the amazing machine which routed traditional farm labour, minimalised the workers themselves and turned my nine fields into one. Combines were invented in Hitler's Germany in 1936 by Helmut Claas, reshaping eventually the earth's agriculture. Although not quite. There are not many days when I do not glimpse wooden ploughshares and bent backs on the screen.

Wind and Fire

Huge October winds, some when the rain hits the earth like silver javelins, some during brilliant sunshine. Yesterday there was a great scream as they tore off the limb of a willow which has been hanging low above the kitchen garden, drawing up the vegetables to hopeless heights. I was just about to get the tree surgeon, but the gale got in first. My neighbour Bernard can have half the wood if he brings his chainsaw to it. We are writing the names of the dead for All Souls, young and old folk long gone, many of whom had never heard of our village. Youths with their mouths full of sand in the Western Desert, Robert the priest, aunts who would not have been comfortable with such a public calling out of 'Matilda' or 'Doris' forty years on. Death makes the living rather familiar. Giving the funeral address for a neighbour of celebrated propriety in all such matters, I use her Christian name for the first time and would have thought that I deserved it if the pulpit reeled under my feet. She had been educated at the school founded by John Mason Neale at East Grinstead, the St Margaret's Sisters, and I imagined her singing his peerless translations of 'Jerusalem luminosa' and the very ancient Alleluyatic Sequence,

They, through the fields of Paradise that roam,
The blessed ones, repeat through that bright home – Alleluya!

Her fields ripple with winter wheat.

Matins at Mount Bures is thunderous with gales, and more like a clipper than a church. Now and then the congregation looks anxiously above as though hoping that the crew is taking in more sail. I preach in a crescendo, all about Jeremiah and King Jehoiakim, how as they read the prophet's book to him, the king cut the read pages off with a penknife and threw them into the fire, and about the Church burning Tyndale's Bible, and the stormtroopers making bonfires of the books which they believed had been made obsolete by *Mein Kampf*. Roaring flames, roaring weather and a friend so hot in the front pew because of the one-bar electric stove over his head that he surreptitiously works his way out of his coat. 'Now the king sat in the winter-house in the ninth month, and there was a fire on the hearth burning before him.' And into it went what he could not bear to hear. Jeremiah, of course, like all sensible authors, had a second copy but the poor young king's dead body 'was cast out in the day to the heat, and in the night to the frost'. Just before his troubles I sat next to Salman Rushdie at lunch and anyone less Satanic it would be hard to imagine, nor could he at that moment have dreamed that here in Britain they would have burnt one of his books. Metaphorically speaking, only one's boats should be burnt.

Midnight. Max will be measuring the cosy stove with his furry length. I lie with the window open to the valley and the curtains blown horizontal, and with the gale noisier than ever, honking and hollering its way upstream.

A Ploughing Match

World-wide thunder and grumpy rumblings all day. But the sky in Himalayan mood with gorgeous clouds in pile upon pile. Picking blackberries before it pours, I suddenly remember a painting by Harry Hambling of a fat woman doing likewise, her bottom to the lane, her engrossed face buried in the bush. He was an old friend, and Maggi's father. When he retired from the bank she put him to work with a paintbox. His pictures contained the hard Suffolk light and his blackberrying woman is a study of absorption. When you pick fruit, particularly wild fruit, you hurry greedily from berry to berry like a child. I have to stamp nettles down to get at the best of them, and there is a flash of lightning.

A bird is carrying on alarmingly overhead – I am taking the very bread out of its beak. But the hedges, I tell it, are loaded, and men too must eat. There is still the occasional wild rose in bloom. More sizzles of lightning on the hill like a faulty electricity circuit, jumpy and dangerous. The afternoon is bright, yet at the same time dark like polished iron, and huge spots of rain fall. Then in spite of this overture the approaching storm goes off to Ipswich, leaving me in timid sunshine.

A farmer chats about the autumn ploughing match. We watch the Punches taking to the field once more. Their manes and fetlocks have been given the full beauty treatment. As for their harness, it would do for Bucephalus. They pull the plough-shares through stubble like a silver wire through Cheddar cheese. Almost as well turned-out are their young masters as they totter and lurch towards the markers. They speak loving words to their horses, private endearments which we cannot catch. What a sight. The spectators' faces shine as they take it in. But the seagulls are puzzled. All this flesh and blood in the field instead of that obliging machine which did ten rows to this solitary furrow. It was hardly worthwhile flying from Felixstowe.

NOVEMBER

*R*onald Blythe loves what he describes as November's 'lovely but sad days', and in his Wormingford diaries he captures the sorrowful complexity of the month. November is the Month of Remembrance, the month of the red poppy, the symbol of life's brevity, made briefer by humanity's capacity for sending its young into the killing fields to be slaughtered, in Wilfrid Owen's phrase, 'one by one'. And so, on Remembrance Day, Blythe preaches 'on poppies, botanical and symbolical, blood-coloured and bloody'. He quotes Binyon's famous lines about the dead not growing old, 'as we that are left grow old', informing us that as a boy he always thought these lines would have brought cold comfort to the young dead soldiers who had hoped, like the rest of us, for a long life.

But November is also the Month of Remembering, the month that looks back as the year fades towards its end. As a countryman, Blythe remembers the snowdrops of February and the violets of March; he remembers the smell of new-mown hay in June; he recalls the sight of the harvest moon in September and the hunter's moon in October.

That's why, in spite of the riches of the other months, I am sure November is the month he loves best — the month of his birth. It is the month for the burning of the leaves and the pulling down of blinds, the saddest month of the year — perfect for melancholics like Blythe.

Richard Holloway

Summer's Ending

Sometimes it is too cold to work, sometimes too hot. This morning it is too beautiful. A sugar-icing frost and a fierce sun are warring it out. Leaves are the main casualty. Ash leaves like old men's hands and hazel leaves like a fortune in gold rain down. The universe beyond the window is both sombre and glittering. I am meditating, I tell myself, not idling. And did I not work a mighty act re the brambles yesterday, and have I not the lacerations to prove it? So do naught and watch the fall. The deciduous (*decidere*, to depart) leaves let go and must receive a thought or two. The poets have viewed them from extreme positions. Shelley called them 'Pestilence-stricken multitudes' and Milton unforgettably had likened Satan's countless legions to their deathly prolixity. 'Angel forms, who lay intrans't. Thick as autumnal leaves that strow the brooks in Vallombrosa.' The image arose from his youthful visit to Italy where he had actually seen the density of leaf-fall on the surface of the little rivers. The year before he arrived the mother-house of the Vallombrosan Order, dedicated to perpetual silence, poverty and manual work was being rebuilt twenty miles from Florence, and clearly was no mustering spot for the fallen archangel. But the quantity of the lifeless leaves on the water there hung in Milton's memory.

John the seedsman, en route to Mount Bures for the service, gives me an excellent botany lesson on autumn colours. Leaves fly alongside the car and dance on the bonnet. At matins I have the cheek to preach on wisdom to a dozen or so wise old folk. 'Whence hath this man this wisdom?' they said of Jesus. I said that they might have considered his family history. A great-great etc. grandfather had written, 'I myself am a mortal man, like to all, and when I was born I drew in the common air. When I prayed an understanding was given to me. I called upon God and the spirit of wisdom came to me, and I preferred her ... Wisdom is the brightness of the everlasting light, the unspotted mirror of the power of God, and the image of his goodness.' Barry, who attends matins in one church and evensong in another, and who rings bells in each, was obliged to listen to me on wisdom twice.

The ancient house is as quiet as that Vallombrosan mother-house except for the noise of a deluded bullfinch pecking at a pane. I think of grandmother's funeral in the country church all those years ago and the shush-shush of the mourning procession to the grave, and this full of leaves, so that her coffin went shush-shush too as it settled. The children are still playing conkers, tenners and twentiers (boasting) and illegal bakers – i.e. hardened in the oven. On the radio the markets yo-yo up and down as unwisely as possible. Hang Seng, Dow Jones, Footsy, mammon-talk. But, as a very different angel said,

Everyone to his own.
The bird is in the sky, the stone rests on the land,
In water livest the fish, my spirit in God's hand.

Angelus Silesius

Crossing the Ford

All Hallows. A furtive sun, a drift of, mercifully, unblemished ash-leaves. They sail across the study window, semi-shrivelled and blotched like old hands. But the rose John Clare flowers, and a yucca promises to, any minute now. Which is unwise of it. The season is both lively and deathly. Winter wheat is ruled across the fields down by the Stour. And, to maintain the geographic pattern, echelons of geese fly over the old roof as regular as clockwork.

My old farmer neighbour, a Framlingham boy, has died. His sons are into onions in a big way. Strings of them, red and white, dangle in my larder. Enough to last a year. I have taken the tender plants in from the frost, scythed the orchard, and am about to tidy up, in a fashion. For nothing approaching neatness will be accomplished until after Christmas. At the moment 'The King of Glory passes on his way.'

James, from the University, arrives, to confess that he does not write letters. He emails. Sloth, of course. He devours cake. Never? He shakes his head, and I shake mine. I point to two shelves of *Letters* in my library, and there he is, a professor, without a letter to his name. A succession of visitors make their way down the muddy track, and are granted audience. The white cat sits on them in turn, dribbling with joy. The village is pensive. The surface of the lanes shines. The hedges are machine-cut to within an inch of their lives. They are what is called a parallel universe.

But the water beneath the bridge swirls about any old how on the surface, though with deep, dark thoughts. Another fall, another bitter time to come. This is where Widermund kept the ford. I see him as one of those St Christopher young men, splashing across shallow rivers with dace and carp swimming between his legs. He would have waded a dozen steps from Suffolk to Essex, heard the watermill, witnessed the kingfisher. 'Do you keep a diary?' I ask the letterless teacher. He shakes his head. 'Through gates of pearl streams in the countless host.'

Ladies appear to sell me a poppy. People on the telly wear them weeks before Remembrance Sunday. Why is this? It seems more to do with respectability than with mourning.

Last Sunday, I preached on Amos, a hero of mine. An unlicensed preacher, this young fruit-farmer from Tekoa had the nerve to 'lift his voice'. He lifted it against liturgy and contentment, and against national happiness. God said: 'Prophesy unto my people.'

'He showed me a basket of summer fruit and said: "Amos, what do you see?" And I said: "A basket of summer fruit." And God said: "The end is come upon my people."' We hear the sadness in his voice.

Summer fruit ends the orchard year. Only this year, there was no fruit. Not a pear, not a plum. I imagined Amos and God in the sycamore-fig orchard. A burst of October wind rattled my trees. Now and then, civilisation begins to crumble, and an unprofessional person says what has to be done. And those in power say: 'Who gives him leave to speak?'

God tells his orchardman, 'I will smite the winter house with the summer house ... I will not hear the melody of your viols ... I despise your feast days.' This was too much for the high priest. He told Amos to go where he couldn't hear him and prophesy there. Minor prophets can be a trial, especially when they write so well.

The Kiddush

The first log fire of the autumn crackles, the saucepans simmer, the cat puts on his starved face, the wind rises in the dark garden, the acrid leaves pile up on the wet grass, the wine is warmed and we wait for Joachim to join us after his journey from Berlin. Guests, and the table properly laid. I am approached with a request. As it is Friday evening, may Joachim say the Kiddush? Ashamedly realising that I would not have said Grace, I reply, 'Of course, of course!', cease cooking and do what I am told is necessary. Place a napkin over the bread, light the candles, pour some wine into each of our glasses and stand with the others to listen to Joachim asking God to sanctify the Sabbath. He breaks the bread into fragments and sprinkles them with salt. He prays in Hebrew the prayers which the Lord prayed. We drink a little wine. The Kiddush – the blessing of the day. I rush back to the kitchen to poke the potatoes and think of all the families who have lived here since the time when this best of all vegetables first made its appearance in an English farmhouse, and how puzzled they would have been to hear the Kiddush. Joining in each others' prayers is properly humbling, properly elevating. How prayers overlap, interweave, take thoughts and praise and thanks from each other.

All Souls, so I read out the names of the departed and think of the school register. Alan Bryan – 'Present, sir.' Alan Bryan – no answer. Familiar faces come and go. Christina Rossetti saw them in 'Light above light, and bliss beyond bliss' where 'our names are graven upon his hands'. She is now regarded as the finest poet of the Oxford Movement, better say some than John Keble. She is forever seeking, searching. For her, death was a meeting with 'your own Angel', the messenger 'who have hedged us, both day and night'. All Saints, so we process through the churchyard and into the glowing aisle, lime leaves hissing and crunching under our feet, and past new graves, and singing of course Bishop How's multitudinous hymn. Obligingly, the weather backs up both our mortal and immortal responses, now thrillingly sad, now utterly glorious. Later, I walk to take a grandstand view of November from the path to the aerodrome, where Essex sweeps across to Suffolk and the larches stand firm on their knoll. We should cleanse our eyes in scenery – use it like lotion. George Herbert liked to gallop up to Old Sarum to see the sights and to draw in the strong air. And, when he was at Cambridge, to gallop out of the fens to the pure upland of Newmarket.

This is the year for the great replanting, something I have promised myself for ages. Plants appear to have not only roots but legs. How else do I discover the borderers bang in the middle? It is what some friends describe as a wild garden, looking at me worriedly in case I misjudge their meaning and take offence. Wild it may be, but not free to do what it likes, I tell it. An old French rose is set where it will be long after I am a new name on the All Souls list.

All Souls

R eading the ever-growing list of those who have, to quote
Henry Vaughan, 'gone into the world of light', I am suddenly
struck by the thought of how swiftly they vanish. Here today and
gone tomorrow. Why has the village not collapsed as prop after
prop is taken away? How does the parish church remain standing
when warden, retired general, choirmaster, the inhabitants of
'farmers' pew', the great ladies in the front seats, the gentle figure
by the second pillar have all gone?

As I add my parents' names, and those of close friends, to the
All Souls roll call, how is it that tears do not disturb my rationality? The ballpoint scrawls on the lined paper require all my attention. Both morning and evening congregations kneel and listen
so as not to miss Aunt Doris and poor John. Here come the priests
who helped us out during the frequent interregnums, here is a
tower captain, here are the good old regulars, here is a boy. Here
are my brief pauses and a mounting silence. But how is it that,
churchwise, they have all gone without leaving an unfillable
space? Something strange here. Is this what mortality is?

In less rational times people would hang around the church on
All Souls' eve, waiting for the year's dead to process across the
grass, chatting, engrossed and apparently not missing the living a
bit. Why, the grave-earth hadn't greened, and there they were, not
even noticing. St Paul's cheerfulness about his own death must
have struck young Timothy and the others as a mite selfish. 'I shall
be with Christ, which is far better!' And landing them with the
infant Church!

Ancient friends type out their funerals and put them in the
post. No fuss. I am to do the committal in church as they don't
want me to 'trek all the way to the crem for a couple of sentences'.
When, finally, I come to the end of the All Souls list, I say my
favourite blessing, the Mosaic one – 'The Lord bless us and keep

us, the Lord make his face to shine upon us and give us his peace.' It comes after the laws on 'separation' in Numbers. After which we all creakily resume our seats and find Isaac Watts's 'How bright these glorious spirits shine.'

How golden bright it is outside where the lime leaves fall in their millions – well countlessly anyway. The cars are being carpeted. The air will be delicious, a kind of dying freshness which is full of movement and colour. The Hall trees wave gaudily and the farm hedge will be rattling with birds. We too are deciduous in our way, bursting newly on the scene but ultimately tumbling down like the poor crooked scythe and spade. Then mulching, then living as we never lived before, caught up as we will be in the divine love.

Between services I mow the sopping lawns, anxious on such a blowy leafy day that autumn should not impact them. I scrape mashed cuttings from the blades. The white cat kindly comes outside to watch. The farmer from the Wiston air-strip does his Sunday afternoon Amy Johnson routine, crackling around over-head in a neighbourly fashion. Well-bred gliders look down on him. The clocks having been put back, teatime arrives soon after lunch. I listen to *Poetry Please* on the radio, nursing the cat. They should have read Thomas Hardy's 'At Day-close in November' in which

Beech leaves, that yellow the noon-time,
  Float past like specks in the eye.

'The poor crooked scythe and spade'

Two blackbirds gorge on berries below the study window. They stand a yard apart, eating and balancing. But no fruit in the orchard for me. Not an apple, not a plum. And the wheat harvest is way down, and were we living in Thomas Hardy's day we would be saying the prayer 'In the time of Dearth and Famine'. 'And grant that the scarcity and dearth, which we do now most justly suffer for our iniquity, may through thy goodness be mercifully turned into cheapness and plenty.' But it was the summer rain, not my iniquity which did it.

In John Donne's Holy Sonnets, he remembers:

All whom war, dearth, age, agues, tyrannies,
Despair, law, chance, hath slain . . .

Dearth is dearness. I no longer know the price of anything – butter, eggs, pyjamas, bacon, the cinema. And now this harvest's bread. I buy three loaves, and put two in the deep-freeze. A charming soil-tester comes and tells me what I have never been told before about our village fields, stones and all.

At the optician, a young man asks me to read A Z L M O, etc. 'Try the next line.' In the High Street – the same down which the Romans wandered – the young and old make their way. I buy next year's Gardener's Diary. How efficient I am.

Changed and in my toiler's rags, I prepare the orchard for the scythe. Everything must lie low. E'er the winter storms begin. I am the great leveller. I think of Oliver Cromwell, of harvest supper, of the last chapter – how to begin it. In church, I must remember not to mention St Luke's little summer, so that people do not exchange looks and give little smiles. 'Wait for it – he will tell us that it is St Luke's little summer.' But what shall I say instead? Shall I leave dearth alone? The farmers and their wives pray. As do the Waitrose customers. All bowed. Honeybees, fruit and veg, the token sheaf, the rich scent. The sun on the painted saints, on the Lord himself.

'I can't bear it,' the old friend used to say as she watched market-day from her car. Meaning that it would all go on when she was 'gone'. The stalls, the schoolchildren on the bus, the swing-doors of the shops, the town hall flag, the plane flying low, the people chatting, the church clock striking, the girl laughing at the counter, the lovers holding hands, the October air. Everything would go on. She couldn't bear it.

Three labourers have spaded their way down to where the Romans trod, raising a mountain of blond rubble. People look down on them. A wit: 'Have you lost something, mate?' On they dig. I take a short cut through long Victorian roads, which are named after Cromwellian generals, and get lost. Most of my short cuts are a long way round. Surprisingly, a villa calls itself a Russian Orthodox church. What a squeeze it must be. Incense and icons in the front room. Rich responses climbing the stairs.

And now, home. What shall we sing on Sunday morning? Do we know 'Light of the minds that know him'? It is a prayer of St Augustine of Hippo, and is about our treading out our own Emmaus road. A little rain falls.

Widermund's Ford

November and the garden seat covered with books and coffee cups — and cat. Skimpy yellow clouds sail on high. Ash leaves like withered hands caress us as they tumble into wet grass. There is a nice whiff of rot. I stroll to the river to make my autumn observance and the dace — I think — flash under the bridge. The iron rail is hot and the mill-pool offers a swim. In my head global warming fights with bliss. I think of Widermund the Saxon setting out the sarsens which the plough has turned up to make stepping stones in the ford so that people could cross the Stour from one kingdom to another without wetting their feet. Widermund's ford, due to much ancestral garbling, became Wormingford — the Dragon's ford. In vain do I teach etymology to the neighbours — 'ety-what?' In vain do I wonder that boys are not christened Widermund — instead of Charlie, say. Widermund's face doesn't appear in the stained glass but the Dragon's does as he munches a virgin. Her snowy bare legs dangle from his jaw and so concentrating is he on his dinner that he fails to see George. A new altar has been set beneath this alarming scene.

Theologically, dragons are only afraid of the panther, not George. In his *Book of Beasts* T. H. White says, 'What Solomon pointed out about Christ is symbolised by the panther being an animal of so many colours that by the wisdom of God the Father he is the Apprehensible Spirit, the Only Wise, the Manifold, the True, the Sweet, the Suitable, the Clement, the Constant, the Established, the Untroubled, the Omnipotent, the All-Seeing. And because it is a beautiful animal, the Lord God says of Christ: "He is beautiful in form among the sons of men".' But no panthers in the north aisle and, a mile or two upstream, above the north door of Wiston church, it is a dragon that gloats over those whose fate it is to be buried 'on the dog' (bestiaries tend to go rather wild and have never heard of David Attenborough). 'On the dog' means the north churchyard, an unhallowed spot crammed with unmarried mothers, unbaptised babies, suicides and paupers. Dragon food. Ours at Wormingford contains some very grand tombs, including those of John Constable's uncles who ran the mill by Widermund's ford and whose chief dragon was the collapse of agriculture after the Napoleonic wars.

I miss filling up my Wild Flower Society Register but having done so a dozen times there seems no point in writing, 'Wild teasel, *Dipsacus fullonum*, Garnon's field bank' for the thirteenth time. For there it may have been since Widermund scratched himself on it. But one feels guilty when one ceases to take note of plants. Those who did so incurred the wrath of John Clare. He was a rural looker. Nothing growing, flying, running, swimming, taking to its bed in autumn escaped his eye, and he would lash out at villagers who stumped to and fro in Helpston, apparently not seeing a thing. But they and he both saw ghosts, of course. You might miss *Dipsacus fullonum* but you would never miss a ghost. The closest he gets to dragons is a crocodile which recognises 'the Ichneumon (mongoose) as its destroyer'. Yet all the mongoose wanted from the crocodile was its eggs. Clare bridges all the science and mythology of the English countryside in his poetry. We see where we came from —and where we are going. His river was the Nene. It glitters and frowns in his work, sucks at the fenny ground, fills sluices, widens into little paradises.

Rushes

Peter has been filming the river all spring and summer, and now the time has come for me to do the voice-over. Our film is based on John Constable's simple acknowledgement that 'These scenes made me a painter.' In attempting to list the credits for our existence we do not always sufficiently credit geography – even the geography of a native street – for helping to make us what we are. Constable's local scene was emotionally extended by the fact that his family owned much of it. Windmills, watermills, a paper mill, dozens of barges, small farms, landing stages, water meadows, locks, sluices, thousands of willows and poplars, alders and elms, a new mansion good enough for a Jane Austen girl to marry into, and a fine cargo ship, the *Telegraph*, to ply to and fro to London. 'These scenes' of his were bustling and profitable, and bursting with Georgian farming commerce. The sheer idleness of his river as Peter and I walked its banks would have shocked him, the same loveliness of its twists and turns he would have taken for granted. River dwellers remain a race apart, even now. Currents seem to wind through them, pulling their thoughts along. They never quite grow up because of their river's never being able to segregate work from play. They possess a different concept of mortality, one of being borne along downstream to estuaries and seas, of life flowing out of sight rather than ending. Watching the rushes of our Stour film with Peter, seeing the spring and summer of only a few months ago fill the screen, and finding words to say over them, I realised that even river dwellers are apt to know no more of their local river than the few yards which run beneath the local bridge or occupy the local stretch. Miles and miles of Stour are now virtually left to themselves by the inhabitants of its valley. The Jordan would have been like this, noisy and teeming in spots, a silent, lonely desert waterway for long reaches.

My white pheasant runs on the hill, sprinting alongside rabbits and rooks, but with a sense of his rarity. He would not be out of place in the wall paintings of St James the Less at Little Tey, I sometimes think. These ghosts of the sacred came through, as it were, the resistance of the ancient walls to today's synthetic modern paints, which caused flaking and peeling until gradually and wonderfully pictures such as Noli Me Tangere, The Last Supper, The Three Living and the Three Dead, and a complete Passion Cycle paled into view. I balance on pews to stare into them. The table in the upper room is covered with cups and dishes, each in pencil outline. In the Washing of Feet, the Lord is forcibly holding down Peter's foot in the bowl as the apostle raises his hand in horror. A towel hangs over a rail. The church is tiny and apsidal. Scabious is in bloom outside. Half a mile away, trucks thunder down Stane Street. A thousand years ago a shrine was set beside it.

'They shall grow not old'

Lovely but sad days. The leaves fall, the sun shines, in church we muster for the Remembrance. It has become a kind of saints'-day, filling the aisles with its devotees. We turn to its memorial, and I say its liturgy. Its words are by the librarian-poet Laurence Binyon, and were published in *The Times* long before the Western Front massacres had begun. 'They shall grow not old, as we that are left grow old.'

As a boy, I used to think that these soldiers would have found this cold comfort, and would have very much liked to have enjoyed a long life. But their melancholy suits the Georgian language of the Remembrance. We sing Isaac Watts's 'O God, our help in ages past'. Charlotte Brontë has a girl, 'her voice sweet and silver clear', sing it in *Shirley*. Our voices, though darkened by time, do justice to this masterpiece. And so the service goes on, inside and outside. I preach on poppies, botanical and symbolical, blood-coloured and bloody.

It was the Jewish poet Isaac Rosenberg in 'Break of Day in the Trenches' who released, as it were, our emblematic poppy, the one we button-hole. A rat touches his hand 'As I pull the parapet's poppy to stick behind my ear'.

Flanders was traditional farmland. Corn and its wild flowers had grown alongside there for centuries. Just as its birds sang above the din, so did its poppies bleed in its mud. The imagery seems to grow more intensely every Remembrance, and my sermons ever more botanical.

But our greatest time-hymn, 'O God, our help in ages past', says more and more to me about mortality and immortality. Or so I find. It is grand, sonorous, truthful, accepting, tragic yet comforting, and it first appeared in Wesley's *Psalms and Hymns* in 1738. A poignant verse was left out long ago, but it uncannily suggests the Western Front:

Like flowery fields the nations stand
Pleased with the morning light:
The flowers beneath the mower's hand
Lie withering ere 'tis night.

Too far to walk, we drive from our church to a steel memorial by the side of the road. It is to the American airmen who came to Wormingford on St Andrew's Day in 1943. Some 200 of them were killed – too many names to read out and halt the Sunday traffic racing by. Their colonel, almost a hundred, sends a message from the United States.

My father, a teenager at Gallipoli, refused to attend these rites, the band playing, the mayor in his robes, the snowy war memorial in the little Suffolk town. Once central, it has long been put at the side of the road so as not to delay a flood of cars. Otherwise you would have taken your life in your hands.

I say Binyon's words all over again. They float in the mild air. I remember my friend John Nash, who painted both the trenches and the Second World War docks, and Christine, his wife, who ran a canteen at Portsmouth for the sailors. John told me that 1939 never meant as much to him as 1914. His brother Paul painted the Battle of Britain, the Heinkels and Spitfires like stars in the Kent sky. And so it continues, the reality and the dream.

Between services, I rake-up fallen leaves, mostly from the giant oaks which stare out of the valley into the next parish. They are all in line, their roots in the everlasting stream, their tops spying Little Horkesley.

How it Happened

The Rememberance once more. There is a palpable element in this annual grief. It announces its arrival in the bare trees, in the dawn skies. I find that a leaf, sailing down from the stripped ash, becomes a poppy petal on the brow of a teenage soldier in the Albert Hall.

Long ago, the Westminster Abbey librarian, Mr Tanner, described to me the burial of the Unknown Warrior, at which he had been present. All this came back to me, as it were, because the artist who had painted Harry Patch had come to stay, and I was telling him about this conversation.

Harry was 107, and had spent much of his life trying to get the trenches out of his head. His longevity was to fix both the war and himself together for ever. The world stared at the thin old man on the screen, still breathing, still speaking. The Unknown Warrior, explained Mr Tanner, was the idea of a young padre, the Revd David Railton, who would later become Vicar of Margate.

After the Armistice, after the millions of 'the fallen', as the poets of the time liked to call them, cried out, like Dido, 'Remember me!', the question was: 'How?' How did a nation remember such an unprecedented slaughter? And then, said Mr Tanner, came this extraordinary suggestion from someone who had been in the thick of it all.

One evening, in 1916, wrote the padre,

I came back from the line at dusk. We had just laid to rest the mortal remains of a comrade. I went to a billet in front of Erkingham, near Armentières. At the back of the billet was a small garden, and in the garden, only six paces from the house, there was a grave. At the head of the grave there stood a rough cross of white wood. On the cross was written in deep black pencilled letters, 'An Unknown British Soldier', and, in brackets beneath, 'of the Black Watch'. It was dusk, and no one was near, except some officers in the billet, playing cards. I can remember how still it was. Even the guns seemed to be resting.

Now that grave caused me to think. Later on, I nearly wrote to Sir Douglas Haig to ask if the body of an 'unknown' comrade might be sent home. I returned to Folkestone in 1919. The mind of the world was in fever. Eventually, I wrote to Bishop Ryle, the Dean of Westminster . . .

The only request that the noble Dean did not see his way to grant was the suggestion I gave him – from a relative of mine – that the tomb should be inscribed as that of the Unknown Comrade – rather than Warrior . . .

The celebrated text on the grave, 'They buried him among the Kings because he had done good toward God and toward his

House', had already been in use on an Abbey tomb for almost 600 years, though the Dean did not know it, because he said that he was indebted to a north-country archdeacon for it. But Richard II had had it inscribed on the tomb of his friend the Bishop of Salisbury in 1395.

At first, George V shrank from the suggestion of this anonymous body arriving at the Abbey. It was novel, and could be sensational. 'His Majesty is inclined to think that nearly two years after the last shot was fired . . . a funeral might now be regarded as belated, and almost, as it were, reopen the war wound which time is gradually healing.'

Remembrance does not seek to heal.

Colin, Master Book-mender

Was there ever such a delectable autumn. I am playing Last Across with the geraniums and the marvellous spire of yucca blossom, leaving them outside until the first rumours of frost. Hazel and ash leaves sail over them, through them. Thinning trees let in pale shafts of morning light. Fungus rots at their roots. The air is both morbid and sublime. I find it hard to stay in. Books topple in the study, paper stays wordless, gobbledegook messages remain uninterpreted on the answerphone. Like the flowers, I must make the most of it, this St Martin's big summer. He was an army officer whose feast falls on 11th November but he suddenly proclaimed himself a conscientious objector – 'I am Christ's soldier; I am not allowed to fight.' He was hugely active, hugely right, excitingly important. On his day the poppy petals fall on the young faces in the Albert Hall.

Colin the farmer's son arrives to say goodbye with new-laid eggs and some mushrooms he has gathered en-route from Maltings Farm to Bottengoms Farm, a tramp of half a mile. He and his wife are seeing the world before settling down. That is, he is mending ancient books in Adelaide. He is a master-restorer of old volumes. Bindings, foxed pages, collapsed texts, dim illustrations are healed by him. But he gets homesick. Australia is a curiously homesick-making country, I found – although no land could be more unlike England. It is deep in drought at this minute. It is a place of harsh renewals. Strangely, talking to Colin, pressing on him something to read on the long haul, I find myself visitor-sick for a glimpse of the blue gums and blue water below my brother's house near Sydney. I am in that very English room once more. There is the marble fireplace in which fires are never lit. There are the piles of books on English gardens and English cathedrals. There are the prints of Suffolk. There, in the hallway, is the larger-than-life brass rubbing of Sir Robert de Bures from Acton, our birthplace, irritable in his armour and in his isolation.

Now and then I steer my way down the mile-long track late at night. Darker and darker it becomes until, as I feel my steps entering the orchard, there is a kind of crescendo of the old rural darkness, an opacity which is almost palpable, hanging from my body as it moves through the fruit trees. Most villages possessed this blessed darkness until a few years ago. But now they are told not to bear it, to regard it as a danger, to wage war against it. Darkness is good for you, this natural daily absence of the sun, that is. Its artificial destruction in the countryside itself is a tragedy. Forget its religious and social symbolism, return to its naturalness. Feel it on your skin. Let it become a part of your wakefulness as well as your sleep. The visionary American poet Theodore Roethke said that even just philosophically 'In a dark time, the eye begins to see'. Physically the loss of each day's darkness is one we should not endure.

St Martin's summer notwithstanding, birds, beasts and insects are taking flight, laying in supplies, making beds. At dusk a river of rooks flowed overhead, and a badger crossed the lane. At dawn a pair of bluetits fed wildly on berries with something of the fervour of a crisp-gorging woman who sat opposite to me on the train. Stuff, stuff, for the hungry day must come. Frosts too.

Herbert in the November Garden

The dead russet apple is to be cut down. There was no lingering in its demise, no withering here and there. Two springs ago it was its usual world of blossom (though no fruit later), then it died. It was a grand member of the orchard which John Nash planted after his demob as an official war artist in 1945. When it was really alive its russets rained down, so many that we would beg the postman, the passing children, the passing anyone, to take twenty, fifty, all you can manage. But tomorrow the saw, Joachim on the ladder, Ian and I below to haul away its heaviness, for newly lifeless boughs weigh a ton. A bow-saw will make them manageable, will provide food for the fire and apple-wood for Stephen the carver, twigs for kindling and a ten-foot trunk to grow a Rambling Rector up. So today it is clearing the ground before we make a start. I feel like the barber of the Bastille clearing aristocratic necks for the blade.

It is an exquisite November day, very still, very subdued and with heart-catching colouring. Various creatures come out to observe these austere preliminaries, robins, chaffinches, a late bee or two, a nice dog. The earth is still dark with the final russet leaves and I can hear the critical chock-chock of pheasants. So many rooks fly over that they darken the sky. 'Try this russet,' we used to say, 'take some home'. I think of the unkempt trees in William Dyce's *George Herbert in his Garden*, the dead branches poking from the ivy and the cassocked poet beneath them, one hand holding a book, the other raised in praise or a gesture of farewell. There is fishing tackle to remind one that Izaak Walton was Herbert's first biographer and in the distance the pale spire of Salisbury Cathedral to point to the poet's weekly walk to sing in the choir. And between Bemerton and the city, the River Nadder, chilly and uninviting. All this in 1861. All of Herbert's physical existence over by 1633. Vikram Seth bought his rectory in 2003 and will be swimming in the river when it is inviting. A house-keeper led me to it just before he arrived, and just before nightfall, and I forgot to see if the trees were pruned. Herbert believed that gardens should be medicine-chests as well as pleasances, utilities and dreams. The rose itself cannot escape:

> What is fairer than a rose?
> What is sweeter? yet it purgeth.

The Music Girl

The sumptuous November days continue. Golden leaves hide the lawns, particularly those from the hedge hazels. Rain-water stays in the ruts. The ponds are glassy, the skies aquamarine and noisy with homing birds. Now and then a drenched fox or rabbit lopes across the greening field where the winter wheat is showing. A solitary figure descends the church tower to pack up, his task done. The time-wrecked finials which Sir William fanci-fully placed on its corners when Shakespeare was writing *All's Well that Ends Well* have been replaced. Now all that is needed is fifty years' weather to blend them into the scenery. John, our Admirable Crichton, has also come down from on high, having taken advantage of the scaffolding to paint the clock. I watch these conclusions from where I am brushing lichen from John Nash's gravestone where in less than thirty years his name strug-gles to be read. Whereas on the grand neighbouring tombs of the Constables the deeply cut inscriptions continue to defy botany. The churchyard is a great untidy bed of seared yellow coverings through which the dead poke their names and pleas, yet again.

It is the feast of St Cecilia. I mention her at matins. She was first buried in the cemetery of St Callistus on the Aurelian Way, this long ago girl who 'sang to God in her heart', sharing ground with a pope who had done time in a Sardinian quarry. But now she has her own church of St Cecilia in Trastevere, where a statue shows her, naturally if unusually, lying on her side, sound asleep. There she is, say all the composers, this remote person from whom traditionally flows the Church's glorious music. What would she have made of the BBC's *Songs of Praise*, I wonder? Had she composed a hymn they would not have mentioned her name. They first celebrated Cecilia at a service in London in which Purcell's *Te Deum* and *Jubilate in D* were sung. Then, a century or so later, came the Cecilian Movement itself for the reform of Roman Catholic church music. Now and then we 'hear her', as it were, singing in a quire window silently, as she nurses her emblem, a toy organ. 'What passion *cannot* Music raise and quell?' asked John Dryden in his 'Ode' to her. We sang, 'My tongue shall never tire of chanting with the choir', I hope truthfully.

On Wednesday the Powys contingent bumped down the old track, old friends from the Welsh border. I lit an ash-log fire to welcome them. I remember their tiny church at Discoed. It would have been a kneeling place for medieval shepherds. The poet Edward Storey has these past few years refilled it with singing. We have lunch at the pub in Nayland, leaving the car on the hard where John Constable's father's barges dumped coal and anything else which travelled easier by river than by road. The weather then started to become a bit wild, or less serene, and the willows thrashed about and there was a mighty rustling. 'More what you expect, like,' said a pleased old chap. Exactly. I thought of the reduced light of Radnorshire, how it is diffused, how it avoids brilliance.

Whereas the light in East Anglia avoids nothing. It just pours down like one of those gifts from St James's Father of lights, no matter if the sun is in. Thus the Stour goes on gleaming in its sullen fashion as the days darken.

What to tell them on Sunday? Parables, poetry and history flicker across the flimsy pages. There are two kings, reminds the Lectionary, Edmund and Christ. Also there is Isaac Watts, hymnwriter, d. 1748. And there is Stir-up Sunday. But how about the young Saviour standing on the Temple steps listening to the singing and joining in?

Barbara Pym

Dank days. Mulch. Slanting rains. The first leaf-carpet is ash and aspen. The latter's grand name is *Populus tremula* from the trees' trembling in the wind, but now their music is reduced to a squelching under my feet. Scores of seagulls wheel fretfully over the hill, presumably searching for something better than horse leavings; for they rarely descend.

The atmosphere is richly sad – pensive. No humans about. Does the ancient farmland mourn its labourers? Just David now, who seeds and reaps it, slashes its hedges into shape with 'the murderer', and commands it from on high.

Our faith, like most faiths, is drawn out of pastorality, out of agriculture, out of days like these, when mud and rottenness, wet feet, and cold hands had to meet as part of the bargain.

A dizzy climber on the east wall breaks its strings and falls flat, which allows me to give it a good back and sides before tying by the door. My ladder sinks before settling, as we all must, I suppose. (You see what a wet November afternoon does to the spirit.)

Tugging off my boots, I might read a favourite Barbara Pym, *A Few Green Leaves*. She wrote this lively novel on her deathbed, and when she was writing to me about the reception of T. S. Eliot into the Church of England, which took place in her village church on 29 June 1917, St Peter's Day. It was Finstock, Oxfordshire, Barbara's own church. Here the doors were locked before Tom had the waters of regeneration poured over his head in the presence of his godfathers, B. H. Streeter and Vere Somerset.

Barbara thought that the following lines from 'Little Gidding' might refer to this mighty episode in the Church of England:

Thus, love of a country
Begins as attachment to our own field of action
And comes to find that action of little importance
Though never indifferent. History may be servitude,
History may be freedom. See, now they vanish,
The faces and places, with the self which, as it could,
   loved them,
To become renewed, transfigured, in another
   pattern.

In *A Few Green Leaves*, Tom the Rector finds Miss Lee 'doing what she called "her" brasses'. He also finds, to his shame, that the lectern is not brass but oak, and that although he had been in the parish for years, he had noticed the polishing but not what was being polished. Did Miss Lee sometimes regret that it was not a brass lectern? 'Oh, no, Rector, I love that old wooden bird, and I love polishing it. A brass one may look more brilliant, but wood can be very rewarding, you know . . .'

Our lectern at Wormingford is made of wood, and was carved by Joliffe Tufnell, our squire. Should this eagle fly off, it would be out of the north door. It is a mighty creature, fully armorial, non-benign, and heavy with message. The Authorized Version is spread on it, and shortish people have to mount a box to read it. A microphone carries its lessons near and far.

Mr Clegg is the gamekeeper in *A Few Green Leaves*, and one is grateful for it. There are no flying bishops, only flying words, not all of them kind. The dark afternoon falters and streaky yellow bands are coldly illuminating for an hour or so.

Knowing When to Go

Although we are apt to imagine that earlier generations worked until they dropped, retirement has a long history. It has been described as an act of falling back, or retreating from a position, a deliberate withdrawal into seclusion and privacy. One of my little jokes as the retired proliferate around me is to declare that 'writers never retire' and to put on a hard-done-by face. Certainly poets, novelists and artists remained outside the bureaucracy of retirement which controls most working lives, and with the effect of obliterating in their subconsciousness the conventional retirement ages, sixty, sixty-five or – for the clergy – sixty-nine, etc. This particular Damoclean sword does not hang by a hair over the self-employed writer's or artist's head to impress upon him that one day he will have to put his pen or brush away, give himself a little party and 'take early retirement'. Not *have to,* maybe, but there are many voluntary retirements in literature, Shakespeare himself giving up his trade while still in his fifties in order to become a gentleman. Still the most amazing retirement of a great poet is that of Arthur Rimbaud who, at twenty, abandoned literature for a life of action in Africa. Disillusioned, self-hating, the dazzling youth had returned home on All Souls' day 1873 and made a bonfire of his manuscripts, the most marvellous being *Les Illuminations* and *Une Saison en Enfer.* Thankfully there were published copies. Rimbaud lived another half-century in a retirement whose pain is still felt by those who examine it. Enid Starkie has come closest to understanding it. She said that Rimbaud was one of those people who make big mistakes, a violent man who could take the knife to himself and cut out, as though it were a canker, his own genius.

Far gentler retirements have been happening. Michael's at Westminster Abbey, our Archdeacon's still in progress, as it were. I sat in Poets' Corner at the Dean's farewell Eucharist, and by the side of the Archdeacon at what was for him a farewell patronal festival in Wormingford church, and all in less than a week. And then this same week I gave a talk to the monthly gathering of Suffolk clergy, young and old, at Bury St Edmunds, reading to them R. S. Thomas's matchless statement on the rural priest's lot. He is both retired and non-retired, as I daresay both Michael and Ernie will be, though for a different reason. The parish has gone but not the poetry. Nor will it until Thomas has 'gone'. And this is what most unretiring writers and artists pray for – that work will last until the end.

Church Music

Early morning just before Advent, with the dawn making the most of it. A bright yellow wedge prises the fields from the sky, and there is a glimpse of countless crazy birds, then a retreat into darkness.

The white cat sprawls on me as I drink tea and contemplate St Cecilia, who 'sang in her heart to God', who was martyred in the third century, and who has a church named after her in the Trastevere in Rome. In spite of all this, she more or less disappeared until the seventeenth century, when John Dryden's 'A Song for St Cecilia's Day', 1687, returned her with delightful panache.

The poem praises each instrument in turn – trumpet, flute, drum, violin and finally organ, possibly suggesting Britten's *Young Person's Guide to the Orchestra*. St Cecilia's Day was his birthday.

Watching the morning, I think of us walking on the marshes with the blue-black Aldeburgh sea thudding on the shingle, all this a long time ago. Dryden said that Cecilia raised music higher than Orpheus, the latter being a pagan. But then he had only a lyre: she was able to pull all the stops out.

I preach on church music on the feast of Christ the King, and read the psalm that he and his friends sang in the upper room,

'When Israel came out of Egypt . . . and the Lord turned the hard rock into a standing water, and the flintstone into a springing well.' The latter is more or less what we still do ecologically at Wormingford. I also read George Herbert's enchanting 'Church Musick', that 'sweetest of sweets' which he helped to make in Salisbury Cathedral every Thursday.

On the radio, Colm Tóibín's musical voice attempts to philosophise on the Irish dilemma – which makes a change from Stephanie's fiscal hauteur and Evan's wicked grin. The great novelist puts his own spin on what his nation has been up to in good times and bad, and it is as acceptable as all the other remedies. And nicer to listen to.

The Irish use language so beguilingly, so seductively. That building spree! That finding the cupboard bare! Well, what can you do about it, whatever? What'll you have? He brings in Henry James, who never earned much, but did well. What is beyond doubt is that the incessant money talk of the present time is wrecking life, and that something must be found to put it in its place. If our lives are not to be half-lives, that is.

Jesus put money in its place, and coolly. As did Matthew when he descended from the Customs and Excise. There is an aldermanic tomb in a church near here that declares that its owner, being both laden with goods and charitable, passed through the eye of a needle. As must have done the builders of our wool churches. It was (sacred) economics, stupid.

I found a marvellous music hymn by F. Pratt Green, but, alas! we did not know it. Now here was someone who sang to God in his heart. He once drove me to a poetry society in Norwich. In his hymn 'When, in our music, God is glorified', he reminds us of that scarcely to be imagined fact, Christ singing. It would have been a beautiful voice from, maybe, Temple training. And it would have been heard more than once, but no one recorded it. 'And did not Jesus sing a psalm that night . . .?'

Advent

A spring feeds the old house as it ultimately feeds the river. Now and then I visit it under the elder and blackberry copse, and see silver beads trickling across dark earth. Just a few steps on they are a runnel, then a gravelly stream, then water in a well, then water under my roof. Its purity was famous not so long ago for the making of beer. What I cannot use overflows into a horse-pond, into the lake, into the Stour. I hear them as I write, as I wake, the spring, the stream, the river, adding to each other in their catchment, their water table. So it has been for centuries.

Inside me, just as incessant, runs what the experimental novelists of the inter-war years recognised as a 'stream of consciousness', a description by the philosopher William James of that unstoppable flow of thoughts and feelings which runs through all our heads. Virginia Woolf was able to drive her stream of consciousness into all kinds of readable directions. The clergy are only too aware of the wastage of ideas, of inspiration, of words. How they stream past too quick for pen or tape. There is no getting them down, not the best of them. Writers too are often in a quandary due to knowing that what gets onto the page is no more than a sad shadow of what, that very minute, had been pouring through their brains. William James paid homage to this marvellous 'stream of thought, of subjective life'. He said that, although its usual metaphor is that of a stream, there was an irregularity in it which also reminded him of a bird's life, with its flights and perchings. So every now and then the divine process does hesitate long enough for us to seize something from it. But these must be fragments of 'one protracted consciousness, one unbroken stream'.

The religious mind has, more than any other mind than that of poet and artist, tried hard to navigate this stream, to follow it, to chart it. It sometimes sees its current as a help to discursive prayer–meditation. I see it as a tantalizing part of an intelligence which first allows me to see, and then whisks out of sight, all the things I would like to talk about on Sunday, or set down in Chapter One. It is bitterly cold and might be mid-winter. Several oaks have shed their leaves in a night, the rest creak. The sheep move up the hill field in dense bundles. The horses breathe plumes. It is Advent and my consciousness revives, rushes ahead of manageable thinking, which is all very exciting but not much use when one has to preach for ten minutes.

The Dark Day

I walk to Advent matins in a thin cold drizzle. Supermarket shoppers zip past. I can hear our bells getting into their stride. How pleased widow Sturdy would have been to know that the bell she created in her foundry was in good ringing order all these centuries later. The footballers are not yet in their stride. Damp, noisy and listless, they trot up and down to keep warm. Their dogs gaze from car windows telling each other, 'More fool they!' In church, strangers take up an entire pew. Well! I light the Advent candle, say the Advent words, sing the Advent tunes:

Ring, bells, ring, ring, ring! Sing, choirs, sing, sing, sing!

And there, long ago, is dear Mr Pratt Green waiting for me at Norwich Station.

Long ago, prophets knew
Christ would come, born a Jew.

What a dark day it is. Black shiny lanes, lightless furrows, horses in their gloomy blankets, shadows tramping home with the Sunday papers, but my little white cat illuminating the ebony piano, having knocked all the photos down. Shall we light a fire? Shall we read all afternoon? Shall we garden? Shall we heck! as Gordon would say. I listen to Bach's *Goldberg Variations*, or some of them, and although it would seem impossible the day grows darker without it actually falling into night. Returning via the orchard I had noticed the reluctance of the leaves to reach the ground. More sticks than foliage had been shaken out of the oaks, and the walnut was deathly in its sodden un-shed growth. There were lots of wrens, tiny feathery balls with tails cocked and, fast as lightning, having supper. The vast ivy on the ancient pear rustled with inmates and had become a bird town. Everywhere, inner Advent light and outer darkness.

Roger Deakin arrives and we discuss wood. Wood as a material, ours being a part of the country which lacks stone. We have flint, of course, flinty fields, flint mines even, but little that one could call stone. So we have done what we could with wood. East Anglia is for wood architects, wood artists, wood saints, woodland poets and wood crafts. Looking around at the uses we have put it to you would think that there would not be a tree standing – but we remain heavily wooded. The dark day polishes the beams of Bottengoms, showing off the adze marks. How many trees were chopped down to make this small farmhouse? Have a guess. It is Tudor Ikea plus straw stuffing, all the beams slotted into place for eternity, and the brick floors scrubbed hollow. Visitors coming to it at nightfall, such as the poor vicar, are apt to wander around in a botanical version of outer darkness, shocked by startled pheasants going off like rockets. Or lacerated by yuccas. I comfort them. Are they not experiencing the genuine one hundred per cent authentic rural November teatime? They should praise God for it.

Sparks thread their way overhead. Each contains hundreds of folk on their way to New York, Rome, Moscow, those by the windows staring down at my spark.

St Andrew

A freezing coming for St Andrew, our village's patron. Hoar-frost and light sprinklings of snow have delineated the land, accenting the autumn drilling, giving every twig its due. The recently dense copse is now a lattice through which I can watch the hares on the far field. They are not skylarking but thump about heavily, 'frawn 'o cold', as they say here. This would have been the time for one of my old friend John Nash's window pictures. Now and then I come across one in a gallery, sometimes with glazing-bars but usually just framed in the window-space, views of the icy garden with trailing pheasants, of the neighbouring farms, of his loved seed heads and floral senescence. Inside work, as he called it. Winter work for every pane in the house. His first and greatest snow picture is 'Over the Top', a recollection of himself and seventy-nine other soldiers in action near Cambrai in 1917. He and a dozen mates survived. The khaki against snow also survived on his palette, to be used for the rest of his long life for weeks such as this.

A window in a painting draws my attention away from what is happening in the room, the Annunciation, Jerome translating in thin sunlight, some horror connected with martyrdom. The Italian masters are always saying, 'Take a look outside.' Like so many others who share the fairly recent passion for landscape, I have pored over Julian's famously scanty views of medieval Norfolk seen, of course, from her window on the world. She saw hazels which one cannot see now, so they are to be put back into the picture by Dr Ellis Roberts, *Corylus avellana*, or 'that which exists now and forever, because God loves it'.

The proto-Christmas card has arrived, Frans de Momper's *Village in Winter*, where there are a hundred seventeenth-century windows looking out on the anti-hypothermian revels of Flanders to see skating, huggings, snowballing, anything to keep the circulation going. I can hear the river cracking, the rushes whipping, the crows protesting around the spire, and I am relieved to contrast this cold snap with that cold season, in which one had to play to stay alive. The windows there are black holes which say, 'Go out to get warm.'

Quite my favourite window mishap is in Acts 20. Poor young Eutychus goes down in Christian history as the first man to doze off during a sermon. He is sitting in the window listening to Paul preaching when he falls asleep and tumbles three storeys to the ground. Paul, ever practical, rushes down to resuscitate him, then returns to continue preaching until the *morning*. As for Eutychus, who cannot have been the hero of many sermons, his friends 'were not a little comforted' to have him back alive. This high window was in Troas, just up the lane from Troy, and it looked out on what had once been Helen's prospect. Winding up at last, Paul sets sail for Mitylene, city of great men.

The Everlasting Circle

The sacred year ends with a fisherman and begins with a craftsman. Andrew and Eloi the metalworker meet at midnight on the last day of November, and the seasons repeat their rounds. In the village there is a blurring of the old distinctions due to there being perhaps no more than a score of its inhabitants still on the land and to changes in the weather not getting into the houses to any dominant extent. There has to be a heavy snow or a heavy blow for us to say things like, 'It got right into the house!' Until double-glazing etc., weather had every intention of breaking and entering, and if you lived in the country it was November inside and out. All the same, November in the valley was always more late summer than early winter, though tinged with loss and decay. Its last Gospel is about that impromptu picnic when five loaves and two fish, distributed to the Twelve by Christ, and by them to multitudinous mankind, proved to be more than enough to satisfy its hunger.

It gets harder and harder in rural life to keep liturgy and everyday experience in meaningful rotation, to keep worship out of the theme park, to get a chilly wisp of November into the church. Out of the all-the-year heatwave of the car and into a vast old room which, in spite of switching on, at enormous expense, every bar an hour before the service, strikes, if not exactly cold, well, as though the days are pulling in. The congregation is annually puzzled by the everlasting circle and can never make out why it should run from Eloi to Andrew, and not from New Year to Old Year.

I walk in the woods. They are perfectly liturgical. By late November their leaves are down and they are structurally naked and soaring. Homing creatures scuttle about. I wade through this year's leaves, through a damp sinking and senescence, and past this year's nests all open to view. And in what the poet John Clare describes as 'the doubting light'. He wrote an everlasting circle book called *The Shepherd's Calendar*, but his idiot publisher complained of its realities. There's no avoidance of these in the Faith-According-to-November, I tell the congregation. The countryside may be running down but we have to stir ourselves up. It says so here – 'Stir up the wills of thy faithful people.' 'But', they protest, 'you say the year is at an end with young Andrew!' The year but not the circle. Every oak knows that. Round and round we all go, the living, the departed, the abundance, the dearth, the planets, the prayers, the holiness of things, all our new toys and comforts notwithstanding.

Scratchings

A long walk to the village on the last day of November. Willows, horse chestnuts and ashes have dropped their leaves, but oaks and sycamores burn with colour and are putting on a show. Rossetti's gold bar of heaven blocks the way to Bures. Children burst from school into cars and are whirled off to hot rooms when they should be shushing their way home through fallen leaves and yelling like freed slaves. The churchyard wall tips towards the lane, though can never fall, it having been locked in this position for as long as anyone can remember. 'The dead are having a stretch', is what they used to say.

I pay calls on the dead. Here is Mrs Constable, John's aunt, aged twenty-eight. Here are the Everards and Nottidges and a better class of people than some I could mention. Here are Mr and Mrs Green who died in 1742, just missing the first performance of Handel's *Messiah*. And here are neighbours who have hurried ahead and who I would have passed on a nice autumn day like this. Their modest memorials lack religious confidence but observe to a T *The Churchyards Handbook*. The church strikes cold and is making its usual noises, clicks and clunks and little sighs. The new *Common Worship* books gleam by the font. Here on a pillar, well-scratched, are the names of T. Scarlett and G. Scarlett who in 1673 decided to be immortal. Further up the aisle a Tudor hand has carved an antler and what looks like a poem or love-letter. And here is a pentagon to keep the Wormingford witches away. There is Jabez on the war memorial. His name means pain.

DECEMBER

*R*onald Blythe wanted to be an artist until they pointed out at art-school that he was in fact a writer. They were right but his writings owe much to the sharpness, precision and delicacy of what he sees and hears. He thinks in images, and he can envisage a whole month as a drawing: 'It has been what I think of as a pencilled December, all fine lines and sepia, with the white horse in his grey field no more than a chalk smudge.'

His hearing is as acute as his vision. He enjoys the racket of rooks in a roost, 'like squawking rags high in the trees', or East Anglian bell-ringers tucking into their Christmas pub-dinner: 'Fifty eating ringers and their guests make a fine roar'. He has read hugely, and his conviviality makes no great distinction between people in the past and the present. Two men laying a hedge 'might have come straight out of a fourteenth-century missal', but for their hard-hats. He always speaks kindly to telephone cold-callers because they 'often sound young and desperate'.

I'm going to end with something Blythe himself said about two men he greatly admires, Dr Samuel Johnson and Rowland Taylor, a Suffolk rector who taught the local weavers so well that people said he turned the wool town of Hadleigh into a minor university in the sixteenth century. Blythe summed up the pair of them in words that might equally apply to himself: 'The earth is the greater for his birth, his books, his brave opinions, his teachings, his weightiness.'

Hilary Spurling

Bare Altars

An early December afternoon, with slanting sunlight. The feast of Nicholas Ferrar, to be exact. Does he have a feast? So he left Little Gidding in Advent. Thinking of him, I see such a sun drawing long shadows from a group of elms that Vikram Seth and I noticed growing there. In a circle, but too close together.

Two horses on my meadow crop the muddy grass and will soon be moved on. The sky is pink and yellow. Now and then, a handful of starlings pass in full flight. A few miles away, in both directions, high streets will be crowded with shoppers and plangent with canned carols. The white cat dozes among geraniums.

Girls call out from polished horses. 'It is coming!' we shout – not Christmas, but the storm. Only it often misses its way, in spite of the forecasters' directions.

I take a funeral and prepare two Nine Lessons and Carols. Winter is all departures and arrivals. The former is back to front as usual, the cremation preceding the service. An old friend, now with God, wanted ten hymns.

'You can only have three.'

'Oh, very well.'

A relation from the other side of the world would talk about her with tears. No flowers in church. And the Second Coming pushed to the back of our minds. And the sweet scent of trampled grass, and the squabbling rooks in the near-naked trees. But youthful winter wheat in all directions, and the river is high. It tugs at the iron bridge that ties Essex to Suffolk, where the Saxon ford would have been. 'No heavy traffic.'

A summer boat has been hauled up and lies meditatively in the rushes. Will we have snow? Who knows? 'Don't forget the bell-ringers' service,' Brian says at the door. 'You don't have to do anything, just the welcome and blessing.'

He does so much – they all do, and not only here, but in thousands of parishes. Such music, such words. Only don't rely on the organ at Mount Bures, which goes up when it should go down, or something like that. I actually delight when, *in extremis*, we sing unaccompanied.

We are to think of Samuel Johnson, my boyhood hero. His statue looks towards Fleet Street from St Clement Danes, where Mother went to Sunday school. He would walk from City church to City church, hoping to hear a decent sermon. But his ears failed him, dear, good man.

His prayers are self-reproving. His virtues were marvellously Christian. He housed a trying female, fed his cats on oysters, made a black boy his son, suffered from multiple aches and disfigurements, and confessed that the ultimate of human happiness was to ride in a swift carriage with a pretty woman.

I once carried Boswell's *The Life of Samuel Johnson* round the Hebrides, reading it wherever he went, not so much in his footsteps as in his complaining shadow. It was early summer, and I was youthful. It was my first glimpse of Scotland.

Pressed flowers, bog cotton, campion and heather stain its pages. May on Skye! Bare feet in the burns. And the telling-off by my Wee Free landlady for swimming on the sabbath. And in my ears Dr Johnson's grand put-downs. Poor young Boswell. I'm not surprised that he got drunk.

But now Advent all over again. The coming of Christ. Its haunting language. Its bare altars. Its wheeling birds. Its heartbreaking music. Its fear and its glory. And all those names for Jesus – Adonai, Dayspring of Nations, Emmanuel . . .

The Quince Tree

I find myself relishing the failing light, the brief afternoons, the cross birds waiting for me to pack up, chiffchaffs and pheasants mostly, joining in noisy protest as I continue to garden when, at

4 p.m., every decent December creature should be in bed. The sun sets like a watery egg and the top field becomes a black wall. But still I clear the orchard. At the moment it is the desperate task of sawing dead wood from the ancient Portugal quince and I feel like one of the surgeons in Nelson's navy – 'Bite the bullet, my lad. You'll be better off without it.' Off comes a vast limb. Half the quince flourishes, half has gone wherever quinces go when they are past bearing. But the tree has a history parallel with my own in the wild garden and I sense that I am losing part of myself as the boughs fall – though not very far, for they writhe in their Laocoon fashion only just above the grass. Once there was so much fruit I could hardly give it away, the locals not wanting 'the trouble'. All except my farmer neighbour William Brown who came to beg a few 'for my wife'. Welcome, welcome dear quince lover. John Nash, who may have planted the tree, liked to place a fat quince on the dashboard of his Triumph Herald, there to scent the car out. I made quince cheese, or put a bit of the fruit in an apple pie 'to quicken it'. Alas, wonderful *Cydonia oblonga*, how you have come down in the world! Once you scented the temples of Venus. A quarter of you is in late leaf so, rid of death, and with my having let the light in, pull yourself together and bring forth in abundance your hard-as-wood, yet delicate, yellow fruit just like you used to. For there remain a few of us who will take the trouble to make of you 'a precious Conserve and Marmalade, beeying congealed with long seethyng, and boiled with Sugar, Wine and Spices'. It is now as dark as midnight and the tools are swallowed up, enveloped, lost, and an owl cries imperiously. I feel my way home. On a shelf of cookbooks going back to the year dot I discover one published in Calcutta in 1919. Quinces, quinces, the yellowing pages turn. 'Quince cheese – press into tins lined with brandy papers'? 'It will take hours.'

A monthly evensong for just half a dozen of us – more when it is light – but 'here two or three are gathered together in my Name', etc. And anyway it is a favourite service, sung without an organist, spoken with alternative voices, the candles wavering, the nave roof somehow floating and indistinct, barely above us, the Advent prayers. It is all so perfect, so beautiful, so 'enough'. But of course it won't save the world. What will?

The bell-ringers' dinner looms into the calendar and we crowd into the Crown, wear paper hats and devour turkey. We spy strangers from towers near and far, captains and masters who make the valley tumultuous when they have a mind to. Our bells reach from the Wars of the Roses to World War Two, and our Attempts reach dizzy numbers, as our peal boards boast. Some of us are ringers, churchwardens and organists all in one. You get your money's worth in the Church of England. I think of my father standing in the dark garden when there was ringing practice, just to listen, just to soak the sound in. The noise in the pub is less listenable to, though there is no choice. Fifty eating ringers and their guests make a fine roar.

Bird-rage

Working late into the early December afternoon, lopping the fallen willow with a bow-saw, I become aware of a mounting intensification of every kind of wild sound. As the light drains away, the birdsong turns to bird outrage and the clicking, rustling of the wind to a roar whose clear intent is to drive me back inside. The usually benign thicket which encloses the ancient garden rocks and rattles with inhospitality. But, so long as I can see to do another half-hour's wooding, I refuse to be threatened in this fashion. These are still my old familiar acres, my towering hollies, my silver bubble of a spring, my cold ponds, my last leaves showering down. So there! Yet the familiar landscape disputes these claims. So do all the creatures which abound in it, some of which – I remind them – take the bread out of my mouth. Be off! they are shrieking, howling. That poet of yours who said

423

something about your 'History is now and England while the light fails on a winter's afternoon' was quite wrong. The truth is that at the ebbing of the light the countryside, rid of humanity, comes into its own. Those old farmers who lived here since the year dot, did they ever tame your scrap of it? Of course not! Their deepest ditch, that patch dug for centuries, what are they but brief marks on the face of the land! The clamour grows. Even the white pheasant, who I have thought of as a mate, turns her wild eye towards me and has the nerve to make an attacking little run in my direction. I continue sawing to everyone's rage. In fact, the primitive shapes and cries of the darkening scene are having quite an effect on me and I shall probably be back at the house as earthy as one of those woodwoses which prop up our Suffolk fonts. I arrange the willow boughs, wigwam fashion, around an apple stump which now only bears honeysuckle, and then grope for the tools which are already settling into the mulch. Call it a day.

Sister Elizabeth from St Saviour's, Hackney, arrives for our patronal Eucharist, driving all the way down the A12 to speak to us. We sing Cecil Alexander's 'Jesus calls us o'er the tumult' and I pounce on the word. Tumult. Tumult is what happens when you stay out late and prevent the birds from roosting at 4.30 p.m. She tells us about her calling, and I think I might be called by such a voice but never by somebody calling in Wembley Stadium. She talks of the 'ordinariness' of Andrew and in the context of us being so extra-ordinary at Advent, what with our musical cries of 'Veni, veni, Emmanuel' and other dramas, I – we – find ourselves brought wisely and simply down to earth by that quiet 'Follow me.' After lunch Gordon guides her car through our already blackening lanes to the motorway. From then on it will be blazing lights all the distance to Hackney, and with nature on either side kept firmly in its place with our concrete.

All That Matters

It suddenly struck me that the straight line of twelve oaks which lead to Bottengoms and which mark the parish boundary would have been planted when oaks were scarce due to the huge felling caused by Nelson's navy. Entire forests went to sea during the Napoleonic wars. My *c.*1800 trees shed their leaves with aggravating slowness so that there can be no complete rake-up before Christmas. And then, wonderfully beautiful and youthful though they are in full dress, stripped naked they reveal the pitiful lacerations of the great 1987 gale. Broken boughs, hang-limbs, wounds like those under the bright uniforms of naval officers, are bared for all to see. Every year I wait and hope for the winter winds to bring them down, but still they swing high up against the sky.

I am planting bulbs, dibbing them in swiftly with a robin to help. Tipped with green, they say, hurry, hurry, hurry. Then to a redundant church to buy cards. Stalls for other goods have crept in and the tall grey aisle along which the snowy choir processed with cross and banner is now a little market. Tractarian angels stare down. 'It doesn't seem right', say the ladies taking my cheque. A golden reredos catches the early afternoon sun. A tape plays carols below the fine organ. I note Gainsborough's uncle, the one who sent him off to London to be trained as an artist, is half-way down the Incumbents' Board, the Reverend Humphrey Burrough M.A., his mother's brother. The boy was thirteen and returned home, they said, well versed in petticoats. Shopping in sacred buildings, a bit of business in the holy place, has a long history. Never mind. D. H. Lawrence wrote:

All that matters is to be one with the Living God,
To be a creature in the house of the God of Life.
Like a cat asleep on a chair

at peace, at peace
And at one with the master of the house . . .
feeling the presence of the living God
like a great reassurance . . .

The small Suffolk market-town of my childhood sparkles with Christmas in every way it can. The pubs are cosy and decorated. The sun goes down below the roofs with a gory crash leaving behind an insipid moon. Country buses squeeze through old streets saying, 'sorry, sorry' as they lumber along. We like to think that poetry is bred on mountains and fields, but it frequently comes from pavements. W. B. Yeats was a 'solitary man', in a crowded London shop when

While on the shop and street I gazed
My body of a sudden blazed;
And twenty minutes more or less
It seemed, so great my happiness,
That I was blessed and could bless.

It is Advent and Isaiah and Amos thunder and sing to us in turn, the Official and the self-confessed unofficial prophets, entrancing speakers both. It was actually Isaiah who followed Amos's inspired outbursts, the theme of which was the need of their nation to have a higher concept of God than that which prevailed in the Temple services. So they sang his glory, Isaiah in the process reaching those heights of Messianic prediction which echo in our Advent hymns. As with pregnancy, Advent is more disturbing than the actual birth. It is full of fear and dread. Advent – God's adventure is entering his own creation. Its language is unsparing, its consequence incalculable. It follows me into the bank, into Marks and Spencer's, into the library, and makes severe argument with the pleasant trash of the season.

St Nicholas

Thin sunshine continues to filter a surprising warmth over our Advent fields and we are told that there has been nothing like it since sixteen-something. So we bask in the rarity of this mildness. Billy's calendar tells her that there will be lambing on Christmas Day, Anthea's calendar tells her that it is less than a week to her wedding-day, Barrie's calendar warns him that the annual bell-ringers' dinner at the Crown is upon him, and has everyone ticked his preference, turkey or beef? Little cardboard windows in the kitchen calendar have to be prised open each Advent morning. At Wormingford we sing 'O come, O come, thou Dayspring bright!' and at Horkesley there is an entire service of pleading carols. They have (said Percy Dearmer) a dancing origin, 'expressing the manner in which the ordinary man at his best understood the ideas of his age'. The extraordinary women too, I find myself amending, as I remember Elizabeth Poston.

The toys of faith are never quite put away. This notion occurs to me as we wander cross-country to Hadleigh, taking the twisting boyhood route from River Stour to River Brett, an up-hill and down-dale journey along lanes with towering banks and still a few flowers. At this mild rate the winter wheat will be cut in March. This is the way I used to travel with John Nash. Now and then he would brake the Triumph Herald to take stock of some excitement in the landscape – 'That's a good bit' – and tucking its detail into his head until it could be put into his sketchbook.

And so to Hadleigh church, which could be called an almanac for the entire English religious experience for those who know how to turn the page. There dangling from the spire is the angelus bell which told the medieval ploughmen to call it a day, there is the room in which in 1833 the young rector Hugh Rose inaugurated the Tractarian Movement and from which in 1554 the old rector Rowland Taylor began the horrible *via dolorosa* which led to his burning on the common. There too, among the sprawling arches, is where two of the translators of the Authorized Version sat as children.

'I'll put the lights on for you,' says the lady who would have been doing the vases, only it is Advent, a fearful time, and one which the Church must meet in all its gaunt reality.

Poverty

The Christmas-card snowstorm brings in an atlas of my life. Views of every parish I have been to: familiar parishes, glimpsed parishes, parishes I have worked in, parishes in which I have felt the presence of artists and writers. And priests, of course. And naturalists. And those adopted by retired friends.

Long ago (for I doubt if the courtesy is still observed) an incumbent would offer his successor the convention of moving at least five miles away, so as not to get in his hair, so to speak – although, once addressing the retired clergy of East Anglia, I was aware that it is often during the final years of ministry that a priest and his wife, or her husband, are apt to make their most important friends.

I have been in Wormingford, on and off, since I was twenty-two – first of all as the friend of the artists John and Christine Nash, and later as the dweller in their remote farmhouse. My feet have kept the track to it open, if not level, and the view from it familiar.

On this near-Christmas day, I stare from its high north window, just as John once stared from it when he placed a canvas on his easel every week, and, cigarette between teeth, would transfer sketchbook drawings to oils.

The studio in those guiltless days was a homily to dust. Tobacco dust, mortal dust from plants and insects, and, to a degree, from the artist himself. It was never swept, and a single 40-watt bulb gave a discreet account of it.

During the summer, when John went to Cornwall or Scotland (never abroad, if he could help it), he would kindly dust a patch where I could write. I never told him that I never wrote a word in his studio, but always in his lovely garden; for summer went on for ever at Bottengoms. Still does. Even at this moment, with Christmas at my heel, the valley within a valley which contains the old house has its own climate. Should it snow, everyone knows that I won't be able to get to the top. The dip will fill up, hedges will disappear, familiar posts will vanish, and ditches will sound with loud but invisible water. Only no one could imagine such a sinking out of sight today, and the postman's van flies towards me with a flourish, and yesterday's cleared desk hides under the avalanche.

Few birds sing, but a squirrel scuttles in the roof, and the white cat is torpid. The News creates a strange unease. People are going to foodbanks. Dickensian activity on cards is one thing, in twenty-first-century Britain, quite another. The poverty of the Holy Family resumes its traditional reality, and is no longer an old tale. All but the well-off would have had no difficulty in identifying with it since Christianity began. In our day, just now and then, it became academic, and below the surface of our time, but it never went away. It was always there, the fragility of human life, and in our world, not the Third World. With the poor and meek and lowly lived on earth our Saviour holy. It was and is true. Politics fail, especially in winter, and spectacularly at Christmas.

Yet the divine birthday is here again, and its light contains no variableness, neither shadow of turning. It is the perfect gift for Christmas. We should see by it. It exists for this purpose. Comprehending our childishness, it tolerates the tinsel. We are young now, whatever age we are.

Seasonal Happiness

It is snowing. Flakes are building up on the flowers and melting on the warm backs of beasts, leaving a sodden gloss. Max looks out in disgust before selecting the softest, warmest chair in the kitchen in which to winter. His green eyes close in prayer as he thanks God for creating men to wait on cats. It is not as cold as the forecasters insist but very wild and dark. The study is covered with letters from the Western Front which are waiting to go into a book. One is blotchy and hard to make out, for which the writer apologises. He is scribbling in a shell-hole, he tells his girl, and it is filling with snow. His pencilled words run. He is a young artist and as the generals prepare for Passchendaele, he prepares his career. The snowy directions are about which London galleries she is to take his paintings, and how to hang them, and what to charge for them. For each of them the war has become a grotesque irrelevance and they don't care if the censor knows it.

I stop work to draw a Nine Lessons and Carols poster to hang in the Thatcher's – the pub at Mount Bures with the wonderful view. I hope the Church of England appreciates my skills. At the bell-ringers' dinner at the Crown I make my usual little speech of praise for the servants of the Temple, that host of choirs, organists, cleaners, embroiderers, flower arrangers, graveyard gardeners, ringers – and John, of course, to whom at Wormingford we naturally turn when there is anything we can't do. Meanwhile, feasts, Christingles, meetings and the like jostle each other more than ever they did, and there are moments when I have a sneaking envy of Parson Woodforde who, if you remember, was begged by his parishioners on Christmas Day if they might sing a carol. 'Yes, but not until I am out of the church.' Woodforde measures his communicants by the rail. 'One and a half rails this morning.' Few attend the Christmas and Easter services but his church is packed when it comes to giving thanks for a military victory, or for the recovery from sickness of a member of the Royal Family. Life at the rectory was, well, boisterous, with 'saucy' servants and prodigious meals. The Norfolk cold pierced them through and through. All the poor men of the village had dinner with him at the rectory on Christmas Day, nor over forty years did he ever take fees from the poor for their weddings, baptisms and funerals. East Anglian winters blast through his pages. On Christmas Day 1796 it was so cold he could neither eat nor sleep, and his curate 'trembled' as he took the service. Singers tended to rile him and he never understood village music. Frozen breath and frozen fingers at the west end. And carols if you were not careful.

Winter at the Window

The day is barely light and has been pencilled in. The sheep can only be detected by their movements in the wet grass, the rooks wear their best black and the oaks are stripped at last. The local Adult Community College arrives at the church for a talk, then a walk. O'Connor stained glass (1869) is as rich as fruitcake and contrasts with the grey outside. My class sits in the frigid pews, the vicar introduces me and then vanishes to snugger climes, and we settle to candle stubs and icy wall tablets, a glimmering reredos and the clunk of the tower clock. I tell them about quoins and bellfounders, place-names and farming, nightingales and knights, dragons in meres and spandrels, the 1870 Education Act, set-aside and the River Stour whose ford gave us birth, and no one blows on their fingers.

We walk to see the churning millrace, and there is Neil laying a hedge, so cameras out. His plants are five-year-old maple. He makes a long, daring slash in each stem, slants it over and ties it. A friend assists. They wear helmets and these apart the pair of them might have come straight out of 'December' in a fourteenth-century missal. They are standing where Wormingford began. In the warm pub, drinking coffee I suddenly think again of the wall tablets, of their harsh whiteness and arctic surface, especially the one to a young man who failed to come back from the Raj. Tennyson, grief stricken by the death of his friend Arthur Hallam who died abroad and who had a similar memorial put up to him in his West Country church, wrote, 'There comes a glory on the walls.'

> Thy marble bright in dark appears,
>   As slowly steals a silver flame
> Along the letters of thy name,
>   And o'er the number of thy years.

'At the Yeoman's House'

The first hard frost. All nature bends before it. The ancient rooms themselves feel crisp. The white cat flies through her flap with panache to settle on the ladder-back chair for the day. She gnaws the strange white stuff from her toes. The chair is old enough for Dr Johnson to have sat on with Hodge. Boswell could not abide cats, but nor could he omit them from his masterpiece.

> I frequently suffered a great deal from this same Hodge. I recollect him one day scrambling up Dr Johnson's breast, apparently with much satisfaction, while my friend, smiling and half-whistling, rubbed down his back, and pulled him by the tail; and when I observed he was a fine cat, saying, 'Why, yes, Sir, but I have had cats whom I liked better than this'; and then, as if perceiving Hodge to be out of countenance, adding, 'But he is a very fine cat, a very fine cat indeed.'

My cats succeed each other in an equality of love – I think. Wintry rifle-shots of frozen branches will honour their graves in the wood.

The question is, will the congregation recognise an Advent sermon that I preached in 1999? Oh, the wickedness of man, who shall know it? Only thou, O God.

The frost delineates the landscape, sharpening it, making the garden tidy. 'We can see where you have been,' say the walkers-by. Where you haven't been, they mean.

I must go to the charity Christmas-card shop without delay; for robins and angels are already flying through the letter box. More importantly – in the long run, that is – I must start to walk the acres that once belonged to my shrunken property, in order to describe them in a new book.

Carrying a Georgian tithe map, I shall trespass into Duncan-land and Grange-land, Garnons-land, and no-man's-land, and the neighbours will look through their double-glazing and wonder what I am up to. The soil will be cruelly ridged and the puddles frozen. Crump, crump.

But what shivering there is to be done will not be done from the cold this year, but from the Crunch. Whatever happens, it will never be like the farming penury of 1908. A little history, and some faith, could put even this economic tumble into its place, as it were.

Cold-calling on the telephone reaches new heights of imper-tinence. This week, I have been rung up by the Guild of Will Writers and a moneylender. When I was a child, there were gates that read, 'No Hawkers. No Gypsies'. Theirs was, I recall, a warm-calling of gentle smiles and pleading tongues. There was the Indian with his enormous suitcase filled with silk ties and head-scarves which slid on to the doormat. And there were country folk for whom the annual round of the higgler was as important as a feast day. How else could they get *Old Moore's Almanack* and other necessities?

Cave Canem read some tradesmen's entrances. Sir Osbert Sitwell declared that when he was walking in Little Venice in London he saw a gate that said, 'Beware of the Doge'. Telephone cold-callers often sound young and desperate, and I answer them kindly. What a job, I tell myself. All that slamming down of receivers, all those hostile voices. Seventh-Day Adventists have given up coming to save me, put off by the muddy track.

Benton End

The historian or the naturalist views a place with maybe a knowledge that casts either a cloud or a brightness that even its residents lack. Thus myself shopping in Hadleigh, Suffolk (there is a Hadleigh, Essex), the day darkening because of its Counter-Reformation martyrs, who I see stumbling to the stake along Angel Street. Particularly the great Rowland Taylor, Rector of this wool town and pupil of Erasmus, and who, they said, taught the weavers so well that he made it a little university.

As a boy, I would cycle to where he was burnt on the common, shocked and excited by his fate. Yet the Christmas shoppers mill along the pavements, and the corporation decorations move in the faint wind, and the lady in Boots has to decide whether I am a safe person to whom to sell razor blades.

Hadleigh High Street is a late medieval dream of small palaces and big cottages on which the pargeting has been picked out with gold leaf. We – Vicky is with me – visit the Farm Shop for homemade bread and fine vegetables, after which I show her Benton End, the far happier scene of my youth, when I came to the East Anglian School of Painting and Drawing. It was a wonderful 'France in Suffolk' institution run by Sir Cedric Morris and his partner, Arthur Lett-Haines. Also a superb iris garden.

The ancient structure hung over the River Brett, and was full of students who were being unashamedly taught, either in the manner of the late Impressionists or in the style of the early twentieth-century Modernists. The grounds sprouted easels and stretched way back. A bell clanged for tea. 'You're not an artist,' they said. 'You are a writer. Write our catalogues.' It was a kind of bliss.

The enemy was the bourgeoisie and his – in Suffolk, at the time, more likely her – values; for Cedric and Lett-Haines were very old and very witty about ancient struggles. Vicky and I sat in the car, looking at the silent garden, the tall windows shining in the patched walls as the sun went down, the beautiful, lumbering old dwelling settling once more for this night. And I imagined old whiffs of garlic and red wine, turpentine and paint, and old voices – somewhat grand – telling tales out of school.

Hadleigh was where Fr Hugh Rose convened the Tractarian movement. Confusingly, its Rectors are Deans of Bocking, and its church is an archiepiscopate peculiar. Do the holding hands lovers in the High Street know this? On the way home, we visit a perfect village bookshop for a gossip and a celebration; for such delights are more likely to be closing down than recently opened. It, too, faces the westering sun.

Can I get more books into Bottengoms Farm? That is the question. Whole walls of them topple about. Possibly a few slender poets. The bookseller himself is a poet. I tell him how Boswell and Dr Johnson met in a London bookshop – the one so youthful, the other so ancient, if only in his fifties; for multiple failings were distressing that mighty frame. Johnson and Taylor had presence, majesty. The earth is the greater for their birth, their loud voices, their brave opinions, their teachings, their weightiness.

But what weather. It is keeping the leaves on the trees, and deceiving the roses. It does not seem to be interested in finance.

Brickwork

The morning after the PCC is delectable. Sun-pierced river-mist with the gold breaking through. I see it from my bedroom window, and with a new proprietary air; for have I not this week been made patron of the Dedham Vale Society? Who would have thought it?

But the pre-Christmas scene is indecisive, with trees floating about, and neighbours' houses only half present. Mild isn't the word. 'We shall pay for this,' an old chap says. What with? I rake up the last sodden leaves. Not a bird singing. The white cat asleep until April, the first cards toppling about on the piano, the shopping list hanging out of a book.

We held the PCC in the pub, with the agenda and the menu in tune with each other. The big question, as always, was the wall. What now seems generations ago, the churchyard wall, exhausted by having to keep in the dead, gave up. Thus PCC after PCC it has dominated our affairs. One day it will stand, mended and perfect, and then what will we do?

And the cherry tree, too, has given up. Trees die, we die, walls tumble down. Think of Jericho. Bodging used to be the answer. Better than handing over good money to experts. My ancient house is witness to the bodger's hand. 'Who on earth mended that?' I ask myself. Only to remember it was me, donkey's years ago.

Two Nine Lessons and Carols have to be sung in neighbouring churches. One after the other in the late afternoon. It may not be exactly King's College, Cambridge, but it is breath-taking all the same. The darkening church, the tremulous first verse at the door, the whiff of mulled wine, the full pews. 'Once in royal David's city' first appeared in Mrs Alexander's *Hymns for Little Children*, and the service itself first appeared in Truro Cathedral. It holds its haunting quality and continues to cast its spell.

How is it that something so repeatedly sung, done, or said can remain spellbinding? Fragments, mere wisps of liturgy, hang about in our hearts and cannot be excised by unbelief. Familiarity itself becomes unfamiliar. There is no knowing what is happening. Poets know not to grapple with it. To let it be.

My old friend Richard Mabey has given me his selection of Richard Jefferies' writings, knowing how I love his work. There is a passage in it that repeats a passage in my life when the ancient house in which I was born burnt down. This was some years after we had left it. I once took Richard to see it.

Jefferies wrote: 'Such old-fashioned cottages are practically built around the chimney; the chimney is the firm nucleus of solid masonry or brickwork, about which the low walls of rubble are clustered. When such a cottage is burned down, the chimney is nearly always the only thing that remains, and against the chimney it is built up again.'

But my birthplace was never built up. There it stood, for years and years – as I once said, like a great charred tooth – until a smart bungalow dismissed it to history.

I would have been three or four when we moved. All I can remember was the night a wild swan came down the chimney and beat about the papered bedroom in terror, creating havoc, they said. My parents' shouts remain in my ears like an equal terror.

The house was thatched, and birds and rats slept in its roof. No country person had a dwelling all to himself then. The youthful John Clare and his wife, Patty, made love in their company.

In the great space above me at this moment, unwed farm labourers had their bothy: beds of straw, elm pegs for smocks, dormers fore and aft, now lined with bricks, which would have given great views of the Stour Valley. They went to bed by 'a pair of stairs', then by ladder. Elm floorboards ran 'bushes' into their bare feet. Their bathroom was the cold stream which ran through the kitchen floor for convenience.

An immense stone sink, in which the children were scrubbed, contains my late geraniums, now tempting the frost. When the Cambridge people arrived to list my house, they said it was c.1600, but economically rebuilt with the timbers of the previous structure, wood from the late Middle Ages. It would have heard the earliest carols.

Now, it hears carols from King's College, Cambridge, and, because he was born a hundred years ago, Britten's Christmas music.

The white cat turns over on a bookcase and says: 'Let me know when it is spring.' But I stay awake, as faith demands. I watch the light failing, the dead leaves clinging to the panes, the horses in quiet conversation in the field, the cards tottering on the shelf, the marker in a novel, the larder groaning, the postman at the door – 'Somebody loves you, my holly hedge shining.'

The cherry by the church gate will not see another December. Lopped, propped, it must go. Whether the dizzy rooks are celebrating or mourning, it is impossible to tell. They whirl and cry amid stars and planes, disturbed by bells. I have supper by ashlight, the furniture glimmering. 'Just like the old days,' murmurs the cat, the squirrels running the length of the roof, the gulls whitening the furrows.

With the December days so warm, it is hard to believe that there will be at least one snowdrift ahead. The dip in the track will be topped up. The ponds will blacken. Some trees will bear more than they can take, and shatter. Winds will take off, the entire village will rattle, commuters will stay at home. Hearths will hiss.

Before and after Christmas are two very different times. Christmas itself, in spite of high spending and dense sociability, has moments of pure happiness and silence. Or a sublimity which must not be missed in the uproar. How to find it – that is the question. It is likely to be as much in the High Street as in an old farmhouse; in a family-packed room as in a chancel. It comes and goes like firelight – and all that preparation! And wrapping paper 'up to here'. As the poor mad poet Christopher Smart said:

Where is this stupendous stranger?
prophets, shepherds, kings, advise:
lead me to my Master's manger

438

Show me where my Saviour lies.
Under Christmas? Hidden by it?

To Console

The view from on high – i.e. my study window from which centuries of farmers would have woken up to find snow. The window too from which John Nash, a snowophile, would sometimes paint the white garden. What he particularly liked were moderate falls which allowed the brown winter grass to poke through. His first great winter picture was *Over the Top* in which a group of heavily clad soldiers scrambled out of their trench, their khaki and the snow creating the colour mood which the artist looked for all his life. He once told me that he had given one of the soldiers the face of a singer he had heard at the Queen's Hall just before he joined up in 1916 'to show the death of civilization'.

Helmeted riders jog past just as I am looking out and give little nods. Blackbirds scuttle under the Butcher's Broom (*Ruscus aculeatus*), a glossy Mediterranean shrub much admired by Virgil. A surprisingly hot sun then enters the smeary glass. The radio can't keep up with snow chaos, as it calls it. Ian telephones from Edinburgh to tell me that the city is an enchantment and that he too cannot cease staring at it from his Prince's Street eyrie and 'O that we were there!' I make do with the Stour Valley, stopping every few yards to regain breath, the cold snatching it from me. Lapwings have arrived, snow or no snow, and are parked with their customary neatness across the levels. Soon the 'lapping' of their wings will precede courtship. At the moment they are standing stock-still, crested and bright, and all turned to the west.

I am reading Kazuo Ishiguro's novel *The Unconsoled* just as Bishop Harries talks of consolation on 'Thought for the Day'. He speaks of the failures of consolation and about Iris Murdoch pronouncing it a fake. There are moments when one must not attempt to console, when the word must not be uttered to the parents of murdered children. When one should keep one's mouth shut. 'In Rama was there a voice heard, lamentation, and weeping, and great mourning, Rachel weeping for her children, and would not be comforted, because they are not.' Yet consolation is among the Church's gifts and many Christians found it best expressed in an ancient book called *The Consolation of Philosophy* by a writer who was thought not to be a Christian, Boethius. He wrote it in prison during the sixth century. King Alfred, Geoffrey Chaucer and Elizabeth I, each translated it, and the whole of Europe read it, for there has always been a need to be consoled. Boethius was a wise statesman who spoke up for a friend who was wrongly accused of treason, and who was executed. To be without a philosophy, to lack a philosophical language in religion, would certainly make me disconsolate. Cast down. To be acceptable, consolation must be pushed past kindly platitudes and could take the shape of a silence in which an immense sorrow can begin to heal.

A tramp to the village school where the World War Two air-raid shelter has been turned into an office for our Headteacher Mags. The Bishop of Chelmsford is here to bless it. St Andrew's School itself is of ecclesiastical flint and cut stone and is redolent of the 1870 Education Act. We talk of epic snowfalls such as that in 1947 when the bus slithered through arctic canyons below Sandy Hill. The thing about snow is that it is not very interesting except at the local level, when it is enthralling. The air-raid shelter has in turn been loos then a store for defunct desks and now a carpeted and computered den for Mags. The newest pupil cuts the ribbon to declare it open yet again. Never throw away an air-raid shelter, it is sure to come in handy.

On the Shortest Day

This is a date which held for my father some portent he was
unable to explain. He had to announce it without fail, 'This
is the shortest day!' Looking at the tall bare may-hedge and the
colourless sky, this time it is certainly one of those English understated days, the kind which Thomas Hardy found dismally to his
taste, to his inspiration even. Job once admitted to having said
things which he did not understand – 'things too wonderful for
me, which I knew not'. And Coleridge confessed to suffering a
similar dilemma. 'Did I say that?'

They are saying that a quarter of our farmers have left the land
these last two years – plus their men of course. It is like a re-run
of that 'flight from the land' before the First World War when the
great agricultural depression spelt ruin for master and man alike.
It was set in motion by endless rain and by the huge grain imports
from the prairie farms of North America and Canada. We in East
Anglia called it 'the coming down time' as the old family farms
collapsed. What a slide into the abyss it was. The government
asked the Norfolk farmer-novelist Henry Rider Haggard to make
an inventory of the disaster, this in 1900. It sits on my shelf, this
village by village account of the fields being deserted and the
people fled. Rider Haggard quoted Judges on the title-page –
'The highways were unoccupied ... the inhabitants of the villages
ceased'. Looking at the A12 and at Wormingford, one could hardly
say this now, but looking at our fields you would be lucky to see
anyone at work in them. The countryside now has a new kind of
resident who is neither rural nor urban, or suburban, but is as yet
unspecified. In certain circumstances it is not possible to say who
or what we are, only time will tell us this.

This shortest day is mild and still. Primroses are in bloom. So is
the brave *minimus narcissus*. A few of them trumpet goldenly on
my desk, an early Christmas present. In the half-light I cut out

brambles and rake up black leaves. Towards evening I join the army of shoppers in the High Street, our swollen plastic bags shining like huge pearls under the festive lights. Young families with beautiful faces pass. Plaguing children tug at hands. Worn to shreds taped carols go on and on. A kind of human goodness passes and repasses. People seem to retain a serious thought in their heads as they buy foolish things, reminding me of what the Irish poet W. R. Rodgers wrote:

> To welcome gravity, and to forego fun
> Is still their fate who seek the heavenly One
> And choose the Star.

Christmas in Cornwall

Not a madeleine, but a pale-yellow spotty apple from a Cornish garden. A fat cooker that no self-regarding super-market would stock, but which, for me, belongs to the epulae (feast) shelf. A poet friend, James Turner, planted this apple long ago, made this garden, hid it behind a five-barred gate, and allowed me to weed it.

Eventually, his ancient home fell into later hands, those of an artist, and she has brought me this evocative Christmas present. I core it, run a sharp knife round its girth, pack it with raisins, and, oh golly, what a rush back over the years to the Cornish Christmases.

I would leave Suffolk at dawn, get to Paddington, make sure to be on the left side of the carriage so as not to miss the red desic-cated rocks at Dawlish, and arrive at Bodmin Road in the early evening. The poet and his wife would then emerge from their little car in their duffel coats, show muted gratitude for my brace of Suffolk pheasants, brag about the eternal spring of the Cornish climate, and carry me off to the lovely house in the watery valley.

Their neighbours were an outspoken old lady who sold camomile plants to make camomile lawns, a silent old man who read ten library books a week, and some wildish dogs. Their house stood next to what might have been a medieval cell for a monk or two.

On Christmas morning, James and I drove to the eight-o'clock in a bitterly cold church, where he would purposely kneel on the damp stone floor, and I would carefully balance on a big stuffed hassock. The communicants dotted themselves around the nave, and our prayerful breath left our lips in little clouds.

In the churchyard, the dead crowded each other in their shiny slate graves. But we — the worshippers — were careful to space ourselves out so as not to cry 'Happy Christmas!' Then home to an enormous breakfast. And an enormous lunch-cum-dinner; for it seemed to go on all day. And talk by the blazing logs — mostly, where James was concerned, about the iniquity and folly of publishers. And, on Boxing Day, the long walk along Constantine Bay, where, contrary to church, we yelled at everyone we met.

James's friends included Charles Causley. The three of us would be in a more accepting mood where publishers were concerned as we drank bitter in the pub. Charles was dry and merry and had just been given the Queen's Gold Medal for Poetry. When he gave me his books, he would change a line here and there with his fountain pen. There were other writers, too, for literature is usually made up of small gatherings in scraps of landscape. Charles knew eastern England; for he had had his teacher-training there, but his epicentre was, of course, Launceston, where he was on speaking terms with every cat.

Three more Treneague cookers to come; three more evocations of the Cornish Christmases and their winter guests. Blowy drives to the Cheesewring on Bodmin Moor. Searches for Thomas Hardy at Boscastle. The weather always a bit wet. Never-ending drinks with friends on clifftops: 'Don't go, don't go.' Shy glimpses of John Betjeman at Daymer Bay, and later to his grave by the

church, which his father had rescued from the sand, once to find
rabbits dining on it.

And always, surprisingly, wild flowers in bloom without a
winter break.

Christmas Eve

Christmas Eve. A small gift for the postmen – they have a rota
– on whose endless kindnesses the logistics of this remote
farmhouse turn. My towering holly hedge is snowily tipped with
old man's beard but the lower boughs are a glowing mass of
orange and dark green fruit and foliage. Blackbirds hustle out as I
cut branches to hang over the pictures and fireplace. A 10.30
'midnight' at Mount Bures in order that the vicar and myself can
get to an actual midnight at Wormingford. We speed through the
black lanes. Among the new arts of being multi-beneficial is that
of appearing to have all the time in the world when one has
another church full of communicants three miles and one hour
away. Most particularly at the midnight. And Mount Bures, such
a sacred little temple on its military height, doesn't make this easy.
It is a church to dream in. Brian plays the organ which commem-
orates the passing of Queen Victoria. A starved-looking John the
Baptist, the parish's patronal saint, looks down at the Eucharist.
Night has rubbed out the window-pictures. Joyce's new candles
waver in ancient draughts. I read the Epistle and John 'In the
beginning was the Word . . .' After the service we stand saying
Happy-Christmases at the door as though we have all the time in
creation. Then a scamper down Old Barn Hill, past cottages flick-
ering with television, up Sandy Hill, by the Crown and down to
St Andrew's where, mercifully, the only restiveness is in the belfry.
And now, of course, the art of showing no sign that we have said
and done all these great things a few minutes before. It is nearly
two in the morning when Gordon drives me home where, now

wide awake, I have a whisky and a read. Lights in the valley go out one by one as the congregation sleeps.

At Little Horkesley matins – crowds of families and famous singing – I preach on time and timelessness, the temporal and the eternal. I ask the children:

> And is it true? And is it true,
> This most tremendous tale of all,
>   Seen in a stained-glass window's hue,
>   A baby in an ox's stall?
> The Maker of the stars and sea
>   Become a Child on earth for me?

They think about it.

A Defined Immensity

'O come let us adore him!' we shall sing at St John's, whilst I, with the three-mile drive through black lanes to St Andrew's to be considered, have to keep my first 'midnight' sermon in check. Behind me glitter a lifetime's 'midnight' country churches odorous with evergreens, wax and, dare one say it, a different form of celebration. But also warm with that undeniable love which suddenly invades the very fabric of all these ancient buildings and turns their good-natured congregations into saints for the time being. Thus we tumble into old attitudes of adoration.

Teilhard de Chardin wrote that to adore 'means to lose oneself in the unfathomable, to plunge into the inexhaustible, to find peace in the incorruptible, to be absorbed in defined immensity, to offer oneself to the fire and the transparency, to annihilate oneself in proportion as one becomes more deliberately conscious of oneself, and to give of one's deepest to that whose depth has no end.' One can hardly do all this with one eye on the clock. A verse in the processional arrangement of the magnificent hymn brings its heady adoration down to earth, though because of all our midnights there is never time to sing it.

Child, for us sinners
Poor and in the manger,
Fain we embrace thee, with awe and love;
Who would not love thee,
Loving us so dearly?

Who would not love Benedict on his first Christmas Day? There he will sit on the rug next to the cat, the pair of them with firelit eyes and with a single obsession – the next meal. We adults know our place with these adorable creatures and will bring new logs and fetch food and make ourselves amusing. Now and then the cat, in wrecking mood, will stroll across the dresser bringing down all the cards. But Benedict does nothing wicked and only geography stops him from being a possible Dalai Lama. How intellectual he is, how contemplative, how lost in the unfathomable, how totally he offers himself to the fire and the transparency! For now it will be late Christmas afternoon, the time for walking off one meal to make room for another. The darkening garden will be full of homing birds which have abandoned the leafless oaks and poplars for glossy holly and bay tree hides, there to shout and twitter and kick up a shindy. It has been what I think of as a 'pencilled' December, all fine lines and sepia, with the white horse in his grey field no more than a chalk-smudge. I have a bursting longing to read, except I was told when I was a bit older than Benedict, 'It is rude to read in company.' In company one must talk. I have given myself Richard Holmes's *Coleridge* and there it lies, burning a hole in my armchair. Just a chapter? Just a page? How Coleridge talked! And read! And rocked Hartley's cradle. And sermonised. And adored.

Other People's Christmas

December 25th. The diarists and letter-writers squeeze against each other on the top shelves otherwise where would I be? Glued to their confessions and not working a minute. But happening to check on one of their Christmases, I cannot stop. Here is John Wesley:

> At the Love-feast which we had in the evening at Bristol, seventy or eighty of our brethren and sisters from Kingswood were present, notwithstanding the heavy snow. We all walked back together, through the most violent storm of sleet and snow which I ever remember; the snow also lying above the knee deep in many places; but our hearts were warmed, so that we went on rejoicing and praising God for the consolation.

Here is Parson Woodforde in 1777:

> Dec. 25. I went to Weston Church this morning at ½past 10 and read Prayers and administered the H. Sacrament there, being Christmas Day. About 24 Communicants ... Being Christmas Day the following poor people dined at my House, old Rich: Bates, old Rich: Buck, Thos Carr, old Thos Dicker, old Tom Cushion, Robin Buck and my clerk Js Smith ... I had for dinner a fine surloin of Beef roasted and Plumb puddings for them.

John having made guards for our pew heaters, I remembered Colette at school:

> Sometimes a baby pupil, who had tried to warm herself by sitting on her footwarmer, would let out a squeal, because

she had burnt her little bottom. Or an odour would spread in the room from a chestnut, a potato, or a winter pear that one of us was trying to cook in her footwarmer ... Surrounding us was the winter, a silence disturbed by crows, the moaning of the wind, the clatter of wooden shoes, winter, and the belt of woods encircling the village ... Nothing else. Nothing more.

Daphne du Maurier, old now, finds herself at Menabilly alone:

It's so queer having no one down here for Christmas. I have not done my routine decorating, but have put all my cards around, and have lovely flowers everywhere, and an arrangement of holly on the centre table in the Long Room, and so it all looks very cheerful. If I thought about it too deeply, I might be rather sad, but I don't ... I think the thing is always to look ahead in life, and never look back, except in gratitude ...

Francis Kilvert, the young curate of Clyro in 1870:

Sunday, Christmas Day. As I lay awake praying in the early morning I thought I heard the sound of distant bells. It was an intense frost. I sat down in my bath upon a sheet of thick ice which broke in the middle into large pieces whilst sharp points and jagged edges stuck all around the sides of the tub like cheveux de frise, not particularly comforting to the naked thighs and loins ... I had to collect the floating pieces of ice and pile them on a chair before I could use the sponge ... The morning was most brilliant. Walked to the Sunday School with Gibbins and the road sparkled with a million rainbows ... The church was very cold in spite of two roaring stove fires. Mr Venables preached.

Katherine Mansfield is malcontented in Hampstead a month after the Armistice:

> I wish we were all in France with a real Xmas party in prospect – snow, huge fire, a feast, wine, old old French tunes on a guitar, fancy dresses, a Tree, and everybody too happy for words. Instead we are wondering to give the postman 5 shillings ... or 3 ... This cursed country would take the spirit out of a Brandied Cherry.

On Christmas Day 1844 Cornelius Stoven, a Lincolnshire farmer, walks to the Methodist chapel at Binbrook:

> When I reached the brow of the hill my ears were regaled by the sound of a band of music. Though the air was thick the clouds formed a good sounding board to carry and diffuse the Binbrook harmonies far and wide ... The air was keen and frosty enough to stiffen my beard with rhyme[rime]. I enjoyed the prayer meeting and had the additional pleasure of reading Talmage's sermon on Amos's basket of summer fruit.

The nineteen-year-old Queen Victoria confided to her diary at Christmas-time that Lord Melbourne 'said that he thought almost everybody's character was formed by their Mother, and that if the children did not turnout well, the mothers should be punished for it. Lord Melbourne is very absent in company often, and talks to himself now and then, loud enough to be heard but never loud enough to be understood.'

On Christmas Eve 1974 Stephen Spender was in Jerusalem:

> After dinner, to the Church of the Nativity, for Midnight Mass. The Church is large and bare, the Mass was intoned in Latin, with some dignity ... The most beautiful part of the

449

evening was after we left the service and walked back along the road the two miles to Rebecca's Well, where our car was parked. We heard, from that distance across the valley dividing us from Bethlehem, the voices from the Church still singing, which the cold night air seemed to purify of raggedness and wrong notes, so that coming from the hill above us, they seemed those of a heavenly choir.

Going Back a Bit

Actually, word from Debach, my old home. How often I have walked 'the street' at that most sated hour of the year, 4 p.m. on 25 December, and marvelled why some family-packed cottage did not explode from all this compressed blood relationship, ritualised obligations and eating. The flocking back home of the brood from digs, jobs, colleges, regiments and vague addresses to briefly create a curious and distinctive atmosphere in pub and church, at the local parties and Boxing Day football. The custom of walking it off has very nearly vanished, and it makes me feel virtuous and adventurous to be alone, outside, cold; beyond the feast, as it were. When I was a boy whole families walked it off, flaunting their presents, kinship and strength.

Back at home I walk into a scene which has little to date it. Small typical East Suffolk fields stuck around with gaunt trees, spreading icy ponds. It is what I see every morning from my desk. I watch it emerging from the night; I see what I always see at Christmas, phosphorescent islands which are farmer French's sheep, rooks like squawking rags high in the trees, all facing the one direction, lapwings and gulls. There are still a few roses out Lear said, 'At Christmas I no more desire a rose than wish snow in May', but he would have to put up with them at Debach when there is rarely a time when they are wholly absent. I investigate the toppling Bramley in whose seamy bark I tucked last year's mistletoe seeds. Nothing. Mistletoe is often unisexual and can be capricious. Its name means 'mistel-twig', but as they used to call basil mistel, it is easy to come to a philological halt. All the festive plants were once simply called 'the Christmas'.

Working as a writer in the depths of the country is popularly thought to be a protected existence. In fact, it is quite the opposite. The cruelties and idiocies of the world are not held off by virtue of some kind of impregnable natural innocence, nor does the immutable process of the agricultural year create a fatalism which stops one from struggling along the common path of the age. Yet the myth remains and continues to be nourished by poets and advertisers. *O fortunatos nimium, sua si bona norint, Agricolas! Quibus ipsa procul discordibus armis* ... – 'How blest beyond all blessings are farmers, if they but knew their happiness! Far from the clash of arms ...' wrote Virgil.

Not so any more. Not decidedly so in tiny ancient Debach with, like Wormingford, its ghostly 1940s aerodrome cancelling out so much of the old map. Edward Fitzgerald tramped these vanished lanes. Their destroyed cottages provided him with the roses of his version of Omar. I easily imagine him strolling these table-level fields which are now ruled across by concrete runways and thinking about the brave music of a *distant* drum. Christmassy-eyed Americans from the NATO base would appear at our services to join us in '*In Dulci Jubilo*'. At the base, Santa in lights sparkled above the nuclear pile.

Christmas Afternoon

Home from Little Horkesley church and a turmoil of children to a roaring fire and a blizzard of cards. I have said farewell to the medieval wooden knight and his ladies and seen that they are stuck with holly, and to Jane Austen's ancestor in the sanctuary, and to the cheery mob, and now the feast is my own. I

will eat chicken and drink port and read a life of John Winthrop
and answer telephone calls from Sydney. They will begin with
banter about the weather, their heat, my cold. Their beach, my
snow-laden house. Except it is not un-springlike, a nippy wind
notwithstanding.

John Winthrop lived a few miles from Wormingford. The entire
area was known as the Godly people of the Stour Valley, Puritans
all and determined to be the Godly people of Massachusetts Bay.
As a boy I used to imagine them setting out in their wagons for
the coast and turning at the crossroads to watch their farmhouses
vanishing from sight, this house maybe. I thought of their first
Christmas in 1630, an abolished feast, and some lurking hanker-
ing for a revel. Winthrop, the new Governor of this fraction of
Massachusetts, and as such the ancestor of the White House, wrote
in his journal: 'The wind comes from the northwest very strong
and some snow' and that it was 'so cold as some had their fingers
frozen and in some danger to be lost'. On Christmas Day they ate
clams, mussels, ground nuts and acorns, and made such big fires to
keep warm that they burnt some of the houses down. Hezekiah
Woodward said that Christmas was 'the old Heathens' Fasting
Day, in honour to Saturn their Idol-God, the Papists' Massing
Day, and the Profane Man's Ranting Day, the Superstitious Man's
Idol Day, the Multitude's Idle Day, Satan's – that Adversary's –
Working Day and the True Christian's Fasting Day', and that he
was persuaded 'no one thing more hindreth the Gospel – than
Christmas'. So Scrooge was right after all. Curiously, the new
Governor allowed some Valentine customs. He had been married
three times and wrote exquisite letters to his second wife. 'Thou
must be my Valentine, for none hath challenged me.'

And then I remember Christmases in Cornwall. Though not as
far as Massachusetts they are now remote. How we walked along
Constantine Bay, how we – all the post-dinner walkers – were
spread out in such faraway groups that there could only be passing shouts. How the tide hissed in and out and the gulls wailed.

How my Cornish friends boasted about the Cornish warmth, as compared with the Suffolk climate, and how wrong they were, although I was too polite to say so. All this is now pictures in the fire. The cats rise from the hearth and stroll through the cards, toppling them over, and there is enough food in the old brick larder to feed the five thousand without a miracle. Television on Christmas Day is forbidden and CDs play holy music, and the pages turn.

There is, many have 'heard' it, a birthday singing in the air. Poets have orchestrated it, so it must be true. It is like the everlasting rise and fall of the Cornish sea or the oceanic voice in shells. The Godly folk at Massachusetts Bay might have cut out the romps – including ball games in the muddy street, but would they not have talked so much about Scripture that their tongues drowned out the angels' song? God must have a special earplug for Christmas so that he can listen to such words as the Eastern Orthodox Church kept by them for this annual happiness.

'Christ is born, give glory, Christ comes from heaven, meet him. Christ is on earth, be exalted. O all the earth, sing unto the Lord, and sing praises in gladness, O all ye people, for he has been glorified.'

But now we have two Bethlehems, the 'little town' of the carol, like the Child lying so still, and that concrete city on the screen with the tanks blundering through Manger Square, and yet they remain one and the same Birthplace. And so the year ends once more, profoundly among the pretty litter, the log ash and the soft rain.

Holy Innocents

The snow has arrived and has settled in. It came down via the coast and smells faintly of the sea. The air is so keen that I am mildly surprised when it doesn't splinter from contact with my face. Streaky blood-red dawns announced the snow and less gorgeous prophets declare there is more to come. Anxious voices ask the perennial question, 'Will I be cut off?' From civilisation at the top of the track, they mean. I hope so. It is the historic prerogative of ancient farmhouses to become inaccessible now and then, and to create consternation.

Supper at Wood Hall – one of the rites of the season. The children (i.e. large young men from London) are home and there is a new dog. Chosen from hundreds at the Dogs' Home, she lies in front of the blaze stupefied by her good fortune. To be the only dog in the house! She stretches her long brindled legs to us and the flames in turn. She may be called Bramble. When I leave she follows me across the yard, anxious not to lose a fraction of this new windfall love. It is unbelievably cold and the geese pile up on each other in their pen to make a living feather bed, the trees crack and the moon is made of ice. Two sets of fox feet imprint the top field. Where are they off to? Prayers for Lady Mallalieu, it is suggested. Countrymen – and women – continue to talk more rubbish about this creature than about any other animal. The next morning a vixen trots through the garden, nose and tail held out, and looking neither to left nor right. I stomp to the village. 'Crump', the poet John Clare's word would best describe the winter-walking sound. The church is a magnificent refrigerator and all the tombs are ice-boxes. Birds are tucking in to the berries on the holly wreaths. The view towards Bures is arctic and spectacular.

It is the Feast of the Innocents. How can a century in which elected governments have bombed, gassed and burnt millions of children deal with those two-year-olds? At the Christmas Communions I asked the worshippers not to leave the Child himself in the cold church when they drive home but to take him with them. Congregations in all three parishes were bigger than for years. True warmth and goodness existed, more than I have felt for a long time. Hackneyed carols rose to the great occasion and retreated to their original freshness. It was very beautiful. And now – the snow. And what will happen if you can't get up to the road? Nothing. That will be the bliss of it. I shall drink port and read Elizabeth Taylor, feed the wrens – and the vixen, should she call again – and have no end of a time.

New Year's Eve

The last morning of the old year. Swift saffron-and-black clouds, and motionless trees. Christmas, which took such an age to arrive, has gone in a flash. Liturgically, we have arrived at some kind of hiatus, as St Stephen, St John and the Innocents seem to go with it. The Church has no Feast of the New Year, but this is what they will expect tomorrow. And so I will do what I have always done, draw Stephen out from under the litter of Boxing Day and translate him to January 1st. This because of the only fully memorable sermon from my boyhood when a fat old bishop, long retired, stood-in for the rector and preached so marvellously on Stephen, and without notes or gesture, that I have ever after held both sight and sound of him in my head. We shall also sing Psalm 8 in which a youthful new argument silences the enemy and the avenger. The gales en route from Scotland will have reached Little Horkesley by then and will be roaring round the roof.

The farmers will be deep in seed catalogues distributed by my neighbour on the far side of the valley, Mr Church. Lorries filled with billions of seeds will soon be navigating the Stour lanes, taking us to the verge. I can see them from the house, those slow containers of scents and food, discreet as pregnancy. Mangle, swede, clovers of all kinds, evening primrose and borage – 'Sow in the spring at 8 kilos per acre and swath in July when seed-drop is imminent'. Ignorance of what comes up in our fields is now widespread. It reminds me of the Victorian undergraduate who, informed by an angry farmer that he was riding across corn, replied, 'I am so sorry but I am not a botanist.' The farm, still the biggest entity of most villages, has become the least seen, the least recognised aspect of rural reality. Crops nowadays are a kind of blank space between destinations, and even for those on their way to church, where they provide so much of the imagery.

The last afternoon of the old year, with the sky darkening and the wind rising. I am trudging across the wartime aerodrome. Hundreds of plovers wheel and shriek ahead. Tomorrow we shall hear of unprofitable mountains being flattened into useful fields by Isaiah's 'new sharp threshing instrument'. He would have approved these seed-beds which lay as flat as pancakes between the concrete runways. I think of Stephen and so the walk becomes a sermon-walk. The plovers think of snowstorms and so John's brassica becomes a desperate dinner interrupted by the birdscarer. Distant lights from the glider club suggest that, Christmas or New Year, celebration is no stickler for dates.

The last evening of the old year. Albert Camus's discovery – 'In the depth of winter, I finally learned that within me there lay an invincible summer.'

For Ronald Blythe

Right hand and left make ten. Earth rings the sun.
On these two truths we mark your hundredth year.
Nature performs its heartless, witless run.
Art presses us to see and smell and hear.
Lucid and strange, your words transmit the sound,
Discordant and concordant, of Earth's round.

By fallow and by field, by rust and rose,
Little or large, by whimsy or by worth,
Your transitory histories disclose
Two truths encrypted in the transient Earth.
Hearts that can sing educe the blackbird's song.
Elms that stand far enough away live long.

Vikram Seth

A Note on Contributors

Julia Blackburn was born in London in 1948, the daughter of the poet Thomas Blackburn and the painter Rosalie de Meric. She has written ten books of non-fiction including her memoir *The Three of Us* (2008), which won the JR Ackerly Award, *Time Song* (2019), which was shortlisted for both the Wainwright and the Hessell-Tiltman prizes, and most recently *Dreaming the Karoo* (2022) and *The Wren* (2022). She has also written two novels: *The Book of Colour* (1995) and *The Leper's Companions* (1999), both of which were shortlisted for the Orange Prize. She is a member of the FRSL, the Society of Authors and PEN, has been a judge for the Ondaatje Prize, and she teaches a memoir course at the Faber Academy. She lives in Suffolk.

Mark Cocker is an author and naturalist who lives on the street in Buxton where he was born. He writes and broadcasts on nature and wildlife in a variety of national media. His thirteen books include works of biography, history, literary criticism and memoir. *Crow Country* (2007) was shortlisted for several awards and won the New Angle Prize for Literature while *A Claxton Diary* (2019) won the East Anglian Book Award. His new book *One Midsummer's Day* is to be published in 2023.

Ian Collins is a writer and curator. His biography *John Craxton: A Life of Gifts* won the 2022 Runciman Award. He has also written monographs on artists James Dodds, Rose Hilton, Joan Leigh Fermor,

John McLean and Guy Taplin. His books on East Anglian art and features for the *Eastern Daily Press* led to the 2013 'Masterpieces: Art and East Anglia' exhibition and a record audience for the Sainsbury Centre in Norwich. He has worked with the Aldeburgh Festival, British Museum, Yale Center for British Art in New Haven, Benaki Museum in Athens, A.G. Leventis Gallery in Nicosia and Mesher in Istanbul. He lives in England and Greece.

Maggi Hambling: Artist.

James Hamilton-Paterson's writing has spanned fiction, narrative non-fiction, children's books, poetry, travel writing and autobiography. His journalism has appeared in the *Sunday Times*, the *Times Literary Supplement*, *Granta* and the *New Statesman*, among others. In fiction, James won the Whitbread First Novel Award for his debut *Gerontius*, and his comic novel *Cooking with Fernet Branca* was longlisted for the Booker Prize 2004. In non-fiction, James has written extensively on subjects as diverse as the sea (his collection *Seven-Tenths*), classical music (a book on Beethoven's *Eroica* in the Landmarks series) and especially aviation. For many years he divided his time between Tuscany and the Philippines, and currently he lives in Austria.

Alexandra Harris was born in West Sussex in 1981. She studied at Oxford and at the Courtauld Institute in London, and wrote her doctorate on art and literature in the 1930s. She worked at the University of Liverpool for ten years until 2017 and is now Professor of English at the University of Birmingham, where she started the 'Arts of Place' research network. She is the author of *Romantic Moderns* (2010) – winner of the Guardian First Book Award – *Virginia Woolf* (2011), *Weatherland* (2015) and *Time and Place* (2019). Alexandra Harris was a BBC 'New Generation Thinker' and is a Fellow of the Royal Society of Literature. She lives and writes in Oxford.

Richard Holloway was Bishop of Edinburgh and Primus of the Scottish Episcopal Church. A former Gresham Professor of Divinity and Chairman of the Joint Board of the Scottish Arts Council and Scottish Screen, he is a fellow of the Royal Society of Edinburgh. His books include *On Forgiveness*, *Looking in the Distance*, *Godless Morality*, *Doubts and Loves*, *Between the Monster and the Saint* and *Leaving Alexandria*, which won the PEN/Ackerley Prize 2013 and was shortlisted for the Orwell Prize 2013.

Olivia Laing is a widely acclaimed writer and critic. She's the author of six books, including *To the River* (2011), *The Trip to Echo Spring* (2013), *The Lonely City* (2016) and most recently, *Everybody* (2021). Laing's first novel, *Crudo* (2018) was a *Sunday Times* top ten bestseller and won the James Tait Black Memorial Prize. She's a Fellow of the Royal Society of Literature and in 2018 was awarded the Windham-Campbell Prize for non-fiction. She lives in Suffolk and is currently working on a book about gardens and paradise.

Richard Mabey became a full-time writer in 1974, after working as a lecturer, then as a Senior Editor at Penguin Books. He is the author of some thirty books, including the bestselling *Flora Britannica* (1996), winner of a National Book Award, *Gilbert White*, which won the Whitbread Biography Award in 1986, and most recently *Turning the Boat for Home* (2019). His memoir *Nature Cure* (2005) was shortlisted for the Whitbread, Ondaatje, and J. R. Ackerley prizes. He was made a Fellow of the Royal Society of Literature in 2011. He is President of Waveney and Blythe Arts, Vice-President of the Open Spaces Society, and Patron of the John Clare Society. He lives in Norfolk, in the Waveney Valley.

Robert Macfarlane is the author of a number of books about nature, people and place, including *Mountains of the Mind* (2003), *The Wild Places* (2007), *The Old Ways* (2012), *Holloway* (2013),

Landmarks (2015) and *Underland* (2019). He is presently working on *Is A River Alive?*, a book about the Rights of Nature. His work has been translated into thirty languages and widely adapted for film, stage and music. Robert is a Fellow and Professor of Environmental Humanities at Emmanuel College, University of Cambridge.

Vikram Seth was born in 1952 in Kolkata, India, and is a poet, novelist, travel writer and biographer. He trained as an economist and has lived for several years each in England, California, China and India. He is the author of three novels, *The Golden Gate* (1986), *A Suitable Boy* (1993), which was an international number one bestseller, and *An Equal Music* (1999). He has also written several volumes of non-fiction and eight volumes of poetry including *Beastly Tales* (1991) and *Summer Requiem* (2015).

Hilary Spurling was born in Stockport in 1940. Educated at Somerville College, Oxford, she was the arts editor, theatre critic and subsequently literary editor for *The Spectator* during the 1960s. Her biographies include lives of the novelists Ivy Compton-Burnett, Paul Scott, Pearl Buck and Anthony Powell. The second volume of her biography of the painter Henri Matisse won the Whitbread Book of the Year Award in 2005.

Frances Ward is a theologian, researcher and writer, preacher, speaker and teacher. She is Priest in Charge of St Michael's and St John's Churches in Workington, Cumbria. From 2010–2017 she was the Dean of St Edmundsbury in Suffolk, a member of the General Synod and a Trustee of the Church of England National Society. From 2006–2010 she was a Residentiary Canon at Bradford Cathedral, engaged in inter-faith work with Muslim women. She is the author of a number of books on theology, most recently *Like There's No Tomorrow: Climate Crisis, Eco-Anxiety and God* (2020).

Rowan Williams was, until 2002, the 104th Archbishop of Canterbury, and is an acclaimed theologian, writer and pastor. He was a lecturer at Cambridge University and held the Lady Margaret Chair of Divinity at Oxford University. He has been Canon Theologian of Leicester Cathedral, Bishop of Monmouth in the Church of Wales, and Archbishop of Wales. He is the author of several books, including *A Ray of Darkness* (1995) and *The Dwelling of the Light* (2003). He is now retired and living in Wales.

Picture Credits

Page viii: Foxglove, *Poisonous Plants*, 1927.
Page 9 January: Tree Stumps in a Wood, 1921.
Page 45 February: Frau Karl Druschki Rose, *Céleste*, 1929.
Page 83 March: Sheep and Lambs, 1919.
Page 119 April: Horses Grazing 3, 1920.
Page 157 May: Landscape with Trees, 1919.
Page 193 June: Water Hemlock, *Poisonous Plants*, 1927.
Page 231 July: Goat and Kid, 1920.
Page 269 August: The Cornfield, 1919.
Page 307 September: Cows, 1921.
Page 345 October: Autumn, *Flowers and Faces* by H. E. Bates, 1935.
Page 381 November: *When Thou Wast Naked* (page 18) by T. F. Powys, 1931.
Page 417 December: Black Cat 1 – Cat on Chair, 1919.
Page 457: Bee Orchis, 1920.

Index